THEN THE WORLD MOVED ON

THE BRUTAL TRUTH BEHIND THE
MAX BAER—FRANKIE CAMPBELL FIGHT

**

Catherine Johnson

Brown Glove Books
California
2024

Library of Congress Cataloguing-in-Publication-Data
Control Number: 2023912744

Then The World Moved On
The Brutal Truth Behind the Max Baer-Frankie Campbell Fight/
Catherine Johnson
p. cm.
Included bibliographical references and index.

ISBN: 979-8-218-24347-0 (paperback)

1. Campbell Camilli, Frank, 1904-1930
2. Baer, Max, 1909-1959
3. Boxing (Sports) — United States — Biography
4. Sports Rivalries — United States — Biography

Book Cover/Design Layout by Catherine Johnson
Printed in the United States of America
First Edition - August 2024

DEDICATION

To the late great Gabriel "Hap" Navarro: matchmaker, master storyteller, boxing historian extraordinaire, and a true gentleman. Successor to Frankie's manager Cal Working as the Olympic Auditorium's matchmaker, it was Hap who confided that the stories that have come down through the decades about the Baer–Campbell fight, were a coverup of the truth. In the hopes I've done you proud, this book is dedicated to you. You are missed.

****

I am the scribe called.
I breathe life into your bones.
I resurrect the memories of your existence.
I mark your journey to render you unforgotten.
- Catherine Johnson

TABLE OF CONTENTS

FOREWORD

RAY MANCINI

Boxing by its very nature is the most unforgiving of sports. The aim of a fighter is to knock a man down and see him counted out. The greatest feeling in the world is to stand over your opponent as he's on the canvas. But you always want to see him get back up.

Boxing is a physical, mental and emotional challenge. It was always a test of myself, of my skill level and conditioning, of my courage and resilience, an almost primitive urge to take combat to the raw outer edges of sanity against a worthy opponent. Boxing is two sides of the same coin: at its best, it can be an honorable and virtuous contest. At its worst, it can be a vicious and savage spectacle.

Boxers are also part of a fraternity. There is usually a certain level of mutual respect and admiration for your opponent as a fighter and as a man, an appreciation for his substance and skills, a basic code of honor and sportsmanship.

There were none of these things on the part of Max Baer when he fought Frankie Campbell. He possessed no honor. No sportsmanship. No respect. This was the wholesale slaughter of an opponent that was obviously out cold and defenseless.

The revelations within these pages is nothing short of a seismic shift in everything boxing fans think they know about this fight and about the men who fought it. As the saying goes, history is written by the survivors. Here lies the story of not only the life and death of a decent man, but the truth exposed of every myth and manipulation by the fighter who lived to remold the story.

****

Ray Mancini held the Ohio State Lightweight title, the NABF Lightweight title, and the WBA Lightweight title over his illustrious boxing career. He is an IBHOF inductee, a boxing analyst and commentator, a film actor, producer, and documentarian, an advocate for worthy causes via his foundation, the pride of Youngstown, Ohio, and a genuinely honorable fellow.

PROLOGUE

IT WAS NOT THE TRUTH THEY WANTED.
BUT AN ILLUSION THEY COULD BEAR TO LIVE WITH - ANAÏS NIN

In the summer of 1934, United Press sports writer Jack Cuddy, caught Philadelphia Phillies first baseman Dolph Camilli in a contemplative mood, as he huddled in the dugout, watching the rain pour down at the Polo Grounds before a game with the New York Giants.

Dolph admitted that in his quieter moments, riding on trains, resting in hotel rooms, sitting in dugouts, he often dreamed of a different outcome to the Frankie Campbell–Max Baer fight. One in which his older brother's hand was held aloft as the winner of that deadly fight in 1930. One in which 100,000 voices chanted Frankie's name as he was declared Heavyweight Champion of the World. Then the dreams faded, and Dolph was left with melancholy for what would never be.

"I hold no grudge against Baer," he shrugged, as the lie rolled uneasily off his tongue. "But naturally I have no love for him.... I know Frankie could have beaten him then or at any other time. Frankie had everything—speed and a terrific punch with either hand. Only death could have prevented his becoming champion."[1]

The short life of Frankie Campbell has become a footnote attached to the early boxing career of Heavyweight Champion Max Baer. The two men's names are forever linked together like leather-fisted revenants in an endless, ghostly waltz from a bygone era. What was unquestionably one of the most savage battles never captured on film took place between them almost a century ago. And as victory seemed about to slip through his gloves, Max Baer sneered at the rules of the game, threw sportsmanship away like a casually tossed cigar butt, and beat to death with grim determination the last man who stood in his way to fame and fortune.

The assault occurred on the twenty-fifth day of a foggy August evening in 1930. The setting was a squared circle situated over home plate at Recreation Park in San Francisco, California. The fight was promoted as part of an elimination tournament between the top two western heavyweights for the unofficial title of

1

Pacific Coast Champion. The winner would be set on a solid path to an eventual shot at the World Heavyweight Championship title.

For Frankie Campbell, the fight was his thirty-seventh battle. It was a chance to provide a good life for his pregnant wife and baby boy. And it soon became clear he had started to turn the battle his way. For Max Baer, the bout was his twenty-seventh; it was not only a gateway to support an already lavish lifestyle and pay his mounting debts, but to attract the attention he so desperately craved.

Seldom do we have the courage or the desire to pull back the curtain on our long dead heroes. Nobody wants to turn over that rock, only to discover with dismay and discomfort the rot underneath. But Frankie's death in the ring was no mere accident. Max was not some novice who threw a couple punches which turned deadly. This was a lengthy and deliberate act. Max not only knew the exact punch that knocked Frankie unconscious, he propped him up against the ropes, and continued to throw at least twenty more unanswered punches at Frankie's head and jaw, until his brain was knocked loose from his skull and effectively turned to jelly. As Frankie's lifeless body slowly sank to the canvas, as blood flowed from the ruin of his sliced-up face, and spinal fluid leaked from his ears, Max purposefully followed him down to pummel him some more. When the referee finally pulled him away, Max fought him in order to administer yet more punishment.

At the resultant investigations which followed, Max's own manager didn't deny that racketeers might have approached his fighter. Max was already friendly with known "sports" who had funded the outcome of at least two of his early fights, and he admitted he had repeatedly placed bets on himself to win in specific rounds. A crooked referee confirmed he kept the fight going through grievous fouls because gamblers had stayed his hand. Frankie's own chief second was a plant who played the role of a Judas. Testimony was heard that Max's father assured others, the expected outcome had the blessings of not only racketeers, but of the district's boxing commissioner. One of the sport's most preeminent syndicated columnists scoffed that Max's actions against his opponent were hardly accidental. A former Heavyweight Champion called his conduct in the ring that night bloodthirsty, unsportsmanlike, and cowardly.

Influential people in the Boxing Commission, the District Attorney's Office, and the State Legislature all worked together to ensure a promising fighter's ascent to the title, and to protect the continued legality of a sport now hanging by a tenuous thread; to have acknowledged the truth then would have endangered the future of boxing in the state. They buried the truth to continue to enrich themselves, and created a version of events palatable to enough people to put any lingering questions to rest.[2]

Contrary to Max's own claims that he fell apart after the fight, while Frankie fought for his life in a hospital, Max was observed two hours after the bout, as he smiled and laughed in a hotel lobby. Within hours of Frankie's death, while his handlers plotted how to divert the blame away from him and onto a dead man, Max's main concern was not the death of his opponent, but how it would affect his career. Within days, Max had gone to Reno where he sparred and gambled, danced and fell in love, while his handlers actively planned his next fight. Within weeks, Max repeatedly pled the fifth at the coroner's inquest and grand jury trial, so as not to incriminate himself. Within months, Max was back to the exact viciousness in the ring that had taken a man's life. Throughout the years after Frankie's death, Max wove one outrageous story after another, about the fight, its aftermath, and his interactions with Frankie's family, which bore no resemblance to the truth.

From the beginning, Max and his handlers floated rumors and fed carefully crafted lies to the press that, in the moment and over time, have become accepted as gospel. Max falsely claimed to have multiple heartfelt meetings with, and provide extensive assistance, to Frankie's widow and son. In reality, Frankie had been dead five years before Max participated in the one and only benefit held for them, and he had to be publicly shamed for months before doing so. Max created from whole cloth a second son of Frankie's who did not exist. He professed a paternal-like pride for the successes of the first one, who died before he achieved any. He invented meetings with that son which never took place, because he never once bothered to meet the boy.

Depending upon who asked the questions, like a conjurer, Max invented fantasy scenarios of the night he killed Frankie, which solidified into appalling delusions in his mind. He physically acted them out and embellished upon them in Oscar-worthy performances before the press. Often the stories literally changed from one newspaper to the next, or one paragraph to another in the same interview. Max lied and exaggerated as easily as he drew breath, while he moved the tales around like chessboard pieces, to produce the reaction he desired at a given place and a given point in time.

Who was there to contradict him really? The fame of both Camilli brothers had already resulted in family members who jealously guarded their privacy. The family blamed Max, and believed he intentionally hurt Frankie. But they clearly realized the firestorm any public disgust would produce, and realistically, nothing would bring back their dead boy. It quickly became apparent to them, that those who could hold Max accountable chose not to, instead doing everything to smooth his almost certain path to the title, anything that would continue to feed the cash cow that was prizefighting in the state—including whitewashing the truth.

Unlike today, old newspapers were not instantly available to anyone's online fingertips; print from the fading past was kept in dusty bound books in each paper's basement morgue. Sports editors who had been ringside that night grew old, they retired, and died, taking their memories of the truth with them. Young new scribes just wanted a story, any story, from "The Champ." If they noted any contradictions, to challenge them was considered bad form.

And so Max could embellish and weave and change history freely without question or condemnation. And he did. He fed it and nurtured it and shaped it like a prized rose bush. He manipulated and distorted the facts behind the veneer of a

3

depreciative smile, an errant tear, and closets full of handmade suits, until somehow, he had become the injured party and his dead opponent was just a victim of bad luck. His own friends confided that despite his repeated public expressions of grief and remorse, he barely gave the fight further thought, and boasted repeatedly of the kill. Max had no desire to move on from the tragedy, while others pulled him back in to the story of that night. He himself repeatedly brought the fight up. He used Frankie's death as a public relations tactic. He yanked the specter of Frankie's uneasy ghost up out of his grave to intimidate his opponents and frighten their families. The public and the press were played like a fiddle, and Max Baer held the bow.

Frankie Campbell was born into turmoil and he left it the same way. He survived the kind of childhood that has left many a man broken. He instead emerged not only a thoughtful and decent fellow, but a hometown boy who fought to honor his family and his city, a game and determined slugger with a fighting heart, a quietly sparkling personality, and a beautiful left hook, whose two-fisted attack was such a thrill he was called a "Second Dempsey."

To date, shockingly few actual facts have been written about Frankie Campbell, in either historical or contemporary discussion. He was not a talkative, endlessly quotable fellow in life, and his story began to be rewritten while his body was still warm. Claims and quotes that are not only incomplete, unsourced, and untrue, have now progressed to generational myths passed down with a minimal basis in fact. Most classic boxing fans are familiar with Frankie Campbell solely as the fighter who died at Max Baer's hands. But the man he was, the life he lived, and the people who loved him has been erased like a faint name on a weathered headstone.

It is long past time that Frankie Campbell's life and death is viewed as something other than a distorted afterthought. The manipulation of facts, and the coverup from that fight, has never been carefully examined until now. The truth demands to be revealed, and the record to be set straight. The story should not remain in the twisted mouths of those who had a hand in his death, but heard afresh from objective voices, from people who were often innocently present during damning moments. These voices, heard across the decades and meticulously pieced together like a jigsaw puzzle, reveal an all-too-brutal truth. Max Baer made a Faustian bargain that robbed Frankie Campbell of a bright future and laid waste to his family, while he lived a life that would've made Dionysus envious.

At its center, this is the story of a lie. But before there was the lie, there was the boy who became a fighter, before he ever donned boxing gloves. Once upon a night so bright with possibility, this sensational son of San Francisco—who was conceived in abuse, fought his way through a horrific childhood in the Mission District, pitched baseballs with the Independent League, worked the heavy bag in gyms of the Tenderloin, and thrilled his fans in boxing rings across California— had the brass ring within his grasp, but at the age of twenty-six, was instead viciously and purposefully beaten into his grave entirely too soon.

CHAPTER I

FROM ITALY TO LITTLE ITALY

I AM THE SHORE I LEFT BEHIND AS WELL AS THE HOME
I RETURN TO EVERY EVENING - LUISA A. IGLORIA

When Frank Camilli entered the professional fistic wars in 1924 at the age of twenty, he adopted the name of Frankie Campbell. He did so for two reasons; to hide from his parents the fact that he had taken up boxing, and to appeal to the vast population of Scots-Irish fight fans in his adopted city of San Francisco.

His origins however were purely Italian. He was born and baptized Francesco Camilli on April 13, 1904, in the Mesabi Iron Range mining town of Hibbing, Minnesota. He was the second son and the third child of Italian immigrants Alessio Camilli and Albina Eliza Tassi.[3] [4]

The Camillis were bricklayers and laborers in the parish of Sassoferrato, in the Le Marche region of central-eastern Italy, the muscular 'calf' of the 'boot' that shapes the country's eastern border against the Adriatic Sea. A stunning land of lush mountains, oak-studded hills, and medieval towns, with ochre-walled homes stacked atop each other along cobble streets, its beauty hid the harsh realities of simple survival for many of its citizens.

Near the end of the twentieth century, the economy across most of Italy lay in tatters, as political and religious factions battled among themselves for power and dominance. Existence became a constant struggle between dire poverty, exploitation, and malnutrition for people like the Camillis. Life was a daily drudgery for Alessio and his siblings. From the moment the Camilli boys toddled up onto two legs, they were given a pickaxe or a shovel. Six days a week, they pried the local majolica limestone out of caves for bricks, which were then shaped by hand to build the homes and line the streets, or they were pushed below ground to labor in the nearby sulfur mines, which was extracted for use in production of gun powder.

By the time he was twenty-one, Alessio Camilli had grown into a young man with hard edges, any trust or empathy beaten out of him by men and circumstance. But he possessed a level of courage and cunning that those around him knew meant he would land on his feet if simply given half an opportunity to thrive. With their blessings, in the early spring of 1899, Alessio shook hands with his father, Sebastiano Camilli, kissed the cheeks of his mother, Catarina Barzoni, as she pressed a satchel of food into his hands, and without a backward glance left home forever. The burden to prosper and provide, as he made his way to that gambler's paradise across the sea, that literal land of opportunity known as L'America, intoxicated and intimidated him equally.

As the steam ship groaned and rumbled its way west in May 1899, Alessio contemplated the wood beams above his berth, where those who crossed before him had carved x's to mark the passing days. He knew stories about the streets of America being paved with gold were fables. But in the last corner of his hard heart, he secretly hoped it was at least a land where you truly made your own destiny; a land that offered freedom from wants and resentments, from conflicts and scarcities.[5]

Immigrants enter New York Harbor (1909) Image by C. Edwin Levick
Courtesy of the Library of Congress

After about two weeks at sea, with a stench in his finest suit, and determination in his solid stance, Alessio stood quietly among the milling throngs crowded onto the port side of the deck. As cheers of relief and excitement filled the air, the Statue of Liberty began to emerge from the mist rising off the water, beckoning them into New York Harbor.[6]

Once Alessio passed a doctor's exam for signs of physical or mental weakness, he walked down a wide set of stairs. At the bottom, was a railway ticket booth, a currency exchange, and a post office to inform his family he had safely arrived. He dashed off a quick note to his mother, and traded his Italian liras for U.S. dollars. He stuffed thirty-five bills into his pocket. He parted with a third of them for a steam train ticket. Meals and a bed were extra, so Alessio curled up on a wood bench seat for the ride northwest to his final destination. He rolled another thousand miles, around the southern shores of the Great Lakes to Michigan's Upper Peninsula, where he made his way to Iron Mountain. The lure and luck of the place where Alessio landed, may have been irresistible in more ways than one. "Sassoferrato" loosely translated into English means "Iron Mountain." So many Italian immigrants from his parish eventually settled there, that the two later became sister cities.[7]

The city of Iron Mountain boasted a population of over 9,000 when Alessio arrived, and was practically splitting at the seams with prosperity. Along with thousands of other immigrants, he gained employment as an iron ore miner, in an area which played an integral part during the Industrial Revolution, and in the emergence of the United States as the world's leading iron and steel producer.

Birds Eye View South Stephenson Ave, Iron Mountain, MI (1897)
Courtesy of Menominee Range Historical Museum

Mining was a difficult, dirty, and dangerous way to earn a living. Death, dismemberment, and permanent injury were appallingly common. Before the area's mines became open pits, for one to two dollars a shift, miners worked sixty hours a week in dark, cramped, airless tunnels to a depth of 1,000 feet underground. Mine captains held an authority over their workers similar to wardens over prisoners. They demanded followers, not leaders, and barked incessantly at their crews for the slightest infraction.

With hard eyes, Alessio often gazed mutely at his boss while he stroked his mustache in thought. Then he shrugged. He had endured worse in the sulfur mines back home. He tightened the strap on his leather helmet, and lit the candle on the crown. He didn't come to America to work for someone else. He would bide his time; laboring below ground was only a temporary occupation.

Though these were no fabled streets of gold, like all new immigrants, Alessio couldn't help but share a blind faith in the prosperity promised by an honest day's labor, in an America that was an industrial powerhouse whose growth and expansion was often so rapid, the fast pace of construction literally made it dangerous to be on the street. His letters home were evidently positive enough that by the end of the year, his brother Giovanni "Joseph" Camilli, and several of his cousins had joined him in Iron Mountain.[8]

****

About the time Alessio had watched Europe speed by from the seat of his northbound train to the seaport at La Havre, France, Frankie's maternal grandfather Achille Tassi, had sent travel money and ship passenger tickets home to his wife and child as they waited in Rome, Italy.

Albina Eliza Tassi, the girl who would become Frankie's mother, was almost three years old, yet she had only a vague recollection of her father. Before she had taken her first steps, Achille had immigrated to America with visions of easy riches and a quick return home as a prosperous man. But life had other plans.

When he alighted in November 1887 at New York's immigration station at Castle Gardens, the bright copper glow of the newly erected Statue of Liberty greeted him. Achille spared her barely a glance; he still had a 2,000-mile overland journey ahead.

On the final leg of his trip, he hopped a narrow-gauge train west on newly-laid rail lines dynamited out of the sheer mountainsides, which led directly to the town of Ouray, Colorado in the San Juan Mountains. He joined a few cousins, and a rush of thousands of farmers and laborers eager to become gamblers, to work a claim in the vast silver mines that threaded the metal-laden peaks.[9]

The remote wilderness of southwestern Colorado silver mining towns was genuinely as rough and lawless as the old Wild West tales claim. Miners could expect adventures below and above ground. The chance of being buried under collapsed mine shafts, drowned by flash floods, or having some fingers blown off by a dynamite charge, was only slightly less likely than being beaten over a bad card hand, maimed in a drunken shootout in the muddy main street, often over possession of a soiled dove from above the saloon, or being hung from a vigilante gallows without benefit of a trial.

Ouray, Colorado (1901) William Henry Jackson Courtesy Library of Congress, Prints & Photographs Division, Detroit Publishing Company Collection

Achille Tassi chipped away for two years in the dark, ten hours a day. Like Alessio Camilli, the only light to guide his pick, was a candle strapped to his leather helmet. When the endeavor didn't pan out as he'd expected, he hopped a train northeast, where he traded one hellhole for another. He joined his Tassi cousins below ground at Iron Mountain.

****

When Frankie's grandmother Felicina Larini stepped off the train from Rome at the port of La Havre in June 1889, she had Achille's tickets clutched in a death grip. Albina's fingers held tightly onto her mother's skirt so she wouldn't get separated in the crowd. As they approached their descent into the hold of the ship, Felicina paused as her gaze swept over the vast body of water.

She had grown up running the cobblestone streets of Quiesa, in the Renaissance-walled city of Lucca in Tuscany, Italy. She had never been on a ship upon the ocean; the rising sun set the tips of the waves afire, but the sea was a fury, and the horizon was frighteningly unending. Letters home from those who had gone before her, warned that the ship's officials were robbers and thieves, and the passengers not much better. With a shove and a curse from behind to get moving, she squared her shoulders, and guided her child down into the dark.

After interminable days on waters that rolled like a carnival ride, Felicina finally held Albina aloft in the fresh sea air. With a tiny American flag in her grasp, she waved her chubby fists in delight at Lady Liberty as they entered the harbor to Ellis Island. When they finally alighted from the train at Iron Mountain, Achille Tassi swept his wife up in a warm embrace, their daughter pressed tight between them. Felicina released a long-held sigh of relief that their journey was over, and the family was together again.[10]

Achille Tassi and Felicina Larini Tassi (1935)
Courtesy of Camilli family

Though they arrived in America from different parts of Italy, fatefully Frankie's parents' families lived next to each on the same street in Iron Mountain. In what was likely an arranged marriage, Alessio Camilli exchanged vows with Albina Tassi on March 30, 1900.

They made a stunning couple. At twenty-three, Alessio was in his prime. He sported black curls, a square jaw, and a muscular physique. Still at the cusp of womanhood, Albina was a slim and lively girl barely past her sixteenth year, with hazel eyes that crinkled merrily at the corners over a wide, generous smile. A year

10

after their union, the Camillis welcomed Frankie's eldest brother Albert in April 1901, with his eldest sister Laura following along in July 1902.[11] [12] [13]

Millie Mine, Iron Mountain, MI (Mar 1896)
Courtesy of Menominee Range Historical Museum

While Frankie's father worked in the iron ore mines, his uncle Joseph ran a bakery with his new wife, the widow Anetta Ferranti Passeri. The couple produced loaves of bread and pastries out of their home long before the sun rose. As dawn broke, Joseph and Anetta loaded up their horse and wagon with baked goods still warm from the oven, and delivered them door to door, to the families who lived along the streets that beat a pathway to the mines.[14] [15]

****

By the spring of 1903, the Camilli brothers and their families were on the move from Michigan to Minnesota. Michigan provided a direct pipeline of labor to an open-pit iron ore mining industry newly developing in northern Minnesota. The Camillis sensed opportunity not available in Iron Mountain. They were in a good position to cater to the service needs of a rapidly expanding labor market, during a population boom that was just getting started.

The Mesabi Iron Range was the most ethnically diverse area in the state, yet tensions existed among the immigrant groups. Newly arrived Italian immigrants with their 'swarthy looks' were among those southern European immigrants shunned as 'not white enough' by northern European immigrants who had settled years before, and were by then deemed to be properly assimilated into American culture.

One so-called learned Yale University PhD candidate who conducted a study before the Second World War of the areas mining communities for his thesis, claimed that "Italian 'Dagoes' were black, greasy, ate dandelions, sniffed snuff, kept chickens, were unkempt, toadying, too prolific, unreliable, double-crossers, and 'knivers.'"[16]

Initially, it appeared the Camilli brothers made the right decision to move. By late spring, they had settled in Hibbing, Minnesota, a town which proudly lays claim to being the childhood home of folk singer Bob Dylan. It was also one of the origin points of a bus line that later become the Greyhound Bus Company. Then as now, it is among the top five largest iron ore producers in America.

Hibbing, Minnesota (1900)
Bloom Brothers Printers Minneapolis MN

Unlike Iron Mountain, the outskirts of Hibbing in 1903 was still largely made up of shanty camps; the town was only ten years old. With a population just over 3,000, the majority of miners and lumberjacks, both single and married with families, lived in clusters of tents and shacks. They were within walking distance of five separate mines, and surrounded by dense forests of valuable white pine, being rapidly logged to vast fields of stumps, to supply lumber to build the Midwest. While retail establishments had only recently graduated from conducting business under sagging canvas, to sturdy wood and brick buildings, the area still retained a frontier mentality.

Mining ruled supreme, so both homes and businesses could expect their walls to shake as the clatter of steam shovels and the blast of explosives filled the air day and night. If the concussion didn't swallow a structure whole, rocks and debris flew through roofs and windows. Great pitted holes were created along the dirt streets, which turned a carriage ride or a casual stroll downtown into a frantic scramble for a safe pathway, or shelter from the fallout.[17] [18]

Undaunted, Alessio Camilli settled his family downtown on Third Avenue at a boarding house next to a saloon, and within shouting distance of a shanty camp to the north, which surrounded the Seller's Mine. Alessio and Joseph bought two lots nearby on Washington Street. Alessio set up accounts with a wholesale grocery supplier in Duluth. In a building on one lot, he opened a mercantile. From a commercial oven in back, his brother Joseph produced baked goods, which his wife Anetta sold with a smile at the store's front counter, to families rapidly settling into fine new homes in the area.[19] [20] [21]

The winter of 1903-04 in Minnesota was especially brutal. The bone-chilling cold continued to hold on with icy fingers well into the spring. It was during a mid-April Hibbing snowstorm, that future prizefighter Frankie Campbell entered the world swinging as Francesco Camilli. At the sound of his lusty cry, Albina smiled in relief and gratitude at the midwife. Alessio grunted at the thought of another mouth to feed and turned away.

Frankie's grandparents, Achille and Felicina Tassi, and his young uncles, Albert and Nero, did not move with the Camilli family to Minnesota. The Tassis had lost their nine-year-old son, also named Frankie, to sepsis after an accidental shooting, in which a bullet that had pierced his skull became infected. Felicina had given birth to four more babies, one right after the other, but all were stillborn. The East Coast held too many memories best left behind, and too many tiny coffins buried in potter's field.

Achille Tassi's cousins, who had emigrated directly from Italy to San Francisco, where they worked as butchers and fishermen, sent word that the Bay Area was thriving. Achille was still young enough to have long-range eyes. The opportunities out west that his cousins described soon became too irresistible to ignore. He moved the family clear across the country to California.

The city of San Francisco in particular, had lured Italians to its possibilities since the days of the Gold Rush. With its rolling hills and rich pastures, coastal cliffs and endless oceanfront, the area called to Italy's farmers and fishermen, to its artists and entrepreneurs. It reminded them of home.

Frankie's grandparents fell in love with their new city. They were both children of vibrant towns embraced by hills. But they missed their only daughter. As Albina shivered from winter temperatures in Hibbing that often dropped to minus thirty degrees, the boarding house desk clerk regularly handed her postcards from her parents which made her sigh with envy. The small images seemed to capture paradise.

View of San Francisco Bay from Russian Hill (c1900)
Courtesy of OpenSFHistory / wnp37.03797

In the end, peace and prosperity in Hibbing remained elusive for Frankie's family. At the time of his birth in 1904, the ships pilots of the Great Lakes cargo fleet went on strike. Movement of iron ore out of Lake Superior ground to a halt. Miners saw their wages reduced, and a sense of shared peril bred solidarity among workers of all trades. Dock workers and then miners joined labor unions, and protests spread across the region, part of a wave of strikes that demanded better wages and safer working conditions. Families tightened their purse strings, and the businesses of Hibbing suffered. Alessio's once-thriving mercantile began to barely break even.[22]

As the miners' strike dragged on, one evening an armed group approached a mine entrance. Two strikers were shot dead by security guards. During the ensuing riot, an estimated 500 shots were fired. The miners and their families were in an uproar. Saloons were booming as workers gathered to commiserate, but Alessio's mercantile continued to bleed red ink. Once he closed the store for the day, he often joined the men to tip back a few shots. After he was good and drunk, he staggered back to the boarding house, where he took his frustrations out on his family. Now that Albina's parents were not nearby to be a witness to it, Alessio regularly began to abuse his nineteen-year-old wife, and terrorize their three small children. Their earliest memories were of fists against flesh, broken furniture, thrown plates of food, their father's shouts, and their mother's cries.[23] [24]

Albina managed to get a letter to her father, requesting money for train tickets and travel expenses so she could bring the children to California. Near the end of October 1904, while Alessio was at the mercantile, Albina hurriedly packed a small bag. Her heart thundered in her breast as she hugged six-month-old Frankie tight, and quietly guided Albert and Laura, both still toddlers, down the back stairs of the boarding house. As the thick coughs and drunken shouts from tents in the shanty town echoed in her ears, she and the children raced four blocks through the snow to the train station.

When they alighted hours later in Duluth for the transcontinental connection west, the police were there to greet them. Alessio had reported his wife for desertion. He vowed to swear out a warrant for her arrest unless she returned. The laws of the era considered a wife as property, controlled by the whims of her husband. Effective consequences for domestic assault weren't even a glimpse on the horizon at the dawn of the new century for a married teenage girl.

The Duluth paper reported that, "as the elder children clung to their mother's dress and stared in wonder at the police, Mrs. Camilli took her arrest calmly. She did not deny that she had left her husband, but explained to Sergeant Fiskett in the Italian language that Camilli had been treating her unkindly, resulting often in abuse." Police escorted the family onto a train back to Hibbing, where Albina and her three children were locked into a jail cell while the situation was investigated.[25]

The family's plight attracted the sympathy of the entire police department. Plenty of blankets for she and the children were supplied, and warm suppers were ordered. Chief of Police Peter Wring asked the night men at the jail to "afford the woman and her babies all possible attention." Albina was eventually charged with larceny due to the contents of the bag she had packed, which legally belonged to her husband. The next morning, to pay for her freedom, she used some of the money her father had sent. She then led the children behind her frighteningly silent husband back to the boarding house to await her fate. Once Alessio had closed the door of their rooms, with a scowl he snatched the bag from her grasp, took the rest of the money, and shoved it in his pocket.[26]

The abuse continued unabated. Near the end of November 1904, Alessio was arrested for assault and battery, and he too became a guest for the night in Hibbing's jail. A fellow lodger overheard Albina's cries as she was being beaten and called police. But Alessio was released the next morning. Albina was too afraid of the consequences to press charges.[27]

Alessio managed to hold on to the mercantile for another year. But by early 1906, the property taxes were in arrears, and his account was overdrawn to the wholesale grocers in Duluth. After months of court appearances, he lost the store and the land lots. The court eventually ordered a public auction of all his assets on the front steps of the county courthouse. While his brother Joseph's family went on to bake and prosper in nearby Itasca County, Alessio Camilli was out of options. With his reputation in Hibbing in tatters, he simply walked away from his debts. He bundled his family aboard a train headed west, to see what kind of advantage he could take in California, in the aftermath of a natural disaster of epic proportions.[28]

CHAPTER 2

CITY BY THE BAY

SAN FRANCISCO IS POETRY. EVEN THE HILLS RHYME
- PAT MONTANDON

On April 18, 1906, San Francisco experienced what became known as the Great Quake, followed by the Great Fire. Though the 7.8 magnitude temblor lasted less than a minute, the upheaval burst gas pipes that ignited the Great Fire. Water mains were ruptured, which meant no water for firefighters to douse the flames.

View from Alamo Square of San Francisco burning (18 Apr 1906)
Courtesy of SFMTA Photo Archive | SFMTA.com / U00822

The fire lasted four days, engulfed over 28,000 buildings, and destroyed almost 500 city blocks. It killed an estimated 3,000 people, and left almost half its 400,000 residents homeless. What wasn't reduced to rubble or vanished completely during the Quake, was gutted or destroyed by the Fire, or dynamited to dust in an attempt to starve the flames of fuel.[29] [30]

The situation seemed overwhelming. But San Franciscans were nothing if not resilient. They could take the rough with the smooth. They declared that their city would rise up better than ever. There was an immediate need of workers in all trades to help rebuild. While Alessio had no specific building skills, he was good with his hands. Several of his Camilli cousins who had settled in the city, and nearby in the North Bay, were carpenters and loggers who taught him the trade.

The city fathers were desperate; even a novice was welcome if he could swing a hammer with confidence. Alessio and his family were among an estimated 6,000 people who initially immigrated to the city to help survivors clear the ruins, rebuild the city, and nurture their ever-evolving version of the American Dream.

In the late spring of 1906, when he and his family boarded the train out of Duluth, Frankie Camilli was two years old. It was the same rail line that Albina and her three children would have taken had her earlier escape succeeded. Upon their arrival in San Francisco, the Camillis temporarily settled on Cotta Street, four blocks away from Albina's parents, where the Tassis had built a home on San Jose Avenue in the neighborhood of Sunnyside.

Neighborhood of Sunnyside (1912)
Courtesy of OpenSFHistory / wnp15.1592

While it's hard to imagine a San Francisco with miles of rural country roads, despite decades of development downtown, before the Great Quake and Fire, much of the city's outskirts remained wild open land. Sunnyside at the time, was considered the sticks, with free-range dairy cows, and flocks of sheep its most numerous inhabitants. Real estate developers had experienced varying levels of success selling land lots in Sunnyside; the area was still largely bucolic and undeveloped. After the Quake, property owners who in the past, were less inclined to sell lots to immigrants, now regularly sold them to Italian newcomers, who developed and cared for their "truck gardens" in the fertile flatlands, and sold their produce locally, or out of the backs of truck beds.[31]

Cotta Street was unimproved land. The Camillis lived in a shack on someone else's lot. Building supplies after a natural disaster were scarce and of inferior quality. With no utilities, it was barely a step up from camping for Alessio's family of five. But as people from every corner of the globe swarmed into the area, to obtain good-paying jobs related to the rapid rebuild of nearby quake-damaged streets, they needed homes, and Sunnyside began to grow.[32] [33]

Trolley car accident in front of the Tassi home, San Jose Avenue (July 1906)
Courtesy of SFMTA Photo Archive | SFMTA.com / U00922

As expansion proceeded at a breakneck pace however, Sunnyside's infrastructure lagged behind. Most residential streets were dirt or wide-planked wood; dusty in summer and muddy in winter. As more train and streetcar tracks were laid, many of the road beds resembled a war-zone. Families dug wells for water, and built outhouses on their lots. Electric lines weren't strung that far out, so homes were lit by oil lamps and candles. There were no gas lines either, so heat came from potbelly stoves, and family meals were cooked in wood-burning kitchen ranges.[34] [35] [36]

Alessio bought a small plot of land on a rise within a stone's throw of Albina's parents. As the Camillis continued to live in a shack, Alessio slowly built a small home on Circular Avenue. Once the last nail was hammered in place however, it was already a tight fit for his growing family. The youngest son, future professional first baseman Adolph "Dolph" Camilli, was born at the shack on Cotta Street in 1907. The birth of the Camillis' youngest daughter Florence Mae christened their new house when she entered the world in 1910.[37] [38] [39]

Camilli house at 1 Circular Ave (arrow) (1914)
Courtesy of OpenSFHistory / wnp37.04189

The location of their new home couldn't have been more miserably situated. The noise level was deafening around the clock. Tracks for interurban electric streetcars were laid in the roadbeds around their lot. A nearby powerhouse smokestack belched coal dust day and night. There was a constant cacophony of whistles, bells, and engine noise from passing trains down the hill. A saloon a block away was the site of a number of disgraceful brawls, often witnessed with equal parts horror and amusement by passing street cars. Horse-drawn fire engines, with bells blaring, raced by the house day and night from the nearby fire station. It was akin to living along a parade route where the procession never ended.[40] [41] [42] [43]

Despite the juggernaut up on the hill at the Camilli house, Sunnyside was still largely rural. Most needs were satisfied within walking distance of home. There were plenty of daily chores for Frankie and his siblings to help their folks. Firewood was gathered for cooking stoves from the edge of the forest along the slopes of Mount Davidson. Coal that had dropped from passing Southern Pacific cars was used for home heating. Freshly slaughtered beef, goat's milk and cheese, and vegetables grown nearby were purchased for a day's meals. Wind-powered well pumps provided water for cooking, bathing and laundry. The boys likely drew lots, or challenged each other to a fistfight, to see who got to clean the outhouse on their tiny plot of land.[44] [45]

When the chores were done, Sunnyside was an equally idyllic and thrilling place for adventure. Sleds were made from cast off wood, or even from metal vehicle bumpers tossed up from accidents at train crossings, for a slide down the hillsides. Mushrooms were picked from the slopes of Mount Davidson. A team of Clydesdale horses delivering beer for Budweiser, passed by the Sunnyside Grammar School on its way to Ocean Avenue. If the alarm sounded at the Ingleside Jail, everyone knew a prisoner had escaped; their foot races home to safety were equal parts angst and excitement. Children used the unique sounds made by either the passing trolley or the freighters, to tell when it was time to go home.[46]

Families knew each other. They took care of each other. Crime was largely unheard of in Sunnyside. Doors were unlocked, so friends freely walked in to visit, to feed the sick, and to quietly help the needy. In one rare occurrence, an unlocked door did result in a crime which directly involved the Camilli family. When he was age twelve, eldest son Albert walked headlong into a burglar in the hallway of the family home. By the time he had run to get his grandpa and the two returned armed with a baseball bat, the burglar, along with his mother Albina's purse and twenty-dollars, was long gone.[47]

By 1910, Alessio Camilli had a few seasons in the carpentry trade under his belt; he specialized in home building. By 1916, he was doing well enough to rent out the little home on Circular Avenue, and purchase a three-story house down the hill on Diamond Street to shelter his family of seven.

Their new home was a definite step up. It was large and located in a nice neighborhood within an easy stroll to streetcars and shops. The streets were paved. There was electricity and gas. The glorious smell of a big pot of pasta sauce greeted anyone who opened the front door as it simmered all day on the stove. Most importantly there was the miracle of city plumbing; it was the Camillis' first indoor bathroom.

The Camilli house at 2945 Diamond Street (arrow) (1923)
Courtesy of Western Railway Museum

Alessio was proud of his achievements, and evidently, he wanted to flaunt his successes a bit. A decade earlier, the automobile was deemed such an unreliable novelty, and a dangerous mechanical fancy, that some cities had banned them from their streets. But within a few years, it had become a status symbol, as close as some men could get to their definition of the American Dream.

In 1918, when the average cost of a family automobile was around $450 and only 12% of state residents owned one, Alessio put a down payment on a fancy new Elgin convertible. At almost $1,700, it was a luxury few families could afford. But he enjoyed being the dandy about town. He reveled in the respectful nods of acknowledgement from other men, and the demure smiles from women as he tipped his hat with a flash of white teeth against tanned skin. Yet while the Camilli family appeared to their neighbors to be rising economically, the reality was much more precarious, and shortly it became a juggling act to stay afloat.[48] [49] [50]

CHAPTER 3

AS A BOY YOU FOUGHT

NO ONE LEAVES HOME UNLESS HOME IS THE MOUTH OF A SHARK
- WARSAN SHIRE

As a home building contractor, Frankie's father soon learned his chosen profession entailed some uncertainty, of feast or famine, and he was not a savvy businessman. He repeatedly took clients to civil court for non-payment of bills on poorly written contracts, and failed to plan for times when demands for his skills waxed and waned.

Although Alessio now drove to his jobsites in a spiffy set of wheels, Albina wisely continued to squeeze every penny given her, and the family lived frugally. But quietly, she fretted. Her husband was a hothead who took too many risks as a shortcut to success. One unwise decision, one unplanned incident, had the potential to put them underwater, and Alessio was a magnet for such situations.

As it grew, the little hamlet of Sunnyside, and the broader Mission District in general, became a diverse, solidly working-class area. Blocks which had housed families from Italy and Ireland, now hosted people from a multitude of nations. As homes sprouted up and down the town's hills like spring mushrooms, the rich and poor lived and came together with varied degrees of harmony. Like so many young men of the times, the first seeds of Frankie Camilli's future career were germinated out of environment and upbringing.

In the vacant lots and city alleys of neighborhoods across America, as a boy, you fought. You fought because you'd rather be called a bully over a sissy. As an Italian, you fought the Irish and the Jewish boys, either because you had dared to enter their zealously home streets, or to uphold perceived ancestral superiority learned at your elder's knee. As an abused or neglected son, you fought out the smoldering anger of a powerlessness that was mentally crippling, and for which you had no other outlet.

If you fought well, you had a certain power. You were admired or feared, and you soon achieved status in your neighborhood. If you didn't regularly sport a shiner, or a bruised cheek and a loose tooth or two, your status level was suspect. Some older boys may have said you were a natural fighter, or the toughest on the block. As you peered through the windows of the local boxing gyms, the photographic gazes of fistic nobility like Heavyweight Champs, "The Manassa Mauler" Jack Dempsey, and "The Boilermaker" James J. Jeffries, scowled down from the walls upon the fighters as they worked the bags; boxers that you idolized and wanted to emulate.

Inside the gyms were boys not much older than you, many of whom dressed well, lived well, and ate well with their winnings. Their trainers kept an eye out for good prospects, and notified the right people of which fighters showed promise. A young man didn't need a degree to be a prizefighter. He didn't need book study. There were no bosses in dingy factories or stuffy offices to kowtow to. A few bucks for a license and a cup, the capacity to power through the pain of battle and not lose your lunch at the sight of bruised fists or a mangled face, these were the abilities that meant your prospects were promising.[51]

Friction out on the streets near home, and the need to defend himself with his fists were not the only challenges Frankie was exposed to at a young age, not the only way his body and mind were hardened to a degree suitable for a future fighter. Unsurprisingly, Frankie's father continued to drink and be violent and abusive to his family. He was strong and solidly built from a lifetime of labor, a fireplug with hard hands that his sons inherited, and he was aggressive and unpredictable while drunk. With little provocation and flimsy excuses, Alessio not only still abused his wife, he beat and whipped his children for the slightest infraction. His son Dolph later said he often struck the boys with chains.[52] [53]

Alessio Camilli (c1920s) Courtesy Camilli family

23

Events that occurred in early 1920 became a catalyst that changed the course of the future for the entire family. The first week of April, after what had been several months of litigation, the State Superior Court ordered a sheriff's sale of the rental house on Circular Avenue for default on the mortgage. There went the money for car payments.

The tense atmosphere that existed in the house on Diamond Street was so charged, it practically threw sparks. After years of battling emotional and physical upheaval to herself and her children, one day in April, Frankie's mother packed a few bags. As if her feet had wings, she hurried her daughters Laura and Florence out the front door, and rushed them up the street to her parents' home. This time, her escape was successful. This time, the state's domestic abuse laws gave her protections.

Less than a month later, Albina filed for divorce. For Frankie's mother to take the steps she did was not only an uncommon rarity for a woman in the era, it was remarkable for a Roman Catholic Italian immigrant, and it indicates how severely Alessio's abuse had escalated. For Albina to have endured years of abuse, then so suddenly take her daughters out of harm's way, meant that nothing was off-limits to Alessio; his abuse toward the girls had become sexual.[54] [55]

But she left the boys behind. And soon the last safeguard for Frankie and Dolph was gone too. As the eldest son, Albert had done everything he could to protect them, even if it meant he bore the brunt of Alessio's fist. He was the tallest of the brothers at 6 feet and would eventually reach 200 pounds. But Albert was a lover not a fighter, the one with the quickest smile and the best wisecracks. There came a point when he needed to save himself. He moved up the coast to the North Bay. Frankie was the big brother now. It was his responsibility to protect Dolph. Yet they were alone in the house with a violent man whose world was crashing down around him; they were convenient victims to vent his anger. Stops at the saloon on the way home at the end of a work-day, or after another failed court appearance, only fed the flames.

When Frankie was fifteen, and Dolph was thirteen, Frankie walked through the front door of home, and into a nightmare. Alessio was in yet another drunken rage. He had Dolph pinned up against the wall and was beating him bloody. With a punch that started from the floor, and contained a lifetime of pent-up fury, Frankie delivered a devastating blow to his father's jaw. Alessio was knocked senseless. For a moment as he and Dolph stood there shaking with adrenaline, Frankie looked down on his father and considered whether to continue. He wanted to destroy him. It had felt good to finally give back what he had received all his life. Instead, he turned away, grabbed Dolph's hand, dragged him stumbling and breathless down the stairs, and they too fled the house on Diamond Street.

But they had nowhere to go. Their grandparents couldn't or wouldn't take them in. The Tassi's home was small and already packed to the rafters. Albina's younger brothers still lived with their parents. Now she and her two girls had shown up asking for shelter. Family members slept out on the back porch, in the living room, and in the basement between casks of homemade wine the Tassis sold during the Prohibition era. Grandpa Tassi came from the Old Country. If he laid down the law that the house was full, there was little the women in the family could do to alter his decision.

The brothers worked at a neighborhood grocery store, stocking shelves and tidying up. The store owner Salvatore "Samuel" Ganci had a shop on Chenery Street, a few blocks east of Diamond Street. Samuel, his wife Concetta, and their two small children also lived on Diamond, only a few doors away from the Camilli family. In the close-knit Italian community, he knew the boys, and had observed the horrifically abusive situation at their house. The brothers slept on cots in the storage room at the back of his store. They were told to help themselves to the food lining the shelves, but not wanting to impose, and aware of their precarious position, they ate only cold canned beans.[56]

All children ages eight to fourteen were required by law to attend school part of the year. Frankie never graduated from grammar school. At fifteen years of age, he didn't have time for a formal education. Now it was about simple survival. To live in the back of the grocery store was a short-term option. For a time, he lived up north in the seaside town of Eureka, where Albert now worked as an automobile painter. Though he pleaded with him, Dolph refused to go with Frankie. Dolph thought the boys should have stuck together. He felt Albert had abandoned them. It would take him time to forgive his eldest brother.[57]

After Frankie left, Dolph tried to stay in the neighborhood. But he needed to work. He dropped out of Polytechnic High School. Initially he lived on the streets. He worked full-time on the docks, and slept under the porch of a barber shop at night, the gravel digging into his body. Kind strangers and worried friends gave him food. In his troubled dreams, his one constant comfort continued to be baseball. Baseball was his way out. On the weekends, he had begun to make a name for himself, playing against grown men in the Saturday Industrial League.[58]

Local friend and future Hall of Famer Joe Cronin, who had long observed Dolph's burgeoning skills in pickup games at Funston Field in North Beach or with the school baseball team, changed the course of Dolph's life. He introduced him to Father George, the principal of Sacred Heart High School, who along with Sacred Heart's parish priest Father McQuaide, was well known for helping homeless and abused children. Dolph was given room and board in the visitor's housing at the parish priests' living quarters, known as the Brothers' House. In between his studies, and after practice with Sacred Heart's baseball team, he helped with the upkeep of the House and the church grounds.[59] [60] [61]

Frankie effectively lived a hobo existence between Eureka and the city; he drifted anywhere he could find work and shelter. Dolph didn't know where he was half the time, and when he asked his brother about it, he was met with silence. The brothers did not see their mother and sisters again for almost three years. This decision was by choice. The nightmare of their experiences on the streets as they struggled to survive, was equal to the horrors Alessio had inflicted upon them as children; they thought Albina should have tried harder to persuade her father to take in his grandsons.[62]

Albina Eliza Tassi Camilli
Courtesy Camilli family

When Dolph was seventeen, he literally ran into his mother on a neighborhood street in Glen Park, where she now rented a flat. Dolph embraced her in a hug so exuberant, it lifted her off her feet and momentarily stopped her breath. All was forgiven at the sight of her dear face. Through grins that mirrored each the other, she asked him to move in with her and the girls, to find Frankie and tell him to come home. The brothers re-established solid and loving contact with their mother and their sisters, but they remained forever wary around their father. Interaction of most any kind was avoided, though Alessio avidly followed his sons' sporting careers for the rest of his days. [63]

Frankie later told a reporter from the *Los Angeles Times*, it was beatings by his father, and forced manual labor beginning almost from the time he could walk, that helped make him the fighter he became. Alessio had brought his Old-World ideas to America on how children should be raised. Just like his own father had done with him, as soon as Frankie and Dolph were old enough to handle a pick and shovel, Alessio made them do a man's labor.[64]

"You've no idea how hard my dad used to work me," Frankie recalled, while he leaned back as if to distance himself from the grim memories. "Sometimes as I look back over my boyhood life, it seems like a nightmare to me. It was work, work, work all day, until I felt as though I would drop. I and my brother Dolph both used to love to play ball, and we'd sneak away from work for a game. Always we'd return to the inevitable beating my father gave us. My father was a big man, and oh how he could hit!" As a sudden smile bloomed on his lips he continued. "Still, we loved athletics and we'd run away to play ball."[65]

The boys had no money to buy new baseball gloves. Dolph said they initially played bare-handed. He broke two fingers that way, and eternally carried crooked joints on his right hand because of it. But in a tough neighborhood, they were badges of distinction. It was almost a fluke Dolph ever became a famous southpaw first baseman. As a kid, he played pitcher and outfielder with right-handed gloves. If he chanced to play first baseman, he put a borrowed glove backward on his left hand. When the prize for one of Frankie's early fights was a certificate for sporting goods, he gave Dolph a brand-new southpaw first baseman's glove. Suddenly, all the stars and moons aligned, and Dolph was finally able to properly master the position he had been born to.[66] [67]

San Francisco's Mission District was the birthplace of professional baseball in California. The first official game ever played in the state was held there in 1859. The Mission was once home to several baseball fields, or a field could be improvised; the brothers regularly joined a game in one of the vacant sandlots found between houses; teams worked together to create a field up in the hills, or they played street ball in the alleys, a diamond painted on the black-top.

On weekends, the brothers hitched a ride or took the streetcar out to Southside Playground, on Seventh and Harrison Streets. The park boasted three diamonds, and the park director Father Crowley, could usually be coaxed to umpire a game. Kids would also peek through the knotholes in the fence during a semi-pro game at Recreation Park. Bleacher seats cost ten cents, but after a game the boys often gathered and returned seat cushions to the park employees, which earned them a free pass to the next game. On Friday afternoons, youngsters were admitted free; the absentee rates at the schools that day were predictably high.

Huddled under the bleachers, the boys gambled photos of local baseballers, furnished in every package of a nickel confection like Zee-Nut, which was a compressed popcorn, peanut, and coconut concoction similar to Cracker Jacks. A stealthy jump onto the back of a passing streetcar, made for a free trip downtown to the Penny Arcade on Market Street, where one cent slotted into a vending machine dispensed photographs of famous baseball players, as well as boxing champions and their leading challengers.[68] [69] [70]

Albina encouraged her boys to play sports. Alessio's opinion was that athletics was a waste of time. He couldn't comprehend how someone would ever get paid a good wage to play a game. He told them to give up such foolishness. He wanted them to continue working as laborers for him and eventually learn a trade, or follow in his footsteps as builders.

That Alessio was adamantly against something the boys loved and excelled at simply drove their aspirations harder toward sports, as not only a small, meaningful declaration of their independence, but a potential path toward success. In the years before she had left the house, their mother could be counted on to run interference. After giving the boys a list of chores, as soon as Alessio left for a job, she insisted they go play ball; she would do the work.

Sandlot Days in San Francisco (1912)
Courtesy of OpenSFHistory / wnp27.5950

Despite his abusive upbringing, Frankie grudgingly admitted he thought Alessio's beatings taught him how to take punishment, in the same way he was able to take heavy punches in the ring.

"I actually grew to hate my father during those terrible days," he admitted with troubled eyes, "but I can see now where his treatment of me played no little part in the building up of my body. Our family moved to San Francisco when I was young, but I finally rebelled from my father and ran away from home." As an onslaught of memories flashed through his head, he ended with quiet steel in his voice. "I have been knocking around in the world ever since and had to learn to fight for myself in a section where only those who could and would fight got along."[71]

FOUR–ROUND ERA

While Frankie's fighting abilities should have been a natural segue into boxing when he grew up, like his brother Dolph, his first and truest love was baseball. As a student at Glen Park Grammar School, he pitched the Glen Park Nine to a city championship for the Public Schools Athletic League. At the same time that he first actively fought in local boxing rings, he was one of the leading stars of local semi-pro baseball teams with the Independent League. He was an exceptional pitcher. In a March 1924 game with the Glen Park Giants, he struck out fourteen batters. Mission District natives distinctly recall one Sunday afternoon in 1925, when Frankie came in from his position as shortstop to pinch hit the last four innings of a nail-biter against the Cartman Tires team.[72][73][74]

Earning a living in the ring was not Frankie's first nor even his second choice as a profession. He initially went into the sport simply because he had both a passion and an aptitude for many sports, and wanted to give boxing a try. He was not only a mound mainstay on the baseball fields. He would have given a mermaid pause in the pool. He had a fearsome backhand in tennis. He wielded a wicked mashie on the golf links. He dribbled a basketball like it was a yo-yo.[75]

He took up boxing in earnest quite by accident, though numerous influences were at play to get him there. A long-time Sunnyside neighbor said his father was an avid boxing fan. As a young boy, chances are Frankie sought a shared interest as a way to connect with Alessio, to still his fists.

Boxing was part of everyday life in America in the 1910s and 1920s. Sparring exhibitions were held at virtually every trade union, fraternity club, and city-sponsored picnic, at athletic games, and ethnic festivals. Before evenings of vaudeville, and even of opera, a pair of fellows would sling some gloves for the opening act.

Frank Camilli (1924)
Courtesy Camilli family

When the "Galveston Giant" Heavyweight Champ Jack Johnson, was done training at the old Seal Rock House resort above Ocean Beach, in between races through Golden Gate Park, he stopped his luxury automobile to chat with Mission District children at their grammar schools, which certainly made an impression on young boys. Realistically though, by the time Frankie was a teenager, he was already fighting like an adult, because for so long he had had to defend himself against a grown man at home.

His brother Dolph claimed his role as a punching dummy may have had something to do with it. "I used to box with him quite a bit, and I think that he got most of his confidence for his future success in the ring knocking me out."[76]

Most importantly, the era and the area in which Frankie came of age, almost predestined him to gravitate toward what was rapidly being marketed as a glamorous sport, in which its successful fighters were portrayed as pugilistic royalty. As a child of San Francisco, Frankie grew up in a location that, since the days of the Gold Rush, was recognized as one of the hottest boxing meccas in the nation. It was once coined a "Cradle of Fistic Stars" for the number of boxers who either fought there, or called the city home. An endless parade of champions, and near champions, from John L. Sullivan to Stanley Ketchel, from Peter Jackson to Jack Johnson, regularly came to town to do battle. James J. Corbett and Joe Choynski were beloved local boys.[77]

Some of the most brutal, bloody, and now legendary brawls, occurred across the San Francisco Bay Area. They were fought in every local location imaginable: from a barn in Fairfax, to a grain barge off the coast of Benicia, and from hastily constructed arenas in Colma, to a public pavilion across from City Hall. Under London Prize Ring rules—where head-butting, eye-gouging, hitting below the belt, kicking, biting and wrestling were allowed—fighters engaged in largely illegal and often secret bare-knuckle fights to the finish, meaning the fight went on until an opponent quit or was knocked out. But the gloved era was on the horizon. The last important major bare-knuckle bout in America was 75-rounds fought in 1889 between John L. Sullivan and Jake Kilrain.[78]

With the adoption of Marquis of Queensbury rules, created to address the social stigma around boxing—deemed by some as uncivilized and only suitable for the lower classes, and judged by the gentry as a duel of the fists, which was less dangerous than one with pistols—the ten-count, the three-minute round, a one-minute rest between rounds, emphasis on technique and skill, and standards of fair play were established. San Francisco adopted the new rules early on. A challenge "with hard gloves under the Marquis of Queensbury Rules," appeared in an 1881 *San Franciso Examiner* sports page, with the irrepressible "Uncle Billy" Morgan as ring announcer. By the First World War, one- to three-ounce gloves—which merely gave fists a thin layer of leather—had given way to horsehair padded four- to six-ounce gloves. Fights to the finish had largely been replaced with 12- and 15-round contests. Prizefights were deemed more gentlemanly affairs, and "the manly art of self-defense" had become a more common catchphrase.[79] [80]

Then one Independence Day, a young man with animal instincts, an inner fury, and a lust for battle, later known as the "Manassa Mauler" Jack Dempsey, seemed to burst onto the scene hotter and brighter than any fireworks display. His childhood had been one long string of hopes dashed, homelessness, deprivation, and barroom challenges for a buck or a plate of food. Unlike previous prizefighters, there was nothing gentlemanly about Jack's style; he didn't box, he launched himself at his opponent as if it was a desperate fight to the death.

In what is still considered among the most brutal nine minutes of boxing in history, on the Fourth of July 1919, before a crowd of over 50,000 spectators, Jack Dempsey slipped between the ropes and into pugilistic history. He stood 6 feet 1 inch tall and tipped the scales at 187 pounds. The heavyweight title holder, the "Pottawatomie Giant" Jess Willard, towered over him at 6 feet 6 inches and 245 pounds. When the bell sounded the opening round, in a ring centered atop a pine wood bowl built on the banks of the Maumee Bay in Toledo, Ohio, Jack Dempsey proceeded over the course of three rounds to brutalize beyond recognition the Heavyweight Champion of the World.[81]

As Jess Willard teetered on his stool just before the fourth round, from his many wounds, an ever-widening pool of crimson soaked into the canvas. He was beyond done. A bloodied white towel of surrender fluttered through the hot still air to land almost at Dempsey's impatient feet. Willard had been utterly destroyed. His jaw, which Jack Johnson had cracked in Havana, Cuba when Jess took his title in 1915, was now broken in several places. He sported a fractured cheek bone and a broken nose above eyes which had swelled shut. On top of what Johnson had managed to bruise, Dempsey caved in several more of Willard's ribs. He later suffered permanent hearing loss. Several spectators reported that half a dozen of Willard's teeth spewed from his mouth "in a rainbow of bloody mist." There followed a mad dash by fans to collect them as souvenirs.[82] [83]

Jack the Giant Killer's ferocious blood-soaked victory immediately caught the nations' eye; young fighters began to emulate his brutal two-fisted attack. They attempted to imitate how, instead of a flat-footed stance, he bounced on his toes, kept up a constant feint and weave, crouched and ducked under attacks. One-hundred years after Pierce Egan coined the term the "sweet science," the epithet for prizefighting had undergone quite an evolution.

Such slug fests as those Dempsey provided soon became fan favorites; the style immediately thrived in the rough and tumble corners of San Francisco, where many of Jack's early fights were held. And just as Jack hit his stride at the cusp of the Roaring Twenties, young Frankie Camilli was there to eagerly occupy a front-row seat, to what is considered the Golden Age of American Sports. He also grew up with technology which exposed him to boxing in a way unlike any other time to date in modern history.

****

On the afternoon of the Fourth of July 1910, the soft clatter of a carelessly dropped fountain pen made spectators flinch, as row upon row they perched tensely on the edges of the wood seats inside San Francisco's Dreamland Rink. The teletypewriter clacked and rattled atop the center table, set upon a crudely constructed stage of plywood and two-by-fours.

Dreamland Rink audience receives news via teletype of the Jeffries-Johnson fight
(1910) Hamilton Henry Dobbins

32

All eyes were on the operator as he awaited the bell that signaled "end of message." He finally yanked the transcription from the roller. The results of round fifteen quivered under his damp palm. The paper rustled as he lifted it up to the extended hand of a man with a megaphone, who paused to read the dispatch. He frowned deeply. Grim-faced, he lifted his horn to make the announcement no white man in the assembled audience wanted to hear.

Jack Johnson still held the title. He had annihilated the former champ James J. Jeffries. The "Battle of the Century" was over, and the black man had destroyed their last and greatest White Hope. A groan, long and low, rumbled from the throats of the throng of nattily dressed boxing fans.

While the results of early twentieth century title fights were received and relayed in a laborious manner, the popularity and affordability of counter top radios soon offered an alternative to regular folks that had begun to take off like wildfire. Radio created a land of listeners, first in crowds at local storefronts, and eventually from the comfort of home. Radio entertained and educated, angered and delighted Americans of every age and class. Eventually radio ownership became a necessity not a luxury. Folks would sooner give up their kitchen appliances than part with the box that connected them to the world.[84]

Crowd listens to World Series broadcast via storefront radio speaker (1926)
Courtesy Curt Teich & Co postcards

Moving pictures remained largely silent until the late 1920s. But the concept of a broadcast that featured a speaking voice, announcing play-by-play live events while they occurred, as a viable medium to the masses, had rapidly gained in popularity. In 1921, radio was still in its infancy. Until loudspeakers were invented, folks shared earphones plugged into their crystal sets to listen in. When over 400,000 East Coast fans tuned in to one of history's earliest live sports broadcast, as Jack Dempsey beat Georges Carpentier in defense of his heavyweight title in boxing's first million-dollar gate, promoters and the press knew they had something.[85]

Radio broadcast towers sprouted like oil derricks after a gusher atop skyscrapers all across town. All three of the Camilli boys regularly gathered downtown with friends and fellow sports fans, to listen to storefront radios, as Babe Ruth's homeruns and Jack Dempsey's knockouts were breathlessly relayed by a newspaper sports announcer.

The brothers were hard pressed to scrounge up the cost of a ticket to the nosebleed seats at a boxing event, but sometimes their father took them. Or they odd-jobbed their way through the doors; as a glove boy, handling the fighters' gloves during the evening for $2.50 plus tips, or selling fight magazines like *Boxing News* or *The Referee* for ten cents at the front entrance.

As Frankie yelled along with the rest of the jostling, screaming crowd at a local bout, cigarette smoke drifting in a haze along the ceiling, eyes locked in awe as two fighters engaged in bloody, sweaty battle lit by the hot, blinding arc lights, he might have imagined himself receiving the admiration and applause he saw lavished on the boxers. To watch them absorb brutal punishment and return it twofold, to move with a maestro's grace and dexterity one moment, and blindingly blunt savagery the next, fighters appeared to the paperboy, the factory worker, the longshoreman, as real men, as heroes worthy of respect. To the child of an alcoholic, who unconsciously still yearned for approval and affection, perhaps to imagine his hand held high in victory, was to imagine a time when his father would give him that long-sought approval, regardless of whether it held any honest value.

****

The juncture when Frankie became a professional prizefighter could not have been more perfect. After ten years, the end of boxing's Four-Round Era in California was on the horizon. On the evening of August 22, 1913, in their third match together, future Heavyweight Champ Jess Willard, flashed a hard right uppercut to the jaw of John "Bull" Young, in the 11th round of a 20-round bout at the Vernon Arena in Southern California. Bull dropped like he had been poleaxed. His head bounced on the floor. Some say the punch was so true it shoved Bull's jaw into his skull. Or perhaps because the canvas was stuffed with only an inch of horse hair, which bunched up with use to expose the wood boards, he was knocked unconscious upon impact.

Young was a virtual novice, and like Willard, at heart was a gentle soul. He was as ill-fitted to the boxing game as a large St. Bernard dog. But Willard had recently been on the losing end of two disastrous fights against fellow title-chasers. A rematch with a big green kid whose moves he knew, would make Jess look good in the ring. As Young lay in his hospital bed, Jess stood alone outside all night to await word of his condition. Young died at mid-morning of a cerebral hemorrhage. He was to have married his sweetheart, the widow Ellie Wright, that afternoon. When Jess caught sight of Bull's brother Noah, the two staggered into each other's arms to cry out their distraught hearts.[86]

Jess Willard was charged with manslaughter, which was later dropped to state law violations governing prizefights. Jess' lawyer argued it was not Jess, but the surgeons who tried to save Bull's life, that had killed him in a botched surgery. An autopsy later discovered that Young had a thyroid condition, and multiple issues with his heart. He was a soft touch with health conditions who had no business being in the ring.

Former champ Jim Jeffries, who had been a sparring partner at Young's training camp, was among those who posted his bail. Jess was eventually acquitted by a jury in the State Superior Court. But after Bull's death, a well-coordinated petition drive was begun. Backed by the Christian lobby, its purpose was to give boxing the heave-ho; a condition that already existed in thirty other states. 30,000 signatures were needed for a ballot initiative. With support from "family-minded" newspapers, almost 50,000 were obtained to amend the State Constitution. Known as the "Anti-Prize-Fight Measure" its passage would make the sport illegal.[87][88][89][90]

On Election Day in November 1914, Proposition 20 succeeded by a narrow margin of 56-44%. The "yes" vote on the amendment was largely a rural one; it lost big in the metropolitan areas of San Francisco and Los Angeles.[91]

There was however one loophole in the law, but it forced fighters to perjure themselves; they technically could register as amateurs, since professional fights were outlawed. To circumvent the rules, promoters held what were coyly termed "amateur exhibitions." Even the press recognized the law was a sham. They put quotes around the word "amateur" to announce the next slate of upcoming cards.

'EIGHT-NINE-TEN AND OUT;' KAYO GREETS SPORT

Midnight Marks Passing of the Fight Game, California's Specialty for Years.

Prizefighting becomes illegal
in California (18 Dec 1914)
Courtesy Oakland Tribune

The law stipulated fighters received only medals, trophies or certificates; prizes valued at no more than thirty-five dollars. Winning fighters were even handed a cheap chalkware figurine painted gold that clubs reused over and over. They were merely part of a misdirection a magician would admire. The true value of the "medals" main-eventers fought for was arranged on the quiet, and known only to a small circle of people. Behind closed doors, the winners presented their gold statuette in exchange for a previously agreed upon sum of money.

Preliminary club fighters were often given rings, watches, or a gift certificate of sorts by the promoter. They could exchange the items at a specified mercantile or pawn shop for cash, or an item of equal value such as sporting equipment. If the agreement was for cash, at the same shops they could purchase a cheap bauble, and be given the rest of their cut as cash back. Among fighters, "medals" soon became synonymous with a fighter's purse. "How much medal do I get?" they often demanded. All of these subterfuges assured fighters made professional-level money, even as they remained in defiance of the spirit of the law.[92]

Fortunately, San Francisco Mayor "Mission Jim" Rolph was not only a beloved local boy, he was a big fight fan. With his wink and a nod, city authorities and the local boxing fraternity knew Jim would always try to look the other way, and they could largely ignore the law. Straw-hatted *San Francisco Call and Post* sports editor Edgar "Scoop" Gleason described it as "a period camouflaged under the veneer of amateurism."[93] [94] [95]

****

For ten years, the contorted shenanigans somehow worked in the city. In fact, the number of fighters, and the emergence of athletic clubs for "amateur exhibitions" only multiplied and thrived. Four-round fights were actually more popular with fans. Whereas the twenty-round bouts of the recent past were almost leisurely hour-long struggles, twelve minutes of concentrated combat over four rounds encouraged a furious pace that was more thrilling.

Eventually, politicians realized the law was so abused, ignored, and violated, they figured it was better to get their hands around the sport, and at the same time make some money for government coffers. Wealthy sporting men and venue owners banded together with political factions to draft an initiative for the next election, which would once again legalize prizefights in the state. Opinion pieces touted the fact that over 730,000 American soldiers and sailors had engaged in boxing contests during the First World War, which had made them fit, healthy, and victorious overseas. After the boys returned home, a large number of them wanted to make money in the ring; who were the city fathers to deny their veterans?

Over 100,000 signatures were gathered in support of the initiative. To assuage the public, its backers promised a powerful organizational structure to give the sport stability, enact tighter controls, and exercise solid safety measures. In November 1924, Proposition 7 passed by a narrow 51-49% margin. Californians approved a measure that authorized professional boxing contests for purses with no dollar maximum, and a twelve-round limit for main events. Four-, six-, and eight-round boxing bouts known as curtain-raisers, preliminaries, and semi-windups, returned to an evening's card.[96]

The first State Athletic Commission, with divisions in Northern, Central, and Southern California, was created to license and govern contests, officials, and participants. The state claimed that what had in the past, effectively been a sport that loosely adhered to the laws of the state, and was largely run by men who had a direct hand in its profits, would now be allowed to realize its full potential under the guidance of what was a supposedly objective body. But the boxing commissioners were wealthy businessmen given political appointments by friends in the state legislator. Most were "sportsmen" who didn't know a boxing glove from a volley ball. They eventually became three foxes guarding a very profitable henhouse for a consortium of influential farmers.[97] [98] [99]

In America during most of the twentieth century, unlike today, where multiple fight judges render the decision on a winner, the new boxing commission held fast to the rule that a referee was the one man to declare an official victor in a match. Not until well into the century was the three-judge system used by the majority of states. This historically gave referees an incredible amount of power. It also meant they were easily and often influenced, by personal attitudes, by prejudices, by who their friends and associates were, and whether they were honest or bought men.

California politicians and promoters rubbed their hands together in anticipation, as visions of dollar signs danced in their heads. Politicians had ensured the new law stipulated licensing fees, and a tax on the gross receipts of every boxing card, landed in the State Treasury. Promoters had dreams of being the next George "Tex" Rickard, who had by now promoted more than five East Coast boxing matches to million-dollar gates, and set gate-receipt records that stood for half a century. Most importantly, promoters quickly recognized they were an essential link between money, politicians, and the courts. Of not only the promise of taxes and profits, but protection, power, and political patronage. Each back happily washed the other.

Wholly unaware of just how quickly and deeply the corruption in the sport would eventually run, history could not have aligned more perfectly, for an ignorant but hungry, punch-savvy, supremely athletic youngster with anger issues like Frankie Camilli, to enter the fight game, and see whether he could wallop his way to somewhere that mattered.

CHAPTER 5

BUCKET OF BLOOD

TO ME, BOXING IS LIKE A BALLET, EXCEPT THERE'S NO MUSIC, NO CHOREOGRAPHY,
AND THE DANCERS HIT EACH OTHER - JACK HANDEY

During the Roaring Twenties, as more states legalized the sport, boxing reached unparalleled levels of popularity in America. It eclipsed baseball in terms of attendance figures and newspaper coverage. Compared to today, the majority of fights in the era were brutal blood-soaked contests; fans could expect wars on the level of an Arturo Gatti–Mickey Ward fight every week at their local clubs. If a fighter wasn't either knocked out or sent to his corner badly beaten, spectators were sorely disappointed.

Promoters and the press made boxing glamorous. News columns written by master wordsmiths Westbrook Pegler, Grantland Rice, and Damon Runyon turned fighters into legends. They plucked metaphors and idioms from the writing gods, to weave wry humor and vivid imagery into a tapestry that was irresistible. In San Francisco, a robust press was sustained by five newspapers, each of them with multiple daily additions, and boxing coverage took center stage.

Jack Dempsey became boxing's first superstar, and was eventually as revered as silent screen actors Rudy Valentino and Mary Pickford. Dempsey became so popular, he literally helped remake the sport into mass spectator events. In 1923, a throng of over 15,000 people stood outside the *New York Time's* offices, just to breathlessly follow fight bulletins shouted out an upstairs window, for Jack's bout in Shelby, Montana, against Tommy Gibbons.

A top fighter could also amass more wealth than other sports figure. Jack Dempsey's largest single fight purse of over $770,000, for his 1926 title defense against Gene Tunney, nearly equaled Babe Ruth's entire career game earnings of $856,000. For the 1927 Dempsey–Tunney rematch, Gene was reported to have given Tex Rickard a check for $10,000 so that his $990,000 purse became a cool one million.[100] [101] [102]

It was into this new prizefighting era of promise that Frankie Camilli came of age. He was certainly physically suited to fight; he stood just over 5 feet 10 1/2 inches tall, weighed just under 170 pounds, and had a reach of 75 inches. He was blessed with incredible strength of bone, extraordinary hitting power, and a lean but solid overall physique.[103] [104]

When San Francisco held its first card under the new state law on the evening of January 2, 1925, Frankie already had five bouts under his belt, four by knockout in the first round. He also had a manager, the man who first induced him to consider the sport as a profession. When Frankie entered a boxing gym in early 1924, it was purely to try something new. He had brawled his way through childhood, but he soon found himself intrigued by the physical, tactical, and mental challenges of fighting as a sport.

When Frankie first slipped between the ropes to spar, his talent as a slugger was apparent. Bert Valerga had decades of experience as a fight manager, and he was a registered trainer and corner second. But his boys had never advanced beyond club fights. As he watched Frankie muscle his way around the ring, a slow smile split his face; he immediately saw the possibilities in this aggressive young fellow. Now he just had to induce him to give his heart over to the game.[105]

Studio photo (April 1925)
Courtesy author's collection

Albert Bartholomew "Bert" Valerga was the successful son of San Francisco Italian and Irish immigrants; he was also a decent man. In 1907, when he was twenty-six, he testified as a witness in court against a man he saw abduct, brutally beat, and attempt to rape a young lady one spring night, among the community vegetable gardens in a dark corner of the Tenderloin. The man served seven years in San Quentin prison for the crime.[106] [107]

Bert was a boisterous fellow with a hearty laugh. He was tall and stout with the Irish blue eyes of his mother. He wore coveralls no matter the occasion or the weather. Father to nine children, he lived on Joost Avenue, just a few blocks west of Frankie's boyhood home. His background was in elevator construction and inspection for Bethlehem Steel. He was also the manager of Chutes Athletic Cultural Institute; a fancy new name to go with recent upgrades made to what locals knew simply as Bill Hopkins' Gym. Located next to the M&M Hotel, the Chutes Gym offered a fully-equipped gymnasium, indoor and outdoor arenas, and training quarters; it became the camp of choice when Mickey Walker fought in the area. Perhaps most importantly, Bert Valerga might have provided the steady encouragement of a father figure that a twenty-year-old aimless young man needed.[108] [109] [110] [111] [112]

The Chutes Gym (arrow) next to M&M Hotel (c1920)
Courtesy San Francisco to the 1920s

Located near the corner of La Playa and Balboa Streets, the Chutes Gym was in the center of everything intoxicating along Ocean Beach. The gym had rows of windows which overlooked the water. While the boys trained, they could ogle ladies in the risqué new bathing suits—which some considered entirely too revealing because legs and arms were shamelessly exposed—as they splashed in the surf. Streetcars disgorged hundreds of working folks onto Balboa Street, where they strolled along the new Esplanade, above a vast beach endlessly smoothed by an arabesque of waves which stretched beyond sight.

The rich swells in furs and black tails, glided by along the Great Highway in their gleaming, chauffeured limousines for caviar-stuffed artichoke hearts and Clicquot Club champagne atop the bluff at the Cliff House Restaurant & Bar. Out the front windows, amusement park rides and games of chance could be had at Chutes on the Beach. Fringed by establishments that offered every luxury, every vice, and an array of food, drinks, and entertainment, the "Western Coney Island" made a Roman bacchanalia seem tame.

Bird's Eye View of Chutes on the Beach (left) the Great Highway (Hwy 1) and Ocean Beach, San Francisco (1927) Courtesy The Process Photo Studios

Bert continued to teach Frankie the rudiments of the game, but boxing in his mind was still just another sport he enjoyed. Then Bert dangled the promise of a $20 purse. That was more money than Frankie made in a week's work as a laborer; he snapped at the hook cast his way. Bert then convinced him he needed a manager; someone to promote him and find him matches that tested his abilities; someone who understood how to draw up a contract and dicker for a bigger cut of the purse before he scratched a pen to it. Frankie was reeled onto shore by a master angler. After the two shook hands to seal the deal, Bert slipped through the sweaty throng of boys on the gym floor, closed the door to his office, and picked up the phone.

Frankie later credited that phone call for the fluke that gave him his ring name. It was first coined by National Hall matchmaker Bobby Johnson. Bobby couldn't understand Bert Valerga's pronunciation of Camilli over a poor connection on the telephone. It went something like, "Did you say Frankie Cameron?" he yelled to Bert through the line. "No, Camilli!" shouted Bert. "Oh, okay Frankie Campbell, good Scots-Irish name, got it!" If by such a fluke Frankie could hide from his parents that he was now a prizefighter, and appeal to an ethnic group who made up the majority of ticket sales, it was something he was happy to agree to. The decision to adopt a Celtic moniker was so popular among fighters at the time, one

Italian newspaper sniffed that at least thirty-two local boxers who had taken such names were actually their boys.[113]

Frankie's first professional fight was a four-round preliminary, held at National Hall on August 27, 1924. His opponent was Bobby Barrett. It was Barrett's first fight too. The *San Francisco Examiner* reported the next day that "all the preliminaries at the National last night were corkers. Plenty of action and hard socks galore," and that Frankie knocked Bobby flat in the first round. The aggressive power of his punch was a harbinger of things to come; Barrett never again laced on a pair of boxing gloves to engage in a professional fight.[114] [115]

Fighters in action at National Hall (1923)
Courtesy of Deborah Stevenson Stirling Collection

His next nine bouts were held at the National. Located at 1975 Mission Street off Sixteenth Street, sanctioned, recorded bouts were held within its walls every Wednesday night, alongside non-sanctioned, unrecorded "smokers." It was well known that National Hall didn't confirm your age before you slipped through the ropes. At the time, smokers were typically fought by underaged and unattached fighters—unattached meaning a fighter was unaffiliated with a club or a trainer, likely had no real training, and was effectively a step up from a street fighter with visions of grandeur.[116] [117] [118]

Nicknamed the "Bucket of Blood" arena, spectators knew they could watch fights at National Hall that were anything but cleanly fought. They demanded brutal action, not skill, and you'd better produce or you wouldn't be welcome back. The hall could seat around 1,500, maybe 2,000 in a pinch for a big draw bout if fans agreed to share a seat. A fighter had to have a decent pair of lungs to survive not only his opponent, but the smoke from the thousands of cigars and cigarettes that hung in a haze over the ring. The gallery extended out on three sides, so patrons had a close-up view of the action. If fans thought opponents clinched too much, derisive suggestions to "Kiss him why doncha?" rang out from the galleryites. If a fight was slow, they hurled disdainful hoots of "Oh waltz me around again, Willie." If opponents didn't provide enough fireworks, shouts of "Toss the bums out!" backed up by all available projectiles at hand, often including a barrage of rotten vegetables, were thrown with disgust and deadly accuracy into the ring.

Only main-eventers rated new gloves for a fight. Preliminary fighters were given well-used, filthy gloves, which had loose seams, flattened horse-hair stuffing, were often mildewed, and harbored an array of bacteria and viruses. A hit to the eye could produce infection or even blindness. Fighters had to duck to get inside the dressing room tucked under the stage, where the changing area was a couple wood benches and a table. Showers were upstairs next to the public toilet, so a flush meant a cold-water shock as the boxers lathered up.[119] [120]

Original National Hall entry (1914)
Courtesy of SFMTA Photo Archive | SFMTA.com / U04752

Entry to the hall was up a steep flight of stairs and down a long hallway that led into the arena proper. On fight night, every inch of its length was jammed. Old-timers held the walls up, guzzled beer, and reminisced about the days of Stanley Ketchel and Joe Choynski. The National was a roughshod, solidly blue-collar venue; it was terrifically popular with the Mission fight faithful.[121]

From the dawn of the new century, National Hall's promoter Al Young, was an integral part of boxing's rise in the city. Born Albert Yung in Germany, he was the fourth of seven sons who, at the age of eight, immigrated to San Francisco with his parents. In his youth, he devoted every moment of his free time to fighting as a young amateur boxer. By the time he reached adulthood, Al was built like a tank, squat and solid with a flattened nose, and a round face that bore the scars of his trade. At the ancient age of twenty-seven, he took the welterweight Gold Medal for Boxing in the inaugural year of the sport at the 1904 Summer Olympic Games held in St. Louis, Missouri.[122] [123] [124]

His Olympic medal still warm in his hand, Al took ownership of the Hawthorne Athletic Club, the gym he had long trained and fought for, and where he was a regular instructor, to use as a promoter's front for professional fights at local venues. To hold prizefights during this era held more challenges than trying to put a brassiere on a gazelle. California held a love-hate relationship with prizefights that harkened back to statehood in 1850. Each election season saw a constant evolution of anti-prizefight laws. But as the hub of boxing in the state, San Francisco blithely passed local ordinances that conflicted with state laws; those in positions to enforce the laws, largely declined to. Before the First World War, boxing was third in profits for the city, behind nickel slots and liquor permits.[125]

Al Young opened a saloon across from the Hawthorne Club in 1908. It was located next to a vaudeville hall called the Victoria Theater and just across from a dance club called National Hall. Al had an ulterior motive in renting that particular property. Under the auspices of the Hawthorne, he continued to host legal, sanctioned pro-fights at large venues. His newly incorporated Association Club however, was a business front dedicated to illegal four-round prizefights.

Through a door at the back of Al's saloon, in a stuffy windowless shack where he occasionally hosted legitimate events as varied as shuffleboard tournaments and election parties, he began to hold fights every Wednesday night. Eddie "Pie" Hennessy, who was one of Al's first glove boys, remembered it as "an old stinking place. They had to open the door to let the smoke out after every round. It held maybe five hundred.... There were bleachers with six rows and the fighters dressed underneath them. Al's brother, Chick, was on the door." Local boy Roy Duggan used to scale the fence of an empty lot out back, where you could watch the fights for free when the door was open.[126]

When passage of the National Prohibition Act, to provide enforcement of the Eighteenth Amendment—a federal alcohol ban which stated you could own it and drink it, but couldn't buy it, make it or move it—saw the country go dry in 1920, Al claimed to have converted his saloon to a soda fountain. After he was fined and jailed one time too many for illegal sales of hooch, he began to devote all his efforts as a matchmaker and promoter. The press called his place a lofty "Al Young's Resort" or "The Association," as if he were an honest merchant who had some spare ropes and poles lying around, which somehow assembled themselves every week for an impromptu slug fest.

As Al's reputation grew for well-matched fights and entertaining cards where anything goes, so did his need for a bigger building. But he went out with a bang at the old club in back of the saloon. A triple main event was held to great fanfare the first week of February 1923, before he closed the doors and moved to National Hall across the street.

Al brought in scrappy former featherweight Bobby Johnson as matchmaker. His weekly prizefights every Wednesday night soon became a San Francisco institution where future title holders and title hopefuls cut their teeth. During the Four-Round Era, victors of the Wednesday Nights Fights at the National had an easy jaunt across the street to Al's "soda shop" to get payment from the ornate brass cash register at the redwood bar. Like so many club and gym owners who always seemed to own saloons, Al likely offered free bowls of hot stew to his boxers, which for many of the boys, was their one and only daily decent meal. Fight fans would often stream out the National's door, stroll over to Turk Street to tip a few frosty mugs, and relive the evening's card, in a private room at the back of Redman's Hall.[127] [128] [129]

National Hall's new marquee (1940s)
Courtesy of OpenSFHistory / wnp14.3579

Frankie Campbell may have been green as grass in the ring, but Al Young and Bobby Johnson recognized a game brawler, whose hell-for-leather style had already made him a darling of Mission District fight fans. He soon became their number one crowd-pleaser, guaranteed to park fannies in every last seat of National Hall.

CHAPTER 6

K.O. KING OF BERNAL HEIGHTS

AFTER YOU HAVE SEASONED YOUR GLOVES WITH THE BLOOD, SWEAT AND TEARS
OF YOUR OPPONENTS, ALL ELSE IS ANTICLIMACTIC - BRIAN D'AMBROSIO

As the rising sun pushed the fog back to the coast, Frankie gazed into the tiny mirror above the sink of his one-room walkup in Bernal Heights, a largely Italian neighborhood just north of his Sunnyside stomping grounds. As he slicked a dab of hair grease through his dark locks, he felt the ache of swollen knuckles. He tilted his head, to examine the yellow-green hues of a faded bruise along his brow. Dressed in sweats and a pullover, with a deft scoop he swung up a grip that held

James Julius "Moose" Taussig
National Archive passport photo (1922)

his boots, gloves, wraps, and jump rope, then walked out the door and down the stairs into the rapidly thinning murk. Up the block, he hopped a streetcar and made his familiar way to one of the two best gyms in town. [130]

Taussig & Ryan's Gym was owned and operated by two fierce devotees of the game, who molded their fighters from the hard-scrabble heart of the Mission District's Tenderloin: James Julius "Moose" Taussig and William James "Paddy" Ryan.

Moose Taussig was one of the "South of Market Boys," a name given to neighborhood toughs born and reared in the densely-packed, blue-collar blocks known by locals as "South of the [cable car] Slot," before the Great Quake leveled the area. The streets produced a lower crust and an upper crust of hard boys and resilient men from the horse and buggy days, many of whom later thrived in the Mission District, and others who went on to become legends and leaders of sports, government and industry.

It was said that during his six decades in a cut throat sport, Moose Taussig achieved the impossible; he never made an enemy in the game. During his long career, Moose was everything from a boxing commissioner to a cornerman of over fifteen titleholders. He had an engaging personality and a mind like a steel trap for boxing minutiae. Long after he retired, boxing fans lined up like eager schoolchildren to hear him weave tales of the golden days of fistiana, which typically placed him at the center of the adventures. With his easy demeanor and owlish features, from his second-floor Ellis Street business offices, for Christmas every year, Moose would don the necessities and ho-ho-ho his way down below, to play the perfect Santa Claus in the lobby of the old Continental Hotel.[131]

It was Moose who gave future Champ "Babyface" Jimmy McLarnin his nickname when he was sixteen-years-old. In 1924, Jimmy and his manager "Pop" Foster landed in San Francisco and toured the local gyms looking for a fight. Moose peered down at the earnest angelic face of a boy barely over 100 pounds and two inches shy of five feet. As he shook his head in consternation, he remarked dubiously to Pop, "No wonder you can't get him a fight. He's got a baby face." The name stuck. Within four years, fans carried him on their shoulders to the dressing room, after Jimmy had claimed the World Lightweight title.[132]

Paddy Ryan referees a Bastille Day event (July 1924)
Neptune Beach, Alameda, CA

Moose Taussig's partner Paddy Ryan lied about his age to join the US Navy in 1896; he was sixteen. During his twenty-year stint, he became not only a boxing instructor and referee for the Navy Fleet's fights, he was Fleet Light-Heavyweight Champ. Paddy was stationed in the Hawaiian Islands with "Sailor Tom" Sharkey, before fighting all the greatest heavyweights of his era was even a dream on Sharkey's horizon. After discharge, Paddy shot to local prominence as a trainer across the bay in Alameda County, then had a short stint in early 1925 as manager of Al Young's new gym above National Hall, before he partnered in late 1925 with Moose Taussig to open a gym in the heart of the Mission District.[133] [134] [135]

Taussig & Ryan Gym interior (1929)
Illustrated by Howard Brodie

By the standards of the day, at 6,000 square feet, Taussig & Ryan's Gym was not only large, it was the fat beneath the fancy. Located in the former Grand Ballroom underneath the 180-room Cadillac Hotel on 312 Leavenworth at Eddy Street, the Cadillac was a four-story, luxury short- and long-term boutique spot. Guests could check their furs at the front desk on street level, while fighters pounded the heavy bags and grunted in two 16-foot rings rimmed by bleachers filled with gym rats and neighborhood kids, in the cavernous space below the hotel guests' well-shod feet. To the hotel's dismay, the odors of liniment and sweat, jarringly blended with cigarette haze and the pungent aroma of soiled and spongy gloves, often drifted up from below into the lobby.[136]

Just a few blocks away, the Royal Athletic Club was located in the basement below the Hotel Arnoux on Turk Street. The Royal was owned and operated by Dolph Thomas. Born Adolfo Gaggetti in Lucca, Italy, at the age of three, he became a son of the Mission District. He initially cut his teeth in boxing around 1910 as a bucket boy, where he watched and learned the trade from the bottom up.

By 1916, he was a matchmaker who headed a team for the Parkside Athletic Club, which provided fighters for the Dreamland Rink. A lean and hungry Jack Dempsey fought on one of his cards in 1917. When Dempsey dumped his manager of six months, Fred "Windy" Windsor, and before he hooked up with Jack "Doc" Kearns," he pleaded with Dolph numerous times to take him on. Dolph declined, and later was often known to give himself a few good swift kicks for passing up such an opportunity.[137] [138] [139] [140]

Dolph Thomas was a notorious neat freak. After he took over operation of the Royal in late 1923, the gym quickly became known for the cleanliness of its equipment, and the lack of blood and gore residue on its ring canvases. He had polished brass spittoons placed strategically around the training area, and was known to banish fighters from the gym if they spit on the floor. He didn't like people to loaf on the ring canvas either. He had it wired to give a hot seat for any dopes who dared to park their fannies on the apron. Jack Dempsey once hid out in his office for two hours waiting with glee to give somebody "the treatment."[141] [142] [143]

Dolph Thomas at his Royal Athletic Club
Courtesy David Thomas Rosenberg

Known as the "Dean of all Fight Seconds," his work as a cut man, one who patches up fighter's wounds between rounds, was legendary. A doctor once remarked Dolph could patch an eye cut better than most surgeons. He carried cobwebs in his kit, one of the best remedies at the time to stop a bleeding wound. Seldom was a fight stopped for cuts with Dolph in the corner.

****

Though press coverage hadn't initially kept up with the excitement he brought to the spectators, under the quiet tutelage of such revered veterans, Frankie Campbell racked up win after win at National Hall, to close out the year 1924 in several four-round preliminaries. In a "night of knockouts" on September 4, he kayoed Jack Desmond in the first round. Jack LaVelle went down and out in the first on September 17. He finished the month with a technical knockout in the third round; Harry Edwards had provided a bit more of a challenge. In November, he

49

was back on track; his relentless blows knocked Frank Howard out cold to the canvas in the first round.[144]

As his reputation grew, Frankie's purse for one fight soon equaled more than a month's salary for the average laborer, who in 1924 made about forty-cents an hour. His brother Dolph Camilli recalled a time when Frankie burst through the door, eyes bright from a recent win, and threw handfuls of greenbacks into the air of his mother's parlor. As they fluttered to the floor like confetti, some landed too near the stove. While his sisters danced to catch them mid-air, Albina's wide grin belied her chiding tones as she grabbed a broom to sweep the rest into a careful pile.[145][146]

Word began to spread of Frankie's sensational, lightning-quick knockouts; he rapidly attracted interest beyond the National Hall regulars. Fans appreciated this new slugger, who waded in with both fists and hit with such devastating force. His appearances at the Wednesday Night Fights guaranteed a sellout crowd. He had obtained celebrity status about town. As he ran the streets of home at dawn, the milkman and the paperboy shouted encouragement when he jogged by. Groups of kids clustered to watch him every afternoon as he trained in the gym. From the bleachers, people cheered him on as he sparred in the ring. These were his stomping grounds. These were his people. To a boy whose father had made him feel like a burden, the feeling of being loved and admired was indescribable.

The majority of Frankie's bouts to date had been against untried fighters with little or no ring experience. When Bert Valerga matched him to fight on December 3, 1924, against welterweight "Gunner" Isaacson, it was expected his mettle was about to be tested. Gunner was a U.S. Navy veteran of the First World War. He had fought aboard ship his entire stint, before he turned professional after the war ended. He had sixteen respectable wins under his belt when he and Frankie touched gloves. His experience meant nothing. Frankie dominated every round. Near the start of the third, he swarmed Gunner like an octopus on espresso; the punches seemed to come from everywhere, until a solid right knocked him out cold.

Frankie wrapped up the year with a four-round bout as a light-heavyweight, against a quick hard-socking southpaw out of Oakland. "Young Frankie Campbell," wrote the *San Francisco Examiner*, "who has been winning consistently at National Hall, hung up another win when he trounced Charley Martino in the special attraction." The *San Francisco Bulletin* noted he "handed Charley a bad lacing, taking the verdict with plenty to spare."[147][148]

Two things happened as the New Year rang in 1925; the game-changing new boxing laws were comfortably in high gear, and Al Young was pleased enough with his recent performances to advance Frankie beyond the curtain-raisers at National Hall. Bobby Johnson matched him as a light-heavyweight in his first six-round bout; the semi-windup to the Joe Miller–Billy Alger main event on January 8.

His opponent was fellow San Franciscan Art Titus, who held kayo victories over "Sailor" Joe Hughes and Johnny Tillman. The local press enthused that "Campbell is a Bernal Heights boy that has made a big impression with the Mission fans. He has won his last bouts with knockouts, though Titus is pretty hefty with his mitts." They predicted fight fans should expect a battle.[149] [150]

Titus was a 168-pound main-eventer, known to pack a deadly punch in both gloves. He had a reputation of mixing things up at all stages. The night of the fight however, with a series of blistering blows that drew screams of encouragement from a packed gallery, Frankie connected a right uppercut to Art's chin that lifted him off the canvas. As whoops of joy raced through the crowd, Titus went down like a felled tree, two minutes into the first round.

Boxing Tonight
NATIONAL HALL
Two Great Six-Round Bouts
Billy Alger vs. Joe Miller
Art Titus vs.
              Frank Campbell
Four Speedy Preliminaries
Ladies cordially invited
New ventilating system in-stalled, change of air every five minutes.

National Hall Wednesday Night Fights advertisement (Jan 1925)

The sports sections of newspapers up and down the West Coast began to carry the results of Frankie's fights. Sports editor Jim Powers of the *San Francisco Illustrated Herald* listed him in his picks for 1925 Pacific Coast boxers to watch. Frankie had become enough of a fan favorite that up-and-comers "Soldier" Burke and "Sailor" Joe Hughes vied for a victory, with Frankie as the promised prize.[151] [152]

When "Sailor" Joe Hughes took the win, the two were matched in mid-February as light-heavyweights in a six-round go at the National. Hughes had fought twenty-three fights in the Bay Area in 1924, and emerged the victor in sixteen of them. He was a Sacramento slugger rated as a real tough battler, who had destroyed the hopes of a lot of boys who endeavored to climb over him for a chance at the big money.

Frankie was confident he could give the Sailor some lessons in knot tying. His growing fan base at the National found no cause to hurl projectiles when the two touched gloves. Over six slashing rounds, as spectators enthusiastically spurred him on, Frankie rolled over his opponent like a backhoe. Joe was staggered so many times, he left the ring covered in blood and sported a newly bloomed cauliflower ear. Joe rallied to take the fifth round, yet as the final gong rang, the bout was Frankie's on points alone. Even "Sailor" Hughes could feel the heels of Frankie's shoes on his shoulders.[153] [154] [155]

In less than six months, Frankie Campbell was the talk of the town. But while he may have been street smart, he was effectively a babe in the woods, who soon became a tasty morsel to be tossed around by the wolves that controlled boxing. The resultant physical and mental toil would repeatedly cause him to question every aspect of his chosen profession.

CHAPTER 7

THE HOUSE OF QUARRELS

HE'S NO ONE PUNCH FINISHER. BUT WHEN HE LEANS ON ONE. IT HAS ALL HIS LOVE
AND BEST WISHES FOR AN UNDISTURBED SLUMBER - CLAUDE NEWMAN

Al Young matched Frankie on February 21, to fight "Brownie" Proctor of Oakland, in a six-round main event at the National the following Wednesday. Proctor, whose given name was Paul Linnet, had just come off a fight where his opponent, Johnny Tillman, mistook Proctor's arm for a beefsteak. After Johnny was knocked down twice, he came up for a second time a bit dizzy. During the excitement, he got his teeth mixed up with Brownie's right arm and took a chomp. The referee promptly disqualified him, and the press promptly dubbed Johnny Tillman "The Biter."[156] [157]

The morning of the fight with Proctor however, the club physician pulled Frankie from the event. An x-ray revealed during training he had damaged two knuckles of his right hand. The press reported he already had sustained injuries to that duke from the "Sailor" Hughes bout. Hand problems continued to hound him, but Frankie was on a roll and in high demand. His hands were wrapped tighter, and he was told to keep his mouth shut.

At the end of March, fighting in a curtain-raiser, he was back in action. He also had his first taste of a massive crowd. 20,000 people jammed the stands at Recreation Park, as Frankie made hard-socking Oakland light-heavyweight "Young" Franklin, look like a day laborer who had wandered in off the street, and been handed some gloves.

Fans paid over $40,000, the largest gate in San Francisco boxing history, to see the main event between the "Philly Phantom" Tommy Loughran and "Young" Will Stribling. It was a lackluster affair, but over the course of ten rounds, Stribling so violently wrestled Loughran in the clinches, with repeated blows to Tommy's short ribs, Will broke three of them.[158]

Frankie later recalled his short-lived career as Will Stribling's sparring partner while he had trained for the Loughran fight. "Pa" Stribling advertised a request for warm and willing bodies to help get his son up to snuff; Frankie was among those who offered themselves as paid punching dummies.

"I knew my place was a sparring partner and I kept the faith as nearly as I could." Frankie paused to fight a grin as his audience smirked. "But when Stribling started a left hook from the floor, I lost my job. I cracked the 'boy wonder' on the button and he wilted." Once the snickering died down, he went on, "I might have knocked Stribling out that day. And if it is my good fortune to fight him, I'll prove that I can still do it." He was being modest. Reports reached all the way to the East Coast that Frankie had knocked Willie cuckoo.[159] [160]

In mid-April, Frankie was paired as a light-heavyweight with 168-pound Joe "Racehorse" Roberts for the semi-windup of his first eight-rounder. Born Clement Robert Lombardi in Lucca, Italy, Roberts was a southpaw with a long straight left based out of the East Bay. Known as the sun-kissed son of Alameda to his local fans, Roberts boasted a record as long as a circus poster. He had over 100 professional contests across the state under his belt. He hadn't had a loss in seven months, and had yet to be knocked out.[161]

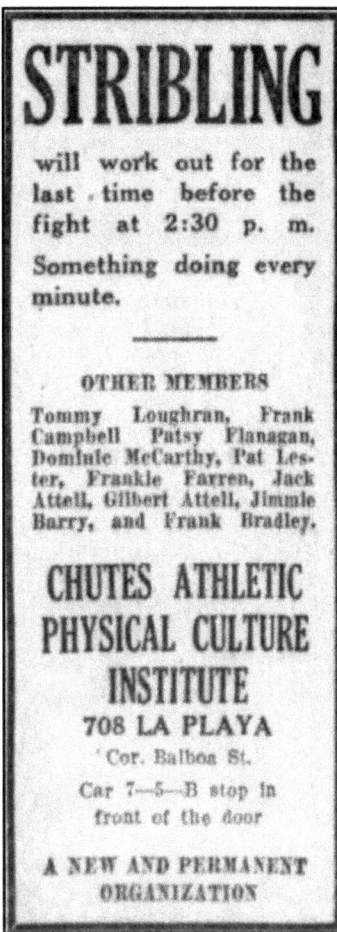

Ad for Young Stribling's training camp before Tommy Loughran fight (Feb 1925)

Frankie was at the top of his game, and already a decided favorite of the press, yet surprisingly little was reported about the fight. Frankie put the skids under Roberts when he tried to make it a brawl, and won decisively on points. It would be their rematch in July, which supplied fireworks that burst across the nation![162]

Frankie next touched gloves with eighteen-year-old George Barach, known as the "School Boy," for another eight-round go in mid-June. Barach was a fast-hitting light-heavyweight, said to carry a mighty wallop in his left and "a right like Judgment Day." Serbian by birth, George had twenty-one fights on his resume. He could take a blow on the button without slowing down. He had twice been a main-eventer, fighting before packed crowds all over the Sacramento Valley. Now he had set his sights on the Bay Area. [163] [164]

Frankie found his opponent to be a willing catcher for his punches; he dominated the first three rounds. George kissed the canvas twice. Those who sat ringside heard the snap, as with body blow after body blow, Frankie cracked three of his ribs in the fourth. In the eighth round, a brutal hit over the heart had George down and unable to leave the ring for a full ten minutes.[165]

Frankie's popularity with Bay Area fans continued to be white hot. Al Young regularly had to turn hundreds away anytime he appeared at National Hall. His manager Bert Valerga had recently surrendered his position over at the Chutes Gym, to devote more time to fight management. He teased that he sought a better class of boxer outside of the Bay Area. Frankie now fought locally for 20-25% of the gate. Bert thought he could get a higher percentage in Southern California. Al Young was worried he might lose a scrapper who had proved to be as popular as chicken at a church picnic. To keep him local, Al matched Frankie for his first ten-round main event at National Hall.

Publicity Photo (15 Apr 1925)
Courtesy author's collection

His opponent was Johnny "The Biter" Tillman of Oakland. The press enthused both fighters were such hard hitters, "that a knockout will surely terminate this setto." But Tillman had not been reinstated since the whole biting incident last February. Jimmy Ross stepped in as a last-minute substitute.

The fight was a fast affair while it lasted. The two went at each other hammer and tongs until the fourth round. Frankie launched a hard right to Jimmy's chin, and he folded like a cheap chair, out cold to the canvas; he now had thirteen straight wins under his belt.[166]

"Young" Franklin and "Sailor" Joe Hughes were hot on Frankie's trail for rematches, but Bert was out for bigger guns and better purses. When attempts to match him with more challenging opponents fell through, he accepted a rematch with "Racehorse" Roberts for a ten-round co-main event on July 29 at the National. Roberts claimed he had not been in his best condition during their first setto. He was anxious to prove his worth to the fans. Nothing filled the gallery faster than a rivalry between two

Bay Area boys. The turnstiles clicked merrily until the house was sold out the day of the bout; several hundred were again turned away at the gate.

When the two touched gloves, Roberts initially put up a game defense; he had not only vastly more ring generalship, he had superior speed and hitting power. Despite Roberts' experience, Frankie led the affair for several rounds, before he put him down for a nine-count in the ninth. Roberts was thoroughly exhausted. Frankie had buried a parade of punches into his ribs, until his torso was contused from the battering. He came out groggy for the final round, and decided to endure the prescribed three minutes through one prolonged clinch.

Referee Joe Gorman became increasingly incensed that Roberts balked at his verbal and physical efforts to separate. Gorman finally stepped forward with purpose oozing from his pores. The crowd expected him to end the fight. Instead, he gave Roberts such a terrific tug, he went whirling headlong through the ropes and landed outside the ring. Roberts made no effort to rise. For a moment, he just blinked up at the sea of faces which surrounded him.

The hall was in an uproar. Fans rushed the ring. Somebody threw a bucket of water at Roberts in an effort to revive him, but it hit the referee. The timekeeper was so flustered he lost track of the second hand. Gorman leaned dripping over the ropes, peered down at Roberts rolling around at the spectators' feet, and promptly counted him out. Two State boxing inspectors at ringside ruled it a valid knockout, and said they would report it so to the State Boxing Commission. For a solid week following the fight, sports writers from coast to coast and across Canada skewered the entire affair.[167] [168]

Nationwide headline compilation
Campbell–Roberts fight (31 Jul 1925)

The press reported the first day of August 1925, that Frankie had again sustained a right-hand injury during the Roberts fight. He was placed on the inactive list for an indefinite period. Despite his injuries, area sports editors now recognized Frankie as the hardest hitter in the region and one of the area's most promising light-heavyweights. Boxing fans agreed. When Bert matched him to fight Frankie Muskie in a ten-round main event on September 25, his popularity demanded the bout be held at the larger Dreamland Auditorium.[169]

The original Dreamland Rink (arrow) (1907)
Courtesy of OpenSFHistory / wnp5.50390

Built within months of the Great Quake, the Dreamland Rink was originally designed strictly for roller-skating. Two festive flags waved over its entrance on Steiner Street, where it was tucked behind the National Theater. It was pressed into service as the city's main boxing venue, after both historic fight centers, Mechanics' Pavilion across from City Hall, and Woodward's Pavilion in the Mission District, were destroyed by the Great Fire.

The first boxing match was staged at the Dreamland on August 31, 1906. There was a streetcar strike that week, but it didn't deter several thousand fans from walking to the event. Seating capacity was 3,000 on the main floor, and another 2,000 in the gallery. After various upgrades over a decade, it was referred to by the press as the Dreamland Auditorium or Pavilion. Fighters and fans fondly called it

"The House of Quarrels." One dandy sniffed that it was "a disreputable, ramshackle barn. Just a few boards nailed together shortly after the Fire. No comforts, no ventilation, nothing but four walls, a roof, some hard benches, and some common kitchen chairs." [170] [171] [172]

Down in the basement, there was a row of open-compartment lockers, but only one dressing room. Friendly opponents at an evening's event joked around good-naturedly as they changed into their fighting togs. However, with no separate facilities, those engaged in a grudge match often started the fight before they ever gained the stairs to the ring. [173]

Frank Schuler was the Dreamland's matchmaker from its inception. He had held the position at Woodward Garden's auditorium before the Great Fire leveled it. Along with two brothers Ed and Chester Lynch, and former boxer Toby Irwin, they formed the Observatory Club as a business front for the venue. Local press called them "The Four Horsemen of Steiner Street." They had a monopoly on bouts held at the Dreamland, and claimed to have established the tradition of Friday Night Fights in the city. [174] [175]

Little red-headed Terry Murnane, who barely scaled five feet, but carried the lofty name of Thomas Francis Meagher Murnane, was the city's main ring announcer, and held a regular stint at the Dreamland. Terry had a penetrating, high falsetto voice which easily reached clear to the top of the eighth row of the gallery. If the boys in back failed to settle down, he would raise a hand for silence and bellow, "Chentlemen, it's time to pipe down now, tank youse!" [176] [177] [178]

Toby Irwin was the Dreamland's head referee. He first met Frank Schuler when he fought at Woodward's. His right name was John Francis Daley. He was a former lightweight, who in the early 1900s, had largely boxed out of San Francisco and Oakland.

He owned a liquor store in his native Telegraph Hill district. One reporter remarked he resembled a bow-tied Kewpie doll groom on a wedding cake.

As referee he would play a direct part in the death of Frankie Campbell. [179]

Toby Irwin (c1910s)
Courtesy author's collection

Ed Lynch (28 Jun 1928) New
Dreamland Auditorium
Souvenir Program

While his brother Chester quietly worked behind the scenes, Edward Jerome "Ed" Lynch was the public face of the Dreamland as its promoter and building manager. Ed's physical appearance was somewhat mild, almost professorial. But he loved nothing better than to place himself at the center of internal strife within the club.

When he reached a boiling point, with blue eyes blazing, he was known to carefully roll up his sleeves before he flung himself at referees, fellow promoters, and matchmakers he disagreed with. The steam that occasionally boiled from his ears was tolerated because he regularly presented some memorable wars.[180]

Though the Dreamland was viewed by some as a grimy and musty place, in its heyday, its walls had welcomed such boxing greats as Jack Dempsey, Jess Willard, Billy Miske, and Gunboat Smith.

To fight the main event at the Dreamland meant you had arrived; you were considered among the elite of the San Francisco boxing fraternity. Now Frankie Campbell had joined their exalted ranks.

CHAPTER 8

THE PERSONAL EQUATION

THE FIGHT IS WON OR LOST FAR AWAY FROM WITNESSES-BEHIND THE LINE IN THE GYM,
OUT THERE ON THE ROAD, LONG BEFORE I DANCE UNDER THOSE LIGHTS - MUHAMMAD ALI

Frankie's opponent for his début at the Dreamland was born Frantisek Muska in Sázava, Czechoslovakia. Frankie Muskie was a light-heavyweight fighting out of Saint Paul, Minnesota. His manager Leo Levitt had brought his three most promising fighters to California to sample the thriving fight metropolis; Muskie was one of the trio. Mere months into his freshman year, Muskie had taken the state by storm with six sensational battles. He had vocally pressed for a fight with Frankie Campbell. Fresh from victories in Southern California, just before Muskie stepped on the train headed north, Leo Levitt wired a direct challenge; Muskie would meet Frankie anytime, anywhere, any number of rounds.[181] [182]

The press had coined the upcoming bout, "The Battle of the Two Frankies." It was deemed a "natural" and was looked forward to with great anticipation. Like Frankie Campbell, Frankie Muskie was seen as a sensational crowd-pleaser, rapidly on the rise up the pugilistic ladder. Both fighters were confidence personified. As fans jammed the little room above Chad Milligan's cigar store on Ellis Street, where weigh-ins for local bouts took place, Muskie told the press he'd wipe the floor with his opponent. Frankie shot back that he would fight Muskie in a winner-take-all, and place a side bet on himself as the victor.[183] [184] [185]

"The demand for tickets has been the largest in all my experience as a promoter," boasted Ed Lynch. Interest was so intense the entire house was nearly sold out in advance. The local papers made the fight one of the most talked about encounters in months to occupy the spotlight at the Dreamland. It was front page news the week before the bout. Some declared it could be the Battle of the Year. There was more anticipation of this fight than the big main event over at California Hall, between the "Idaho Assassin" Mickey Rockson and "Sailor" Joe Hughes.

Despite the fact Frankie was purely a puncher, while Muskie could punch and box, meaning he possessed good defense and offense skills, he went into the fight a 10-to-8 favorite. His sparring sessions at National Hall's gym were standing-room-only events. It was expected this would be Frankie's baptism by fire. He had quickly knocked over most of his opponents but never been forced to assimilate much punishment to achieve victory. Reporters remarked he needed to further develop his ring generalship, and learn to lead; he was content to let the other fellow force the action. Could he wade in confidently and take three to give one, or would he flinch? The coming battle was the moment to find out.[186]

The day of the fight, a group of over 250 Mission District folks teamed up with a local eight-piece musical orchestra. In a long column of flower-festooned vehicles, his name on signs upon the doors, Frankie stood in the lead car like a Grand Marshall at the head of a parade. As the band played popular jazz tunes, he waved and smiled, his eyes damp with emotion as they drove through his neighborhood streets. Friends waved and wished him good luck, then everyone gave a great cheer as they arrived at the Dreamland.[187] [188]

Brass band auto parade for a local fighter (1925)
Courtesy author's collection

The crowd was not disappointed. Frankie's performance that night was said to have added "new laurels to his fistic record." Alex McCausland of the *San Francisco Examiner*, famous for wearing a tuxedo to local fights, called him the "Glen Park Ring Demon." It was a slashing ten-round affair. At the opening gong, Frankie pummeled Muskie across the ring with stiff rights and lefts to the body. Just when it seemed he'd make short work of it, Muskie came back and pounded him soundly until the bell. The second round was a corker. Muskie initially touched gloves with a left eye slash, which hadn't properly healed from a recent bout with Lew Rollinger; with a cracking right, Frankie split the cut wide open. Muskie's corner could not staunch the wound. Blood splattered both fighters and the ring canvas in a steady spray for the remainder of the fight.[189]

Through the middle rounds, the spectators, who had crammed the place to such capacity they taxed the rafters, stood on their chairs and screamed themselves silly. Frankie's Mission District fans, who sat together in a block of hundreds-strong, shook the walls with yells of encouragement, while their orchestra repeatedly broke into musical celebration. Frankie's bombshell rights to the head and chin sent Muskie reeling to the ropes. Muskie tried to land his big right on Frankie's jaw, but time after time he slipped them to counter with a tattoo of hard body shots.

Battle of the Two Frankies article image
(24 Sep 1925) San Francisco Bulletin

Frankie kept up his rushing tactics with a bombardment of one terrific right cross after right cross. Muskie's knees sagged, but he weathered the storm until the bell. Several times Frankie appeared on the verge of a knockout, but he couldn't put Muskie down, which won him the admiration of the crowd. He seemed to absorb punches like a sponge. Frankie added a split lip to give Muskie's slashed eye some company. Muskie showed some life in the fifth, but Frankie kept his cool. With a barrage of heavy lefts and rights that boomed through the purple haze of tobacco smoke floating listlessly over the ring, Frankie forged back into the lead until the final gong rang.[190]

The crowd surged to its feet in a roaring wave of applause. The press deemed Frankie Campbell's fifteenth fight as the best in his short career. Some said it was the best fight seen in years at the Dreamland. Over 5,000 spectators witnessed the affair, the most to fill the pavilion in many months. As the crowd streamed out into the night, some wended their way up to Ellis Street for an early breakfast at the Waffle Inn. In between fluffy bites of scrambled eggs and crisp bacon, over the clatter of silverware and the clink of porcelain mugs of java, they shared grins of contentment at full bellies and the reliving of a good card.

In a September article about promising young fighters, which opened with "All the World Loves a Socker," Jim Powers of the *Los Angeles Daily News*, who had been ringside at the fight, remarked that, "While Signor Camilli is a nice gentlemanly fellow out of the ring, he is certainly a raving maniac when he pulls on the gloves. He has knocked out ten of his fifteen opponents since he started juggling the leather mittens. Up north they think [World Light-Heavyweight champ Paul] Berlenbach is a powder puff puncher compared to Campbell."[191]

It was said jovially, but was an apt description. Outside the ring, Frankie was a good-time Charley. But when he stepped through the ropes, one expected steam to jet from his nostrils like an enraged bull as he pawed his shoes in rosin dust. He not only fought for the honor of his district; when that bell rang, he unleashed the rage which resided inside a part of his heart that was still a cornered boy.

Article illustration Jack Lustig
(27 Sep 1925)

Harry B. Smith, sports editor of the *San Francisco Chronicle*, noticed the devotion of Frankie's fans, and chalked it up to the fact that Frankie was simply a decent fellow. He took his successes without having to increase the size of his hat. He fought to give the regular folks a thrill, fans and friends with two bits in their pocket, when those coins were often dear to part with.

In an article titled, "The Personal Equation," Smith mused:

"Turn any way you desire, and you'll discover the personal equation enters very largely into life. We had an example of it the other night at Dreamland Rink, when Frankie Campbell, a strapping big fellow of 169 pounds, fought and defeated Frankie Muskie."

"Campbell is a product of Glen Park where, judging from appearances, he has friends by the legion. They packed one section of Dreamland Rink on Friday night to overflowing; had a big banner to tell the world they were there to cheer for Campbell, and an accordion to grind out some music."

"Campbell as a fighter has much to learn. He's big and he's strong, and he's got a punch. So, these Glen Parkers are not just raving over Campbell merely because of his being a fighter. True, he has won something like twelve of thirteen starts. But there unquestionably is that personal equation of a chap who is popular. Naturally his friends like him for his successes, but that wouldn't be a sufficient inducement to bring about such a demonstration. There's nothing like being liked for yourself."[192]

Sports editor Larry Lavers at the *San Francisco Bulletin* was smitten. He suspected Frankie had started to put himself in line for some big-time bouts, and hoped he wouldn't forget his local fans. "Here's a few words, Frankie, from one who wishes you well: Don't go too fast; you're young yet and you've got a lot to learn before you'll be champion. Don't go away for a while; stick around here and give us a coupla more fights like you did last night. The fight game hereabouts needs you."[193]

Publicity photo (1925)
Courtesy San Francisco History Center,
San Francisco Public Library

While Frankie was well on his way to pugilistic heights in the Bay City, he still hadn't fully left baseball behind, though it had become a part-time commitment. Fighters who also played baseball with the semi-pros was common in the Twenties. An entire stable of Oakland fighters with the Imperial Gymnasium had developed a successful team that often challenged their rivals across the bay. Throughout the autumn, the press reported any noteworthy successes as Frankie continued to play with the local ball clubs. But where before, his name had been merely a line item, now sports page mentions on team performance singled him out.

"Frankie Campbell, the sensational Glen Park light-heavyweight scrapper, pitched the Lindberg-Freese Nine to a 4-to-3 victory over the Lundstrum Hatters yesterday," and "Frankie Campbell will be on the mound for the Lindberg team next Sunday when it tries conclusions with the Cohen

Jewelers at Southside Playgrounds." He moved easily between positions; sometimes he was relief pitcher, other times he played shortstop or first baseman. He loved baseball, but the lure of battle and the excitement he provided fans, as he notched more knockouts in the ring onto his belt, had become addictive.[194] [195]

Around this period, Frankie also clearly began a stretch where he experienced mixed results in the ring. But not due to juggling two sports. His manager wanted him to become a more well-rounded fighter, with less slugging offensively and more boxing defensively. Yet Bert Valerga failed to provide any consistent training, and without guidance, Frankie started to noticeably flounder. His draw to fans was *because* he was a slugger. Bert then began to over-match a youngster who was still effectively learning the ropes of his profession, against those who vastly outgunned him in experience; opponents who were adept in ring wars and possessed good overall skills. Bert's percentage of Frankie's purses had grown to such a tidy sum, he built an addition onto his home with the profits.[196]

An Associated Press fight announcement which ran nationwide in mid-October was characteristic of Bert's growing greed. He accepted a match with southpaw sensation, Theodore "Tiger" Flowers on November 14, for the main event in an open-air ring over home plate at Recreation Park. The "Georgia Tornado" was a sturdy middleweight who called Atlanta home. At the time, he was the most heralded black fighter in a generation. His manager had expressed interest in what became his second successful campaign on the West Coast. He had an astonishing record of 108 wins, 13 losses and 5 draws (108-13-5). He had just racked up his sixteenth straight win, and had most recently fought against eastern veterans Jock Malone, Joe Gans, Jack Delaney, and Ted Moore.

Then the Flowers fight was put in jeopardy. Tiger's manager Walker "Walk" Miller was suspended by the New York State Boxing Commission. For months, Walk had circulated rumors that Tiger's previous opponent, Jack Delaney had something besides his fist in his glove, when he had knocked out Tiger last winter. Walk's claims resulted in so much publicity, that the world's foremost boxing promoter George "Tex" Rickard, who never passed up an opportunity good or bad if it stood to make money, later stepped in and promoted a Delaney–Flowers rematch at Madison Square Garden which made him a killing.[197]

****

Just after Halloween, Bert Valerga secured 30% of the gate for Frankie's last bout of 1925, set for mid-November. His opponent was the "Idaho Assassin" Mickey Rockson. Al Young reported he had pushed Frankie's bout with Tiger Flowers to December, but eventually the match faded away with no explanation, and no indication of a revisit. Given Flowers' level of expertise, it was a gross mismatch that Al and Bert should never have considered. Just months later, Tiger took the title from the "Pittsburgh Windmill" Harry Greb, to become the first black American in U.S. history to win the World Middleweight title.

Frankie Campbell and Mickey Rockson had both just come off of what were unanimously deemed two of the most exciting local slug fests in years. Sports writers were hard-pressed to decide which of the two fights had been the most sensational. Interest in their bout reached a fever pitch. Promoters expected a sellout crowd. It was an event that caused considerable interest by boxing aficionados. "Campbell's last showing, when he trounced Frankie Muskie so decisively, just about made him. Rockson is just the type of a fighter that will bring the best in Campbell to the surface. It ought to be a great fight, with plenty of hard socking in sight."[198]

Fighting out of Boise, Idaho, Mickey was a light-heavyweight with sixty-seven bouts. He was a rough, aggressive boxer-brawler, who made his opponent step at top speed. He sported an iron jaw, a stomach that was steel riveted, and a sledgehammer right, which had rendered more than one of his opponent's unconscious. Rockson was an immense crowd-pleaser. In between arrests for hot rod races and dance hall brawls, he had been fighting 12- and 15-round bouts up and down the Pacific Northwest while California was still hostage to the Four-Round Era.

With his thick dark locks, and an endearing dimpled smile that lit up his face, Mickey could charm the birds from the trees. He looked 'black Irish' but was actually born Nikola Rajković in Yugoslavia. Like Frankie, his ring alias was to appeal to Scots-Irish boxing fans. Mickey's charm later resulted in a desperate attack that cost him his eyesight. During a heated dispute with a fellow in Boise who claimed Mickey had tried to romance his wife, sulfuric acid was tossed into his face. On his Second World War draft registration forms, a tortured approximation of his signature, was followed by comments that the 39-year-old was blind, wore dark glasses, and required a service dog. [199] [200]

Despite reports that he had again injured his right hand during his fight with Frankie Muskie, and that Mickey Rockson was the more experienced fighter of the two, Frankie went into the bout a 2-to-1 favorite. Both fighters had trained for close to five weeks, and were in the proverbial "pink of condition." At weigh-in, Frankie tipped the scales seven pounds heavier than Mickey, one of the few times in his career he weighed more than his opponent.[201]

As the opponents waited in their corners, the crowd was already out of control. It was the biggest, most raucous house that had ever wended its way into the Dreamland. At the sound of the bell, rather than slug it out, Mickey elected to stand off and box, and Frankie attempted to follow suit. But Mickey danced and circled easily as he kept stabbing Frankie with repeated jabs to the mouth to take the first round.

Honors were about even for the middle rounds. Frankie was largely the aggressor, with short hard lefts and damaging rights to the body which made Mickey wince. But the fame of Frankie's hard punches failed to daunt him. Mickey was ever on the go, as he repeatedly rushed in, taking the play away. On the retreat before Frankie's rushes, he did so gracefully, as he slipped over left hands while

Frankie sought in vain to land a haymaker. Frankie was noted to be overcautious during moments he could have put Mickey down; he failed to take advantage of the few openings given him.

The fireworks started in the sixth and seventh rounds. With a recklessness that pleased the big crowd, they finally stood toe-to-toe, lashing out wildly. Frankie abandoned any thoughts of boxing. He swung repeatedly with jolting lefts to the head and stiff rights to the body. He fought savagely in the seventh, battering Mickey from pillar to post. A terrific right to the jaw, perfectly timed, seemed to rock him back on his heels. But Mickey just grinned widely like a possum eating fire ants and came back for more. Iron jaw, indeed.

In the ninth round, Mickey took the fight away. With the fury of a mid-western tornado, he sent two lefts to the ribs and a smashing right to the jaw. Frankie's eyes were glassy as he stumbled groggily to his stool at the bell. Sensing blood, Mickey tore out of his corner in the tenth. With a mad, desperate do-or-die onslaught, he threw all cautions to the wind. He pounded Frankie about the head, smashed two left hooks into the body, then he stepped back, and copped him with a beautiful right, square on the nose. Frankie's knees sagged but still he replied with a hard left and a right to the jaw

The house was in an uproar. The din was deafening. A sea of faces and a cacophony of languages, all stood on their chairs, cheering lustily as they screamed at Mickey to finish him off. He gleefully slammed away, with rights to the stomach and lefts to the head. Frankie reeled out of clinch after clinch, balanced on a razor thin edge between defeat and survival. The sound of the final gong found Mickey still flailing away with tireless energy. When the referee raised both arms, to announce to the wildly applauding crowd that the bout was a draw, the cheers turned to a thunderous chorus of boos that vibrated the window glass.[202] [203]

****

With some wounds to lick, and a lull in boxing due to the year-end holidays, Frankie eagerly turned his sights back to baseball. He had missed his true love, and embraced her with all the pent-up energy and devotion of a besotted fool. In mid-December, in the position of shortstop, during a game against the Lundstrom Hatters, Frankie's double-play, followed by a triple-play, helped clinch the Lindberg-Freese Nine to a win of the Independent Winter League Championship of 1925.[204]

While Frankie helped to win local baseball games, Tom Laird, occasional local ring referee and sports columnist for the *San Francisco News*, was back east to cover the World Series. When Tom ran into fellow columnist, Damon Runyon, he spoke excitedly about a fighter he expected to be the next Light-Heavyweight Champion of the World. Runyon noted that Tom was not commonly given to praising green fighters, "but he waxes so enthusiastically about this chap, that at one time he was standing with his hands raised in the manner of an exponent of 'The Manly Art of Scrambling Ears,' showing how the next champ delivers his blows."

"I saw Jack Dempsey when he started out in the four-round game on the Pacific Coast," said Tom. "He had none of the promise of this Campbell.... Here is a natural socker. He knocks 'em bow-legged with a punch.... He likes to smack 'em around the body, and he can pick openings about as nicely as anyone you ever saw.... I think he is the best prospect I have seen in many years."[205]

Runyon's tolerant skepticism bled through the pages, but Tom Laird's opinions on future prospects in sports came to be taken seriously. In 1935, he informed dubious New York writers, that a San Francisco Seals outfielder from a crab-fishing family in North Beach, who had just signed with the New York Yankees, would make them forget Babe Ruth. His name was Joe DiMaggio.

CHAPTER 9

BERNAL HEIGHTS SLUGGER

WORDS CANNOT DESCRIBE THAT FEELING OF BEING A MAN. OF BEING A GLADIATOR.
OF BEING A WARRIOR. IT'S IRREPLACEABLE. - SUGAR RAY LEONARD

Frankie Campbell mopped up the floor in a decisive rematch as the New Year ushered in 1926. Frankie Muskie wanted to avenge what he considered a close loss the previous September. Mickey Rockson's manager Abe Matin pursued a rematch just as vigorously. Abe claimed the draw last November was an unfair nod to Frankie for being the hometown boy. On December 22, Mickey received an early Christmas gift. The fighters signed on the dotted line for a New Year's Day ten-round main event back at the Dreamland. Bert and Frankie received the gift of 30% percent of the gate.

On the morning of New Year's Day however, Rockson's manager announced his fighter was a patient down at Stanford Hospital, suffering from a bout of influenza-related pneumonia. A nationwide flu epidemic that winter had resulted in fatality rates upwards of 40%. The Dreamland promoters sought out either "Allentown" Joe Gans, who had just arrived from the East Coast, or Frankie Muskie as a substitute. Muskie eagerly accepted. He was happy to get a chance to reverse the former verdict of their last bout. Fans and the press were thrilled to get a rematch with two of the hardest brawlers in the game; they knew to expect a ring war. Muskie had just come off a decisive 10-round fight against the now-ailing Mickey Rockson, where he had handily won every round; he was the logical choice for the spot.

Half an hour before the bout, as spectators fussed in their seats, a fellow known only as Joe asked permission to step into the ring and sing a few tunes. To the delight of the crowd, he had a good voice, and he fairly captured the rapt audience as the notes floated clearly up into the rafters. The orchestra, present at every one of Frankie's fights, played a selection or two. The Grand Finale was a dance exhibition, with the band furnishing the accompaniment. Then the referee barked a stop to the whole affair, and the spectators settled down to watch the boys fling some gloves.[206]

Frankie wasted no time easing into the bout. He planned to bend Muskie into a bow knot and present him as a souvenir to the folks back in Saint Paul. At the opening gong, he staggered Muskie with two jolting rights. Muskie's lip split and blood began to stream down his chest. In the second, Frankie shot out a right clip along Muskie's jaw that shook him to his shoelaces. A left to the gut doubled him over, and fans screamed for Frankie to knock him out. But Muskie clinched until the gong sounded.

Frankie battered Muskie around the ring for the entirety of the third and fourth rounds. He took everything Frankie threw at him, but still he managed to survive the onslaught. Whenever Frankie hit Muskie with a particularly hard sock, the band's bass drummer produced a rumbling thud, which caused the crowd to howl. In the fifth, a stiff right uppercut dropped Muskie like a sack knocked loose from the rafters. But he refused to be stopped, and he rose for another go. On through ten relentless rounds, the two traded wild blows like sailors on payday. No less than six different times, Muskie appeared on the verge of being knocked out. Frankie hit him with everything but the corner stool, yet still he staggered to his feet. Granite was envious of his jaw. Blood continued to flow from Muskie's cut lip throughout. The two fighters' chests and trunks were splattered red like an abstract painting.[207]

When the final gong sounded, the crowd erupted in wild cheers and stomped their feet at the ferocious contest. As the referee raised Frankie's hand in victory, they applauded with gusto, both for Frankie, who threw everything he had into the fight, and for Muskie, who survived the endless bombardment of punches. As rematches go, the crowd not only heartily approved, they demanded another, just to experience such a thrill one more time.

****

Frankie now had a record of 16-0-1: sixteen wins, nine of them knockouts, zero losses, and one draw under his belt. The local press proclaimed him the second-best San Francisco draw after National Hall and Dreamland darling welterweight Joe Roche. But Frankie had an entire orchestra playing full tilt between rounds at his events. Joe only had a lone accordion player from his North Beach streets. He had another nickname too: "The Bernal Heights Slugger." Status as the city's number-one fan favorite was in his sights. Damon Runyon ranked Frankie as second among the top three West Coast light-heavyweights to watch in 1926.[208]

When Middleweight Champion Harry Greb came to the coast to fight Ted Moore down in Southern California, he asked that an out-of-weight fight, which would not put his title at stake, be arranged up north. Frankie's name was at the top of the list. His fans were elated at the thought of such a bout. To the chagrin of the locals, Jimmy Delaney was selected to fight Greb in what would be their third fight. Delaney, who had now won twice over Tiger Flowers—who himself lifted Greb's crown mere weeks later—went on to fight and lose to Greb for the third time.[209] [210]

Ed Lynch attempted negotiations with Bert Valerga in early February 1926, to contract a rematch for Frankie with Mickey Rockson at the Dreamland. But after the second pounding Frankie had administered to Muskie, he once again needed to nurse his swollen hands; he would be in no condition to fight until March. He had already hopped a train north. His brother Albert's wife had family up in Mendocino County. Frankie spent hours swimming in the Russian River; he took to the water like a retriever pup. When he didn't hunt and fish in the coastal forest, newspapers reported he often found himself in the role of lifeguard, to rescue inexperienced swimmers caught in the Russian's cold and strong currents.[211] [212]

In early March, Charley Harvey, manager of Britain's Roland Todd, who had taken both the European and British Empire Middleweight titles in 1923, arrived in town on the train from New York. He and Bert Valerga hashed out an agreement for a ten-round main event under promoter Tommy Simpson, at the Oakland Civic Auditorium in the East Bay.

Opened to great fanfare in the spring of 1915, the Civic is a Beaux Arts-style municipal auditorium. At the time, it's 215,000 square feet made it one of only three large convention halls located in the West. It was a very innovative complex for its time and the pride of the citizens of Oakland.

Oakland Civic Auditorium (1915)
Courtesy of Wikipedia

The auditorium boasted a separate concert theater, an arena, exhibit halls, and an art gallery. It once hosted Buffalo Bill's Wild West Show, and had even been used as a treatment center during the Spanish Influenza epidemic of 1918. Prizefights were held in the arena, which could accommodate up to 8,000 people.

Roland Todd was born in Marylebone, London, England. He was the seventh child born to his parents, but the only child to live beyond infancy. He was the great-great grandson of prominent eighteenth-century bare-knuckle pugilist John "Jack" Musters. As he launched his tour of America, Todd had the double burden of country and ancestry to uphold. Only three years older than Frankie, Todd boasted a resume of 81-14-4. He was accustomed to 15- and 20-round fights in the United Kingdom. He sported an aquiline nose that had yet to be broken. Since he landed on American shores, Todd had the temerity to meet fellow middleweights Dave Shade, Harry Greb, and Jimmy Slattery in one-two-three order, all in the month of January alone. Though he decisioned on points in all three fights, he remained upright and battling in every contest when the final gong sounded.[213]

Upon his arrival in San Francisco in mid-March, Todd set up camp at Taussig & Ryan's Gym. Frankie settled in at the Royal Athletic Club. Fight promoter Tommy Simpson arranged for Sabbath day workouts by both fighters at Oakland's Imperial Gym the day before the fight. Bay Area sports writers, and a large crowd of the curious, took the half hour ferry trip across the bay to follow the pugilists through their rope skipping and sparring. Several reported being accosted by dice hustlers, who fleeced several suckers in crap games held on the decks of the boats as they chugged across the water.

Frankie Campbell (left) & Roland Todd (right)
(30 Mar 1926) Courtesy Oakland Post-Inquirer

Once at the Imperial, Todd went four easy rounds. He was said to be a rough, tough, mauler who hooked his punches from every angle, and was a vicious infighter. While a win over Todd wouldn't immediately result in fabulous purses, Frankie realized the doors a solid victory over him would open; the thought made him strangely nervous. His manager reckoned a win over Todd would provide Frankie with a confidence boost. But Bert Valerga still hadn't worked with his fighter on good defense tactics, and he was sending him up against a seasoned veteran.

To a capacity crowd of onlookers, Frankie sparred four rounds for speed with welterweights Joe Fox and Joe Dundee, then pounded away with hard rights to the head of Carl Augustine, a light-heavy known to be a tremendous body puncher. Raymond McNally, editor of the *San Francisco Bulletin*, noted from ringside that Frankie needed to use his left for something other than lifting his hat. "Add a good left hook to his repertoire and he'll be a dangerous man." Frankie trained without headgear, and he had never trained harder or looked in better condition; "a tough kid with a good wallop who likes to tear in where the gloves are the thickest." Bert told spectators to get a good look at Roland Todd's pretty face, because nobody would recognize it after Frankie got done knocking him around. [214] [215] [216]

Just days before the bout, promoter Tommy Simpson announced the winner would fight veteran middleweight Jock Malone at the Civic on April 7. Malone had come out to the West Coast from St. Paul at the beginning of the year looking for fresh opponents. Jock had just won a decisive technical knockout over Joe Roche at the Civic; he demanded a match with Frankie.

F. CAMPBELL (Camilli)

Illustration in La Voce Del Popolo
(31 Mar 1926)

While gamblers waged even money on the shindy, sports writer Bob Shand of the *Oakland Tribune* thought Frankie was in over his head. Todd was a veteran fighter, while Frankie was viewed as a youngster still being brought along. He had knocked over a battalion of brawlers, but had never been put to the acid test against a cagey fighter like Todd, who could adjust his style on the fly. Shand expected Frankie's trainers to send him out to make it a slug fest with an early knockout. If the fight went the distance, he expected Todd, as a skilled campaigner, to take the lead; Frankie was still a bit too green to handle it properly.[217]

The city's Italian paper, *La Voce Del Popolo* agreed. "Campbell has all the requirements to become a great boxer but he must not be pushed forward too quickly. In boxing, especially when dealing with a young, relatively inexperienced fighter, managers should follow the old proverb, 'He who goes slow, goes healthy, and goes far.'" They did however have hopes that one of Frankie's "tremendous clubbing punches" would send Roland Todd into orbit.

****

On the afternoon of March 31, Frankie entered the ring at 168 pounds. As a natural middleweight, Todd typically fought comfortably at 159 pounds. At weigh-in however, he tipped the scale at a surprising 168 1/2 pounds.

The fight was a fast affair. Todd was observed to have an odd powder-puff style that did not impress Frankie's fans in the gallery, who jeered him mercilessly. But Todd's experience carried him over several rough spots. He blocked and slipped punches nicely; many of Frankie's slugging rights and lefts sailed harmlessly by. When opportunities did arise for Frankie to put him down, he failed to use his head, and Todd managed to outsmart him. When Frankie accidentally head-butted Todd in the seventh, a cut opened up over his left eye, which bothered him considerably. [218] [219]

Just before the end of the tenth, Todd landed a left-handed crack to the chin. Frankie's knees sagged and he clinched. The press noted his eyes appeared perfectly clear. They felt the punch did no serious damage. Yet the moment evidently made an impression on Referee Al Wainwright. As the echo of the gong signaled the end of the fight, Wainright threw both arms in the air, signifying a draw. The west side of the gallery, where a rooting section had formed that held thousands of Frankie's fans, groaned like a bloodthirsty throng at the completion of a too-swift hanging.

As many had predicted, the outcome of such a mismatch was somewhat expected. But others thought a draw decision during Frankie's impressive upward climb was not the mark of a possible title-chaser. Some observed he didn't have enough of a killer instinct; that grim determination to sail in with both hands going until a man in trouble dropped to the canvas. Others had unfairly pinned all their hopes on Frankie, as the one to lead San Francisco out of the pugilistic wilderness, and into the championship class; a long drought that stretched back decades ago to Joe Choynski and Jim Corbett.[220]

When he failed to perform to their standards, they were merciless. Bill Moran at the *San Francisco Bulletin* was especially brutal. "The hopes of local fight fans that a new champion was in the making were dealt a hard blow. Campbell was our last hope, and he flivvered. He will never be a champion or even a contender until he changes his style of attack."[221]

PLEASURE PARADE

IF YOU CHEAT IN THE DARK OF THE MORNING.
YOU'LL GET FOUND IN THE BRIGHT LIGHTS OF THE NIGHT - JOE FRAZIER

Frankie shrugged a tailored suit coat onto his muscular frame, and buttoned it over a crisp white dress shirt. From his rooms on 20th Street, the meager glow of a streetlight caught his hazel eyes as he gazed out the window for the taxi. He ran a hand over his freshly shaved jaw; the barber had lightly nicked the cleft in his chin. When the taxi pulled up, he gave a final swipe to settle his glossy locks, snugged his wool tie, slipped a leather wallet that comfortably bulged with cash into his pocket, and jogged down the stairs. Within the hour, his arm encircled a pretty girl, his head was abuzz with bootleg gin, and the Ted Lewis Jazz Band had just launched into "St. Louis Blues." The night was young, the booze was plentiful, and he was a terrific dancer.

The Roaring Twenties was among the most transformative eras in American history, and author F. Scott Fitzgerald seemed to deftly capture it all. "The parties were bigger. The pace was faster, the shows were broader, the buildings were higher, the morals were looser, and the liquor was cheaper."[222]

As America entered the decade, over half of what had once been a nation of agricultural workers, dependent on the whims of the weather, had rapidly become one of city dwellers with steady paychecks. Women entered the workplace in record numbers. They began to express their independence; in thought, in fashion, and in consumerism. They cut their hair into short bobs, tossed away their corsets, and donned clothing that allowed them not only to breathe, but to dance the Charleston. For the first time American culture was dominated by the youth. The "flapper" emerged supreme and her free-spirited allure to men was as irresistible as bees to honey.

An unprecedented winning streak on Wall Street meant regular folks had ready cash, and seemed to suggest the good times would go on forever. An exciting new type of music called "Jazz" captured it all, and every age group had joined the dance. In movies, on the stage, in music, and magazines, and newspapers, hedonistic excess was celebrated. Illicit sex was seen as a sign of glamour and sophistication. Pleasure was something to be enjoyed and celebrated, not shunned. Men became friends with women, not just prospective husbands.

Actress Barbara Stanwyck (1925)
Alfred Cheney Johnston

Frankie had grown up in a traditional household. A kind of Victorian-meets-the-Vatican upbringing. Now a young man in his prime, the appeal of being with a young woman who wore a little slip of a dress, spoke her mind, and had a flask of bootleg brandy strapped in her garter, was unlike anything he had ever seen. He was like a kid in a candy store, who planned to get both hands thoroughly sticky. He became the baton twirler at the head of a seemingly endless pleasure parade of sex and booze, food and fun.

By 1925, Prohibition of alcohol had been in effect for five years. The government soon discovered they couldn't legislate morals; what was meant to eradicate the "evils of drink," instead turned millions of Americans into criminals; they were slinging back more liquor than ever before. Breaking the law became the thrill of the forbidden. The federal government had passed legislation, yet failed to fund enforcement, so many local municipalities ignored the law altogether. Fines and penalties were light, because the jails were full, and the courts were overwhelmed by the sheer number of people happy to break the rules.[223] [224]

Just as local fight clubs had once found a way around the anti-prizefight laws, San Francisco's roadhouse, saloon, and restaurant owners simply viewed the mandate as a challenge. The wide-open city was so wet it was slippery. It was well-versed in the endless efforts to prohibit its vices; during Prohibition it was rumored to have the most speakeasies per capita in the nation. Hidden behind store fronts and tucked away in alleys, they were more plentiful than saloons, who rebranded themselves as soda shops or cigar stores, but kept right on selling alcohol.

Prohibition also inadvertently fueled a sexual revolution. Prior to the law, men and women didn't generally drink together. Proper ladies retired to the parlor for sherry, while gentlemen gathered in the den for whiskey. But speakeasies served drinks to both sexes. The First World War had driven home the point that life was finite, and couples weren't going to waste a minute of it. In 1920, when the invention of a thin latex condom became more popular than its thick rubber cousin, men and women now slept together outside of marriage without fear, and most definitely with pleasure.

****

Frankie's new life was a contradiction to everything he had known as a boy. He had been raised to work without complaint, until his growing bones felt about to break. His father believed that fun was for the frivolous, and he had best do what he was told, or else. His instincts were finely-tuned after years spent reading the subtleties of Alessio's tone and expression for mood, measuring his gait or gesture for sobriety or drunkenness. His childhood had been small moments of joy, sprinkled among endless years of terror and uncertainty. Abuse had made him a watchful lad. Living on the streets had made him wary. He held his feelings close, and kept his circle of friends small and tight. He had suffered in unimaginable ways to survive to adulthood, and though this had made him hard, it hadn't made him ruthless.

Now his pockets were comfortably filled with cash. Worries about his next meal, and where to lay his head at night, were gone. As he discovered who he was, after half a lifetime defined by someone else, he shed some of the demons of his childhood. Like his brother Dolph, he was inherently a quiet fellow, but like his brother Albert, he was also a jokester. His naturally engaging personality began to emerge. He developed a clearer direction of his desires. His star in the ring had risen; because he had persevered and sacrificed, because he had pushed through exhaustion and a succession of injuries without complaint, he found his way to the top of the pugilistic heap.

Yet in the eyes of his handlers, it still wasn't enough, and they began to butt heads. He was told to run farther, punch faster, spar longer, work on your defense dammit, what is wrong with you? Liquor and fried food were frowned upon. Fast women would be the death of his career, and sex would kill his legs. Holidays were for training, not family dinners. His married handlers went home every night to a hot dinner and a warm bed. More often than not, Frankie was expected to refuse his mother's cannoli, and listen to the silence between cold sheets. His team preached the importance of physical and mental discipline, and then seemed aghast at the idea that, as the one who actually put in the work, he might need to let off some steam, have an independent thought, or a difference of opinion. They wanted to orchestrate his career, but that meant they controlled every aspect of his personal life.

Frankie became resentful of his captors. The way he saw it, he had traded one person, the father who controlled the direction of his youth, for a crowd of dictators. He was full up being the golden goose—for his handlers, for the matchmakers, and for the promoters. He had skyrocketed to local fame, he had cash in his pocket, and he spent it on wine, women, and song, with all the exuberance of a zoo animal who had escaped his cage. For the first time in his life, his days daisy-chained together with a contentment he had never known; he had earned this joy. He intended to savor it.

****

News broke the beginning of April 1926, that Frankie's scheduled April 7 bout with Jock Malone was called off, due to lingering hand injuries Jock had sustained in a fight the week before. Frankie was at loose ends while Bert Valerga arranged another match. It was rumored Bert was angry that Frankie hadn't decisively beaten Roland Todd. As if he wanted to punish one of his children for not trying hard enough, Bert signed an open contract with Tommy Simpson for a fight at the Civic the end of April. He told Tommy that Frankie would fight any opponent he cared to select, suitable or otherwise. But Tommy had a hard time getting somebody lined up; matches with Leo Lomski and Tony Fuentes fell through. In mid-April, Frankie appeared in a smoker for a few rounds of sparring at the Disabled War Veterans clubhouse.[225]

Still no new matches appeared on the horizon. The literal and figurative hunger that had driven him before was largely gone. With time heavy on his hands, frustration that he just couldn't crack the code of good defense, and still at odds with Bert, Frankie settled his fedora at a jaunty angle, rapped a secret knock on the door of his favorite speakeasy, and proceeded to wear out his dancing shoes. As the evenings slipped one into another, he began to view the world from the bottom of one too many shot glasses.

He wouldn't admit it aloud, but the scathing words of local scribes that he had let down his city, wounded him. Bert told him when he was on the cusp of truly getting somewhere, he choked. It never occurred to Frankie that he was being expected to perform at a higher level against a more proficient caliber of boxers, but nobody in his camp was giving him the tools to do so. He wasn't shown strategy or technique, he was just told to go out and either slug here or box there, seemingly at the whims of pom-pom waving cornermen.[226]

In time, his exasperation led to more drinking. He tried in vain to smother his scattered thoughts as the sun set, and drown them until she rose again. He lived life with the reckless ferocity of youth, but had become like the moth around the chandelier, until his nights began to affect his days. When the confrontations with his handlers about too much dancing and too little training became intolerable to him, as they struggled to maintain control of him, Frankie took his rebellion one step further. He quit the game.[227]

Frankie in training (May 1926)
San Francisco Examiner

In early May 1926, photos appeared on the front page of the local sports section, which shocked Mission District fight fans to the core. Frankie appeared in a baseball uniform, under headlines that he had signed a tryout contract with a farm team under William H. McCarthy, head of the Pacific Coast League minors, for next year's season. A farm team molded promising young players, with the expectation that if a player became successful, he would ascend to a position with an associated major league-level parent team. The league had room for four more bushers to guide to the majors, and Frankie hoped to win a spot. When asked by stunned reporters about the switch, Frankie responded he felt he would last longer as a ball player than as a fighter.[228]

He agreed to one last fight on May 19 at the Oakland Civic Auditorium. Bert Valerga matched him once again, against someone with vastly more ring experience, veteran heavyweight Chuck Wiggins. The event was a benefit show, put on by promoter Tommy Simpson. His fellow Bill's in the local Elks Lodge needed to raise money to send their band and drill team to a competition in Chicago. Ticket sales were brisk. Hundreds of members who seldom attended boxing matches purchased blocks of ringside seats.[229]

Chicago promoter Ray Alvis had recently arrived in the state with a small but exclusive stable of veteran fighters, which included Wiggins. Chuck had a stunning record of over 200 battles, having exchanged courtesies with all the top-notchers in the last ten years. Nicknamed the "Indiana Terror," he was a notoriously dirty fighter. The "Pittsburgh Windmill" Harry Greb once tried to out-dirty him during a bout by chomping down on his nose. Without breaking stride, Chuck kicked him loose with a well-placed knee.

At a fighting weight of 183, Chuck had ten pounds on Frankie. He sported a cauliflower ear that could win a blue ribbon at any county fair vegetable competition. His best punch was a hard left hook, which he indicated he planned to bury into Frankie's ribs, with hopes to hear them crack. While sports writers reported from the Imperial Gym in Oakland, that Wiggins looked in excellent physical condition, and had lost none of his pep, Frankie juggled fight training with baseball conditioning in the days leading up to the bout. The expectation by reporters was that Wiggins would have an easy victory.[230] [231]

The morning after the fight, it was indelicately suggested by the press, that Frankie should be a wonder in his new profession with the Pacific Coast League. The boys banged away at a good clip and were evenly matched in the opening rounds. Then Frankie just seemed to run out of steam. In the fourth and fifth rounds, he sent in three successive and palpably low lefts. Since low blows were among Wiggins' bag of tricks, he didn't complain about it to referee Al Wainright; the kid was actually a clean fighter. Some scribes wrote Frankie simply appeared to be too

Frankie signs contract to fight Chuck Wiggins (17 May 1926)

tired to keep his guard up. Others suggested he was getting beat and fouled out to stop the fight. Nevertheless, he was warned by Wainright after each foul. A mere minute into the eighth round, he copped another one, and seemed to hold his glove where it landed, to be sure Wainright got a good long look at it. There was no protest, even from his own fans, as the referee disqualified Frankie and held Wiggin's arm aloft in a token of victory. It was Frankie's first loss.[232] [233]

Whether he failed to train adequately for the fight due to pressures with his intended career in baseball, or all the nights out had caught up with him, or he lost on purpose, so what he then perceived as overwhelming expectations, wasn't his burden to shoulder anymore, is purely speculative. After a string of sixteen sensational wins, Frankie Campbell hung up his boxing gloves and slipped his battered hands full-time into a baseball mitt. Whether this was at all a hard decision to leave, or a clear-eyed determination to thrive, is lost to history.

****

As twenty-two-year-old Frankie Camilli struggled to find a consistent direction in life, his nineteen-year-old brother Dolph Camilli's rise in baseball appeared destined to be meteoric.

The year before, he had graduated from Sacred Heart High School. He had excelled on the Fightin' Irish sports teams, as first baseman in baseball, and as a tight end in football. His nickname in school was "Wreck'em" for his throwing power in baseball and his hitting power in football.

79

After scouts observed Dolph in action at the Sutro Heights Class B Winter League, where he had fielded brilliantly, batted an astonishing .714 and was never struck out during the season, scouts from the Pittsburg Pirates, the Cincinnati Reds, and the St. Louis Cardinals virtually camped out on his doorstep for months, to sign him on with their respective teams.[234]

Dolph Camilli (1925)
Courtesy Camilli family

When Dolph autographed a contract as first baseman with the San Francisco Seals, the team's veteran scout Nick Williams, and its Vice President Charley Graham, appeared in competition with each other on who could most herald his praises. In the stocky, 178-pound, unassuming southpaw, they declared they had secured the best player to come out of the Bay District in years.

"I don't usually get excited and enthusiastic," Williams proclaimed "but I really think that Camilli is the best young prospect I have ever looked at." Nick deemed Dolph to have the same kind of educated hands as Charley "Lefty" Grimm, former first sacker of the Pittsburgh Pirates, now with the Chicago Cubs, and that he had an ability to reach in all directions with the same ease. When Dolph fielded a ball, he had soft hands, and possessed unusual strength in his wrists and arms, which allowed him to power a throw like a bullet, and hit a homer clear out of the stands. [235] [236]

The local papers reported on Frankie's progress with his tryouts among various teams in the Pacific Coast League. He was mentioned in June as batting 4-for-4 with the Twin Peaks Parlor team. In July, he held the position of first basemen when Twin Peaks played against the San Anselmo Wildcats. In late September, he pitched for the Lindberg-Freese Nine, then led the team in a 4-to-3 victory over the Lundstrom Hatters in the first week of October. He continued as pitcher at the end of October, against the Seymour Drug team, with a final score of 18-to-2.

In the end, his overall performance was evidently not remarkable enough, and he didn't make the final cut. It was another devastating tear in the already frayed fabric of his confidence. Frankie suspected he had closed the door on his dreams of a career in baseball for the final time.

With the resignation of a penitent before his priest, he packed away his pitcher's mitt, and at the encouragement of his friends, he once again tightened up the laces on his boxing gloves. [237] [238] [239]

Within days of the news, he was seen back at the Royal Athletic Club, where he quietly resumed training. When his manager Bert Valerga announced Frankie's return to the ring, the story reporters were given, was that after weeks of treatment and six months of rest, a physician had pronounced his badly bruised dukes as good as new. No mention was made about his baseball aspirations. No questions were asked how he could have played baseball with injured hands. The fans and the press didn't care, they were simply happy to have him back in the ring. [240]

Frankie comes back (21 Oct 1926)
Courtesy La Voce Del Popolo

In a clear sign he still hadn't learned a thing about how to mold his fighter, or bring him along with care, in October 1926, Bert matched Frankie to fight Australian heavyweight George Cook, in a 10-round main event at the Dreamland. Less than two months later, Cook went on to win the Australian Heavyweight title from "Tiger" Jack Payne. Cook's mixed ring record belied a tough opponent who possessed inexhaustible reserves of stamina, was one of the most difficult men to put down, and was known as a destroyer of fistic reputations. Frankie would also give away sixteen pounds. Considering it was Frankie's first appearance in the ring in months, the suitability of the match utterly bewildered the local press.[241]

To the delight of the spectators, the fight ended up being one of the most bitterly waged, ferociously fought wars witnessed in the city in months. George was a game fellow, and Frankie had a willing body before him to punch out his frustrations. Somewhere along the way, he finally had discovered his left hook. And that left hungered for vital organs. He put up one of the best fights of his career. His performance surprised even his most ardent followers, that he more than held his own against a veteran warrior.[242]

The tide of the battle changed three times during the ten tumultuous rounds. In the opening round, Cook battered Frankie around the ring at will. It appeared he wouldn't survive to the bell. He teetered back to his corner like a circus stilt walker. Then he came out slugging in the second like a house on fire. Through the middle rounds, Frankie staggered Cook repeatedly with vicious left hooks, and uppercuts to the body. A bombshell overhand right opened a gash over Cook's left eye that bled like a stuck pig.[243]

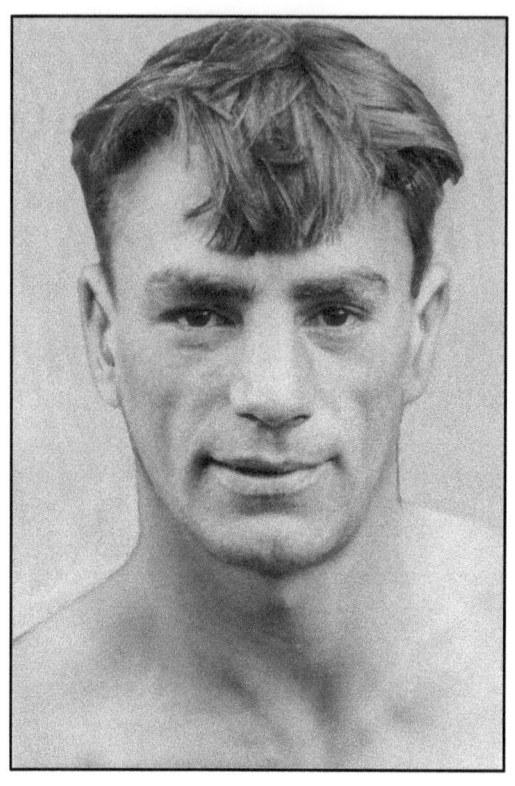

Promo shot for Frankie's fight with
George Cook (26 Oct 1926)

But George Cook was relentless. In the sixth, he landed a right to the head that had Frankie reeling on the ropes. He came right back in the seventh to out-box Cook, with merciless left hooks to the jaw, and unrelenting blows to the gash on Cook's eye. Blood spray smeared across both fighters' torsos like a Rorschach test.

Frankie was spent after the undaunted onslaught. Cook's sixteen-pound weight advantage had finally taken its toll in the clinches. Cook began to batter Frankie with gusto about the body; a left hook split his brow open in the eighth. He survived the round on bravado and sheer temerity alone. Cook began to come fast in the final canto. When the last bell rang, the referee threw up both hands. Cook had managed to earn himself a draw.[244]

Frankie was next matched to fight Joe Woods, in the main event at the Dreamland Auditorium, the first week of December 1927. Born Joseph Kopach out of Painesdale, Michigan to Polish immigrants, like Frankie, he had come to California as a toddler. He was a Los Angeles light-heavyweight who had been last year's U.S. National Amateur Champion. A hard slugger known to have a sleeper punch, he was a promising young protégé of George Blake, who had taken Fidel La Barba out of the amateur ranks down in Los Angeles, and within eleven matches, guided him to a World Flyweight Champion title.

Three days before his fight with Woods, Frankie sparred with his pal, welterweight Joe Dundee, who just months earlier, had dealt an unmerciful pummeling to former World Welterweight Champ Mickey Walker. Despite the fact both fighters were hours from their main events, the session turned into a brawl. Dundee tore right in, punishing Frankie with relentless body blows. Frankie was forced to break ground, but never stopped throwing his two big fists into the smaller man's face and body. In the second round, they stood at center ring and traded wild punches like two gloved kangaroos. The third and fourth rounds were so fast and vicious, the exhibition was considered better than most official fights of the season. When the last gong rang, the two men grinned at each as blood trailed down their faces, while spectators stood up on their seats in the gym bleachers and cheered.[245]

Joe Dundee, who at that time had sixteen consecutive wins to his credit, went on four days later to be knocked down four times in the first round by Eddie Roberts, in a huge upset on a Saturday afternoon fight at Recreation Park. Frankie fared little better in his Friday night fight with Joe Woods.

The day of the bout was declared a holiday in the Mission District by its leading citizens in honor of their pride and joy. Led by a brass band, a merry automobile parade of Frankie's legions of loyal fans proceeded from lower Monterey Boulevard up to the Dreamland, in a raucous, celebratory mood all the way.[246]

The press thought the fight had all the earmarks of a merry tussle. As the bout commenced that evening, the opponents were well matched. They jolted and smashed, and countered back and forth over the course of the early rounds. Frankie had comfortably taken the lead, but in the fifth, he got entirely too cocky. The first few moments of the round, Frankie had Joe groggy, and it appeared he was on the verge of a knockout. When he nailed him with a stiff right on the chin, Joe wisely fell into a clinch.

As they broke away, the two glared at each for a moment from center ring. Frankie smirked up at his friends who packed the gallery, and as if to say it was all a lark, he stuck out his chin invitingly. Joe responded with a right hook that caught him dead on. The punch stunned him. Another right caught him on the jaw, and he went down in a heap like a puppet with the strings cut. Instead of staying down for the count until his head cleared, he gamely staggered to his feet, only to reel against the ropes in a daze. The press later noted it was obvious he was out on his feet; both arms dangled at his side, wide open for another wallop, yet the referee motioned for Joe to continue. [247] [248]

There was nothing else for Joe to do but hit his target. A crushing haymaker found its mark again. Frankie however refused to go down. He stood there like a blackout drunk the morning after a New Year's Eve party. Joe again sent a questioning look to referee Toby Irwin, who frowned at his fun being interrupted, before he finally stepped in and waved his arm to signal an end to the fight. Joe Woods was awarded the victory on a technical knockout. [249] [250]

A collective gasp arose from the throats of Frankie's fans at the abrupt turn of events. Some were observed to have tears in their eyes, as with heads bowed, they silently left the auditorium. The next day, local sports writers proclaimed Mickey Walker—who had upset fistiana in the Chicago Coliseum the same night, with a questionable win against Tiger Flowers, to become the newly-crowned

Middleweight Champion of the World—had nothing on what Joe Woods had done to Frankie Campbell at the Dreamland last night.[251]

In two years of fighting, it was the first time Frankie had ever been knocked down. He later said he was disgusted with his careless performance. The local press ridiculed him, which was a bitter blow to his ego. When word reached them that Frankie might once again do a vanishing act from the ring, Les Cohen at the *San Francisco Bulletin* noted perceptively that after a victory, Frankie was eager to fight anyone, loudly issuing challenges from the ring. But if he was beaten or shaded, he disappeared. Les said Frankie had the stuff to go places. Now if only he could get over this latest blow to his aspirations. "And the blow," Cohen observed, "is purely mental."[252]

In Frankie's mind, he had not only suffered a stunning defeat after a foolish act in the ring, but a loss of pride in front of his people. On the face of it, he took the ribbing of his friends good-naturedly, but privately he felt that if he could barely face himself, how then could he slip between the ropes to face his fans? When Bert Valerga tried to smooth it over with talks of future opponents, Frankie told him there wouldn't be any more. He hung up his gloves and did not enter a professional boxing ring for almost sixteen months.

CHAPTER II

A MERCIFUL ACT

BOXING IS THE ONLY JUNGLE WHERE THE LIONS ARE AFRAID OF THE RATS
- JACK NEWFIELD

As he pointed his car east along Monterey Boulevard toward his rooms on 20th Street, Frankie's stomach gnawed a hole into his backbone. Dolph and their mother lived three blocks away from him on Hancock Street. Albina had promised to make cioppino for dinner. Pounding nails every day into a new roof was hard work. But there was a certain sense of satisfaction in the exhaustion from a good day's labor. His recent stint as a taxi driver up in Eureka had been easier. At least a stench didn't permeate his clothes, as it had after weeks as a cowhand at Albert's in-law's ranch up in Humboldt County. Yet he had desperately missed his family and friends, so he came home. On the weekends, Frankie played shortstop with the San Francisco Nationals. Between time on the field and weeks on rooftops, his olive skin had turned dark. The physical demands kept him muscular, which made him popular with the ladies, but it also built up a voracious appetite. [253]

His stiff and sore fingers drummed a beat on the steering wheel, as he slowed his approach to Monterey Boulevard and Joost Avenue, at the sound of a train whistle. The outbound Market Street Railway streetcar was coming through. He watched idly while an automobile carrying two women and two small children came from the opposite direction. As the train raced toward the intersection, the car didn't slow, it tried to get ahead of the locomotive. But the driver had missed the approach of an inbound streetcar on the other track. She plowed head on, straight into it.

Frankie leapt from the car, and rushed over to a torture of twisted metal. Its occupants lay like carelessly scattered jacks before the ball toss. Everyone sported severe cuts and contusions. Blood leaked from both the children's ears. Desperate moans hinted at possible internal injuries. As others tended to the children and the driver, Frankie knelt to gather the passenger into his arms. When Lillian Victorine began to scream at the sight of her battered children, he shushed her with words of calm reassurance. Fluidly he arose, and turned to gently lay her into the wide back seat of his car, before he sped up the hill to Mission Emergency Hospital.[254] [255]

When not doing good deeds, Frankie typically began work at dawn, so he was done for the day by the early afternoon. His rooms were in an endless row of Victorians a few buildings east of the sprawling Mission Dolores Park. Some evenings when his mind was restless, he threw air punches as he pounded the sunbaked dirt paths which circled the park's grass. He pondered his future among the newly planted palm trees, whose ground once held two Jewish cemeteries. Across the street, he watched the progress of the new Mission High School bell tower, still an iron frame under construction, and wished he had stayed in school.[256] [257] [258]

Over the ensuing months, Frankie quickly ran through the last of his ring winnings. He was the first to admit that once he held a thousand clams in his hand from a fight, the money just slipped through his fingers like a failed steeplechase flourish. Roofing paid the bills reasonably enough, but to escort women out for drinks, dinner, and dancing wasn't cheap. His manager Bert Valerga continued to repeatedly pester him like a kid with a stick in an anthill. Eventually he wore him down and induced Frankie to return to the ring.

****

While he had been absent from the squared circle, use of a rubber mouth guard had started to become more commonplace in fights across America. After Jack Britton's loss in 1921 to Ted "Kid" Lewis at Madison Square Garden for the World Welterweight title, Jack complained the rubber mouth piece Ted wore, "took up the shock of my punches." New York promptly enacted a "no mouth guards" policy, which it had zealously defended ever since.[259]

In March 1927, after the Mike McTigue and Jack Sharkey title contender fight was stopped when an artery burst in Mike's mouth, New York's commissioners finally admitted, that since the "kisser protectors do not afford either fighter an unfair advantage, it was decided to let the boys use them in all future bouts." As New York boxing goes, so goes the nation. Other states eventually followed suit. While it was a positive step forward, the early guards only protected the teeth, cheeks, and gums. The science of protection, which consisted of an ideal oral separation between the jaw and base of the skull, to reduce impact and shock, and prevent serious injury, was years away.[260]

In the early spring of 1928, Bert approached Al Young at National Hall with hat in hand to request a fight. Al was thrilled to have Frankie come back. He knew what a tremendous draw he could be. In a sign of how much luster his star still retained, the Associated Press picked up Frankie's return to the ring, and it was reported from coast to coast. He was given the March 28 main event at 175 pounds. The prelim just before his bout, was a green kid Frankie would soon come to know; Les Kennedy was fighting in his sixth pro fight.

Frankie's opponent was George "Buster" Trenkle, out of Venice Beach. Buster was a bit of an injury prone fellow. Last July, his jaw had been broken in a fight with Dusty Miller. In December, days before a match with Billy McGowan, he fell from a horse and sustained a leg injury, which contributed to his second-round loss by technical knockout, as his leg repeatedly collapsed on him.

Buster had a wild swing, but he was a heavy hitter with a hard right cross and a fair left jab. He had recently dropped a close decision, in a sensational fight against undefeated local light-heavyweight up-and-comer Armand Emanuel, who had stepped into prominence last September, when he fought the semi-windup at the Dempsey–Tunney title rematch.

Despite his long absence, when Frankie touched gloves with Trenkle in his old stomping grounds, he was favored to win. A packed house let loose with a sustained cheer when he entered the roped arena. His Bernal Heights pals had presented him with a big floral horseshoe for luck. Frankie did not disappoint the crowd. He led the first four rounds with ease, as he beat a steady tattoo upon Trenkle's ribs, and buffeted him about at will. In the fifth, Frankie shifted his attack to the head. After he had boxed his ears into a braid, a flurry of lefts and rights to the jaw knocked George to the canvas for a nine-count. As soon as he regained his feet, Frankie followed up with a beauty of a right uppercut to the chin, that sprawled him flat on his back. Trenkle's manager couldn't throw the towel into the ring fast enough.[261]

Banner headlines in the local sports pages announced that at the end of April, Frankie would fight Ted Sluder in the National's main event. Sluder was native to San Pedro and fought out of Los Angeles. He was riding a sensational winning streak of seven consecutive knockouts. During the war, he had held the light-heavyweight title with the Atlantic Fleet. In his twenty-two professional bouts, he had notched seventeen knockouts. None had gone beyond the second round. He was known to be a slugger with a heavy punch and a wicked left hook. He promised to make the ten-round tilt a barroom brawl. [262] [263]

Sluder started the first round with a terrific right to the jaw, then winged over a stiff left hook to Frankie's chin. Frankie just grinned at him, as if to say, that's all ya got? With two hard blows to the chin, he snapped Sluder's head back. In a disjointed pirouette, he sprawled to the canvas. The crowd surged to its feet with boisterous applause, but Sluder was up at the nine, and managed to dance away from Frankie's swarm of body shots until the bell rang. In the second, Sluder nervously pawed a host of jabs as he looked to land his sledgehammer right. Frankie whipped over a brutal left hook and Sluder dropped like a ton of bricks for another nine-count. He gamely staggered to his feet, only to eat another left hook. As his eyes rolled up in his head, he slid in slow motion to the canvas. The count was an afterthought.[264]

Frankie and Bert were hitting on all eights; they were ready for bigger game. When Abe Matin, manager of French-Canadian Charley Belanger, was approached for a match with Frankie at 175 pounds, Bert snapped at the promoter's offer like a trout takes a fly. The winner of the bout was promised a go with Armand

Emanuel. Charley boasted a record of 25-7-3. He was not only an incredibly gifted boxer; he showed an almost super-human ability to take a punch. He was an aggressive fellow, whose long leading lefts were as effective as his brutal close action rights to the head and body.[265]

Bert Valerga couldn't have made a more dangerous decision. In thirty-five fights, Belanger had never been knocked out. Three weeks earlier, he had won Canada's Light-Heavyweight title from Harry Dillon in Winnipeg. At a fight in San Diego just a year earlier, in his début fight, his opponent Harry "Jim" Flack, was believed to have died of an inter-cranial hemorrhage from the brutal blows he had received from Belanger. Abe Matin also possessed an important edge over Frankie's manager. Matin had handled Mickey Rockson when Frankie fought him to a questionable draw. Abe was well acquainted with Frankie's strengths and weaknesses; he looked forward to exploiting that knowledge. Bert naively viewed the fight as a chance to quickly jump Frankie a few rungs up the ladder. The promise of a big payoff blinded him once again, to how mismatched the opponents were. [266]

The fighters would meet the first week of May for a ten-round main event at the National Guard Armory, a beautiful brick fortress located at Mission and Fourteenth Streets. Beginning about 1912, the Armory served for three decades as one of the cities primary sports venues. Prizefights were held inside a ring constructed in the middle of the 40,000 square foot Drill Court. The Drill Court was an open-air arena until 1925; success with boxing events had encouraged a barrel-vaulted enclosure of the roof to hold fights there year-round. Its massive size eventually earned it the nickname "the Madison Square Garden of the West."[267]

Armory Drill Court with boxing ring (1926)
Courtesy U.S. National Guard Armory

A few days before the bout, KYA Radio breathlessly announced that "Microphone Ernie" Smith of the *San Francisco Examiner* would be ringside at 9:30pm, to give a graphic "blow-by-blow, groan-by-groan account of the light-heavyweight fistic imbroglio."

Weeks before, Ernie had broadcast his very first fight. So many fans had written letters to request more of the same that KYA encouraged a second go. Transmitting at 1,000 watts from atop the Warfield Theater downtown on Market Street, listeners from as far away as Seattle and Los Angeles could tune in. [268] [269]

Both fighters did part of their training at Taussig & Ryan's Gym. The weekend before the fight, an informant told the *San Francisco Examiner's* sports writer Alex McCausland, he had overheard Frankie say, after he finally watched Belanger's

BOXING TONIGHT
AT
ARMORY ARENA
Fourteenth and Mission Sts.
Frankie Campbell
of Glen Park
vs.
Charley Belanger
Canadian Light-Heavyweight Champion
TEN ROUNDS TO A DECISION
And Four Other Rattling Contests
Prices—Gallery, $1.25; reserved seats (elevated), $2.20; ringside seats, $3.30.

Campbell vs Belanger ad (07 May 1928)
Courtesy San Francisco Examiner

sparring sessions, that he had lost all confidence in a win. Frankie had loudly remonstrated with Bert for even thinking of taking the match. Frankie's entire mental attitude had shifted. McCausland predicted him doomed to defeat. As was his custom when in training, early the next morning, Frankie went out to the coast for several miles of roadwork on Ocean Beach. As he relentlessly pounded the sand, he scattered seagulls into the air, while he tried to get his head straight[270]

After spectators observed the final afternoon workouts of both opponents, and then McCausland broke his scoop, betting odds which had heavily supported Frankie as the likely victor, switched in Belanger's favor.

As the sun slipped into the sea the night of the fight, a parade of festively-decorated automobiles, packed with a brass band that played some popular tunes, escorted Frankie up to the venue. But as he had waved to block after block of cheering friends and fans, his smile was tight and his mood pensive.[271]

****

The clang of the opening gong still echoed through the air at the Armory, when Charley whipped over a brutal straight right to Frankie's jaw. He dropped to the floor like a bucket down a well. But at the count of two, he leapt up and charged back into battle. The fighters sprang toward each other to open round two, both exchanging hard rights to the head. Frankie rocked Charley with a volley of left hooks, when suddenly Charley's sledgehammer right lashed out and caught him. He was so dazed at the end of the round, his seconds had to jump into the ring at the bell to lead him to his corner. Early in the third, with two rapid rights to the ribs, Frankie managed to stagger Charley, who wisely clinched to clear his head. Frankie abandoned any attempts to box, and gamely tried to clash with his tried-and-true rallies, but while ambitious they were aimless. He repeatedly missed with wild rights that hit air as Charley easily slipped them; it was like trying to catch a puff of smoke.[272][273]

In the fourth, Charley began to work Frankie like a cooper going around a barrel. Time and again, he spun him into a clinch to pop him with brutal head and body shots. Yet Frankie gave him no quarter. He repeatedly buried left hook after left hook into Charley's body. They fought all over the ring, glancing off rope to rope. Frankie was dazed on the retreat to his corner, but once again, he came out gunning to open the fifth. He caught Charlie with lefts and rights to the body until he was forced to break ground. Frankie appeared to have him on the run. His local fans sat breathless as they hoped the tide had turned.[274][275]

But the sixth was only seconds old, when Charley swished a right through the atmosphere, and Frankie's chin was in the direct path of the wallop. He staggered into the ropes, and Charley went in for the kill. He flayed him with both fists to the face. Frankie's head bounced back and forth from the blows, like a fishing cork announcing a big one. After Charley had sent over a dozen punches, and it was obvious Frankie had finally succumbed to the unmerciful bombardment, referee Bobby Johnson waved Frankie to his corner and raised Charley's arm. It was a merciful act.[276][277]

The morning after the fight, you could almost feel the breath of his sigh drift up through the pages, as *Oakland Tribune* sports editor Bob Shand wrote with a heavy hand, that last night, "another good prospect in the box-fighting business was ruined." He noted that Frankie's manager Bert Valerga had unwisely accepted the match, "because it was a 'big shot' and they figured to get plenty of green." [278]

The number of times Charley's right found Frankie's head and jaw, before the fight was stopped, was dismal enough that Harry B. Smith of the *San Francisco Chronicle* warned, "Campbell had best quit the ring or he will be up in Napa making paper dolls" from all the hits to the head, referring to the State Mental Hospital. Smith finished with a particularly prophetic conclusion. "For the last minute of fighting in that sixth round, Campbell was in a neutral corner with his guard down. Belanger was landing vicious rights to the jaw of the local boy, who was unable to protect himself, and the referee did the right thing stopping the fight."[279][280]

Belanger was complimentary after the bout. "He's the hardest puncher I have ever fought," he told the *San Francisco Bulletin*. "I was never hit harder in my life. Leo Lomski does not punch nearly as hard as Campbell."[281]

Thirty fights later—which included battles with title-holders and top contenders, Ted "Kid" Lewis, Maxie Rosenbloom, Ace Hudkins, Tuffy Griffiths, and Harry Dillon and Leo Lomski twice more—Charley Belanger was still thinking of their encounter. He told a Canadian pressman, "That Campbell fight was the toughest I've ever had. It was the only time I came close to being stopped, and he nearly did the trick with a sock to my stomach in the fourth round. But I recovered and knocked him out."[282]

Publicly, Frankie didn't appear to take the defeat as severely as one might expect. "These things will happen," he philosophized to reporters. Then he turned to Charley and invited him to take a cold plunge in the Armory's swimming pool. But privately he had again lost all confidence in himself; attempts at boxing defensively had proved to be a miserable failure, and even slugging away had not gone much better. Once again, he did what he did best, he disappeared.[283]

CHAPTER 12

NO MONKEY BUSINESS

FATE ONLY PICKS ON THE COWARDS AND QUITTERS.
SO GIVE 'EM BOTH BARRELS AND AIM FOR THE EYES - GRANTLAND RICE

For seven months in 1928, Frankie's name was elbowed from the fight pages by other up-and-comers. He was back on the baseball fields with the Twin Peaks Parlor by June. He hit 4-for-4 in a game against the Foster Lunch Nine; as first baseman he helped take the team down the line to a 15-to-6 win. Over the summer, he took some construction work along points between Eureka and the city. Then in September he was seen working out again at Taussig & Ryan's. It was observed he looked in his best shape ever. Bill Moran at the *San Francisco Bulletin* remarked Frankie had been the number one light-heavy threat in the bay until he had embarked on attempts to box. Bill noted with relief he had largely given up on defense work and returned to where he excelled, as a slugger.

After twelve weeks of conditioning, Frankie accepted a match against Bud Doyle for the main event at the New Dreamland Auditorium on December 21, 1928. His comeback was picked up by the Associated Press, and made banner headlines in the local papers. [284] [285] [286]

****

Long before it became the venue for music performances by the world's most popular bands of the 1960s and 70s, Bill Graham's Winterland Arena was known as the New Dreamland Auditorium. The old "House of Quarrels," which started life after the Great Quake as the Dreamland Rink, had begun to fall apart, and was deemed a safety hazard. One night in 1927, Isadore Zellerbach, founder of the paper company, looked around the pavilion during an opera and remarked to his buddy, shipping magnate and Police Commissioner Andrew Mahony, "This in an awful dump. We ought to build a new Dreamland." Located on Steiner Street near Post, the old Dreamland was demolished, along with the National Theater at the corner, to make way for a larger, more modern venue. Price was no object. The final construction cost was said to be a cool $1,200,000.[287] [288]

The New Dreamland was christened on the last Friday in June 1928. Fans eagerly parked their fannies upon 10,000 seats upholstered in midnight blue, which sat upon a floor fashioned of pure grain maple. The floor seating rested atop hydraulic lifts; lowered flat, it was suitable for ball room dancing or basketball; when sections were elevated, with a boxing ring at the center, it afforded spectators a clear and unobstructed view from all parts of the house.[289]

The new structure was a dramatic improvement from its origins as a slapdash fire trap. To assuage those whose visions of the Great Quake and Fire still haunted their

New Dreamland Auditorium (1928)
Courtesy of Western Neighborhoods Project
OpenSFHistory.org / wnp100.00324

nightmares, developers assured the city that in case there was another natural disaster, the New Dreamland was catastrophe-proof. It was built of structural steel reinforced with concrete. It even boasted what was then the novel idea of underground parking for 250 vehicles. The New Dreamland, its financial backers declared, adds to the reputation of San Francisco as, "the city that knows how."[290] [291] [292]

Also making its début was a one-of-a-kind "hydraulic elevator," that with the push of a button, could raise or lower the ring eighteen feet in a few minutes. Fighters who previously had to run a literal gauntlet through the crowd, now stood in the ring, while the lift transported them to and from the basement dressing rooms up to the main floor. [293]

A few unforeseen negatives of the new feature soon presented themselves. If enough patrons thought the action in the ring was too slow, derisive shouts of "push the button!" rang out from the gallery. If they disagreed with a referee's decision after a fight, along with a deafening chorus of boos, they hurled a mountainous hail of seat cushions, programs, and cigars over the ropes, which filled the ring as it sank below the floor. Several minutes trapped inside the ropes became an eternity. By the early 1930s, numerous mechanical mishaps mid-fight finally forced management to disassemble the lift. [294] [295] [296]

Hydraulic elevator at New Dreamland (27 Jun 1928)
Courtesy San Francisco History Center, San Francisco Public Library

Bud Doyle, Frankie's opponent for the Dreamland fracas, was born Louis Oteri, down in the South Bay. He had twenty solid wins to his name, largely in area arenas. Bud had never been knocked out, and had just come off a close loss, in a hard-fought battle the month before at National Hall against Jock Malone. He was determined to prove himself to the San Francisco fans. To gain an edge in training, Jock was hired as Frankie's main sparring partner.

The New Dreamland's matchmaker Frank Schuler, had seen Doyle's recent fights at National Hall and thought the two sockers were a good fit. The fans wanted their blood and gore, yet hated to be played for suckers with a mismatch. But they eagerly filled every seat to see some good scrappers. "There is a lusty demand for action, and you can get more action from two offensive machines than you can from two defensive parties."[297]

To the delight of the spectators, the opening rounds of the fight was a slugfest all the way. Frankie hadn't lost any of his pep. Then a solid right to the chin knocked him bow-legged. Bud followed up with a relentless attack to the body. By the third, Frankie appeared recovered; he swooped down on Doyle like a hawk after a rabbit.

But it was short-lived. Doyle responded with jarring socks to the jaw that had Frankie dazed at the bell.[298]

In the fourth, Frankie was in desperate straits. Not only were the rusty effects of his latest layoff apparent, reporters observed he seemed to have adopted an awkward new zigzagging style, which he used at close quarters trying to evade body punishment. He kept up a barrage of punches, but they were as erratic as a balloon in a hurricane.

The fifth and six rounds belonged to Doyle by a mile. But he had failed to pace himself. In the seventh, Frankie began to turn the fight his way. In the eighth, he hooked and jabbed at will. A left hook to the face dropped Doyle in a heap. His right eye closed tighter than a padlocked speakeasy; until an operation in 1930, Bud kept it a secret that he likely had suffered a detached retina from this one punch.[299] [300]

In the ninth, Frankie tore a muscle in his arm as he hammered over one more brutal left hook. But it did the deed. A collective gasp rose from the crowd as Doyle's jaw went right and his body went left like a vaudeville hook intervention. He collapsed with a thud to the canvas. Spectators went wild as the referee counted him out. Frankie was devoured by the crowd as fans waylaid him outside the dressing room. But he had eyes for only one fan. His lovely new wife.

The end of October 1928, Frankie had married Miss Elsie Ana McGuire. The two had known each other as children. Years before, Elsie was the first girl he ever kissed, though his brother Dolph almost got there first.

Frankie comes back again (21 Dec 1928)
Teddy Burnett illustration

Frankie once asked him if he had ever kissed a girl. Dolph admitted he had not. Frankie suggested he give it a shot with Elsie and tell him how it went; he worried she would slug him if he tried.[301] [302]

When he did finally get his gumption up, Frankie discovered she tasted like sunshine and promise. Elsie had been fetching as a girl, but she had never looked as beautiful as she did a woman fully-grown. She was a flame-haired Irish girl and a devout Roman Catholic. Her widowed mother Mary lived on Randall Street in Glen Park, where she ran a grocery store in the ground floor unit of a triplex. Elsie managed the books and worked the counter as a clerk; She and Frankie often traded winks and wisecracks as she counted back change from a purchase. More than once as he pocketed his coins, Frankie grinned roguishly, boyishly, as he wondered where the skinny girl from childhood had gone. As they continued their dance, Elsie ever so gently nudged open the doors of his heart until he was smitten with her.

Elsie's porcelain skin and fine-boned face hid a spirited, competitive nature wrapped in a physique as lithe as a colt. One blustery December day in 1923, mere months after her father Patrick had died, her rowing team at Mission High School won the school district championship in a cutter race across San Francisco Yacht Harbor. Undaunted by miserably cold and foggy conditions, Elsie and her thirteen teammates shivered without complaint in thin navy-blue bloomers and white middy blouses. Their hands chapped by the chill winds and palms blistered by the big cutter oars, they pulled to victory over five other public city schools, with little finesse but all their hearts.[303]

Elsie McGuire Camilli
Courtesy author's collection

Frankie didn't have anything that remotely resembled security to offer Elsie after they married. The newlyweds moved into one of the upstairs units of her mother's building. But he had finally discovered the love and support of a good woman. She was a quietly feisty gal who challenged him yet looked upon him as if he'd hung the moon. She seemed to make everything inside of him settle. She smoothed the knots of his long-tangled scars and made them bearable. She found his broken parts and began to mend them one by one. She saw him through this time when he was clearly conflicted. He had been approached on multiple occasions with a potential fight, but each time he refused. Frankie was in love and Elsie was all he needed. During his respite from the ring, Elsie became pregnant with their first child.

Los Angeles newspaper sports articles later suggested that in early 1929, Frankie fought Henry "Bad News" Johnson in January, and Harry Richards in February for his début bout, dates and locations unknown. However, the *San Francisco Examiner* reported in early February that Frankie had been in training for twelve weeks and had "been resting since winning over Bud Doyle a few weeks ago." No press coverage that he fought either of the aforementioned opponents exists, though at the time a Harry Richards down in the Central Valley had some purebred puppies for sale.[304][305]

****

There was a story behind Frankie's awkward new zigzagging style. He had dropped Bert Valerga as his manager, and hooked up with the man who helped him stage that rare accomplishment in boxing, the successful comeback. Some stories suggest Carroll Edward "Cal" Working met Frankie while he knocked around baseball fields with the Independent League. Others say Cal had watched Frankie work in the ring, recognized his potential could be better molded, and caught up with him in Eureka, during those months Frankie was not actively fighting, to induce him to return to the game.

Cal Working had cannily zeroed in on the one thing guaranteed to persuade Frankie to his way of thinking, the one thing he was most devoted to: his desire to provide for his family. He convinced Frankie that to achieve success, he simply needed a square fight manager and a better trainer. In August 1928, Cal announced in the Dreamland Auditorium's monthly newsletter that he had become Frankie's manager. They sealed the deal with a handshake in the days when the respect and trust behind such a thing was more meaningful than a signature scratched on a contract.[306][307]

Cal seemed a likeable fellow. He was blond haired,

Frankie with manager Cal Working (1929)
Courtesy Harry E. Winkler Collection,
University of Notre Dame

with merry blue eyes, a toothy infectious smile, and an easy-going personality. Cal was new to the business of managing fighters. He owned and operated C.E.

Working Company as a distributor of paint brushes with an office in downtown San Francisco. Raised in Augusta, Illinois, he was the son of a skilled carpenter who descended from a long line of successful Pennsylvania Dutch landowners.

Cal loved to tell the story of how, as a young stationary salesman in San Antonio, Texas, he once sold 10,000 school slates with chalk to Mexican revolutionary Pancho Villa. Despite his personal inexperience, he had contacts in the West Coast boxing scene. He liked Frankie; he offered to stake him as he trained, until he had padded his belt with a few fights to shake the ring rust off. "I don't want any of your earnings." Working told him. "But I want you to train and follow my instructions, and there is to be no monkey business." [308] [309]

****

Cal had persuaded veteran boxer Dave Shade to try and improve Frankie's dismal defense and tighten up his offensive skills. Dave was an impulsive, fun-loving welterweight from the East Bay. A fast talker, whose words tumbled forth breathlessly from his lantern jaw like a Tommy gun spitting lead, he possessed a keen mind, an easy smile, and piercing blue eyes that didn't miss a trick.

Born Charles David Shade in 1902, on the shores of the San Pablo Bay town of Vallejo, California, he was initially the overlooked son of a boxing band of flashier brothers. When he was only fourteen, Dave fought non-sanctioned smokers for Jack Doyle down at the old Vernon Arena in Southern California. In 1918, he had his first recorded professional fight over at Al Young's old Association Club in San Francisco.

At the time the two fighters hooked up, Dave Shade had an official record of over two hundred documented professional bouts and about the same number in smokers. He was a gypsy of the ring; no town was too small and no city too large for him to fight in, if there was a decent opponent and a reasonable purse.

Dave was one of the most elusive, calculating, defensive fighters in the game. He had mastered his own inventive version of Jack Dempsey's crouching, bobbing, and weaving fighting style; and he was in the slow process of passing that style on to his eager pupil. It was described as unorthodox yet oddly stylish, and often completely confounded his opponents. Dave largely fought a technical, off-the-cuff game, but he wasn't averse to throwing out science and wading in with brutal infighting and effective knockouts.

Dave was a naturally gifted fighter, negligent about training in comparison to Frankie's studious new determination to improve upon his faults. Dave however took his coaching work seriously. Frankie still needed a tutor.

When Cal Working announced plans to start Frankie down in Los Angeles, Dave indicated he would meet them there. The two fighters had already developed a true friendship beyond their profession. [310] [311]

Dave Shade trains at home (Sep 1925)
Courtesy International News

CHAPTER 13

THE THREE WISE MEN

WHAT A BOXER IDEALLY WANTS TO DO IN THE RING IS TURN THE OPPONENT
INTO AN ASSISTANT IN HIS OWN ASS WHIPPING - STANLEY CROUCH

Through the dappled shade of old cypress and pepper trees, the sun warmed Frankie's face, as Cal motored them along through the Hollywood Hills, and down into Southern California in the spring of 1929. A western breeze brought the smell of sage and the sea through his open window.

Hollywood Hills (1926)
Courtesy Water & Power Associates

It was a bright bustling land in the midst of a frenzied boom that showed no signs of ending. As Hollywood studios transitioned from silent films to talkies, they struggled to keep up with the voracious public demand for motion pictures. Oil derricks sprouted inland across hills and valleys, and eventually right down to the sands of Huntington Beach, Long Beach and beyond, as one wildcat oil strike after another produced almost a quarter of the world's crude oil.

Los Angeles Port was the second busiest deep-water port in the nation. Vast livestock yards across the Los Angeles Basin rivaled those in Chicago and Omaha. With almost 300 sunny days a year, the county was an agricultural powerhouse that grew everything from avocados to oranges to wheat which fed the world, and it led the way in development of commercial aviation. The population had more than doubled in a decade to well over one-million people. It was a vibrant metropolis where so many before him had been lured to reinvent themselves; a place where 24-year-old Frankie Campbell hoped to stage one final spectacular career comeback.[312]

During what had already proved to be a difficult pregnancy, Frankie's wife Elsie remained home with her mother in San Francisco, while Frankie bunked in a room at Cal Working's new bungalow on Hayes Drive in the heart of Los Angeles.

They chose the Manhattan Gym to continue Frankie's training. When prizefights were legalized again in 1925, Jack Dempsey saw a bright future awaiting the game in the south. He took over the old Western Athletic Club on South Spring Street and began the laborious task of sprucing it up. The press proclaimed it a "top notch joint" with all the latest modern equipment. The ring posts were varnished wood, and the ropes were wrapped in rich velour. Dempsey's brother Bernie ran the business while his brother Johnny worked the floor. The gym's name was chosen by Bernie on the eve of its Grand Opening in February 1925; at the time, Jack had a starring role alongside his future wife, Estelle Taylor, in a silent film titled "Manhattan Madness."[313] [314]

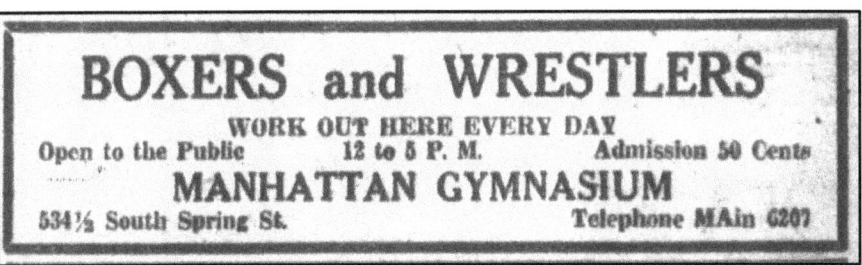

Manhattan Gym weekly newspaper ad
(11 Jul 1927)

Cal realized soon after their arrival in Los Angeles, that not only was he ignorant of the angles of the fight racket, he needed a plan to bring attention to Frankie's talents. He also needed a regular trainer; Dave Shade wouldn't be in town forever.

He hired a man who possessed not only the charismatic charm of a game show host, and the face of a demonic cherub, he had a contact list thicker than pedestrians on Broadway at noon.

Tom Maloney had a spiel that rivaled an auctioneer and a keen eye for potential. If he believed a fighter had skills and that innate charisma which drew crowds, he boosted him better than any head cheerleader. He became not only Frankie's trainer and all-around ballyhoo man, Tom quickly recognized he might just have a dark horse title contender, and he planned to bargain the devil into a corner for him.

Frankie and Tom Maloney (1929)
Courtesy Harry E. Winkler
Collection, University of Notre Dame

He was born Thomas Emmett Maloney on the Fourth of July in 1900 in San Francisco. After his parents divorced, he was shuffled in and out of the city orphanage. He was big for his age and started work when he turned fifteen. He took jobs in the trucking industry, with transport of registered mail to trains, and shipments of gold between the City Mint to the Federal Reserve Bank, which segued into Transportation Manager for the *San Francisco Bulletin* newspaper.

A lifelong boxing enthusiast, by 1920 Tom had drifted into work as a press agent and an advisor to fighters, before he advanced to training and management. He successfully mentored San Francisco light-heavyweight Armand Emanuel into prominence, until Armand left for Europe and Tom's invite onto the ship somehow got lost in the mail.

He had just come off several years' management of Teddy O'Hara, a hard-socking lightweight with a left like a Missouri mule, who had recently retired after his hands blew out. He had the ear of Middleweight Champ Harry Greb, and was one of the few people who could rap on a hotel door uninvited, and Jack Dempsey would greet him with a smile and invite him in.

Tom was familiar with Frankie's abilities. The two had run into each other often enough up at National Hall, when Tom was matching Teddy, and Frankie was knocking them out in the first round at the National's Wednesday Night Fights. It was Tom who suggested Frankie in his light-heavyweight days as an opponent for Middleweight Champ Harry Greb back in 1926, when Greb's manager sought an out-of-weight bout for his fighter in San Francisco.[315] [316] [317]

Tom was known by many nicknames in the industry, though most didn't bear repeating. "Fat Maloney," "Greaseball," and "Blubbery Tom" Maloney took the top spots in the press. Sometimes they even spelled his last name with a "B." He was written about using many colorful adjectives, rarely complimentary. But Tom possessed the gift of gab, like an evangelist who relieved you of your life savings to finance his yacht. He beguiled promoters and the press with an unceasing patter of promises, each more enticing and outrageous than the last. His enthusiasm was hard to resist. With a hint of admiration, sports editor Russell "Stub" Nelson at the *Los Angeles Record* adroitly labelled him, "a big, rotund ambitious ball of fire in the thick ear trades."[318]

Tom generally slurped five malted milks a day. He was known to eat an enormous amount of food at one sitting. He often gave interviews in between forkfuls at the Dairy Lunch, a local diner below the Manhattan Gym. About six feet in height, *Long Beach Sun* sports reporter "Tige" Clinton claimed he sported "320 pounds, three chins and flat feet," though he carried his weight well on his sturdy frame. He had asthma, so was often red-faced and wheezing as he enthusiastically waved his cutlery around, while he exhorted the sensational abilities of his latest new charge.[319] [320]

While some in the press heaped ridicule upon him, others grudgingly lauded him. Tom recognized which fighters had the potential to rise through the ranks with a change in style. That switch was simple. He "Dempsey'd" them, and Frankie became his star pupil. There was no finesse in Tom's training, no clean defense, no plan to take a fight to the last round; his boys fought at a gallop, not a trot. They waded in, never backed up, never stayed down, and launched reckless two-fisted assaults. Tom's motto was, "You can't be whipped if you keep swinging." Most importantly, Tom was a psychological maestro. He not only revamped Frankie's style; he successfully rebuilt his mind. He carved out the doubtful hesitation which had hindered Frankie in the past and bored in decisive self-assurance. [321]

Stub Nelson's appreciation for Tom's tactics was clear; "He's one of the best blow 'em up, steam 'em up, build 'em up, any way to get 'em up, men in the rack 'em up racket."[322]

Despite of all his public bluff and bluster, Tom had his own anxieties. Just before one of his fighters entered the roped arena, he never quite managed to conquer a bad case of the nerves. He often rushed headlong through a crowd, his bulk scattering people like bowling pins, as he ran for the exits to vomit onto the concrete behind the building.[323]

Just as Frankie's last group of handlers had done, Tom and Cal took complete control of his life. This time though, he was more amenable to the idea. At his age he either had to be in it to win it or wind up in the dust. Frankie had a wife and a baby on the way. The time he had once devoted to drinking and dancing, was now redirected to disciplined training and hopes of a rejuvenated career. As the success of their endeavor with Frankie began to bear fruit, the trio of Cal Working, Tom Maloney, and Dave Shade were dubbed by the press as, "The Three Wise Men."[324]

When Three Wise Men Put Another Wise

Three Wise Men (June 1930) Courtesy UC Davis
Shields Library; Archives and Special Collections

All throughout the spring and summer of 1929, Frankie was clay in the hands of a consortium of potters, as his team set about remolding their young charge in both body and mind. Like a control freak that whisks his bride away from her family after the rings are exchanged, Frankie was removed from the influence of people and places he was familiar with. He began roadwork at 5 o'clock every morning, trained all day, and was in the nest by 9 o'clock in the evening.

He punched the heavy bag relentlessly, as if it had mortally offended him; the rat-a-tat of his gloves hitting the speed bag, and the unceasing slap of his jump rope followed him into his dreams. When his eyelids grew heavy, in those few free moments at night as he penned another letter to his wife, he often gazed out the window, his lips quirked in thought. He felt that he was in a good place: as a man, as a fighter, as a husband, and soon-to-be a father. Somehow, while he wasn't looking, Frankie Campbell had quite simply, finally found himself in all the ways that mattered; he was content that the path on which he travelled was exactly where he wanted to be.[325]

****

As Tom Maloney held a stop watch and shadowed his fighter around the gym, he advised him to forget all he had ever learned about boxing. Like Jack Dempsey before him, and Rocky Marciano twenty years on, at just over 5 feet 10 1/2 inches tall, with a fighting weight of around 185 pounds, Frankie was considered small for a heavyweight. While he was solid-boned, the majority of his opponents were likely to be bigger and taller. Tom actually preferred that to be the case. Taking a leaf from the Kearns–Dempsey book, he wanted to avoid fast-stepping heavies, and match Frankie with slower fighters he could flash around, as he power-punched them to the canvas.

Dave Shade had determined Frankie would likely never truly master the chess match of an excellent defense. Being a slugger was the niche he fit into, so Dave worked to make him a smaller target. He continued to train him how to bob and weave and punch from a crouch, how to hit

Dave Shade demonstrates his infamous crouch to Frankie Campbell (1930)

effectively and powerfully with either hand. Tom showed him motion pictures of Jack Dempsey in action, master training by silver screen.[326] [327]

As Frankie mimicked the moves of his idol, the former champ had not fought for two years. After he failed to regain his title in a 1927 rematch—before over 100,000 spectators at Soldier's Field in Chicago, Illinois, against the technical genius of the "Fighting Marine" Gene Tunney—Dempsey quit the game. While Jack teased the public for several more years that he might return, he later philosophized, "What good would an extra million dollars do you when you are walking on your heels punch drunk?"[328]

Tunney had vacated his title as World Heavyweight Champ in the summer of 1928, but he was largely not missed by the public. With his clean-cut collegiate looks, speeches peppered with quotes by Shakespeare, and photos of his engagement in various intellectual pursuits—those that caught Gene having the nerve to read books were especially incendiary—Tunney was viewed as a bit too high brow to appeal to most fight folks. To many fans of the heavyweight division, his greatest misstep on the path to popularity was his technique; while Dempsey came from the school of sock, Tunney came from the school of science.

"Without Jack in the limelight," Bill Smith at the *Los Angeles Evening Express* mused, "folks in general take little more than a casual interest in the doings of the ring.... The fight fans can't seem to forget Dempsey. Most of them have only a hazy recollection of Tunney."[329]

With the title vacant, boxing fans searched in vain for another heavyweight with the same brute appeal as Jack. The press searched with longing for a heavyweight who so effortlessly sold newspapers. Those who demonstrated even a resemblance to Jack's rampaging onslaught of aggressive combinations and stunning knockouts were touted as "the next Dempsey," and could be guaranteed a second look. With Tom's encouragement, Dempsey himself had watched Frankie spar at the Manhattan Gym and liked his looks. Jack's early advice to Frankie only confirmed the style in which Tom and Dave had already molded him; "Never mind the defense, go out and knock them over quick.[330] [331]

"The Three Wise Men" continued to fine-tune Frankie's training regimen, with the eventual hope that he would garner just such a look among fistic fans and the press, especially if he fought as a heavyweight, the magic magnet for good ticket sales. Frankie was trained and conditioned for almost six grueling months, before he was allowed to enter the professional ring against an opponent. His diet was altered completely with the latest nutritional expertise available. Without steroids, and without human growth hormones, Frankie developed almost fifteen solid pounds of muscle mass. But it wasn't bulky muscle to slow him down. He developed long smooth fast-twitch fiber muscles, which wouldn't sacrifice speed or dexterity, but gained him explosive brute strength in both fists.

When his team felt Frankie was as finely tuned as a Stradivarius, and ready to enter the heavyweight-class, Dave Shade hopped a train east to fight at Yankee

Stadium, while Cal and Tom made the rounds of Los Angeles area matchmakers. There were two main event centers that Southern California boxing fans thronged to on fight nights in the late 1920s, the Hollywood American Legion Stadium, and the Olympic Auditorium.

The Olympic Auditorium to this day retains a mystique on the West Coast that is unparalleled in the history of throwing leather. Erection of the 60,000 square foot athletic stadium and convention hall, with a capacity of 10,400, began in 1925 on a 6-acre lot at the corner of Eighteenth Street and South Grand Avenue in downtown Los Angeles. It was named in anticipation of the Olympic Games, where several events were held in 1932. Its cost was initially bankrolled by the Vernon Arena's Jack Doyle, millionaire oil men, and real estate moguls, at an estimated cost of $350,000.

Olympic Auditorium (1925) Courtesy University of Southern
California Libraries and California Historical Society

Jack Dempsey had just emerged from a hospital stay sporting a newly constructed nose—which his surgeon boasted could stand a twenty-five percent heavier punch than the old nose—to boost attention to the Olympic's impending construction. Jack was present as the cornerstone was laid on January 10, 1925; he climbed onto a huge steam shovel to break ground to commence the building

project. Built to completion in six months, it was shockingly over budget at a final cost of over $500,000. But when its doors were thrown open on August 5, the coatless gallery gods, and tuxedoed celebrities, who thronged to the grand opening and filled every seat, declared it a modern marvel. Said to be the largest and finest stadium in the world devoted to boxing, it put the old Madison Square Garden to shame. Current and former fistic champions and major silent film superstars all made appearances. Dempsey was presented with a solid gold lifetime ticket, good for all future events at the venue; later a mural of his image adorned the main entry way. Movie cameras were there to grind away merrily as a record of the event. So many spotlights shot into the night sky that Batman would have shielded his eyes.
332 333 334 335

With rows of ringside seats, cavernous ground level seating, and a wraparound mezzanine, General Manager Jack Root said the venue "was erected with the idea of making every seat ringside." The leather upholstered opera-style chairs each contained fifty-six springs and were said to cost $65,000. It was the first venue in the country to have running water at ringside. Red velour drapes adorned the aisle entrances. Gigantic blow-fans, and two enormous intakes, exchanged the air in the cavernous space every eight minutes, to keep the smell of smoke, beer, and body sweat to a minimum. 336 337 338 339

Below ground were "the Catacombs," which was its own world of hope and angst. Within its subterranean depths, over the next eight decades, warriors celebrated their victories, while others breathed their last breath. The ghosts and the glories of the past permeated its atmosphere, a persistent presence that captivated with both possibility and prudence. There was a rabbit warren of small rooms for athletes to warm up, to get final instructions, or to say a prayer. Their doors opened onto a labyrinth of concrete block hallways. As a fighter began his jog toward the ring, the noise of the crowd grew in volume and echoed off the walls as he neared the main floor. Then it exploded to a cacophony as he emerged up the stairs from the bowels below, ran the gauntlet through the cheering, back slapping spectators, and stepped between the ropes to prepare for battle.340 341

****

When the Campbell contingent approached the Olympic's matchmaker "Wad" Wadhams, to ask for a fight, he was amenable. But Frankie was an unknown in Southern California; his recent past up in San Francisco had been uneven, and he was still adapting to his new style. As expected, he was once again down at the bottom of a retractable ladder looking up.

Hayden Alfred "Wad" Wadhams descended from a long line of land-rich farmers in Litchfield County, Connecticut. His father Edward was the first Wadhams in six generations to unhitch his plow horses and settle his family in the town of Norwalk, along Puget Sound, where he thrived as a sign painter with a shop downtown. After his father's early death, Hayden took the family rebellion one step further.

In 1914, he left his job in a Bethel haberdashery as a curler of felt hat brims, and brought his wife and young son clear across the continent to Los Angeles.[342]

Tall and taciturn, Wadhams was a hard-boiled charmer with dark hair and a thousand-yard stare emanating from his summer blue eyes. Within a year of his arrival to the coast, he bought the Western Athletic Club—which later became Dempsey's Manhattan Gym—from silent film star Thomas S. Hart. Located at 534 1/2 South Spring Street, on the second level of a three-story walkup, the gym's design was a novelty to sports writers used to smelly, dark, and dingy interiors. The entire top floor had been opened up to give

Hayden "Wad" Wadhams (c1920s)
Courtesy author's collection

greater height to its interior, creating a spacious loft where the morning sun striped the oakwood floors, and sought out the sheen of sweat on fighters' busy physiques as they trained.

Despite its bright ambiance, the Western was quite the shoestring operation. Fighters laced up in used gloves, picked up on the cheap from other fight clubs. Blood and sweat from prior battles permeated the leather, and the horse-hair padding was largely smashed useless. While a small regulation ring was eighteen feet per side, the Western's ring was a mere twelve feet. The ropes consisted of some spare rubber tubing and the metal corner stanchions were unpadded. Battles across the small canvas provided fans with not only a higher likelihood of serious injury, but more slugging and less dancing, which made for some thrilling fast-paced fights.[343]

During the Four-Round Era, Wad held a stint of successful smokers at the Western every Saturday night; six bouts for 50 cents. The club was a favorite of actors on set at the nearby Universal Movie Studios. He later captured the eye of Jack Doyle, owner of the Vernon Arena, when actor Charlie Chaplin not only stepped into Wad's ring to referee fights, but ducked, swung, and dodged imaginary blows from his ringside seat—attention that would soon change Wad's life in ways he could never have imagined.[344]

In the heady days of the Roaring Twenties, and in the early years of the Great Depression, Wad Wadhams and Jack Doyle would venture together into prizefight forays that became legendary in Southern California; a history that for a short but thrilling window of time, Frankie Campbell would play no little part of.

CHAPTER 14

A SECOND DEMPSEY

I HAD A LITTLE MOTTO ABOUT GETTING RID OF MY OPPONENTS. THE SOONER THE SAFER.
- JACK DEMPSEY

When Tom Maloney strolled out of Wad Wadham's office that summer of 1929, he had a Cuban cigar clenched in his teeth; smoke drifted around his head from his slow satisfied puffs. As he settled a straw boater into place, he wore a lopsided grin so wide he had to turn sideways to exit the building. With each jaunty step, the contract for Frankie's first official bout as a heavyweight crinkled in his pocket. The purse was a paltry $250. But Tom had the confidence of a cliff diver. He was certain more zeroes would follow.

The match was an eight-round semi-windup against Arizona's Clyde "Roughhouse" Colvin, a game scrapper who stepped at top speed. Colvin's recent past included a furiously fought battle to a decision against rising teenage phenom "Dynamite" Jackson, when Jackson still fought under his right name of Ernest Bendy.

In the Olympic Auditorium's newspaper predictions for the event, Colvin was described as a smart youngster and was a good short-ender, meaning he was an underdog, who possessed the ability to pull off a surprise victory when the odds were against him, but that Frankie was expected to win. Tom had turned down an offer for Frankie to fight the winner of the night's main event, between Dick Daniels and Yale Okun. He said Frankie would be brought along gradually, before any attempts were made to slip him back into the select circle he had once enjoyed up in San Francisco.

Tom floated stories that Frankie's past erratic behavior in the Bay Area, was due not only from failure to take the game seriously, but entirely too many distractions for a single fellow with a pocketful of benjamins. He was now a married man with a baby on the way, who had left his playboy ways on a shelf and possessed the

110

heart, determination, and skill to become a serious contender. Tom bragged he planned to have Frankie up in the big money inside of six months.[345]

****

On a warm July evening, when Frankie's name was announced, from his corner he flashed a confident smile, as he lifted a darkly-tanned, well-muscled arm to wave to the crowd. There was a gasp from those who had watched him fight up north. The Frankie Campbell who slipped between the ropes at the Olympic that night, was nothing like the boy back home. His stance was self-assured, his gaze was aggressive, and he was fine-tuned to perfection; he was 185 pounds of whalebone and whipcord. The press described him as a stocky heavyweight, with blasting powder in either fist, which landed both to the head and body, with the precise regularity of a jackhammer busting up concrete. [346]

The New & Improved Frankie Campbell (1929)
Courtesy Harry E. Winkler Collection,
University of Notre Dame

"Roughhouse" Colvin looked like he had stumbled into a hornet's nest and came near being stung to death. Punch after brutal punch thudded into his face, the sound like a ribeye roast being smashed against a wall. He took a nine-count three times in the first round alone. Frankie then repeated the process with measured pile-driving rights and lefts through the second round. Colvin tried to either hold on in a clinch or backed up throughout the entire third round. Frankie set such a dizzy pace it made the Daniels–Okun main event that followed look like a minuet. A staggering right, which seemed to materialize from the ether, landed flush on Colvin's jaw in the fourth round and rendered him senseless. His corner appeared relieved when the referee finally called a halt to the affair.[347]

The next day, the *Los Angeles Examiner* admitted that last night, "Mister Tomaso 'Fatboy' Maloney had made no idle boast when he said he would introduce a spectacular fighter to the Olympic patronage."[348]

Wad Wadhams, Baron Dougherty, Lou Daro (1927)
Courtesy author's collection

While arrangements for Frankie's next fight progressed, Tom called up his contacts among the press, and induced them to observe Frankie's daily workouts at the Manhattan Gym. When reporters arrived to watch him train, they were suitably impressed. Not only by his speed and strength, and the enthusiasm of the curious onlookers, but by his choice of sparring partner.

Though he was known to maul his man so thoroughly over the first day's sparring session, that they seldom showed up for a second helping, Frankie had been slinging the mitts for a solid week with popular World 'Colored' Heavyweight Champ George Godfrey, and he had the better of the rounds. Godfrey's height and weight was estimated to be at least 6 feet 2 inches and 250 pounds. He was trying to drop weight to 235 for a title defense at the Olympic against "Long Tom" Hawkins.

Godfrey's manager "Baron" Jimmy Dougherty and Jack Dempsey had their heads together as they watched the two men spar. When Frankie hopped down from the ring to discuss his progress with Cal and Tom, Dougherty offered them $10,000 on the spot for his contract. When they hesitated, he told them to name their price. "Why I could put ten pounds on that feller and he'd lick all the heavyweights who are dodgin' George back east," said the Baron. [349] [350]

Frankie conceded fifteen pounds to his next opponent, 200-pound heavyweight Harry Beum, in the semi-windup to the James Braddock–Yale Okun main event, held at the Olympic the end of August. While the main-eventers got most of the press, local sports editor Stub Nelson encouraged folks not to overlook Frankie. "In condition such as Campbell now is, he is a threat. He could substitute for either Braddock or Okun and look good."[351]

Harry Beum was a protégé of George Blake, former trainer of Joe Woods, who back in 1928 was the first opponent to ever knock Frankie down. Blake had by now developed not only Flyweight Champ Fidel LaBarba, he had guided Jackie Fields to a Welterweight title. Blake was considered a man of impeccable character. He did background checks on his prospects before taking them on. His eye for promising fighters was considered top-notch.[352]

Beum was a burly Los Angeles firefighter, a heavyweight champ in the amateurs, and one of the brightest stars to come out of the Los Angeles Athletic Club under Blake's tutelage. Syndicated sports columnist Damon Runyon had proclaimed Beum a promising prospect, and predicted great things for him. He was a sensational crowd-pleaser with sledge hammers for hands, a punishing straight right, and a vicious left hook. Blake had carefully built Beum's resume before he stepped into the Olympic's ring against Frankie, and he was predicted to have an easy win.

****

As they awaited the opening gong the night of the fight, just before Tom whisked the stool away and climbed down from Frankie's corner, he growled in his boy's ear what became his mantra before each of Frankie's fights. "Now go out there and fight like Dempsey!"

The blood and thunder of Frankie's two minute and thirty-four second performance struck the crowd dumb. He completely overshadowed the Braddock–Okun main event. It was reported some fans left during the monotony of the final bout, to tip their eyes to the skies for a glimpse of the Graf Zeppelin blimp, then flying over Los Angeles on the last leg of an historical round-the-world trip. It was the first time on record a windbag ever put a crimp on the gates for a boxing match.[353]

In the opening round, Frankie Campbell threw a gang of left hooks that so stunned Harry Beum, he quivered like a nervous oyster on a fork. As spectators scrambled to their feet in shock, Frankie flattened him with a hard right to the head and another left hook to the body. The echo of the opening gong for the second round still lingered in the air, when Beum face-planted to the canvas in a cloud of rosin dust from a blistering left hook to the short ribs. No sooner had he risen from the nine-count, when another left hook to his jaw knocked him backwards. His muscles noticeably twitched as he flopped all over the canvas, gasping like a carp out of water, while he kicked and rolled in an attempt to rise. As the referee's count progressed, he gave one last valiant effort, only to fall flat on his face again. His manager George Blake disgustedly threw in the towel to save him the embarrassment.[354] [355] [356]

Veteran sports editor Kay Owe of the *Los Angeles Times* was gobsmacked. Campbell, he said had put Beum down with a two-handed attack that no other heavyweight had possessed since Jack Dempsey was in stride. The next morning over their coffee and donuts at the local diners, sports fans were still chattering about it with enthusiasm. The crowds at the Manhattan Gym soon became standing room only, simply to watch Frankie train.

After he had given big Harry Beum such a lacing, the other local heavies were hesitant to fight him. Les Kennedy turned him down. Word was Les' manager thought local favorites Tony Stabenau or Vigo Doman were safer bets. Stabenau and Doman both suddenly found something interesting to peer at out the window upon mention of Frankie's name. When the latter two fighters instead chose a rematch, Tom Mahoney demanded Frankie fight the victor. [357]

"There's trouble ahead for the winner of tonight's scrap, for Frankie Campbell is in line for the bout with the fellow who has his hand raised," proclaimed Fane Norton of the *Los Angeles Examiner*. Frankie had become such an instant sensation, Fane thought if either fighter entered the ring against him, they'd have to run a second show to accommodate the turn away.[358]

Wad Wadhams sent out a feeler to heavyweight Max Schmeling of Germany, who had been beating all comers in New York for the last year, with an offer of

Tom Gallery (14 Oct 1925) Courtesy of Newspaper Enterprise Association

either Frankie or Les Kennedy at the Olympic Auditorium, but received no response. Though Frankie would concede forty pounds, Wad finally matched him to fight Chet Shandel on September 13. Then the fight fell through. He wired Leo Lomski's manager Eddie Eicher with articles for a bout on October 8. Eicher declined. Lomski should have taken the match. He went on instead to lose spectacularly to Frankie's old nemesis, Charley Belanger.

Tom Gallery reported similar issues trying to match him at the Hollywood American Legion Stadium. An arranged bout there for October 18 against Tony Fuente fell through.

The Legion's matchmaker Thomas Sarsfield Gallery began life in the public eye as a silent film actor. Son of a Chicago police captain, he was also a state competitive-level tennis and squash player. He came to Hollywood in 1920. After twenty movie roles, he quit filmmaking to become a matchmaker, and had just marked his fifth year there in the position. He became so successful and well thought of at his craft, that in the depths of the Depression, when most event centers in the state were bleeding red ink, Gallery successfully juggled matchmaking at the Hollywood Legion, and later at the Dreamland Auditorium up in San Francisco, after Ed Lynch was forced out in 1933. He later became a sports events promoter and director of sports for TV, where he pioneered professional football as a small screen attraction.

Tom Gallery could be counted on to present cards that filled every seat of his stadium. Located on El Centro just east of Vine Street, the Legion was considered a luxurious boxing club. But the original stadium had the humblest of beginnings; it was initially an open-air venue which made its début in 1921, two years before the "Hollywoodland" sign gazed across the City of Angels.

The original open-air Hollywood Legion Stadium (1921)
Courtesy American Hollywood Legion Post #43

Seating consisted of folding wooden chairs on a dirt floor. Some folks brought fruit crates to sit on. Flimsy canvas barriers served as makeshift privacy walls, which ended at the backyards of residential homes. If a night's card went past sunset, cars would encircle the ring and use their headlights for illumination. There were no dressing rooms. The boxers stripped for action in a small adjoining club house, then wrapped themselves in towels and bathrobes before they slipped through the canvas walls. As they awaited their bout, they often squatted shivering around stoves located in the aisles, which fans fed with wood they carried in.[359] [360]

The stadium operated at a loss initially; it wasn't until an evening's card held on New Year's 1922, that the venue's backers, American Legion Post #43's treasury, boasted a net profit of $3. But once it found its feet it was a spectacular success. That year the property received some luxurious upgrades. The 5,100-seat venue acquired a roof, full fencing, and dark wood plank walls; it fondly became known as "The Shack." To encourage attendance by Hollywood celebrities, stadium manager Si Masters had spotlights pierce the sky on fight night as if it was a film premiere. He installed ringside box seats with movie star's names painted on them. Each black vinyl seat boasted a wire rack under its iron-framed, wood-back to hold men's hats.

The Shack/Hollywood American Legion Stadium (1923)
Courtesy American Hollywood Legion Post #43

Soon so many fancy cars lined the blocks nearby, tourists were heard to ask whether the President was in town. As limousines deposited their rich cargo, spectators arrived early to seek autographs. Movie folks joined informal gatherings to exchange gossip, while greetings were shouted across rows of seats. Friday nights became "Fight Night" in Hollywood. It was a regular weekly occasion like church on Sundays. It was a classier joint than the typical blue-collar crowd of longshoremen and roustabouts at other venues. Ringside was filled every week with not only the high society crowd, but the hottest stars of the era; Rudolph Valentino,

Al Jolson, Jean Harlow, Clara Bow, Harold Lloyd and Charlie Chaplin were among the regular attendees.[361] [362] [363]

Frankie was at loose ends while Cal and the two Toms worked to close a match for him at the Legion. The press claimed a bout with Tony Stabenau was reported to be in the bag. But with no immediate promising fights on the horizon and time heavy on his hands, Frankie was disinclined to get stale. The playboy stuff was not an option; his wife Elsie would throttle him.

At Jack "Doc" Kearns' request, the first week of October 1929, Frankie signed on to be one of the "Toy Bulldog" Mickey Walker's sparring partners, as Mickey got in shape for defense of his middleweight title against the "Nebraska Wildcat" Ace Hudkins. Training was conducted at "Pop" Soper's Ranch along the Ventura River over in the Ojai Valley—a boxing camp made famous when Jack Dempsey trained there in early 1927 for his match with Jack Sharkey.[364]

Doc Kearns was best known as the man who, along with promoter George "Tex" Rickard, made a household name of Jack Dempsey. He cultivated the persona of a dandy, who favored gold-tipped

Pop Soper at Soper's Ranch (1925)
Courtesy Ojai Valley Museum

walking sticks, and violet-scented cologne. At heart he was a rough hustler whose devious greed bankrupted the town of Shelby, Montana, when Dempsey fought there against Tommy Gibbons. He was a raconteur who mingled easily with the best and the worst of society. He threw money away on the high life as if he owned a mint, yet had a soft touch for a hard luck story. His life was so lavishly and lasciviously grandiose, it would still make an author blush to put an honest pen to paper.

He was born John Leo McKernan in the farmlands of Waterloo, Michigan, where his father raised cattle and grew corn and wheat. At age twelve, his family rode a covered wagon west to Washington State. At fifteen, John stowed away on a freighter to pan for gold in the Alaska Yukon, where he rubbed shoulders with author Jack London, who suggested his name change, based on a character idea for a future book.

The newly christened Jack Kearns became a gambler and a grifter, who tried his hand at a variety of jobs across the west, before he drifted solidly into boxing. Under the name "Young Kid Kearns," he fought eight professional lightweight bouts and lost seven of them. By the First World War, he had settled into prizefight management in the San Francisco Bay Area.

When he found himself cornered and in contemplation of several ruffians about to rearrange his face in an Oakland barroom in 1916, he met the gaunt eyes of a hungry, hollow-cheeked, aspiring fighter by the name of William Harrison "Jack" Dempsey. Jack's brother Bruce had been stabbed in Salt Lake City, and he had stopped in the bar for a drink as he awaited the train home.

Jack "Doc" Kearns (left)
George "Tex" Rickard (right)
(1925) Courtesy author's collection

Doc was so impressed with how easily Dempsey dispatched of the scalawags, that in the summer of 1917 he sent him a letter proposing an alliance. A five-dollar bill and a one-way ticket back to town soon followed. It launched the beginnings of one of the greatest partnerships in boxing history.

Once he recognized the potential in Dempsey, there was no line Kearns wouldn't cross to elevate him to the top. He embraced each of the seven deadly sins like a warm wool coat. Doc was a maestro of ballyhoo. Over a two-year period, he guided the "Manassa Mauler" from a barnstorming tour to a heavyweight title. Within six years he made Dempsey a global superstar. The duo was so effective at generating publicity and dickering contracts, they were often called "The Slick Jacks."

After an acrimonious split in 1925, following Dempsey's marriage to actress and astute businesswoman Estelle Taylor—who questioned just how much of a cut of her husband's earnings that Doc was siphoning off—Doc went on to manage Mickey

Walker through two world titles. In Mickey, Kearns met a true partner in debauchery; the two could match each other drinks to dames until dawn and beyond.

The duo once blew through almost $400,000 dollars on a month-long trip to Paris. "Sober or stiff," Mickey later boasted with his trademark grin, in the ring, "I belted the guts out of the best of them."

Kearns spent over sixty years in the game. He was still planning his next grand scheme from his death bed. When he died of pneumonia in 1963, his son remarked that, "he died with the mind of a man of 20, who had the body of a man of 125, after 80 years of living life to the hilt." Kearns was memorialized with the traditional final 10-count before the second Sonny Liston–Floyd Patterson heavyweight championship. In his obituaries, sports editors fondly called him a columnist's dream, and the greatest con man in boxing history.

Both of the "Slick Jacks" played a part of not only Frankie Campbell's rise in the ranks, but also in his death. The consequences of their intentional and unintentional actions which surrounded the Baer–Campbell fight, would rival a Shakespearean tragedy.

CHAPTER 15

CHEAP ACTORS

With a good word from Doc Kearns, in mid-October 1929, Cal Working and Tom Maloney met with the Mickey Walker–Ace Hudkins bout's promoter Jack Doyle. Frankie was given a six-round semi-windup before the night's main event at Los Angeles's Wrigley Field baseball park.

William Mills Wrigley Jr's eventual focus on chewing gum in the era of a popular new habit had made him a wealthy man. He became a beloved benevolent philanthropist, free with his millions to assist the downtrodden, especially during the Depression. But above all else, Bill Wrigley lived and breathed baseball. In 1921, for the astronomical sum of $150,000, he acquired the Pacific Coast League's Los Angeles Angels as a farm team for his Chicago Cubs. [365]

In 1924, he purchased a 10-acre lot in South Los Angeles, at the corner of East 42nd Place and Avalon Boulevard, to build the Angels a home field park. The western park was designed by Zachary Taylor Davis, who had been the architect for both of Chicago's ballparks, Comiskey Park and Weeghman Park (later renamed Wrigley Field). Construction of the first Wrigley Field in Los Angeles began in 1924. The 21,000-seat stadium, which the press had christened "Wrigley's Million Dollar Palace," bore the Wrigley name before the one in Chicago, which opened the following year. [366]

Frankie's appearance at Wrigley Field provided him with his first major exposure at a southern boxing event. His opponent was Ed Herting, a 185-pound slugger fighting out of his adopted state of Texas. Herting was a former Rice University footballer who wore the Texas "lone star" on his trunks. He had five impressive professional wins under his belt.

Appearance in the bout was a big deal, both for Herting and for the Gulf Coast States. His manager Clay Hite, wrote letters home which were published in the southern papers as the event at Wrigley's drew near. "At last, we are getting our big shot in Los Angeles. Ed is matched with Frankie Campbell, the best heavyweight on the Pacific Coast.... Ed will have the advantage of weight, height and reach.... If we get by this fellow, all of California, boxingly speaking, will know of Ed Herting." [367]

Jack Dempsey continued to take an ever-greater interest in Frankie. He regularly stopped by the Manhattan Gym to watch his progress. He admired not only Frankie's two-fisted attack, and his punishing left hook, so reminiscent of his own, he was fond of the earnest young man. On one such occasion, he presented Frankie with the trunks he had worn at the Luis Firpo fight—a souvenir from a defining moment in Jack's career, in which the champion was knocked clear through the ring ropes, gashed the back of his head on columnist Jack Lawrence's Corona 3 typewriter, yet returned to win the bout by kayo in the next round.

Tom Maloney almost fainted dead away when Frankie showed him Jack's gift. Before the sun kissed the horizon, he had huffed breathlessly down to every single local press office, wildly waving them in his sweaty paw. Frankie, he crowed, would wear Dempsey's trunks from the Firpo fight the night of his bout against Ed Herting at Wrigley Field! [368] [369] [370]

Wrigley Field (Los Angeles) boxing match (1937). Courtesy UCLA
Charles E. Young Research Library Department of Special Collections, CC BY

A crowd of 25,000 fight fans streamed through Wrigley's gates that October night in 1929 to attend the event. Most were blissfully ignorant that the world as they knew it was about to implode. The New York Stock Exchange had crashed the day before the fight on "Black Monday." Panic selling ensued the morning of the fight until the stock market fell to its lowest point in history. That morning's "Black Tuesday" crash proved to be a chimera on the horizon. The Great Depression had been given her first breath of fire and before it was over, along with the agricultural and environmental disasters which produced the Dust Bowl, she and her siblings would consume the nation in the worst crisis America had faced since the Civil War.

While stockbrokers despaired over their ticker tapes, under a striped awning which fluttered in the breeze over the ring at Wrigley Field that night, Frankie dispatched of Ed Herting in the semi-windup faster than it took to boil an egg. The two slugged a furious flurry that pleased the big crowd in the opening round. Herting banged out a few stiff wallops but Frankie shook them of and returned the favor. Ed was dropped three times; the bell that saved him from a knockout could hardly be heard through the mounting clamor of spectators.

Moments into the second, as punches flew wildly and the fighters careened across the ring, Frankie crashed a brutal right to Herting's jaw, followed by a hard left hook that dropped him face-first with a crash like a piano off a cliff. The cries of the huge throng became a tumultuous roar that rent the very air into pieces, as the referee stopped the contest to save Herting the trouble of a count. Through the opening rounds of the lackluster Mickey Walker–Ace Hudkins main event that followed, the buzz of excitement about Frankie's performance continued to arc through the autumn air.[371] [372]

Doc Kearns was so impressed by not only the speed and power Frankie exhibited, but the exuberance of the crowd to watch him fight. This fellow just might be a goldmine. He asked Cal and Tom what the current prices were for heavyweights on the hoof. But Kearns didn't stand a chance to buy such a prospect now. Tom demurred with a Cheshire smile, "I've got a second Dempsey in the making. When a heavyweight is good enough to make Jack Kearns take a peek, it's a good bet that you've got something with a big future."[373]

Stub Nelson at the *Los Angeles Record* declared excitedly, "There is no denying that Frankie Campbell can kick your head loose with either hand!" Scribes at the *California Eagle* were convinced that, "Campbell today is the nearest approach to the Dempsey of the Firpo and Willard conquests of any ring man in the world ... and he punches just as effectually and accurately as Dempsey did in his most ferocious days." [374] [375]

Four days later, Frankie signed to fight Tony Stabenau for the main event on November 8 at the Hollywood Legion Stadium. The next day, Tony's new manager, retired lightweight boxer Herman Langfield, withdrew him from the match. He stated Stabenau had done no hard training and was in no condition to fight since an operation on his broken nose from his rematch with Vigo Doman. Others intimated Tony's avoidance of Frankie was due to other parts of Stabenau's anatomy that ailed him.[376]

In his place, a rematch with Bud Doyle was announced to be in the bag. Doyle wanted to avenge his close loss to Frankie in 1928; he was considered a tougher match than Tony. But then Bud backed out. He decided Frankie had become too tough to take on a moment's notice. Next, Honolulu heavyweight Alex Rowe was presented on a platter. Talk about six degrees of separation. On the same night that Frankie had kayoed Ed Herting at Wrigley's Field, a colorful 19-year-old upstart by the name of Max Baer, fighting up north out of Oakland in the East Bay, with a record of 10-1-0, kayoed Alex Rowe in the first round of a scheduled six-round fight.[377]

Just a week later, Rowe traveled to Southern California. His trainer Tim McGrath, who had introduced the world to "Sailor Tom" Sharkey had offered up his latest new hope as a last-minute replacement. McGrath claimed Rowe was a better prospect than Sharkey had ever been. Fans weren't particular about who was on the receiving end of Frankie blows; they wanted to see firsthand his reputed double-fisted onslaught. [378] [379]

****

A single spotlight shown down upon the head of genial human megaphone Dan Tobey, as he stood in the dark of the Legion's ring that Friday night. Dan was a legend during the first half of the twentieth century. He appeared in twenty-five movies, and was immortalized in a Looney Tunes cartoon, "Bunny Hugged," appropriately enough, as a ring announcer.

Dapper Dan Tobey (1921)
Courtesy American Legion Post #43

A mentor to beloved ring maestro Jimmy Lennon Sr., he cut his teeth at "Uncle Tom" McCarey's Naud Junction and Vernon Arenas, in a fight era before both radio and silent film.

As others adopted microphones, loudspeakers and other new-fangled inventions to speak to a crowd, Dan spurned them in disgust. While the first televised fights, with announcers tethered to a camera, were a decade away, Dan had the freedom to command the ring, and he used every inch of it to build enthusiasm as he worked the crowd like a carnival barker.

Dan wore a perpetual grin, as if he had a pip of a story about the farmer's daughter; he often broke out into an impromptu two-step to punctuate his delivery. In a voice so rich and loud it rattled the molars of the front-row spectators, and carried clear to the last nosebleed seat, he began his familiar opener.

"Ladiessss and gentlemennnn!!" To which fans whooped with delight, "yaaaas!" Then with a grand sweep of his arm he gestured, "In this cornerrr, Frankieee Cammmpbelll, that much talked about heavyweight...," and so it began.

From the clang of the bell, Frankie's bobbing weaving style completely baffled Alex Rowe. He never stood a chance. With twenty seconds left of the first round, Frankie swung a hard right cross to the jaw followed by a straight left to the ribs. Rowe was struck dizzier than a ride on the Tilt-A-Whirl down at the Venice Pier. A great puff of rosin dust marked his landing like the outline of a dead body.

Though he rarely ventured far from his family fireside to watch local fights, former champ Jim Jeffries had heard good things about Frankie. That night he was ringside for a closer peep. "The best fighter I've seen in years," he remarked afterward. Jim was impressed enough that he did something he had rarely done before; he went back to Frankie's dressing room to congratulate him. He invited him to his alfalfa ranch in Burbank, where Jim also raised thoroughbred bulls and was among the foremost suppliers of Holstein-Friesian cattle in the U.S., Mexico, and South America.[380] [381]

A reporter and a photographer followed Frankie and his manager Cal Working to their visit with Jeffries. Images of Frankie show his chest stuck out so far, they had to move the buildings back. But not with arrogance, with pride that he had come to be in this moment, and stood as a guest alongside one of his boyhood idols.

He wore his best Sunday suit to signify his respect for the former champ, and to mark the momentous occasion, a mid-1920s navy-blue double-breasted pinstripe. It was a bit snug on his recently rebuilt frame. He didn't wear it often and moths had chewed tiny holes in one knee. He wore his favorite cap toe oxfords. He splurged on a new tie and a spear point collar shirt.

Cal sported the grin of a successful heist guy driving the getaway car, and the garb of a lackadaisical used appliance salesman the morning after a bender. Jim was pleased to see Frankie, but looked like he'd snugged a hat onto unkempt hair, and switched out his bedroom slippers for loafers.

Frankie Campbell, Cal Working and Jim Jeffries
Burbank CA (1929) Courtesy Harry E. Winkler
Collection, University of Notre Dame

San Francisco trainer Moose Taussig was once asked who were among the best-dressed men in the boxing world. When Jeffries' name came up, he snorted that Jim dressed liked a 'dowd.' Jim didn't give a hoot how he looked; he had a ranch to run. The next day, photos and banner headlines were splashed across the nation's papers to cover the visit.

"It wasn't the knockout or the man he stopped," Jeff remarked to the reporter about Frankie's recent bout with Alex Rowe, "It was the decisive way Campbell scored that I liked.... Too many fighters today are nothing but cheap actors. They want to do a song and dance turn and get away with it. Campbell showed me that he is willing to get in there and take a chance just to put over a punch. This boy can stop any man he can hit." [382] [383]

CHAPTER 16

A RING MIRACLE

LUCK IS WHAT HAPPENS WHEN PREPARATION MEETS OPPORTUNITY
- SENECA

With Tom Maloney pulling the strings like a manic puppeteer, sports editors across the continent began to speculate on the "New Heavy Battler Developing in the West." Tom loved nothing better than to bang out nutty press releases on his typewriter to hype his fighter. He provided endless reams of copy and quotes to the press, which earnestly made the case that this "New Dempsey," while not as tall as Jack, was simply built lower to the ground. That he was the same weight as Dempsey when he kayoed Jess Willard in Toledo, and the same age as Jack when he was crowned the champ. [384]

Frankie's sporadic on-and-off appearances in his early days were held up as a good thing; he wasn't too burned out, he wasn't too beat up, and he'd inadvertently saved his best for today. Even his pleasure-seeking past was excused as simply actions that cost him a position among the top-notchers he likely wasn't equipped to handle as a youth. Tom pointed out that Stanley Ketchel and Harry Greb were both shameless playboys. And who hadn't heard the wild stories of Mickey Walker's night life, who famously wrote, "Few guys raised more hell or had more fun doing it. If I sinned, I sinned happy." Yet look what they had accomplished in the ring![385] [386]

Tom Maloney's ballyhoo bordered on the obnoxious, but it was consumed with glee by sports reporters. Their enthusiasm harkened back to the heady days when Jack Dempsey's exploits dominated the headlines. Frankie could not only be matched with a cigar store Indian and pack the rafters, he regularly topped the daily sports pages. Tom had made him the hottest cookie in town. Despite the hype, some things remained fact; Frankie was in the best condition of his career. The press took to calling him the "San Francisco Adonis" for his finely-conditioned physique. He had matured physically and psychologically, and it showed in his ring work. He was well regarded as an earnest fighter who worked hard to improve at his craft.

If "The Three Wise Men" were accused of trying to "Dempsey" their fighter, Frankie's new style appeared to work for him. Whereas before, he generally stood erect and methodically lashed out with his punches like a mustachioed bare-knuckle boxer, Frankie now had body strength and mental prowess to throw punch combinations with power and precision from either fist, to bob and weave just before he delivered a knockout punch, that seemed to appear like a magician had pulled the proverbial rabbit from a hat.

Stub Nelson of the *Los Angeles Record* observed that Frankie favored a corkscrew punch that dropped over rather than shot forward, which resulted in faster, harder blows, and that his knockout punches typically landed on the temple rather than the point of the chin. But to be most effective he had to drive in close; a big fellow with a long-left hand would put him at a disadvantage. Nevertheless, said Stub, when his blows landed, "None of his opponents fall backward. They fall forward.... His opponents don't pass out cold ... they seem to be stunned and in pain ... one feels like calling for a doctor."[387]

Chances are also likely Frankie was naturally left-handed, coerced at a young age into using his right by a wacky religious-based belief that left-handers were more vulnerable to the Devil's influence and more likely to exhibit mental illness. Southpaws run consistently in the Camilli family, even into the modern era. Frankie's father Alessio, his brother Dolph, and two of Dolph's sons were left-handed. Dolph said their grammar school forced lefties to become right-handed. Instead, they often became ambidextrous. Depending on how his golf game proceeded, Dolph owned two sets of golf clubs to accommodate either grip. Frankie's left hook, which up north had eventually become a thing of beauty, in the south now became one of his deadliest weapons.[388]

****

To take advantage of Frankie's explosive rise into prominence, Wad Wadhams at the Olympic Auditorium immediately signed him to box eleven days later, for a ten-round main event against heavyweight Harry Dillon. Dillon's right name was Joseph Darbell. His manager named him Dillon due to his striking resemblance to former World Light-Heavyweight champ the "Hoosier Bearcat" Jack Dillon. Harry was born in Winnipeg, Canada. The square-jawed son of Ukrainian immigrants, he was not only the idol of his local townsmen, he was a fan favorite across North America. He would be Frankie's first real test in the south. He had been smacking around big, slow-moving heavies. In Dillon he would meet a boxer of his own size; one with not only considerable speed, but a seasoned campaigner.

Harry Dillon boasted fifty-two ring battles. He had hooked up with some of the best boys of his heft. Young Stribling didn't stop him, even after Stribling broke his rib. Neither did Tuffy Griffiths. He lost four teeth during his fight in Portland, Oregon, against Leo Lomski, though Harry boasted he had knocked out three of

Leo's. He had recently fought the seventh of his seven career battles with Charley Belanger; the same Belanger who had trounced Frankie so completely in the spring of 1928. Dillon had twice been Canada's Light-Heavyweight Champ. He had lost the title both times to Belanger.

The Dillon–Belanger battles had been considered especially brutal contests, with both fighters giving and receiving serious injuries. Dillon was described as a busy two-fisted mauler who had over seventeen headliners to his credit. It was expected he would give Frankie the battle of his life. If Frankie won this fight in a decisive manner, against a nationally prominent boxer, he would cement himself as one of the leading heavyweights in the nation. Harry Dillon's skills were so well thought of at the time, that fight predictions in *Collyer's Eye* stated if Frankie emerged the victor, it would stun the boxing world.[389]

Bill Smith of the *Los Angeles Evening Express* suggested if Frankie claimed victory over Dillon, he would have to be included in the select group of fighters who might get somewhere in the chase for Tunney's discarded crown. It was a crown Gene Tunney had defended only two times in three years, before he retired undefeated and was scorned for quitting. Tunney admitted he had willingly discarded the title, after he experienced amnesia for two days from a brutal hit while training for the Dempsey rematch. He later confessed he was not entirely normal for the first seven rounds of that fight. [390]

Both fighters trained at the Manhattan Gym. But Frankie was superstitious; his mental attitude had been destroyed after seeing Charley Belanger's superior ring work back in 1928. He didn't like to see his opponents until they met in the ring. The boys had agreed to book gym time at different parts of the day. When Dillon dawdled a bit too long one morning, Tom Maloney rushed over and yelled at him to get out. Dillon didn't back down. "Get in the ring Tuesday night with the wop and I'll knock both of you out!"[391]

Manager Bill Black, who had brought Dillon to Los Angeles, didn't endear himself to Tom either. He offered a bet that his middleweight Del Fontaine could stop Frankie with ease. He thought that much of Tom's talk about Frankie's hitting power was baloney. "I expect to see Dillon blow this new phenom up inside a few rounds and win by a kayo himself." Dillon wasn't impressed either. "I've fought a lot of them 'second Dempseys,'" he smirked, "but I reckon there was only one." [392] [393]

The *Los Angeles Times* came to the defense of their own. Frankie was a fellow townsman now, not just an invader from the north. He was an official resident who had settled into the city's rhythms. They huffed that Frankie had championship possibilities. That he was in as perfect a form as few fighters achieved. Why, he was in as good a condition as Dempsey was the day he knocked out Jess Willard in Toledo! And just like Dempsey, "he hadn't the interest to carry an opponent for multiple rounds. He tears out and throws with all his might. New management and a changed style," said the *Times*, "seems to have wrought 'a ring miracle.'"[394]

Frankie chocked up his newfound success to the impending birth of his first child. "I didn't take the game seriously for a long time. If I got $1,000 for a fight, I wouldn't take another match until I had spent every cent of it. But all my luck seems to have started when we began to expect the baby. I changed managers and came away from my old playgrounds around the San Francisco Bay." Frankie may have been living down south while Elsie was back home, but never a week passed that she didn't send him a letter. Her advice was straight and to the point: "Knock that fellow out for me and the baby."[395]

Frankie Campbell at the Manhattan Gym (1929)
Courtesy Harry E. Winkler Collection, University of Notre Dame

Doc Kearns and Mickey Walker planned to sit ringside for the bout. Mickey had his eye on the light-heavyweight class, and Doc had been in recent discussions with Wad Wadhams for suitable matches against weightier opponents. Doc said if Frankie knocked out Harry Dillon and all future big-name opponents through January, a Walker–Campbell fight with Frankie at 180 and Mickey at 170, was in the bag at Wrigley Field for early next year. Kearns told the press, "If Campbell comes through and is as good as he looks right now, he'll do.... I'm interested in this Campbell because he can hit. Walker and the Italian would make a great slugging battle. He's getting to be a pretty good card around here."[396] [397]

Jim Jeffries, Tommy Ryan, and Georges Carpentier planned to attend the fight. Jack Dempsey sent a telegram on the eve of Frankie's big test: "Go to it, kid and fight for me." Jack told reporters he had watched his progress with "more interest than any boy he has set eyes on."[398] [399]

****

The most packed house the Olympic had seen in months filled the joint to bursting on the evening of November 19, 1929. The turnstiles hummed and the gate was well over $10,000. As Frankie slipped between the ropes he was greeted with raucous applause. At the sound of the bell, he rushed in with revenge on his mind, ready to knock Dillon right into the faucet end of the bathtub. He opened the round with a hard straight right to the jaw that pushed Harry back on his heels. Spectators sprang to their feet with a clamor. Harry responded with a right and left barrage to the head which sent Frankie reeling like a merry go round. Then he bounced off the ropes and replied with a series of brutal rights and lefts of his own. Now Dillon was staggered. Before his head had cleared, two wicked left hooks to the ribs and a crushing right uppercut to the chin lifted him up on his toes and stretched him out on the canvas. Little birdies still orbited his head as Frankie's hand was raised in victory. [400] [401]

The applause of the crowd was eardrum shattering in its enthusiasm. Frankie had given Elsie and the fans exactly what they wanted, a sensational "off-to-dreamland" knockout, and he did it against a top-notch opponent. There was great jubilation over in Frankie's corner. If Frankie's smile had been any wider, he'd have broken his face. Tom Maloney was so euphoric, he almost levitated into the air. He grabbed Frankie's cheeks and gave him a lip-smacking kiss. He turned and gave Cal Working a big buss too. Tom was so happy he smooched the ring post a few times. Then he made so many bows to the crowd, folks thought *he'd* won the fight![402] [403]

Jack Dempsey phoned his associates in Chicago, enthusiastic about the sensational victory. He instructed them to begin a file of wire clippings on Frankie's successes, as a resume of sorts in anticipation of a campaign on the East Coast. Managers in New York, Boston, Minneapolis, and Cleveland were all in touch with Cal and Tom about future bouts; Cal admitted to being positively overwhelmed by the attention.[404]

Bill Smith at the *Los Angeles Evening Express* started to measure Frankie's brow for a championship tiara. "By tipping over Harry Dillon in the first round Campbell proved he is a much greater fighter than the ring birds were willing to admit. He stood the big test when he receipted for a punch which almost toppled him, and then flashed something that all present and future champions must have—the ability to come from behind and win when the odds seem against them. Some critics thought Campbell was reckless in his brief and thrilling encounter with Dillon. Took too many chances they said ... but there's a prize ring axiom that the best defense is a vicious offense. Campbell believes in it, just as McGovern, Ketchel and Dempsey did, and up to date it has carried him far enough to make him an outstanding performer in the local rings."[405]

James Mitchell of the *Los Angeles Post* wrote, that in stopping Dillon he had put a bright feather in his cap. "They can bring in the big fellows as fast as he is ready for them and tips them over with his thudding thumps.... Campbell is made—no doubt about that—here and around the country. How they love a puncher. How they'll go wild every time Campbell ends a fight with his vicious wallops."[406]

Frankie Campbell was indeed a fighter with a bright future. While other heavyweight title-chasers used stalling tactics, wrestled, and claimed imaginary fouls, Frankie launched assaults like a first-line soldier in the Argonne Forest. In four months, he had become the biggest box office attraction in Southern California. Though the Great Depression had already put boxing events in a slump, Frankie's crowd-pleasing popularity literally broke the Olympic's string of bad gate receipts. He was their most promising prospect to keep the auditorium in the black.

Not only had his dedication paid off, but Lady Luck seemed to have sidled up to caress his shoulder and toss him a come-hither look. When Frankie next went down to the Manhattan Gym to train, he was surprised and pleased to be greeted by the applause of adoring fans, surrounded by an eager press, and given hearty congratulations by his fellow fighters.

Made it, Ma! Top o' the world.

CHAPTER 17

HAPPY JACK

A CHAMPION IS SOMEONE WHO GETS UP WHEN HE CAN'T
- JACK DEMPSEY

Along with Tuffy Griffiths, Paulino Uzcudun, George Godfrey, and the winner of the upcoming K.O. Christner–Les Kennedy bout, promoter Jack Doyle put Frankie's name in the running to fight top title contender Jack Sharkey, as one of a series of heavyweight bouts he had planned at Wrigley Field for the New Year. When Sharkey, a mere six months away from a fight with Max Schmeling for the heavyweight title, demanded at least $35,000 just to drop his robe, Doyle took a pass. [407]

Happy Jack Doyle (1922)
Courtesy author's collection

John Joseph "Jack" Doyle was said to be the second greatest boxing promoter in Los Angeles history. He learned the game at the knee of the first. Thomas James "Uncle Tom" McCarey was celebrated as the man who almost singlehandedly put the City of Angels on the map as a major fight destination. One of McCarey's last gigs as a southern promoter, was the 1913 fight that resulted in the death of Bull Young at the hands of Jess Willard. With McCarey's departure from the scene, Jack Doyle set about slipping his eager feet into Tom's discarded shoes.

Born to Irish immigrants, the Doyle sons were all gregarious entrepreneurs. As a young man, Jack Doyle followed his father Patrick and brother Tom into work with the Southern Pacific Railroad as a fire engineer. Before he became a sports columnist and raced a string of ponies, his older brother Malcolm had developed a successful fight club in St. Louis, Missouri. When "Mal" brought several prospects out to California, boxing lured Jack down from his iron horse. [408] [409] [410]

Around 1902, Jack hooked up with Tom McCarey. Through Tom, he developed a friendship with multi-millionaire, Elias J. "Lucky" Baldwin. Lucky hired Doyle as on-site manager of a boxing training camp in Arcadia, which bordered Lucky's ranch in the San Gabriel Mountains known as Rancho Santa Anita. Doyle began to hold highly successful boxing exhibitions there, for influential guests of Lucky's nearby luxury Hotel Oakwood. [411] [412] [413]

In early 1908, land developer John Batiste "J.B." Leonis enticed Jack down from the hills to the village of Vernon on the outskirts of Los Angeles. Leonis offered free land lots to businesses for use as oil refineries, assembly plants, and slaughter houses. He also encouraged entrepreneurs that catered to the vices of their workers: broads, booze, boxing and baseball. Jack leased a huge lot on 38th Street and Santa Fe Avenue in April 1908, where he initially built the South Side Athletic Club. He erected an open-air ring with a few wood bleachers, and the nexus of the legendary Doyle's Vernon Arena was born. [414] [415] [416]

The origins of Vernon Arena
Dingman Brothers Postcards, Los Angeles (c1910)

Capacity crowds grew so numerous simply to watch the fighters spar, that Jack covered the training ring and added bleacher seats to hold exhibitions. By November he had opened the infamous Central Saloon, known as the "Thirst Emporium" next door, to whet the whistles of thirsty fight fans. Its two eighty-foot bars, which could accommodate 400 pairs of elbows, were manned by almost forty bartenders, each with their own cash register, and all said to have been imported from Ireland. An electric "Bar" sign shone like a lighthouse in a storm as patrons made their way along the dark back roads to the saloon's doors. [417] [418] [419]

Jack Doyle lured Hayden "Wad" Wadhams away from his position at the Western Athletic Club in 1916, and into a spot as Athletic Director at his club, which eventually led to a position as matchmaker for the Vernon. Wad made more matches during the Four-Round Era, with seven four-round fights on every card each Tuesday and Friday nights, than Tex Rickard, "Sunny Jim" Coffroth, and "Uncle Tom" McCarey did in their entire careers. [420] [421] [422]

Jack Doyle's Central Saloon (c1915)
Courtesy Los Angeles Examiner

Doyle opened the Stag Hotel across from the Central Saloon to house fighters, and Doyle's Café to feed visiting fight fans. As Prohibition spread across the state, Vernon was one of the last two "wet" towns in Los Angeles County. The thirsty headed south by the thousands, and the money poured in. Wad Wadhams later said he used to bale up money like hay, load it into an old Ford and drive it to the bank to put it uncounted in Doyle's vault. They often had $30,000 (equivalent to $530,000 today) after a big weekend. [423]

Though fond sentiments would always remain with the old original arena, in 1923, Doyle converted it into a luxury training center, and in a record thirty-five days, built the 7,000-seat Vernon Coliseum nearby; he made sure several of its doorways conveniently opened directly into his saloon. Cinema spotlights lit the ring. Electric-lighted name plates adorned the box seats of prominent sporting men and business firms. Standard four-legged ring corner stools were replaced with padded seats, which swung out of sight between rounds. Running water replaced old water buckets. Wood benches were upgraded to orchestra seats. Jack had a ringside seat—fifty percent wider than ordinary ones—constructed to accommodate Keystone Comedies superstar Roscoe "Fatty" Arbuckle. In 1925 he added balcony seating, and 8,500 fans soon parked their fannies inside to fill it to capacity.[424]

Jack Doyle's Vernon Coliseum (28 Aug 1923)
Courtesy Los Angeles Examiner

But change was on the horizon and Jack Doyle wouldn't miss a beat. Southern California was fight-mad; it was ripe for a larger arena. He often had to turn away as many as 3,000 spectators for popular fights, who then anxiously stood outside the Vernon, or crowded around the saloon doors, while a man with a megaphone announced the results of each round. Jack was among the financial backers for the new Olympic Auditorium. He had hoped to run both arenas to replace lost profits after Prohibition finally shuttered his saloon. But once the Olympic opened its doors, Jack's Vernon Coliseum profits were severely affected.

Undeterred and ever the savvy businessman, in the spring of 1927 he permanently turned his speculative grey eyes north to Los Angeles. He shuttered the coliseum and took Wad with him to run the Olympic and hold outdoor extravaganzas at Wrigley Field. Now that the Vernon was no longer the competition, within months Jack became one of the most successful promoters in the nation. Together Jack and Wad held the first two six-figure gates in California history: the $125,000 gate George Godfrey–Paulino Uzcudun fight at Wrigley Field in 1928, and the $150,000 gate Mickey Walker–Ace Hudkins fight at Wrigley for Walker's middleweight title in 1929. By the time he approached his fortieth birthday, Wad Wadhams owned a home on Hollywood's Sunset Blvd. [425] [426] [427] [428]

Jack Doyle became so beloved, that Sid Ziff of the *Los Angeles Evening Express* penned an ode to honor him when he was around to still hear it. "Eulogies belong to the departed. Rarely are they given the living. Jack Doyle deserves his. When a man's name is the foundation and the savior of so profound a sport, it is high time he be given credit for it.... He protected four-round boxing and under his wing nursed it along until it became virtually an industry here. He guarded his child's reputation zealously. In all the long years that he promoted fights at Vernon his name has never been linked to a framed fight."[429]

****

The end of November 1929, Frankie was matched to fight the first week of December, in a headliner at the Hollywood Legion Stadium. He would finally touch gloves with Tony Stabenau. Tony fought out of Los Angeles via Buffalo, New York. He stood 6 feet 3 inches tall and hovered around 200 pounds. He had come west via Chicago a year earlier. During his West Coast sojourn, he handed Chet Shandel his first-ever defeat, and gone toe-to-toe with Dynamite Jackson. It was after his rematch with Vigo Domain, a relentless roughhouse affair which ended in a draw, that Tony's nose had to be surgically rebuilt. Frankie had high hopes to be the one to rearrange Tony's brand-new proboscis in record time.

An innocuous article in the *Los Angeles Times* dated December 1, reported that Frankie headed the card of an exhibition held at the 'colored' Elks' Hall to aid the cause of old "Dixie Kid," who was dependent on charity. Born Aaron Lister Brown, the Kid was once World Welterweight Champion; in 1904 he took the title from "Barbados" Joe Wolcott. He had battled the likes of Sam Langford, Joe Jeanette, and Georges Carpentier. A victim of punch-drunk-syndrome, he slept in a tumbledown shack near the railroad yards, a dresser drawer filled with dog-eared news clippings of his golden years. Frankie's opponent was not named, but he mingled among some of the finest unsung and long-forgotten black boxers of the era. It was one of numerous benefit events where he appeared to aid a fellow fighter fallen on hard times.[430] [431]

The night of the Campbell–Stabenau fight at the Hollywood Legion, the "sold out" sign had been up for hours, and the walls were bulging. It was deemed the most highly anticipated local heavyweight fight in months. Reserve seats were gone two days in advance. As the Depression was being felt in earnest across the nation, it was the only bout in all of 1929 held at the Legion where over 1,000 fans were turned away; extra police were rushed to the club to control the crowd that milled around the ticket windows. If it had been held at the larger Olympic Auditorium the gate might have surpassed $15,000.[432]

Frankie weighed in at 180 1/2 pounds while Tony Stabenau tipped the scales at 192. Tony had height, weight, and reach advantages, yet Frankie went into the bout a 4-to-1 favorite. Tony had a deadly knockout right, and a granite chin, but Frankie had a brutal two-fisted attack that mowed his opponent down like a scythe through wheat.[433]

****

In the moments before the main event, the serenade of band music wafted through the dense vapor of cigar smoke as it swirled in thick clouds around the gallery. Vendors threaded the aisles with harsh calls of peanuts and popcorn and soda pop. The subtle sparkle of diamonds winked from earlobes and cufflinks. The usual scuffle of feet and rustle of programs battled with coughs of impatience and idle chatter. Tense, expectant smiles cut through the thrill in the air at the thought of the impending battle to come.

Suddenly the music stopped as all but the ring was plunged into darkness. In the pool of the stark white light, the two sweat-slicked, magnificently-muscled gladiators gazed across the canvas with hard, challenging eyes as introductions were made. An impatient bark clashed with the sound of the opening gong. The stare was broken, as with heads bowed and shoulders hunched, like two charging bulls they plowed into each other.

Frankie cut his opponent down to size from the start in spectacular fashion. He kept up such a dizzy pace he might have all but punched himself out near the end. Yet he now had the endurance of a truck horse; he still retained his wallop in the final heat. Tony was dazed three times in the opening round alone with Frankie's favorite combo, a left hook to the body and a right cross to the head. The fans were clamoring for a kayo when Frankie threw two terrific left hooks to the chin like the business end of a croquet mallet. But Tony managed to hang on until the gong.

In the second, Tony was floored twice, with a right uppercut for a no-count, and a right cross for a nine-count. He gamely replied with a succession of right uppercuts, but was so groggy the punches lacked sizzle. As the bell rang, he was bleeding heavily from the mouth. In the fourth, after a terrific assault along the ropes, Frankie threw a brutal right to the head, which sprawled Tony flat on his back for a nine-count. But when he waded in to finish him, Tony was again saved by the bell.

Frankie switched his attack to Tony's mid-section in the fifth, and then returned to his head in the sixth; he did everything but remove Tony's wishbone and use it as a good luck charm. Tony's supporters had their only chance to cheer when he floored Frankie in the sixth for a nine-count. At the opening of the seventh, he knocked Frankie's head back with three more uppercuts. Frankie didn't even break stride. He weaved right back in and whipped over a right cross which banged his foe again to the canvas. As Tony staggered to his feet, in an atmosphere made milky by smoke and rosin dust, Frankie delivered a final left hook that started from the bleachers and ended on Tony's chin. He face-planted into a different time zone.

The referee's intervention went unheard; Tony was seeing more stars than there are in heaven.[434]

Frankie later admitted he had trained a mere three days before he exchanged pleasantries with Stabenau. The stork had been hovering around back home. Elsie presented him with a son, Francis Campbell Camilli, on December 3, 1929. He had stayed with mother and child in San Francisco, until she assured him, she was fine, and their son was hale and hearty.[435]

****

Just before Christmas, Werner Laufer of the *Newspaper Enterprise Association* penned an article titled, "Bored Boxing World Seeks New Champion for Ring," that was carried nationwide. "Now is the time for every good fight manager to look under a boxcar for another Dempsey," he smirked. "In every section of the country there are suspicious looking men prowling about rail yards, looking under gondolas, and around boiler factories, getting a load of the young huskies who dally with the pneumatic riveting machines. They are fight managers, and their quest is for a heavyweight."

He observed that one "Pacific Coast boy who is being groomed for greater things is Frankie Campbell of Los Angeles. He is highly regarded by Jack Dempsey himself to succeed him as a real fighting champion. Campbell has a style similar to the old master's. He punches hard with both fists from a crouch. He is serious about fighting and has rung up nine straight knockouts. Of course, he has only recently passed the Tony Stabenau milestone of his pugilistic journey and may be quite a way off. But there is the possibility that he, like Dempsey, may gather a sudden momentum and breeze right through the heavyweights like a borer through an Iowa cornfield."[436]

Frankie's trainer Tom Maloney was in hog heaven as he held court at the Manhattan Gym. A gaggle of reporters stood with pens paused in anticipation of any personal gems he might share about his star fighter. With a beaming countenance, Tom looked out at the sea of faces and drawled a greeting. "Gemmen…" The ringside bleachers groaned in protest as he leaned back to blow a stream of smoke from his Perfecto cigar. "If you'll wait for ten minutes," he winked, "I'll let you shake the hand of the next heavyweight champion."[437]

Veteran sports writer Bob Shand of the *Oakland* Tribune deemed Frankie the biggest pugilistic shot in Los Angeles. He noted that Frankie's manager Cal Working had offered Max Baer a nice purse to meet his fighter, but Max's managers could not see the match. Baer, he said, is going big but is still green and will be fed the Tony Fuentes kind for some time yet.[438]

CHAPTER 18

LIVERMORE BUTCHER BOY

IF YOU'RE UP AGAINST A BRUISER AND YOU'RE GETTING
KNOCKED ABOUT: GRIN - ROBERT WILLIAM SERVICE

In a mere twelve months, Maximilian Adelbert "Max" Baer had achieved twenty-one wins, twelve by knockout. His most recent battles had largely been against fighters who were nothing to write home about. But as he was pitted against more experienced opponents that he couldn't knock out early, he willingly played possum and, seemingly without harm, absorbed a shocking amount of punishment in the ring. He would often demonstrate just how hard his head was by banging it against the radiators and steam pipes of his dressing room before a fight.[439]

Contrary to repeated claims by Max, and even by his own brother—that Max became a jester in the ring as a defense mechanism only after Frankie's death—he did so from the very beginning. He put on seriousness like the squirting boutonniere of a clown. If an opponent landed a particularly hard punch, Max petulantly stuck out his tongue to show it had no effect, or thrust his chin forward invitingly for another blow. He coquettishly chatted with the crowd and his opponent during rounds. He seemed more interested in what he could do to get a laugh from an audience, than get to work against the guy in front of him.[440]

Several scribes noted he became angry if his opponent caught the crowd's eye and would childishly act out to center their attention back on him. If his haymaker right didn't knock his opponent out cold in the first round or two, he simply clowned—and waited. When he finally decided his foe had run his legs off and tired out his arms, with a feral kind of cunning, in a millisecond a manic snarl replaced the smile. Like a bolt from the blue, he unleashed one-two-five hurricane force rights that had his hapless victim sprawled out like pancake batter on the griddle.

Like Frankie Campbell, Max Baer had been blessed genetically with a build made for athletics. He possessed shoulders so spectacularly wide he moved

Max Baer (circa 1911)
Courtesy author's collection

sideways through doorways. He boasted an incredible 80-inch reach, his weight approached 200 pounds, he measured just over 6 feet 2 inches tall, and he was still growing.

Max claimed he made his lusty ten-pound appearance during a brutal Omaha, Nebraska snowstorm on February 16, 1909. However Omaha Registrars note the birth was simply entered on the 16th; Max didn't discover until 1930 that he was actually born on the 11th. He often shared an elaborate fairytale of his mother being near death's door as she struggled to give birth to him. How Papa Baer heroically braved the storm to get her some medicine.[441]

"The snow-drifts were five feet in height and my old man went out into the teeth of a frozen gale and fought his way on hands and knees to bring the medicine the doctor said might save my mother's life," he told *Topical Times* author Leo Fuller in 1939.[442]

But that was just a fable among many with a foul odor. Omaha newspapers remarked upon the lack of any snow and the unusually "balmy air and bright sunshine" in the area for the entire month of February. Dr. Warren Henry Slabaugh, who had practiced in Omaha since 1888, delivered Max at home on 47th and W Streets in South Omaha. A home Max later professed a desire to develop, "as a sort of shrine" to himself, a place he thought the stockyard workers might enjoy; an intimate nightclub, with "a good band and floor show with no cover charge." If Dora Baer's health had been in jeopardy as she labored to bring Max into the world, Omaha boasted three large hospitals, and police ambulances were available for emergencies.[443 444 445 446 447]

Max's childhood was largely as placid and comfortable as Frankie's had been deprived and difficult. While Frankie spent his youth in a state of terror, abuse and homelessness, Max was surrounded by parents and siblings who shared tremendous family solidarity, along with hugs and kisses when one of them simply left for the grocery store. But that alliance came with a cost.

When Max was age six his brother Jacob Junior, nicknamed Buddy, was born. His mother avidly followed prizefighting, so when her youngest son emerged to tip the scales at twelve pounds, she remarked that surely this big strapping boy would someday be heavyweight champion of the world. As the brothers grew, Buddy became her favored darling; he was spoiled and doted upon. Her expectation that he would be a great fighter persisted. Through the years this piqued Max to jealousy, at the attention focused by his mother upon her future champion son.

Because there was nothing particularly distinctive about young Max, the assumption was he would follow in his father's footsteps as a butcher. He was viewed as the odd one, off in a world of his own. Seated at the family dinner table, small snickers and snorts and cackles would often erupt in between the clatter of flatware. When asked what was so funny, as the grin dropped from his face, with a shoulder shrug, invariably the reply was "...nothin'."[448] [449]

He was rife with phobias and fears. He was afraid of the water and never learned to swim because an uncle once threw him into deep water to sink or swim. He sank. He had such a fear of mice, the blood drained from his face as he scrambled madly onto furniture to escape them. The family thought him a coward because he didn't try to defend himself against schoolhouse bullies. His clothing torn from the grasps of his torturers, he sprinted in a panting panic for home, where his sister Frances would slap his pursuers silly while Max cowered in the house. This angered his mother. She demanded he defend himself. She decried having to mend his clothing. She threatened him with a whipping if his conduct continued.[450]

As a kid in Durango, Colorado, Max excelled in many sports. One story claimed he threw a baseball with the speed and accuracy of a sniper. A home run hit saw the ball sail more than 600 feet into the dark recesses of a fruit packing plant situated just beyond the boundary of center field, and wasn't found until the next day. Max's strength and quick reflexes served him equally well in football and basketball. But while Frankie Campbell eagerly embraced the teamwork, discipline, and respect inherent in team sports participation, Max Baer eschewed them.[451]

When the family moved to California in the spring of 1922, Max's father Jacob, who had learned the trade of butchery and animal husbandry from his father Aschill Baer, leased a succession of small hog and cattle ranches over the next five years around Hayward in the East Bay, and Galt in the Central Valley. When his father had difficulties finding reliable ranch hands, Max happily dropped out of high school while still a freshman to help.[452]

Jacob taught his son the use of cleaver and pole-axe. But instead of disassociation from the feces and the filth, the gore and the smell, Max came to enjoy his efforts. Indifference between life and death and his power over the decision was soon imprinted on his psyche. He swung a short meat-axe after a kill until it became an instinctual extension of his body. "I'd bite clean through muscle, sinew and bone," he later said, "and this was the work that gave me my right-hand punch. I loved it. The gorier the better.... I had the glorious feeling of sheer physical power." Max became a steadfast worker and a skilled killer. Stories would later abound that he bragged how he killed steers with a single punch to the skull— which any butcher will tell you is physically impossible—or slugged swine unconscious with a punch to the short ribs—which is potentially possible. The physicality of his long days in the abattoir built up an appetite. He would often walk into the house covered in blood and muck from head to foot, slice a hunk of bread, slather it with butter, spread homemade jam in a layer an inch thick, and shove it into his hungry mouth.[453] [454] [455]

Max relayed the story numerous times of the moment he decided to become a boxer, though the details shifted like sand in the wind over the years. In one story he said at age 16, "he was cornered by a pugnacious youth at a high school dance and he had to fight." But Max had dropped out of high school at age 14. In another, someone insulted his girlfriend and he defended her honor. The most consistently plausible tale he finally settled on, was that one night outside a dance hall in Galt, where the family lived for eighteen months in 1926-1927, eighteen-year-old Max shared a jug of bootleg liquor with friends, stolen from a truck parked nearby. When the vehicle's owner emerged to whet his whistle only to find his liquor gone, he challenged the group. Max being the tallest was pushed forward.[456] [457] [458]

As Max recollected, the gent was an itinerant painter, hired to daub a nearby church steeple. A solidly muscled brute, he immediately charged at Max. Once he had him cornered, he threw a round-house right, flush on Max's chin. When Max opened his eyes, he was shocked; he was still upright, and the punch hadn't hurt. He grinned widely, and for a moment, the steeplejack was startled motionless. Then he hit him again with everything he had. Max's head thwacked hard against the wall. In abject terror, he swung his right in the way he whipped the cleaver into a carcass. With a thump, the steeplejack dropped to the dirt, out cold. It was the first time Max had ever thrown a punch at another human being. He learned right then that he could not only take a punch; he could really dish one out with devastating effect.[459]

In that one moment, many of Max's fears were wiped away. The cowardice that had so beset him was gone. But the effects of his youthful yearning for more love and attention from his mother, for an indication that he too was a favored son or had redeeming qualities, would stay with him all his life. With the astuteness of a psychoanalyst, sports columnist Paul Gallico later observed that, "Baer's boastfulness and cockiness covers a considerable inferiority complex, which causes him to strut and pose, to boast and brag, and which drives him relentlessly to the spotlight."[460]

****

By the spring of 1928, Max and his family had settled just south of Livermore, California, a picturesque town at the edge of the East Bay. Jacob Baer raised and butchered livestock at a small ranch in Murray Township on Vallecitos Road in Twin Oaks, though Max would later claim in 1930 that Papa Baer was vastly wealthy and ran a 500-acre spread. Max received no wages for his work at the ranch, and took a fifty-cents an hour job at a nearby gravel pit to have some spending money. The work was tough, both at the ranch and in the pit. Sometimes he worked from four o'clock in the morning until nine or ten at night. The result of the ceaseless labor molded his long lean body into a sculpted musculature. [461 462 463 464 465]

Livermore local Charles Calderoni had seen the potential in Max before he saw it in himself. Charles had dabbled in boxing and baseball as a youth. When Max's story about how he had knocked out the steeplejack reached his ears, he offered to teach him what he knew. An old chicken house at Twin Oaks was converted to a crude training area. A sack of feed tied with a rope to a rafter in one corner became a punching bag.

Max eventually saved up enough money out of his paychecks from the gravel pit to buy a 25-pound canvas punching bag; he couldn't afford the leather model. He drew a man's face on the bag and began to bang about with great gusto, lots of noise, and little finesse. Charles donated a speed bag and some gloves. There was no ring in the chicken house, just the dirt floor surrounded by four rickety walls and a low ceiling. As opponents milled around, they had to duck near the sagging corners overhead. [466 467]

Word began to travel around Livermore and beyond about the potential of this hard-hitting youngster. While Charles was on an extended trip back east in early 1929, local man Joe McGlinchey, a player with the semi-pro Livermore Cowboys baseball team, and an enthusiastic supporter of Baer's skills, invited Harry "Spider" Griffin, a guard at the county Veteran's Hospital, where Max often picked up swill to feed the pigs, to watch Max work out.

Griffin was said to be "ring-wise" and offered to train him. Max was soon learning the ropes and sparring nearby in a real ring set up on the property of Manuel Medeiros. Manny provided local boxing hopefuls with a decent training area on a large lot behind his home on Sixth Street in Livermore. [468 469 470]

All of the men who sensed Baer's talent were "of the old school" and believed a fighter should train for months before actual ring combat. But like a tot denied a toy Max was impatient; he insolently demanded a fight. McGlinchey told his boss Percy Madsen, who managed the Livermore Cowboys, about the ferocious strength of the young slugger.

Madsen was a veteran fan of boxing and had an eye for talent. Friends with Manny and Spider, they suggested he head out to Manny's place to give Max a look. "I was awed at the power he used in attacking the punching bag," Madsen later commented. "I thought the bag might fly apart, a kayo of an inanimate object." [471 472 473]

Ray Pelkey (c1920)
Courtesy author's collection

Percy Madsen suggested Max move out to Oakland. An East Bay boxing mecca, a ferry ride away from San Francisco, it offered him knowledgeable trainers, experienced sparring partners, and some serious competition. Papa Baer spotted Max $200 to live on, and to pay for his gym dues and equipment.

Ray Pelkey, an aging but still-active local light-heavyweight whose right name was Raymond Lockwood, supervised his training at the Imperial Gymnasium on 20th Street in West Oakland. He didn't ask for a cent in training fees. Ray recognized Baer's charisma even then. "Baer had a star quality about him," he remarked to *Sports Illustrated* in 1932. "Everybody wanted a piece of him." Max frustrated Ray and Percy during training right from the beginning. He had no interest in learning the fine art of technique or defense. Max had the discipline of a dilettante; he figured he had his knockout right and an iron chin. What else did he need? [474] [475]

Max's move to Oakland took him away from home for the first time. He lived at the Harrison Hotel, a few blocks from "Bash Boulevard" around Franklin and 11th Streets, where the fight crowd hung out. Ray Pelkey found him a $4 a day job at the Atlas Imperial Engine Company in East Oakland, where massive diesel engines for watercraft were machined in huge factories at the port of Oakland. Max loved to show off his boxing skills at work. With the frenetic zeal of a missionary clutching a conversion quota he begged fellow employees to spar him on his lunch break. But he quickly ran out of opponents once word got out how hard he hit. [476] [477]

Max soon attracted the attention of his employer's son, John Hamilton "Ham" Lorimer. Ham was the grandson of a Bonnyton pub owner in Kilmarnock, Scotland. His father John Wightman Lorimer immigrated to America in the 1890s. After a stint as a machinist with the Hercules Gas Engine Company in San Francisco, John developed his love of engineering into formation of the Atlas Imperial Engine Company. Ham worked at his father's company in various vague capacities. Except for a stretch as a Private with the 104th Aero Squadron in WWI, and a brief marriage that bore him a son, Ham lived at the family home, which started as a modest abode in downtown Oakland, and progressed along with his father's success, to a hilltop mansion in the Oakland Hills overlooking San Francisco Bay.

144

Ham was a bored rich kid, an avid boxing fan who later admitted he had visions of being manager of a world champion one day. Ham had numerous contacts on Bash Boulevard, one of whom was former middleweight ring star Bob McAllister, who invited him to the Imperial to watch Max spar. As Ham speculated with narrowed eyes outside the ropes, an idea began to form; a pet project with a promising protégé was right up Ham's alley.

Because Ray Pelkey was in training for his own upcoming fight, Ham whispered an idea into Bob's ear. Bob offered to continue Max's training, while Ray got himself up to snuff, and Percy Madsen tried to get Max a bout. Ham began to regale Max with visions of riches and solid financial backing. He quietly encouraged Max to dump Ray and train officially under Bob, who encouraged Max to dump Percy and sign with Ham. [478] [479]

Oblivious to the knife being twisted into his back, after several false starts in Oakland, Percy Madsen finally persuaded Oak Park Arena promoter "Ropes" Heinemann to match Max for a bout with a $35 purse down in Stockton, south of the State Capitol in Sacramento. [480] [481]

LOCAL BOXER TO HAVE FIRST RING ENGAGEMENT

Local boxing fans and admirers of Max Baer, Livermore's aspirant to fiscal honors, are anxiously looking forward to Thursday evening, May 16th, when he will meet Jack Zariboa, a 190-pounder, at Stockton.

Percy Madsen, who has been managing Baer for the past several months, arranged the contest. He states that Baer is in excellent condition and he expects to see him put up a showing that will bring him many future engagements. Ray Pelkey will act as second for Baer in his initial appearance at Stockton

Max Baer's first professional fight
(09 May 1929) (with name typo)
Courtesy Livermore Journal

His opponent was Albert Baptiste Meldrum. Of Scottish, Sushwap and Ulkatcho Nations ancestry from Cariboo, British Columbia he fought under the ring name "Chief Caribou," and had just landed in San Francisco. This would be Baptiste's fourth fight. The Stockton papers said both fighters had reputations as heavy hitters and predicted the match would end with a kayo. Max had two pounds and one inch on his opponent. But while Max was still wiry, Baptiste was solid as a brick. [482] [483] [484]

On a sticky hot May evening, while he waited impatiently to slip between the ropes as a pro for the first time, Max Baer had a painful thirst. With the impulse control of an overindulged toddler, he guzzled down several bottles of soda pop. When his name was announced, he entered the ring grinning. But when Caribou socked him in the gut, Max hunched over in pain. Not because the punch hurt, nerves and the carbonated drinks had made him nauseous. Realizing he had to either knock the Chief down, or throw up on him, Max began to chase Caribou around the ring like a sandlot pitcher breaking into the majors, almost everything he threw was a wild pitch.

The *Stockton Evening Record* called it, "more or less a glorified indoor street fight," and that Caribou, "was as wide open as a boarding house mouth." But before an otherwise deserted house, to the delight of fifty Livermore locals who attended, Baer's flying fists knocked Caribou down three times in the first round. In round two, as the Chief and the stunned crowd wondered how long this maniac could keep it up, Max struck him a right on the chin with so much force, he seemed to hang suspended in the air for a moment, then toppled over like a bombed building. Max Baer had won his first professional fight.

Percy Madsen, Max Baer, Louis Lippi(?) Stockton, CA (May 1929)
Courtesy Bancroft Library, University of California, Berkeley

After Percy Madsen's cut, he held $25 in his hand; a week's salary for five minutes of punching. As the possibilities whirled and flashed like a pinball machine victory through his brain, Max asked breathlessly when he could get another fight.[485] [486]

When Ham dangled the keys like an enticing baby rattle to a new $3,800 automobile before Max's eyes, if he would sign a contract with him, good until he turned twenty-one, Max decided Ham's riches could take him places Percy Madsen and Ray Pelkey could not. Without a backward glance at the men who gave him his start, before the year of 1929 came to a close, Ham Lorimer had registered with the state as his manager, Bob McAllister was his official trainer, and Max Baer was on his way.[487] [488] [489] [490]

CHAPTER 19

CAT BIRD SEAT

The first week of the New Year 1930, in what was termed the hottest heavyweight natural in Los Angeles in some time, Wad Wadhams offered Frankie Campbell $6,000 to fight Les Kennedy. After he heard the amount, Tom Maloney pulled out a Perfecto cigar, planted his loafers on Wad's desk, and heaved a big sigh as he looked out the window. He knew his fighter was the most sensational prospect in the south and sold the auditoriums out as a main-eventer. Kennedy was viewed as an unpredictable technical boxer; he was considered just a fair attraction to slugger-hungry fans. Tom planned to make promoters cough up the dough.

"If Jack Kearns had Campbell, he'd bid 'em up, wouldn't he?" queried Tom as he waved his cigar around. "Well, Kearns' style of business is good enough for me. I'll use him for a model.... Give us forty percent and Kennedy twenty and the bout is on.... You know who the card is; none other than Mr. Campbell."[491]

Kennedy's manager Herb White had refused a bout with Frankie four months earlier. He told Tom that Frankie needed to build up a reputation first before the matter would be considered. Les boasted impressive wins over local and imported heavies Ernie Owens and K.O. Christner. But Tom had not forgiven Herb and Les for that earlier refusal, and Herb had been quoted in the press calling Frankie a palooka and a joke. Now Tom was in the cat bird seat. "If the truth must be known," said Tom as cigar ash floated onto his polka-dot tie, "We don't feel any too kindly toward White and Kennedy. When we were around here trying to get established ... they gave us the cold shoulder and Frankie needed a dollar then."[492][493]

It was true Kennedy wasn't nearly the same draw as Frankie. The highly touted Kennedy–Christner fight had grossed only $5,800. Frankie pulled in well over $10,000 against Harry Dillon at the Olympic. Receipts were over $7,000 at the

Legion against Tony Stabenau, with over a thousand fans turned away; it would have hit five-figures in a larger venue. But boxing fans clamored for the fight. From across Los Angeles and Long Beach, where Kennedy had taken up residence, they wrote in droves to local sports writers to ask, "why does Campbell duck him?" To which one paper replied, "Ask us something easy. We try to answer sports questions. We can't solve puzzles." [494] [495]

When Wadhams reported Kennedy rejected previously acceptable terms to ask for a higher percentage, he abandoned the match; Wad refused to give more than 55% of the gate. As he scrambled for a suitable opponent that wouldn't bankrupt the house, the Hollywood Legion's matchmaker Tom Gallery swooped in. He liked Frankie's prospects. While up north he had run into Oakland heavyweight Jack Beasley, who sought a fight in the south. Gallery remarked to reporters that all the nice things they had heard about Campbell were true. "I saw Frankie fight in San Francisco. He's a different boy now and should develop into a first-class heavyweight." When he returned south, Tom shuffled some dates around, and arranged a Campbell–Beasley match. [496]

The two would fight the main event the following Friday, January 10. Jack Beasley was a main-eventer whose recent bouts included a first-round kayo of Jack McCarthy and a win on points against Jack DeMotte. He had decisioned Chet Shandel and kayoed Tony Stabenau the year before. While some gushed the event was sure to be sold out, others thought that while there were currently few heavyweights who could best Beasley when he was primed, he was a poor trainer, and might not present enough of a challenge. [497] [498]

Bay Area sports writers, miffed that their hometown boy had found success elsewhere, boasted that whereas Frankie had taken seven rounds to drop Stabenau, their boy Beasley had done it in two. Tom Maloney retorted that Frankie, "had worries when he fought Stabenau that he won't have this week." Frankie's wife Elsie did not have an easy pregnancy and her labor had been especially hard. Over three nights before the bout with Stabenau, Frankie stayed by his wife's side and didn't sleep a wink. But, Tom assured, "Now that that is over with, Campbell is going to be busy accumulating a bank roll to buy the baby shoes." [499] [500]

When Benny Ford brought Jack Beasley down from the East Bay a few days before the fight, he was asked about Max Baer. "The best heavy prospect in years," Benny replied without pause. "He can hit and he can take 'em." [501]

****

As Frankie prepared for the bout, he did so under a new trainer. Tom Maloney wanted to devote more time to dickering with promoters and pounding out ballyhoo for his fighter. He brought in Larry Morrison. Though barely twenty-one, Larry had a reputation as an exceptionally gifted trainer. He started in the game as Bantamweight Champ Bud Taylor's water boy, when Bud picked him up off the streets downtown where Larry sold newspapers. By the time he joined Frankie's crew, top contenders of every weight-class requested Larry for some hard conditioning when they hit town for a fight. He was described as a tall lanky Bostonian with a beezer that stuck out like a lighthouse in a fog. A natural at his trade, he was a stern taskmaster with a soft touch, who had a knack for knowing just when to encourage, and when to browbeat his charge. [502] [503] [504]

The press noticed the change in Frankie's demeanor almost immediately. In addition to his new-found confidence, he had become almost cocky in training. He boldly said he expected to win handily against Beasley. He brashly demanded fights with Max Baer and Les Kennedy after his impending victory. [505] [506]

Obligatory 'reach' image of 75-inches (1929)
Courtesy Harry E. Winkler Collection, University of Notre Dame

Claude Newman at the *Los Angeles Evening Citizen News* had a few predictions about the outcome of Frankie's bout with Jack Beasley, and he wasn't far off. "Campbell packs the sleeping potion in either fist and if the fight goes over three heats, we'll have to admit that our eyesight is bad and our reasoning worse. While we expect to see Beasley carted out feet first, we further expect that he will tag Campbell with a couple knee shakers before giving up the struggle involuntarily. It is no disgrace to be flattened by Campbell. In fact, it's a strong chin that can withstand his wallop."[507]

It was a sold-out crowd at the Hollywood Legion. Reserved seats were gone two days in advance. Golfing great Walter Hagen was at ringside after a day of competition at the Los Angeles Open. Stub Nelson noted that Beasley tipped the scales at a lean 175 pounds. Frankie weighed a stockier 182 and "with strength and cockiness—shaped up like a Greek Adonis when they unveiled him." Though Beasley went into the bout as a short-ender, as predicted by the local press, Frankie doffed his robe, bounced up and down a few times to limber up, and scored a knockout in six punches. It took exactly one minute and one second of fighting in the first round. That didn't include the official ten-count over Beasley's prostrate form.[508] [509]

The first two left hooks to the body unhinged Beasley at the knees. The second two punches were misses. The fifth was a left hook to the jaw and the sixth was a right cross. Beasley landed on his back and lay limp as a dishrag. At the count of nine he barely moved his head. He didn't even blink at the lights. At the ten Frankie rushed over to help pull him to his stool. For several minutes Beasley was groggy. His seconds punched the back of his head to make him pop his eyes open. He staggered out of the ring like a drunken man.

Sid Ziff at the *Los Angeles Evening Express* expressed what he said was the frustration of many, when he sneered, "Such was the record of a terrible setup.... Fans yelled their indignation at the short session. Campbell cannot get by accepting such poor excuses for opposition."[510]

Jack Beasley knockout (11 Jan 1930)
Courtesy author's collection

However, from Stub Nelson's seat at ringside for the *Los Angeles Record*, he noticed that the large gathering seemed satisfied. "Everybody smiled and said 'Wow! Did you see that wallop?!' If two clever but tapping boxers had toiled for ten rounds, the customers would have walked away bored and disgruntled. Yet a couple of hard socks—plus a knockout—gave them the desired thrill."[511]

"A lot of people don't give fat Tom Maloney a tumble," Stub mused, "And yet you can't help but see his assets. He can blow up a fighter—both to the fellow himself, as well as the public—like an air pump on the end of a balloon.... He has put the fire under Campbell.... The results work magic."[512]

Some sports editors in the southern press in early 1930, didn't hesitate to use their columns like a battering ram to bludgeon anyone who didn't toe an imaginary line. Aided over the last six months, by Frankie's breathtaking dominance of the local scene, an unceasing stream of copy that Tom Maloney had carefully crafted to boost his fighter, had worked magnificently. But those in the press who felt they had been a large part of making Frankie a success, now expected their tit for tat. When Tom refused the matches they deemed worthy, they began a campaign to force his choice of opponents.

Frankie wasn't the only fighter with difficult handlers. The tactics were nothing new, and a common dodge employed by handlers of "drawing cards." Wad Wadhams experienced challenges everywhere he turned in his attempts to match big draw bouts for the Olympic Auditorium. Depression-poor spectators needed enticement, but Wad needed to add some tidy numbers in the Olympic's profit column. Managers in every weight division cherry-picked their fighters' opponents. As bank failures mounted, in-demand fighters no longer performed unless given a flat guarantee deposited in advance at a reliable bank. Fighters' handlers made unreasonable demands, and offered miserable excuses, why a match wasn't a good fit. The almighty buck trumped giving the fans a thrill or accepting bouts that tested their charge's abilities.[513]

Frankie's consecutive string of knockouts was impressive for its sensationalism. One scribe said, "they could match him with a visiting longshoreman and pack the joint." But his followers howled for a fight in which he faced an opponent who wouldn't fold up under a punch. Frankie was happy to fight anyone and everyone, yet he seriously ran the risk that his handlers' jockeying of opponents had taken the edge off his work. It had definitely begun to damage his reputation.[514]

"Tige" Clinton of the *Long Beach Sun*, who soon led the charge in a determined smear campaign against Frankie, groused that, "the biggest fistic plum the boxing orchard has produced in many months threatens to spoil." He thought "Rubbery Blubbery" Tom Maloney had placed too prohibitive a price on Frankie's services. That the Olympic's promoter Jack Doyle had played a large hand in development of Les Kennedy and Frankie Campbell's star power, only to get the run-around. The *Los Angeles Examiner* noted, that Tom had recently sniffed in disdain at a $20,000 offer to fight Ace Hudkins, when just a month ago, Frankie's purse was $750, and he was happy to get it.[515 516 517]

The Olympic's manager Gene Doyle, brother to Jack, came to Frankie's defense. His thoughts were that when a fighter begins to show real promise, there was always an immediate cry for him to face tough opponents, which was among the reasons Frankie had quit up north. He argued young fighters had been ruined when their managers over-matched them, because they wanted to get rich quick. He reminded people, that Jack Dempsey and Gene Tunney had their build-up fights, against what were perceived at the time as inferior opponents, and Frankie was entitled to be brought along likewise.[518]

Frankie wears Dempsey's trunks from Firpo fight (1930)
Courtesy Harry E. Winkler Collection, University of Notre Dame

Tom Maloney told friends privately that he wanted Frankie to get better acquainted with his new style; to bob and weave in and out of danger zones without getting his nose pushed from one side of his face to the other, before he accepted stiffer competition.

****

When Tom and Frankie went home to visit family in mid-January, they were interested parties in the audience at the Arcadia Pavilion in Oakland, to observe a fight between Max Baer and Milton "Tiny" Abbott. In the third round, they watched slack-jawed as Max was disqualified on a blatant foul. Abbott still sat on the canvas and was being given the count, when Baer suddenly rushed from his corner and slugged him. The referee immediately disqualified Max, fined him $100, and he was given a thirty-day suspension.

Lou Parente who promoted the bout, had some days earlier offered Frankie $3,500 to fight Max. After the Abbott fiasco, Lou upped the ante to $5,000. Tom Maloney took a pass. Max's manager said he didn't feel Max was ready to handle a fighter of Frankie's experience. Tom was concerned Max was out of control. Only months before, he had been suspended for multiple fouls in a fight with Jack McCarthy; at the time Jack was one of his roommates. When Jack was hanging helpless on the ropes, Max threw a succession of illegal kidney punches at Jack's turned back. When that didn't get a response, Max leaned over and bodily threw him to the canvas.[519]

Sneaky fouls like elbows and eye gouges, head butts and kidney punches, holds and backhands, or 'accidental' hits on the break and after the bell, are all things that will get a fighter suspended today. In the 1920s, they were commonly ignored, as long as the majority of a fighter's punches were clean. Some referees even proudly informed reporters they recognized no such thing as a foul; their bouts were virtual free-for-alls. But for Max Baer, such unnecessarily brutal fouls against an opponent, especially if the shock factor centered the audience's attention squarely back on him, were his forte from the beginning of his career.[520] [521]

Bay Area sports writers, who had covered his early fights in San Francisco, cornered Frankie at the event to ask why a match hadn't been arranged with Ernie Owens or Les Kennedy. He assured the press he was eager to fight both men, and that a match with Kennedy was in the works. He said Cal and Tom had a plan in place, and he had placed his trust in their decisions.

But the drumbeat by the southern press had only gotten louder. Bill Smith at the *Los Angeles Evening Express* had joined in the fracas, and finally ferreted out what exactly Cal and Tom's plan was; its name was Jack "Doc" Kearns. Doc had relentlessly drummed into Tom and Cal's ears to "go slow and give Campbell a good build-up." But by all appearances, they were largely too inept or too inexperienced, to handle the rise of a fighter who had quickly become a potential title contender.

Cal Working avoided the fray so consistently the press called him "Silent Cal." He deferred to Tom Maloney, either because he was great at generating excitement among fans and the press, and enjoyed the battle for dollars with matchmakers, or because Tom simply out-talked him. Tom used the playbook of constant, often outlandish claims, adopted by Doc Kearns to build up Jack Dempsey. But Tom not only lacked Kearns' finesse, he held out for so much money as he shopped around, Frankie was effectively denied good matches as the promoters turned away.

Like a good sycophant, Cal remarked in earnest to Smith, "We feel that Campbell has shown he is a good fighter, and we think he is ready to meet tougher opposition. But Kearns says to go slow. You know what a great manager Kearns has been and he brought Dempsey along. With such an adviser you can't blame us if we don't push Campbell along too fast." Bill Smith closed his column with some advice to his fellow pressmen: "So don't fire all your bricks at Working and Maloney. Level a few at Kearns."[522]

Tom Gallery finally arranged a main event at the Hollywood Legion Stadium for the end of January 1930. A flock of eastern fighters and fans had come west for the winter. Frankie's opponent was Benny Ross, a native of Buffalo, New York. The bout was contracted for 175 pounds. Ross, whose given name was Samuel Rosenberg, had been fighting almost exclusively on the East Coast. He had close to a hundred bouts to his credit, and was touted to have an iron chin. He had met nationally known first-tier scrappers. He came within a hair of a pugilistic upset when he knocked Tommy Loughran to the canvas during a tune-up fight, just before Loughran went on to become Light-Heavyweight Champ. He lost close on points against Young Stribling and Jock Malone, and was handed a draw with Ernie Owens that many felt Ross had won. Benny had never been knocked down, and Ernie admitted it had taken everything he had just to eke out a decision.

KNX Radio, which transmitted 1050 kHz from Paramount Pictures Studios, announced they would broadcast the Campbell–Ross fight from ringside. Frank Orme, who coordinated a list of daily radio broadcasts for the *Pasadena Post* newspaper, often inserted personal comments after each listing. Under copy for the Campbell–Ross affair he wrote, "If I miss this badly, I probably will put an end to such predictions in this column. I'll pick Campbell by a knockout in the third." [523] [524]

****

The fighters met at center ring to a sold-out crowd. Hundreds had been turned away and the joint was jumpin'. Frankie bolted out of his corner and immediately began throwing vicious punches with both fists. Ross caught Frankie during a weave with a snappy right cross which bounced off the left side of Frankie's jaw. Frankie dropped to one knee for a no-count knockdown. With a boisterous rumble of anticipation, spectators sprang to their feet; the stage seemed set for a regular battle.

But before Ross could reposition himself to press his advantage, Frankie shot up like he was spring-loaded. Ross backed into a corner with Frankie hot on his heels. He launched a straight right that sent Ross to his knees. Once he rose up, Frankie buried a vicious left hook to the body and a crushing right cross which caught him flush on that iron chin. Ross dropped to his hands and knees with a thud. He looked like a kid scrabbling for his marbles as he tried unsuccessfully to rise again. At two minutes and forty-two seconds after the opening bell, he was counted out. At the ten, the crowd erupted in riotous celebration while Frankie helped drag Ross to his corner.[525]

Bill Smith at the *Los Angeles Evening Express* reported some of the patrons were skeptical that Ross had tried hard enough. They tossed crumpled programs through the ropes in protest. Bronx cheers lingered in the air like a flock of ducks deprived of their dried breadcrumbs. Smith remarked in frustration that Frankie, "looms as a great fighter in the making, but his managers won't let him prove it."[526] [527]

Benny's manager Lee Moore was dumbfounded. He said it was the first time in his career Ross had ever been stopped. "Campbell is a greater fighter than even his managers were willing to admit." Frankie later professed he was still feeling the effects of the flu, and was a bit sluggish, until that pop on the jaw woke him up.

The Hollywood Daily Citizen's Claude Newman, however, was pleased. "Frankie 'Hurry Up' Campbell stands affirmed today as he never has been affirmed before as a promising heavyweight.... He proved to smart fight men that he could hit the deck and keep his effectiveness. It was the one thing that needed proving and we must admit that Campbell is a vastly underrated fighter." [528] [529] [530]

CHAPTER 20

MYSTERIOUS GUS

DO NOT JUDGE ME BY MY SUCCESSES, JUDGE ME BY HOW MANY TIMES
I FELL DOWN AND GOT BACK UP AGAIN - NELSON MANDELA

In the last days of January 1930, Jack Dempsey—who was involved with charismatic impresario Patrick "Paddy" Harmon, in development of his Chicago Stadium as a premier fight center in the Windy City—had suggested plans were imminent, to bring Frankie back with him on the train for some seasoning against East Coast fighters. While it was an exciting prospect, it would result in even more reluctance by Frankie's team to match him with local fighters, who not only pleased fans, challenged Frankie, and built upon his ring education, but continued to polish Tom Maloney's claims that he was on his way to a title. Tom's attempts to strike a balance would be disastrous. [531]

Worried he was about to lose his number one crowd-pleaser if Frankie left the south with Dempsey, and in a desperate effort to match some real competition, Wad Wadhams offered him a flat fee of $6,500 or 40% of the gate receipts, to fight Ernie Owens at the Olympic Auditorium. That was more than a small-town doctor made in a year. Ernie was hot at the moment, having just made a sensational battle against Dynamite Jackson. Wad said Owens was willing to fight for next to nothing to get a crack at Frankie. Tom Maloney wouldn't even give the offer a tumble. He claimed he was in negotiations with Tom Gallery for a fight with Vigo Doman at the Hollywood Legion Stadium. [532] [533]

Wadhams reached out to Max Baer's handlers to see if there was an interest for him to fight Owens. Just as the southern press did with Frankie, some in the northern press claimed Max was "fattening his record at the expense of a terrible array of set-ups." The rumors were that Baer's handlers might no longer be permitted to hand select his opponents either. One Oakland reporter called it a sin and a shame, that Baer was allowed "to bop some of those cripples rigged up for him ... if he's getting $2,500 for a fight, he should at least tackle a $1,500

156

opponent." A fight with a proven tough fellow like Ernie Owens however would further cement Max's growing reputation.[534] [535] [536] [537]

That week, the doors of all the local press offices were soon banging open, as Tom Maloney wheezed in at full tilt, a telegram fluttering in his meaty paw. The fight with Vigo Doman was on hold; Tom Gallery had wired terms for a March 14 outdoor bout at Wrigley Field. Frankie's opponent would be the "Basque Woodchopper" Paulino Uzcudun. Just as Frankie was a big draw to Italian-Irish fans, Uzcudun had a huge following among Spanish-Mexican fans. Paulino had fought only once in Los Angeles, when he touched gloves in 1928, with Frankie's old sparring mate George Godfrey. The bout had amassed the first six-figure gate in California history: $125,000 at Wrigley Field. A Campbell–Uzcudun fight was expected to pack the ball park to overflowing.[538] [539]

While negotiations droned on, Frankie flew home for a week to visit Elsie and his son. For him to simply board a plane in 1930, effectively made him an aviation pioneer. Commercial airplane travel was still a luxury the average Joe couldn't afford. Frankie was among a mere 6,000 passengers who flew commercially in the U.S. that year. Flight was also not for the faint-hearted. There were no parachutes. Accidents were frequent; fifteen crashes would occur in America in the month of February alone. Air travel was cold, loud, and uncomfortable. Cabins weren't pressurized or climate-controlled. Noise decibels approached that of the front-row at a rock concert; airline employees used a megaphone to communicate with passengers. Airsickness was common, as even minor turbulence caused planes to suddenly drop in altitude. Seats were lightweight affairs typically made of woven wicker; luxury cabin seats might boast a thin leather covering.

Fokker F-10 Interior (1930)
Courtesy SDASM Archives, Wikimedia Commons

But it was one extravagance Frankie splurged on repeatedly with his ring winnings. The window afforded him between training and fighting was so often narrow. A three-hour flight, verses an overnight sleeper on the Southern Pacific's "Lark" out of Los Angeles, was worth the extra cost for Frankie to spend more time with his young family; he was utterly devoted to his wife and son, and was willing to make every sacrifice with them in mind.[540]

Intimations that a Baer–Campbell slugging bee had begun to drift across sports editors' minds, first appeared in January 1930. Frankie himself had gotten the ball rolling when he said he desired the match. Frank Schuler was in negotiations to bring Max Baer into the Dreamland; an indication of Baer's growing reputation beyond the East Bay. Max had expressed a willingness to box Frankie later on, but his handlers still felt he needed more experience before they touched gloves. Despite the fact Frankie was still perfecting his new bobbing weaving style, Max viewed him as a dangerous, seasoned opponent, with a wallop that easily matched his own.[541]

While Frankie was still up north, the Uzcudun bout suddenly went on the back burner due to Paulino's multiple managerial difficulties. Frank Schuler reached out, hopeful to match Frankie with the "Boxing Barrister" heavyweight Armand Emanuel, who had recently earned a law degree, but wanted to go out with a bang against a top fighter. Tom Maloney wanted to bring Matt Adgie out from Philly for a fight with Frankie at the Olympic on March 4. Max Baer was scheduled to fight Ernie Owens that night, but Frankie was the bigger draw in the south. If the fight with Adgie closed, they would garner the spot. It was dizzying to keep up with Tom's juggling act. He was loose with his promises but shy on commitment. The snark by the southern press was off the charts. [542] [543]

"Campbell has a taboo list a yard long and a mile wide," growled Sid Ziff at the *Los Angeles Evening Express.* "He has an eligible list just small enough to be elite, and impossible enough to make it a cinch the man will not have to be fought."[544]

Others continued to press for a Kennedy–Campbell bout. Stub Nelson at the *Los Angeles Record* thought the two were passing up good money by not getting down to terms while the match was hot with the public. "But the more the match is talked about the wider they get apart."

Stub recognized that Frankie's handlers didn't want to hurl him along too rapidly. His new style made him a comparative novice in some ways, and improvement of his defense went by the wayside in favor of quick knockouts; sweet stuff that appealed to punch-hungry fight fans. Nonetheless, Stub still thought Frankie was ready for most anybody. He made him a favorite over both Ernie Owens and Les Kennedy.[545]

****

Then news broke in late January that the Max Baer–Ernie Owens bout had been postponed. Max was in trouble for a third time on more serious charges than his previous suspensions for fouls. He was asked to reschedule all future fights, to testify on evidence that his now two fights with Tiny Abbott had been tampered with by gamblers. Before the first match, heavy bets were placed that Tiny would not survive three rounds—the exact round Max fouled him—and for which he had been fined and suspended; the rematch also had similarly sketchy rumors attached.[546]

In a misguided attempt to help, Max's pal Louis Lippi, sent a letter to the local paper, that Max had in fact carried Abbott; but he did so out of the goodness of his heart to help his roommate. He wrote that Baer knew he could not disappoint his friend Larry Doyle, who bet every cent he had that Max would win in three rounds. "This I believe caused Max to get very anxious in the third round," Lippi wrote, and commit the foul.[547]

Being "anxious" was a common adjective used when Max was involved with racketeers. The word crops up again after Frankie's death. For the current fiasco, he indignantly claimed innocence. But he was lying through his teeth. Max casually admitted in 1948 to Bill Leiser of the *San Francisco Chronicle,* that he and Larry Doyle both borrowed $250 from local jeweler and boxing "sport" Joe Niderost, to bet on Max to knock Tiny out in round three of their first fight. Max felt the $125 purse for the fight wasn't enough.

"For two rounds I hit him, but I can't make him go down," said Max. "In the third I think about that $250, and I hit harder, and finally he does go down, but time is short, and I'm so *anxious* I go over and hit him again before he gets up and [right] there, I lost the whole fight."[548]

The investigation made headlines across the state for weeks. Max was barely eight months new to the game, yet had already acquired some unsavory friends. But he hadn't yet perfected the art of the smooth con; he just humiliated himself as his story kept changing. Fortunately, in Northern California Boxing Commissioner Charles Traung, he had the sole decision-maker of his fate solidly in his corner.

Along with his twin brother Louis, Charles Frederick Traung was the wealthy owner of Traung Label and Lithography. A leading printing corporation based in the city, with sales offices across the nation, the company printed products as varied as fruit crates to maps to event programs.

Traung had once circled the boxing orbit of the original Jack Dempsey "The Nonpareil," but his appointment to commissioner in early January 1927, as one of the last acts of outgoing Governor Friend Richardson, was purely political.

Twins Charles & Louis Traung
Courtesy The American Printer (05 Jan 1917)

Charles Traung did the bidding of State Assemblyman, William Hornblower and Senator Joseph "Jack" Inman; both were boxing "sports" with well-placed friends in the industry. All three men were friends with boxing promoter Ancil Hoffman, who would not only promote the Baer–Campbell fight, he later became Max Baer's manager, and was eventually exposed during a corruption investigation for a bribery scheme between he and Senator Inman. Hoffman was consistently given preferential treatment by Traung and his fellow commissioner James Woods, who was a personal friend of Ancil's.

Traung was regular golfing buddies, and served on golf tournament committees, with the County District Attorney Matthew Brady—who would oversee the grand jury trial of Max Baer—with Assemblymen William Hornblower and Harry Morrison, the latter also a matchmaker, and one of the "fathers of the California boxing law." Traung had business interests with the Dreamland Auditorium, where referee Toby Irwin—who was third man in the ring the night of the Baer–Campbell fight—was on the board of directors. Irwin was said to be "a favored pet" of Traung's as referee for big dollar boxing cards held in the Bay Area, especially those promoted by Ancil Hoffman.

Every single one of these men would later play a role in misdirection of facts, manipulation of evidence, and in prevention of consequences to Max Baer, after manslaughter charges were leveled against him for the death of Frankie Campbell.

For the Baer–Abbott investigation, while Traung worked to bamboozle the public and the press, that Max's actions against Tiny Abbott were nothing of concern, Max awkwardly worked to sow confusion, as to exactly which gamblers he had hooked up with. Traung met privately with Max and Louis Lippi to hash out a plausible story. When they emerged to a clamoring crowd of reporters, Max and Louis nervously declared a gambling mystery man, acting on behalf of someone named "Gus" entered Max's dressing room before the first fight. He offered Max money, and a $4,000 L-29 Cord automobile, to carry Abbott for three rounds. Max said he declined the offer and didn't even know this "Mysterious Gus."[549] [550] [551]

But when it came to shady figures in the fight racket, everyone in town knew who "Gus" was. Reynaldo Augustus "Gus" Oliva was a well-known Tenderloin political fixer. He was called the Emperor of North Beach; a king-pin who made his millions as a rum runner, and was notorious for payoffs to politicians, police and Prohibition agents. Well-loved by the local folks as a philanthropist, he held annual Easter egg hunts at Golden Gate Park, and filled thousands of orphanage stockings every Christmas. He was also a betting fixture at prizefights, who reporters said was seen at both bouts, and was rumored to have bet $10,000 for Max to win against Tiny Abbott.[552]

Scribes gathered around Traung in a frantic gaggle to hurl questions at him. Traung was flustered; he sputtered that he didn't think anyone was interested in the investigation. Allen "A.T." Baum, sports editor of the *San Francisco Examiner* smirked that, "some of us were light-headed enough to believe that part of the public which admires clean boxing ... was vitally interested." Baum scoffed that the boys in the racket, made sure Baer and Lippi's memories were dulled sufficiently to serve its purpose. "The only thing they were quite sure of, is that the bribe-offering rascal wore a hat, had on two perfectly matched shoes, and might have had curly hair."[553] [554]

Traung then inexplicably announced he had removed Max's suspension early and sanctioned a Baer–Abbott rematch for the following week. Reporters were flabbergasted. Baer had so easily dominated the initial fight; a rematch was little more than target practice. Not only were Traung's actions suspect, they didn't buy what Max was selling. Reporters chided that unquestionably both Max and Louis knew the name of "the Mysterious Gus"! Bob Shand at the *Oakland Tribune* had personally observed Gus Oliva with both fists full of money at the first Abbott fight, while his lieutenants had solicited bets that Tiny Abbott would not come out for the fourth round. [555] [556]

The night of the rematch, Gus again stood at the back of the venue, to take bets that Tiny wouldn't make it past the sixth round. Reporters at ringside remarked, it was obvious to everyone Max was playing a waiting game. Instead of fighting, he pawed and chattered and played to the crowd. In the sixth, when he finally re-discovered he had a punch, Max threw two unconvincing punches at a smiling Abbott, who then folded like an accordion. To make it doubly certain, a towel was flung from his corner in a token of defeat.[557] [558] [559] [560]

Max's trainer Bob McAllister privately accused him that night of carrying Tiny for both fights. Bob expected promises to mend his ways, but Max already had the moral compass of an axe murderer. He liked living high, wide, and handsome. The easiest route to fund his expansive tastes were the gambling syndicates, and Bob stood in his way. He announced the next day that he and Bob had parted ways;

when he turned twenty-one in a couple weeks, he would sign a new management agreement with Ham Lorimer and locate another trainer. Ham had already proved he couldn't control his fighter; but he was a vending machine that Max easily charmed money from. A new trainer would have to agree to do his job and park his integrity outside.

****

At the next meeting in Commissioner Traung's investigation, the situation quickly deteriorated into charges and counter-charges. Max claimed Oakland haberdasher Herb Wolf had approached him to say "wise money" in San Francisco would pay him to carry Abbott. Wolf claimed Max had made the approach, to assure him the fix was already in, and to "bet the house." San Francisco stockbroker James J. Lee, who regularly rubbed shoulders with racketeers, testified to deny rumors he had "made a killing" with bets on Max to win in specific rounds.

Max's manager Ham Lorimer squirmed like an irritated toddler with a full diaper when he testified. He admitted he placed a bet for Max to carry Tiny, and felt double-crossed that someone had changed the round Abbott would go down, without telling him. Ham abruptly stopped his own testimony at one point to declare he was tired of the fight game, and wished to return to his father's engineering plant.

Local fight fans were already tired of Max Baer. One night that week during a fight intermission, as he began to slip through the ropes at the Arcadia Pavilion in Oakland to be introduced, he was booed out of the ring. [561] [562] [563] [564] [565]

Bob Shand observed in his column, that whomever Gus was, he knew the kind of auto Baer craved, so he must be fairly intimate with either Max or his handlers. When Max was later seen driving a new L-29 Cord automobile of the exact type the

John Walbridge illustration (07 May 1930)
Courtesy Oakland Post-Enquirer

"Mysterious Gus" had offered, Ham hastily assured reporters he had receipts for the purchase. He claimed it was a birthday gift.[566] [567]

When proceedings resumed, Max and Louis had both pivoted again. Max had reconsidered his checker board, calculating how this would affect his future, and what moves he might make to avoid trouble. Juggling the names of so many gamblers had proved too difficult. Commissioner Traung suggested he point the finger at just one. He and Louis signed an affidavit that claimed the "Mysterious Gus" was in fact Gus Oliva. Gus feigned outraged. He stated unequivocally to reporters, that he would never personally "conduct petty business with a cheap fighter." He had henchmen after all. Why, he had a network of betting parlors in haberdasheries, pawnshops, and jewelry stores across the Bay Area, to coordinate such things without personally getting his hands dirty. Oliva asserted Traung was out to get him for refusal of political and financial support to Traung's pal—the man who appointed Traung as the district's boxing commissioner—former Governor Friend Richardson, during his last, unsuccessful campaign run.[568] [569] [570]

****

When Max testified, Commissioner Traung tiptoed around him like a sleeping newborn. He delicately asked why he appeared to stall in the rematch. Max replied that he did his best, and offered as evidence a cauliflower ear, which he said he received in the contest. However, in 1934 the cauliflower ear story underwent a renovation. Max claimed Bob McAllister was the only man to put a mark on him. "He hit me a wallop sparring and cauliflowered my ear." By 1936 the lie had evolved again. Baer claimed that early on in his career, he asked a friend to give him a cauliflower ear so he would "look like a fighter."[571] [572] [573] [574]

Bob McAllister was next to take the stand. He prided himself on a spotless reputation as a businessman, as a former boxer, and as a boxing trainer. He refused to be linked with scandal. But scandal seemed to attach itself to Max like a remora to a shark. To a stunned gallery, Bob testified Max admitted to him that the "Mysterious Gus" story was fictitious; nobody visited his dressing room with enticing offers. Max had framed various men purely as a distraction, to hide the fact he had not only accepted Oliva's offer of an L-29 Cord, not only placed bets on himself, but at Gus Oliva's request, agreed to which specific rounds to do the deed.[575] [576]

Bob stated that Max could have stopped Tiny at any time. That when he so obviously held back in the early rounds of the rematch, Bob knew Max was in with the gamblers to carry him. Before the first Abbott fight, Bob admitted he had to physically drag Max out of a known illegal betting parlor, fronted by racketeers and run by jeweler Frank Cator, and stuff him in his car, while from the back seat, Larry Doyle repeatedly asked how Gus Oliva planned to bet. Max later boasted to Bob's stenographer that he had cleaned up on the fight via a bet placed with Cator. [577] [578] [579] [580]

Frank Cator was a repeat felon. But he had influential friends, one of whom was San Francisco stockbroker James J. Lee. Cator had been found guilty of not only running gambling operations, but as a fence who bought jewelry stolen from the wealthy, and even federal conspiracy violations of the National Banking Act, for a scheme with local Bank of Italy employees, to fund his gambling ring. None other than attorney and state assemblyman William Hornblower—close friend of Max Baer's future manager Ancil Hoffman—regularly represented Cator in court. Hornblower was either very good at his job, or had bribed the numerous witnesses who pled the fifth at Cator's trials, or had paid off his many friends in the courts. He consistently managed to get all but the federal charge reduced to a paid fine with no jail time.[581][582][583]

When Leo Sullivan, attorney for Herb Wolf, began to question trainer Bob McAllister whether Max and his roommate Larry Doyle had bet on Max's fights, Commissioner Traung nervously cut in, "That will be all for this hearing." It appeared to reporters Traung had Max dead to rights. He instead shocked the press again. Despite the numerous lies and obfuscations made by Max and Louis, despite the personal and professional connections between all the players, despite multiple witnesses with damaging testimony against Max, which included his own trainer, Charles Traung stated it was a matter of "conflicting evidence uncorroborated on either side." As a disciplinary measure for his failure to report the "attempted" bribes, and because this was his third offense, Max was fined $500 and placed on a two-month suspension, retroactive to when he was asked to stop fighting one month earlier. He would not be allowed to fight until April 1.[584][585]

Traung informed the press he would turn over transcripts of his investigation to the Alameda County District Attorney for Oakland, Earl Warren. Warren retorted that because the boxing commission had no rules in its regulations to address racketeers, or any individual not licensed under the commission, it was a matter for the police. He instructed Traung to swear out complaints against the alleged gamblers. But Traung was confident that would go nowhere. Oakland Police Chief Donald Marshall's department was a happy hotbed of vice and gambling. Traung's public song and dance now complete, no complaints were filed.[586]

Commissioner Traung's erratic handling of the situation gained further clarity in the aftermath of Frankie's death. Louis Lippi later testified before a grand jury that he never read the affidavit he and Max had submitted against Gus Oliva; he was pressured by Traung and Max to sign it. Lippi confirmed that Traung wrote it to even a personal grudge against Oliva. The entire affair was so convoluted, it's possible Traung sought to shield the very gamblers with which he had placed his own bets! Of course, he denied any such thing. But his protection of Max continued well beyond his farcical investigation of the Baer–Abbott fights.

Herb Wolf's attorney had followed the right trail of breadcrumbs before Commissioner Traung shut him down. Just like the first Abbott fight, Max later admitted he had again bet big on himself to win in a specific round of the rematch.

"We borrow again, $500 this time, and I win alright, but what? The commission calls me and fines me $500 for not winning soon enough."

Frankie Campbell's manager Cal Working, along with an innocent mother of two, who happened to overhear a parking lot argument just before the Baer–Campbell fight, would later testify before the grand jury which investigated Frankie's death. Commissioner Charles Traung not only coordinated fixed fights with referee Toby Irwin, he regularly profited off of Baer's fights. It's possible he even had a cut of Baer's contract. Just as he made sure Max suffered no serious consequences after the Tiny Abbott fiasco, Traung would bring in the right influential people to shield him again, after the death of Frankie Campbell.[587] [588]

CHAPTER 21

GREEN GOODS—BUT GOOD GOODS

PEOPLE HAVE TO HIRE PRIZEFIGHTERS TO DO THEIR HATING FOR THEM. AND WE DO.
WE GET INTO A RING AND ACT OUT OTHER PEOPLE'S HATE - FLOYD PATTERSON

Down in Los Angeles, Tom Maloney continued hard at work with distracting publicity stunts. In mid-February 1930, a United Press article with the banner "Green Goods–But Good Goods" was splashed across the nation's sports sections. It was said to be the official rating given by Jack Dempsey, after he just happened to stop by the Manhattan Gym to watch Frankie spar. This visit was nothing remarkable. It had Tom's paw prints all over it to further encourage the "Second Dempsey" moniker bestowed on Frankie. Some in the press weren't fooled. They even claimed Les Kennedy or Ernie Owens had rightfully taken the crown from Frankie as "the New Dempsey."

Promoters and the press still sought a worthy successor that could thrill fans and don the crown which had formerly sat upon the head of the Manassa Mauler. As two heavyweights who shared wicked left hooks and used aggressive two-fisted tactics in the ring, Frankie was still the fighter with the best chance to catch the nod.

As Frankie climbed through the ropes to spar, Dempsey remarked aloud he was tempted to don ring togs and have a go, but contented himself to hang on the ropes and yell advice.

GREEN, BUT GOOD--DEMPSEY

Jack Rates Frankie Hardest Hitter He's Seen in Many a Day

Ex-Champion Likens Fighter to Ketchel; Advises Eastern Shipment

By Mark Kelly

GREEN goods—but good goods. That's the official rating placed on the fistic value of Frankie Campbell by Jack Dempsey, who yesterday watched

Green Goods article (12 Feb 1930)
Courtesy Los Angeles Examiner

After Frankie had completed his dog and pony show, Jack declared himself impressed. He likened Frankie to Stanley Ketchel. He viewed him as the stiffest puncher in the game; he didn't waste his blows, and his left hook was "a pippin, but he makes it even better by smart use of his right which has equal punching juice behind it." When he closed his observations of the session, Jack unwittingly issued a prophesy for the future, when Frankie touched gloves with Max Baer. "Campbell is just the type who will upset a lot of apple carts and in turn have his own progress halted by some freaky beezark."[589]

Jack gives Frankie tips for victory (Feb 1930)
Courtesy of San Francisco Public Library,
San Francisco History Center

Tom Maloney's shuffle of the heavyweight deck to hold out for bigger purses, and publicity stunts with former champions, couldn't continue unchallenged without damage to his fighter's reputation. Tom was threading a dangerous needle; if virtually any other fighter looked bad in the ring or suffered a loss, the press would shrug their shoulders and suggest he return to less important bouts for more schooling. Tom had hyped his fighter to such heights, anything other than a perfect performance was bound to be criticized or termed a failure.

Ernest "Dynamite" Jackson was a 215-pound, eighteen-year-old teenage phenom, fighting out of Long Beach. He had first attracted local attention when he sparred with Tommy Loughran in a local gym as Tommy trained for his bout with Armand Emanuel. He dropped the former Light-Heavyweight Champion to his knees. Jackson had since won over two of Frankie's former opponents, Tony Stabenau and Jack Beasley. It was natural for him to request a match with Frankie. Cal and Tom refused. Not because Frankie had "drawn the color line." There is no indication he ever joined the crowd of fighters, who proudly declared they wouldn't fight in a "mixed-race" fight with an "inferior opponent." Jackson was just too damn good. Tom was worried one wrong match would undo his carefully crafted path to a title run.

167

One sports reporter called Jackson a "dusky menace" that every fighter tried to avoid. Earlier in the year, Jackson's manager Wirt Ross had yelled to all and sundry from the apron of a Fresno ring, that he had posted a certified check for $2,500 at the State Athletic Commission as a guarantee to the first person to persuade Les Kennedy, Frankie Campbell, Max Baer, Jack Sharkey, or any other heavyweight, to meet his fighter. Ross sweetened the pot with an offer of a side bet up to $1,000. After extended pressure by the press and fans alike, Les Kennedy finally agreed to meet with Dynamite Jackson in late February. Scribes indicated both fighters had promised to make such a driving fight, boxing fans would demand the winner meet Frankie. [590] [591] [592]

The *Los Angeles Times* sports section carried a banner headline above a discussion of the heavyweight division: "Les Kennedy and Dynamite Jackson Hot on Trail of Frankie Campbell for Ring Date." The fight was highly anticipated. Both fighters were at the crest of a wave of sensational victories. Kennedy's manager had been offered as much as $20,000 for his contract. While odds favored Kennedy, Kay Owe at the *Los Angeles Times* thought Jackson was such a fine prospect, that "if he was white his contract would be worth a lot of money on the heavyweight market."[593] [594] [595]

As Kennedy trained for the bout with Jackson, he was asked about the continued difficulties in finalizing a match with Frankie. Les said Frankie's managers claimed he was on the road to the championship. Les believed he was entitled to a shot at a fight to prove or disprove the declaration. That he'd fight Frankie for nothing in the back alley of the Olympic, rather than agree to his handler's demands for 40-50% of the gate. "If he's that much better a fighter than I am, I guess the fight would be no contest for him."[596]

The Kennedy–Jackson match was a sensational brawl. Fans were in a breathless, edge of the seat, tizzy the entire ten rounds. The bout went up and down like a teeter-totter, with each fighter taking the lead from the other as the meeting progressed. A wild swipe by Les in the ninth tore Jackson's ear, and as the blood dripped to the canvas, frenzied fans were heard to yell, "tear his ear off—clean off!" In a whirlwind final round, an exhausted Jackson, his stamina gone, fought on by sheer heart and courage alone. He threw endless punch after punch at Kennedy until the final bell rang. When his glove was raised in victory, the fans' applause was deafening for the incredible battle.[597]

****

Frankie, Tom, and Cal were not in the audience. They were up in the Bay Area for the big bout of the season: the Jackie Fields–Young Corbett III fight to be held on February 22 at Recreation Park. Frankie was swarmed by old friends and fans as he made his way about town. He still retained a devoted following in the north from his salad days fighting at National Hall and the Dreamland Auditorium. They had avidly read about their transplanted "Bay City Socker," and set up a clamor to see him fight again on his old home turf.

Frank Schuler at the Dreamland Auditorium wanted to take advantage of the huge number of fight fans in town for the Fields–Corbett bout with a card the night before. He lobbied Frankie and his team, and they contracted for a fight with an unknown opponent. Jack Dempsey, who planned to take the train up from Los Angeles to see the big ballpark event, agreed to be third man in the ring.

Dempsey had confirmed that week, that his plans were imminent to take Frankie to Chicago after his bout at the Dreamland. Jack thought that he was a fine prospect, but lacked proper training. He was a good game fighter who could take a blow, was fast to learn, and carried the most important asset of all—a wicked punch. He had two or three faults Jack thought were easily corrected, but he had been watching Frankie's steady progress for some time. He wanted to have him nearby to supervise his training. Jack didn't believe in rushing a boy along too fast.

"We'll take him along slowly back there…. If there is championship caliber in him, we'll find it out about this time next February."[598 599 600]

Frankie greets Dempsey at train station (Feb 1930)
Courtesy of University Southern California, USC Libraries Special Collections

Veteran heavyweight John Lester Johnson, also in town for the Fields–Corbett festivities, was selected as Frankie's opponent; Johnson's last fight had been against

169

Les Kennedy. He was a slippery heavyweight that Dempsey often said hit him the hardest of anyone with whom he had ever touched gloves; Jack left their encounter with three broken ribs. Veteran manager Fred "Windy" Winsor, who was in town with another boxer, had agreed to represent Johnson for the fight.[601] [602]

The following day however, Commissioner Traung indicated he had met that morning with all involved parties. He said while he had no proof, there were rumors the fight was shady. Traung said he would be ringside, and if the referee smelled a rat, he would personally climb into the ring with the police, eject both fighters, and hand out indefinite suspensions. It seemed an extreme statement, given how lenient he had just been with Baer and multiple credible claims of his involvement with racketeers. Winsor said while he thought Johnson was completely on the up-and-up, he didn't want to get in a mess for the sake of handling him in one bout. He pulled John Lester from the fight.[603] [604]

Cal and Tom were outraged. They bellowed that the rumors were designed to damage Frankie's reputation, that Traung obviously had it out for him. Cal asked Traung to reinstate Max Baer to be Frankie's opponent, even though Max was still under suspension for the Tiny Abbott fiasco. For reasons that perplexed the press, but foreshadowed Traung's involvement in Max Baer's successes, he angrily refused. He barked that even if Max desired the match, he would not sanction it. The entire event appeared to be going down for the count. Dempsey said he was happy to referee any bout Frankie cared to fight, but when Schuler couldn't drum up another opponent willing to fight Frankie on short notice for the main event, he abandoned the card.[605] [606]

Jack Dempsey's plans to take Frankie to Chicago also took a dive. Jack developed neuritis in one eye and became a patient at the Mayo Clinic in Rochester, Minnesota. Just over a week later, he announced he had withdrawn from fight promotion work in Chicago. He spent the month of April back at the Mayo recovering from another surgery. Dempsey had not only lost money in the Chicago endeavor, he lost millions in the stock market crash. All present talk of taking Frankie east disappeared, while Jack investigated other efforts for a regular income stream.[607] [608]

For Frankie to have trained under Dempsey's care was a missed opportunity of epic proportions. Once it was gone, he remained with an erratic and floundering management team, his reputation continued to be destroyed by that faction, and all future decisions seemed to herald a perfect storm of calamities and missteps, which set him directly on the path to his death.

****

On the evening of the Fields–Corbett bout, Wad Wadhams waylaid Frankie and his team at Recreation Park's clubhouse. An agreement was reached to match Frankie with Les Kennedy down south in mid-March. Cal and Tom were also in discussions for Frankie to fight the "Nebraska Wildcat" middleweight Ace Hudkins at Wrigley Field. The "Kitty" was on the prowl for the light-heavyweight title.

Frankie was willing, but his team locked horns on terms with Hudkins' manager, who had requested impossible-to-meet weight requirements. While some in the press were hot for the match, others saw no prestige in Frankie fighting at lower weights when his eye was on the heavyweight title.[609] [610]

Frankie's Bay Area pals meanwhile still clamored to see him fight. His team was determined to show off their remade fighter at home. They turned to Oakland Civic Auditorium promoter Lou Parente; Frankie would meet any heavyweight in town. It took considerable juggling of two cards and Lou grabbed the first willing opponent. He signed Frankie to meet Natie Brown, a game scrapper who had been a prelim on Frank Schuler's defunct Dreamland card, for a fight on March 5. In his second professional fight, Brown had lasted six slashing rounds to a decision with none other than Max Baer. Brown had given Baer his toughest fight to date, and twice had him wobbly from right-hand punches to the bread basket.[611]

Brown had just come off a ten-round win against Frankie's recent opponent, Alex Rowe, and had decisively trounced another in Jack Beasley; Natie wasn't an optimum choice from Frankie's viewpoint, but Natie viewed the fight as his first big chance. His trainer Dolph Thomas, over at Frankie's old haunt the Royal Athletic Club, declared Brown's skills were underestimated. He predicted Frankie would have trouble on his hands. Though still on the rise in 1930, just five year later, Natie Brown would become one of only fourteen men to ever go the distance with the "Brown Bomber" Joe Louis. [612] [613]

Now that a local fight was on the books, the sports scribes did everything but give Frankie a rhinestone crown and a brass-plated scepter. Reporters had to push through crowds of spectators, who packed the bleachers at Taussig & Ryan's Gym and spilled beyond the doors, eager to watch him train. Over 300 fans gathered to see him spar at the Imperial Gym in Oakland. He was still the area's same big drawing card he had always been.

The press went into endless raptures of literary bombast in describing the fistic and physical transformation of this "new and improved version." How he could now effectively weave and bob and throw punches like the old Manassa Mauler himself! That he stepped around like a lightweight, and Dempsey himself looked upon Frankie as a "potential contender for the heavyweight crown of fisticuffdom!"[614] [615]

Bob Shand of the *Oakland Tribune* appeared shocked that Tom Maloney's claims about Frankie's makeover were true. "Campbell ... actually boxes like Jack Dempsey." Recalling his early Bay region days, Bob noted that Frankie no longer haunted the bright lights. "He had one fling at that racket and hit the toboggan so fast that he skidded right out of the picture. He is back again, a bigger and better fighter, and he is going to sacrifice a lot of fun he might have in order to accumulate a bank roll."

In a dig at the antics of the merry Max Baer—who had begun in earnest his collection of automobiles, the build-up of a massive wardrobe, and marked carelessness in training—Shand noted that Frankie was a likeable fellow, not addicted to fast motors or late hours, and was always willing to listen to his handlers. "With that kind of a disposition, he is apt to be near the top and copping important money when less tractable prospects are back in overalls." [616]

The day of the bout, Frankie visited one of his old haunts on Turk Street to honor an unwritten tradition among local fighters; he tucked in to a medium-rare steak at the Bay City Grill. It was good to be home. That night, Frankie's old Mission District fans and friends had taken the ferry across the bay, to organize a huge raucous rooting section in the auditorium. After so many months, they were thrilled to finally clear the dust from their long unused vocal cords to cheer on their hometown boy.

At the opening bell for Frankie's thirteenth start since his return to the sweet science, the fighters met at center ring and exchanged a flurry of hard and wild swings. When Frankie weaved in and connected with a brutal left hook, Brown went down for a nine-count and needed every moment of it. At the minute rest, one reporter heard him dazedly ask his cornerman Ray Pelkey, "What happened?"[617]

FRANKIE CAMPBELL
STOPPED NATIE BROWN WITH A FLOCK
OF RIGHTS TO TH' HEAD EARLY IN TH' 2ND ROUND—

Frankie stops Natie (07 Mar 1930)
Courtesy Oakland Post-Enquirer

At the gong for the second round, it was obvious Brown's confidence was shaken; his caution was evident as he left his stool. Frankie tore out of his corner, feinted with a left, then came out of a crouch to nail him with a right on the chin. Natie bounced off the canvas before he settled, facedown and motionless in the rosin dust. When he came out of his swoon, it was as if he leapt out of a nightmare. Muscle memory had him punching a foe who had already left the ring.[618]

Russ Allen of the *Hayward Review* later mused, "Brown was knocked so bow-legged he wanted to fight after the lights had been doused, the cash customers were half way home and the seconds were mopping his brow with a flock of towels. Campbell certainly hits hard."[619]

After the bout, A.T. Baum of the *San Francisco Examiner*, who had by now watched from ringside, both the old and the new Frankie Campbell, offered some astute observations about the fighter. Frankie could hit dangerously hard, but he could still be hit, and hit often. The difference now was that while his chin was wide open, he appeared to have the ability to shake off his opponent's blows without any apparent injury.

His conditioning and appearance were top-notch, and though his style and offense had improved, Baum said it couldn't seriously be compared to the brutal elegance of Jack Dempsey in the ring.

Frankie possessed Jack's unrelenting aggression, but lacked his sophisticated ring-craft. What Baum admired most, was Frankie's seriousness and confidence; he showed he really meant business in the ring, and had discarded his often-careless manner of the past.[620]

The *Vallejo Evening News* was a bit more impressed. "The bout, although of short duration, proved beyond a doubt, that Campbell can hit, and that ain't maybe.

Teddy Burnett illustration "Bring 'em On" (Mar 1930)
Courtesy author's collection

If he is matched with Baer, we look to see him stretch that young gent on the canvas, as Campbell can surely hit and from any angle, with punches that don't travel over a foot. He is nearer the style of the 20-round-days fighters than any boy we have seen in years. His footwork is great and his weaving his excellent."[621]

A growing maturity had resulted in a self-possession that Frankie had slipped on like his first finely tailored suit; something he had not worn easily as a youngster when he first fought in San Francisco. He felt he still had work to do, to erase any lingering bad taste among the press and his fans, put there by his team's uneven decisions. But in his mind, the path to a title was wide open and waiting; now if only his handlers would get out of his way.

Early the next morning, with his wife Elsie's arms wrapped around him, their son cooing to himself in his bassinet, Frankie quietly gazed over the expected criticism in the sports pages, that Natie Brown wasn't enough of a challenge for him.

Frankie picked up the phone, called Tom Maloney, and told him to issue one. "All right—give us [Max] Baer!" Tom bellowed that afternoon to the press. "Give us [Chet] Shandel! Give us [Primo] Carnera!" Frankie would soon get his wish to battle with one out of three.[622]

CHAPTER 22

FLASH OR FACT

CRITICS ARE PEOPLE WHO WALK IN AFTER THE BATTLE AND SHOOT THE WOUNDED.
I DON'T FIGHT FOR THE WRITERS OR THE CRITICS. I FIGHT FOR THE PUBLIC - RAY MANCINI

When the Campbell team landed back in Los Angeles, a firestorm awaited them, and as usual the conflagration was due to Tom Maloney's love affair with bumping his gums. While the team was up north, Tom claimed Les Kennedy's manager had demanded 30% of the gate for the bout with Frankie, and the fight was in jeopardy. "Tige" Clinton of the *Long Beach Sun* came to Kennedy's defense. Tige was a confidante of the Kennedy camp. He knew Les had accepted a flat fee for the fight. He accused Tom of running a bluff; he had been a no-show to sign articles of agreement at the Olympic offices for the bout. Wad Wadhams tried to punish Frankie for Tom's transgressions; if Frankie wouldn't meet Les or another equally qualified local heavyweight, Wad suggested he might not be welcome again at the Olympic Auditorium.[623]

Les Kennedy was matched within hours of the news, to meet the following week at the Hollywood Legion Stadium, against the hard-hitting Vigo Doman. Les said he was still eager to touch gloves with Frankie, but for a fair purse. He proposed to fight him if he won against Doman. Then Les fell seriously ill with the flu. His bout with Vigo was about to be called off. With visions of lost revenue dancing in his head, the Legion's matchmaker Tom Gallery offered the bout to multiple heavyweight fighters.

A Campbell–Doman bout had potential. It was the opinion of the press that Vigo had chased Frankie out of town when a match was proposed back in February 1930. Vigo now boasted twelve early-round kayos to his credit. He had dominated Frankie's earlier opponent Harry Beum, and even given his old nemesis Charley Belanger serious heart palpitations when they met. Tom Maloney and every single heavyweight management team in the area declined the last-minute substitution except for one; Tony Fuentes accepted. It was a wise move on Tony's part. He knocked Vigo out in the second round. [624] [625]

When word reached Wad Wadhams that Armand Emanuel had abandoned thoughts of retirement from boxing to practice law, he proposed a main event at the Olympic with a local fighter. Armand had recently climbed into the ring before the Jack Linkhorn–Gene O'Grady fight up north at the Oakland Civic to loudly hurl a challenge to any heavyweight in the state.

But when word reached Armand that Wad was in actual talks with Tom Maloney for him to fight Frankie, he backtracked; he decided he needed a warm-up fight. Armand had just returned by ship from an unsuccessful eastern bout with Jim Maloney at Boston Gardens. Maloney had sent Armand to the hospital. He was found to be suffering from contusions of his right side, an injury Armand claimed was evidence of a foul blow.[626] [627]

****

An oddity occurred about mid-March in the normally arid southland—an extended period of rainy weather. The storm quieted down local discussion about baseball, track, and tennis temporarily. But it souped up the fistic brethren. A main event between lightweights Eddie Thomas and Goldie Hess, and a semi-windup between heavyweights Frankie Campbell and Ray Spiker, was scheduled for March 25 at the Olympic Auditorium.

Spiker was a First World War devil dog who claimed twenty-five kayos in thirty-nine battles among his fellow Marines. He had broken the jaw of his last opponent with one punch. He held the Fleet Heavyweight title. Spiker outweighed Frankie by twenty pounds; he tipped the scales at a strapping 205 pounds.

He was a free-spoken fellow who barked, "If I can't whip that Campbell I'll enlist for another hitch in the Marines." The press enthused that Ray was schooled in bang and sock aboard a lot of Uncle Sam's fighting forts. Spiker had fought his way all through the war and was one of the toughest sea dogs who ever scowled at you across the canvas.

One afternoon as the rain poured down outside the Manhattan Gym, Frankie took a break from sparring with heavyweight Mac House for a photo shoot. *Los Angeles Record* sports editor Stub Nelson took advantage of the moment to ask him a few questions. He said Frankie loved to fight; it made him tingle from the toes up. Stub discussed the fact that Frankie was the object of much criticism for not rushing headlong into every match pushed by a vocal press. "He itches for battle," said Stub, "it is not his doings that he's held back."

As he posed in the ring corner, Frankie watched Vigo Doman while Vigo trained for his own upcoming bout with Les Kennedy. Many in the press continued to claim Frankie had avoided a bout with Vigo. But as if he had never laid eyes on the fighter before, Frankie turned to Tom Maloney and said, "Get that fellow for me. I like the way he hits."

176

Photo shoot at Manhattan Gym (Mar 1930)
Courtesy Harry E. Winkler Collection,
University of Notre Dame

Frankie shared a story from his childhood, which demonstrated just how solid a streak of determination he possessed. That certainly his handlers had him on a leash, but he was determined to take the title one day. His father, he said, whipped him for playing marbles. He whipped him for playing baseball. And he told him he would whip him down to the bone if he ever became a fighter. But Frankie did what he wanted. He endured the whippings and carried the scars of his resolve on his body. To his surprise, his greatest admirer for his ring accomplishments was his father. When Commissioner Traung and reporters had accused Frankie of picking set-ups, Alessio threatened to whip them too for slighting his son. [628]

He addressed the "setup" label given to his recent opponents by some in the press. He mused that reporters seemed to call anybody who got knocked out quickly a setup. He was sure that's what they would call him if he got nailed for the count in an early round. Because heavyweights naturally possessed a solid punch, any time a blow landed right it was going to collect, and collect big. "Some of the fellows I fought may have even had glass jaws," he grinned as he stroked his chin, "But some of them didn't. Or at least they didn't know it before I came along."

While Frankie chomped at the bit to leap faster up the ladder, he wisely realized he wasn't ready to dive headfirst over a cliff. He reiterated that he hadn't used the weaving and bobbing Dempsey crouch until he moved down to Los Angeles. It was a style change he seemed to have adapted to, while others might try it and it wouldn't work for them. "I'd like to fight all these boys around here the papers have suggested, and I will when they turn me loose.... But people should remember that I'm not claiming I'm ready for the Jack Sharkeys and Max Schmelings yet. I'm claiming nothing.... The matches I had before that, I used to stand up straight. This weaving is all new to me. I'm just going to school now." [629]

****

On March 15, Tom Maloney indicated a match for Frankie to fight Les Kennedy in May just needed both opponents' signatures. But Tom could spin a train wreck into a carnival ride if given half the chance, so despite the long-awaited news, the press attacked him relentlessly. There were calls for the boxing commission to censure him for the earlier fiasco that surrounded attempts to match with Les. Word on the street was that Frankie had even considered firing him for holding him back.

Opinions on Frankie's rise in the ranks continued to be mixed. Harry Levette of the *California Eagle* noted that, "as usual when Campbell is matched with anyone besides Jack Dempsey or Primo Carnera, the chorus sings 'easy pickins'." On the flip side, Tige Clinton of the *Long Beach Sun* called him the "heavyweight dodge of the Golden Gate." [630] [631]

Claude Newman with the *Los Angeles Evening News* shared the opinion of Stub Nelson and Harry Levette. He offered a thoughtful perspective that the local poison pens seemed determined to ignore. He said the suspicion lingered that much of Dempsey's build up when he was a young fighter, was at the expense of battlers no tougher than those polished off by Frankie in hanging up a string of consecutive knockouts. He admonished that there must be a starting point, and unlike many modern managers, Cal and Tom wisely did not think that Frankie should start at the top until he better mastered his new style. To take that route, he risked a fall all the way to the bottom with a loud thud. He needed experience and he wouldn't get it by brawling with the top-tier fighters before he was ready. [632]

Claude figured that Frankie was in a tough spot. If he won against Les Kennedy in April, fans and the press would jump back on the bandwagon to sing his praises. If he lost, they would say they knew he was a bum all along. "He was razzed if he did and razzed if he didn't." [633]

He reminded fans that Dempsey may have fought fifty suckers to reach the top, but nobody recalled it after he battered the giant Jess Willard into submission at Toledo. Frankie's handlers were being careful, even if it gained the contempt of the fans, but it would be forgotten if he reached the heights promised. People seemed to forget that Frankie had been fighting in the south for just over half a year. "One doesn't climb ladders from the top and champions are not made in a day, a week, or even a year." [634]

Yet after Frankie had uncommonly spoken at length to share his side of things, and most of the press now appeared mollified, on March 25 it all blew up. With only hours to go until his fight with Ray Spiker, Tom and Cal pulled Frankie from the weigh-in. They said medically he was in no condition to fight. But Frankie had fought sick and injured before. He wanted to go anyway. He yelled that he would fight with one hand. But his team wouldn't allow it.[635]

Frankie and Ray Spiker (inset)
(25 Mar 1930) Courtesy
Los Angeles Post-Record

That night the Olympic was packed to the rafters. Hundreds of fans who had been turned away stood outside in the rain. Clustered under umbrellas like black beetles around the open doors of vehicles, many of which sported a popular new invention called a car radio, they listened to Zeth Fitzgerald broadcast the affair on KFWB. When the news of Frankie's withdrawal was announced, the thunderous boos in and outside the auditorium, were like the rumble of an unceasing bombardment at the Battle of Verdun.

Ernie Owens was substituted to fight Ray Spiker. Owens hadn't trained a day for the fight. He had played twenty-seven holes of golf, eaten a few hot dogs, slurped down a couple milkshakes, and was about to hit the hay, when his manager Dutch Meyers pounded on his front door, and told him to hurry out to the Olympic. Ernie received a rousing cheer, and the respect of the crowd, when he knocked out Ray Spiker in six rounds.[636]

****

Speculation about Frankie's withdrawal swirled like the first ominous curves of a developing hurricane. Tom tried to get ahead of the bad publicity. He insisted he told the Olympic's physician Dr. Lloyd Russell Mace and promoter Wad Wadhams, three days before the fight, that an old shoulder injury had flared up. At noon the day of the bout, sports orthopedist Dr. Charles Spencer advised Frankie not to enter a ring for thirty days or risk permanent injury to his shoulder. Several physicians, which included Dr. Harry Martin, a future state boxing commissioner, supplied Maloney with affidavits which stated in addition to his shoulder injury, Frankie had several ulcerated teeth and infected tonsils they felt were severe enough to make him unfit to fight. [637]

In the early twentieth century, such infections were possible death sentences even to young healthy men in their twenties. In 1917, beloved Australian World Middleweight Champion Les Darcy died a miserable death far from home, due to poor dental repair which eventually led to pneumonia, blood poisoning, and heart inflammation. In 1925, World Flyweight Champion Pancho Villa died from a severe bacterial infection that spread into his bones and soft tissues, after removal of an infected wisdom tooth. In 1927, former Middleweight Champion Tiger Flowers died of an infection after eye surgery to remove scar tissue. While microbiologist Dr. Alexander Fleming had discovered penicillin two years earlier, wide use of effective antibiotics to treat such infections wouldn't occur for another fifteen years.

When Tom Maloney supplied medical reports to Dr. Mace and Wad Wadhams, they blew it off. They gave him some liniment to rub on Frankie's shoulder, and said not to mention anything to the press, as it would ruin the gate receipts. Despite phone interviews conducted with the seven doctors who submitted their diagnoses, the next morning the local press laid the blame for the entire fiasco on the Campbell team. They admitted rumors had run rampant for days that Frankie might not be able to appear due to a sore shoulder. But they declared Tom and Cal should have informed the press to protect themselves.

Then they pivoted and declared Frankie was so tough, he might have killed a green fighter such as Spiker. Only to spin again and say he should have just fought anyway, because the fight game is a "primeval man-to-man struggle." While the local press eventually reported on the specifics of the situation, the Associated Press simply ran a nationwide blurb with no follow-up that Frankie had run out on a fight.[638]

Two days later, Frankie was ordered by physicians to the hospital for surgery to have his inflamed tonsils removed. Doctors also discovered the cause of his shoulder injury; the infection to his tonsils was so severe it had caused reactive arthritis in his shoulder. He needed reconstructive surgery for scar tissue build up and bone chips in his nose as well, which he admitted impeded his breathing.[639]

The concoction of ether and nitrous oxide used as surgical anesthesia during the era was also fraught with dangers. Middleweight Champion Harry Greb had died just four years earlier, after surgery which included work on his nose. It's posited a reaction to the anesthetic caused him to slip into a coma and die from a resultant heart attack. [640] [641]

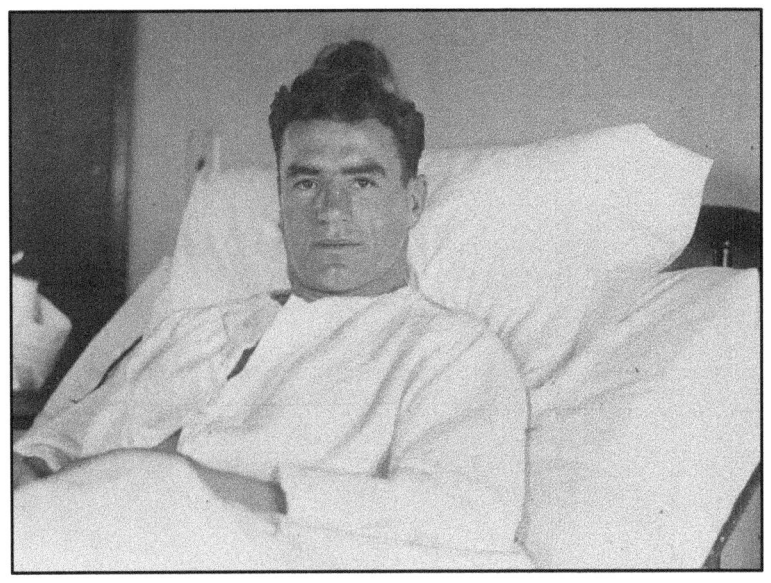

Frankie after surgery at California Lutheran Hospital (28 Mar 1930)
Courtesy of University Southern California, USC Libraries Special Collections

After the Campbell board of directors presented their case at a March 28 hearing, Dr. Mace, and James Wood, the Southern District Boxing Commissioner met behind closed doors. Frankie was indefinitely suspended. His April 15 bout with Les Kennedy was postponed. He wouldn't have a chance to clear himself until the commission's next meeting.

With copies of the doctors' affidavits in his hand, Tom Maloney made several in-person demands that the local press inform fans of the truth. His boy was no quitter. The national press and even the papers back home did no such thing. With no apologies, on the day after his 26th birthday, Frankie's boxing license was quietly reinstated. But the damage was done. Stub Nelson of the *Los Angeles Record* said his reputation was as dead as a mackerel in the ice box.[642]

Frankie was never matched again with Ray Spiker. However, the two fighters may have acknowledged each other in passing five months later, when Spiker walked down from, and Frankie walked up to, a boxing ring situated in Recreation Park, right after Ray had lost on points to Hans Birkie in the six-round semi-windup to the Baer–Campbell fight.

Max Baer had meanwhile just come off his suspension from the Tiny Abbott fiasco, and was about to make his first début in a southern ring. His fight against Ernie Owens was scheduled at the Olympic for April 22. It was his twentieth fight; his first against a technical boxer, and one against an opponent who wasn't a green kid or past his prime. The bout was viewed as an acid test of whether Max belonged in the shuffle of California heavyweights who might get somewhere as title-contenders.

In an effort to wow the commoners, Max made a grand entrance upon his arrival in Los Angeles. He looked like a British frat boy wearing the fashion of the elite: two-tone wingtip spectators with plus six knickers tucked into his argyle socks. A short sleeve polo shirt under a v-neck sweater which hugged his muscular frame was topped off with a snazzy serge cap.

Max Baer & Ham Lorimer at Manhattan Gym (Apr 1930)
Courtesy Harry E. Winkler Collection, University of Notre Dame

At lunchtime one day, the *Los Angeles Record*'s Stub Nelson happened to see Max with his manager Ham Lorimer in a local coffee shop. "I expected to see a rather uncouth rookie. But the good-looking kid handles himself like a drawing room gigolo at an afternoon tea dansant." He noted that whenever Max lifted his glass, he had his little finger crooked into an extension as daintily as a debutant.[643]

As he alighted from his chauffeured L-29 Cord limousine into the spring sunshine, to stroll across the street and into the Manhattan Gym for a training session, the gym rats gaped in utter disbelief. When his handshakes consisted of the extension of a couple fingers, some European gentry thing, they blew silent raspberries behind his back as he passed through the doors.

Unlike Frankie, who had befriended everyone in the gym from the towel boy to the janitor, Max affected an affronted snobbery as if such people were beneath him. He was not off to a good start in his local debut.

CHAPTER 23

NO PHONUS BOLONUS

IF THE MATCH IS COLD, IT'S LIKE TRYING TO HERD A BOWL OF GOLDFISH
UPSTREAM TO CATCH THE FANS' INTEREST - TIGE CLINTON

The night of Max Baer's fight with Ernie Owens, despite the generally positive build-up by southern scribes, the crowd ended up being disappointingly small, with a gate of scarcely over $5,000. Word of Max's egotistical behavior and tendency to clown around in the ring had followed him south.[644]

When he snickered and sneered and laughed through it all, the crowd actually began to boo his performance. Ernie Owens ignored the show, and proceeded to slash Max to ribbons through six rounds, until both eyes swelled shut, and his face was a grotesque gory mess. By the seventh round, quite a bit of the cockiness had been punched out of him. Ernie repeatedly laid Max over the ropes and all but had him down. His late round smiles were sickly and his conversational repartee had faded away to a whisper.[645]

When Owens was all punched out, Baer stopped acting like a half-baked nitwit and got down to business. Playing possum and putting on a performance was over. His opponent had finally run out of steam and was easy pickins'. In the eighth and ninth rounds, Baer let loose with his terrific right to Ernie's jaw, and followed it up with a half dozen more. Owens bounced off the canvas four times. Saved by the bell, he was battered, dizzy, and bleeding at the end of the ninth. It was only his gallant heart, and the ministrations of his corner, which had Owens somewhat revived to come back and take the final round. [646] [647]

While Owens had easily taken seven of the ten rounds, Baer's pummeling caught the eye of the referee. When Baer's hand was held high in victory, spectators booed the decision loudly and at length. They jeered Max as he left the ring wrapped in his blue silk robe with "California Maxie" emblazoned in gold across the back. They gave Owens a standing ovation in what spectators and the press felt should have been a draw.

From ringside however, Jack "Doc" Kearns was thoroughly smitten with the show; "I'm sunk. He's either a great fighter or he's daffy."[648] [649]

The day following the bout, local sport editors made snide remarks on Max's affectations. Sid Ziff was honestly bewildered. "We never expected to see the supreme egotism of the ritzy social climber from Livermore." Max was viewed as one of the oddest characters ever glimpsed in a ring. "He clowned, laughed and carried on," mused Sid, "like he was a leading man giving the small-town natives a treat." Others tapped their heads in significant fashion.[650]

But Sid Ziff noted something important in the scheme of things. "Whatever you say about Baer, he has guts and a cool knowledge of his own capabilities." After Max had knocked Owens senseless to the canvas in the eighth, "he walked nonchalantly over to the other side of the ring. He knew his man was out." An astute observation, given just four months later, Baer and his handlers claimed after the Campbell fight, that Max was a green kid who kept punching because he was too inexperienced to know Frankie was truly "out." [651] [652]

Yet while California's sports scribes thought Max Baer had an insufferable ego the size of Mount Rushmore, to a man the press agreed until they ran out of adjectives, when he finally stopped clowning around and got down to it, he had the power of the gods in his huge right fist.

Ancil Hoffman, a promoter originally based at the State Capitol of Sacramento—who later became Max Baer's manager, and who had muscled full-time into the San Francisco fight scene—took an overnight train to Los Angeles to watch Baer fight Owens. His briefcase held a batch of unsigned contracts.

After the fight, he approached Frankie Campbell with an offer to fight Max Baer back home. Frankie readily consented and excitedly referred him to his manager Cal Working to talk terms. But when Hoffman approached Baer, he refused to even discuss it. After Max's uneven fight with Ernie Owens, his manager Ham Lorimer firmly declined. [653] [654] [655]

****

By the third week of April, Frankie felt good enough after his hospital stays to pitch a few throws and catch up with his brother Dolph Camilli, while together on a local baseball training field. Dolph was now first baseman with the Sacramento Senators. He lived in the Capitol city with his mother. The team was in town and in practice for an upcoming series at Wrigley Field against the Los Angeles Angels.

Despite being out most of last season with a broken leg, Dolph was now among the most outstanding leaders on his team. Sacramento would go on not only to trounce Los Angeles for all five games of their series, but take first place in a race to the pennant for the Pacific Coast League. [656]

THE BROTHERS CAMILLI

Introducing two brothers in a new famous California sports family—at the left, Dolph Camilli, first baseman for Sacramento, and Frankie Camilli, who is a heavyweight ring boxing under the management of Campbell. In their youth both boys aspired to be ball players. Dolph made the grade, but Frankie found that he was more adapted to fight-

ing and hence turned pugilist. Frankie is the hard-hitting member of the family, with twelve straight knockouts to his credit. Dolph's only wish is that he could hit like his brother. He is a fine fielder but a little weak with the willow. Frankie boxes Les Kennedy at Wrigley Field next Monday night in his first serious test.

Dolph & Frankie together (May 1930)
Courtesy University of Southern California; Herald-Examiner Collection, 1920-1961

As they lobbed the ball to each other under the bright blue sky, the brothers smiled with contented ease when their eyes met. Not only was it good to shoot the breeze about news from home, their blood and history bound them. The implicit trust and honesty he could count on from his brother was a rarity to Frankie in the south. It was untainted by greed and his value as a commodity. Despite the back slaps and smiles for a fight well-fought, sometimes he didn't know who to trust in Los Angeles. Sometimes, he didn't know who benefited from the direction his career had taken. Sometimes, he felt very alone.

****

Near the end of April 1930, Frankie officially signed for the long-awaited shindy with Les Kennedy. The bout would be held on May 13 at the Olympic Auditorium. Fight fans up and down the coast were ecstatic at the news. Ticket sales were brisk. Tom and Cal were ecstatic because they had secured a guarantee of $6,500 for Frankie's services, with Kennedy guaranteed $3,500. When two days later, Kennedy gave a severe nine-round beating to Frankie's former opponent Benny Ross, the stage was set for their mid-May brawl.

Leslie Ambrose "Les" Kennedy was a plain spoken, raw-boned fellow, utterly without pretense. "We were always poor folks," he often stated simply and without artifice. Born in Starkweather, North Dakota, he started boxing in high school in Butte, Montana. He worked with his father in the copper mines during the day, then later as a butcher at the local Hansen Packing Company, while he trained after work at the local YMCA. In 1926, he bruised his way to a sensational championship win over several cocky collegians at a Montana State Amateur Tournament. His trainer John "Slug 'em" Sullivan, who claimed he once fought Gene Tunney in an Army-Navy bout during the war, advised Les in 1928 to jump to California for better boxing opponents. Les landed in Long Beach, where he worked on the docks as a stevedore, then drifted into labor at the oil fields, while he trained nights at the local athletic club.[657]

His manager Herb White, a former lightweight boxer, had carefully guided Les to better and successively more challenging bouts across Southern California. When he touched gloves with Frankie, it would be with a solid resume of 34-4-2 to Frankie's record of 29-4-2. While Frankie had been in the southern spotlight for sensational knockouts, Les had met tougher opposition. He had fought all the fighters Frankie had not: Ernie Owens, Dynamite Jackson, and Vigo Doman. Except for the close decision to Jackson, in the last two years, Les Kennedy had neither lost a fight, nor had he been knocked out.

Les was a punishing hitter, and while not normally a kayo puncher, in the last year had added flashes of a two-fisted attack to his repertoire. He favored a short, wicked right uppercut to the jaw, and brutal body shots in the clinches to take the fight out of his opponent. Les had been knocked down in a ring, even knocked for a loop a few times, but his technical game was a thing of beauty, and he unerringly always got back up for another go; he was nobody's lollypop.[658]

It was the opinion of most experts that Kennedy was the better boxer and superior defensively, with a left hook like a battering ram. But with thunder in both fists Frankie was favored to stop Les within four rounds. If the bout went the distance, Kennedy was considered a virtual cinch to win on points. Others thought that while Frankie had been knocking out his men with machine-like regularity, doubts still remained whether he could take a hard punch as well as give one against a solid opponent. Kennedy was just the man to find out whether Frankie was a flash or a fact.

In the weeks leading up to the fight, Les trained out in the high desert at Guenther's Murrieta Hot Springs. Les didn't like the noise and fuss of Los Angeles and preferred the quiet of the desert. He did all his training and sparring with a small circle of friends. He ventured into town only to fight. Frankie had just returned from conditioning at Pop Soper's Ranch. Quiet was a preference to him as well.

When he reappeared at the Manhattan Gym in the last days of April 1930, to continue hard training for the Kennedy fight, Frankie Campbell had gained a few things, and lost a few things. He tipped the scales at 191 pounds. He could breathe through his nose again, and his shoulder felt great. In addition to having his tonsils removed and his nose scraped out, he was minus five teeth. He looked refreshed after his layoff. He was still the same gym drawing card he had always been. The rail birds lingered by the ring as they waited for him to arrive. He did not disappoint the crowd. Before a packed house he vigorously resumed his bobbing weaving style in sparring sessions.

"You don't know how much better I feel now," he grinned at Stub Nelson during a break. "I don't get tired any more. I'm sorry for that Spiker mix-up I got into, but feel that my fighting will improve so much now." He was anxious to touch gloves with Les. "Kennedy will have to fight me. There are four corners in that ring. If I don't catch him the first round, I'll get him in the second." He banged his gloves together and slipped back between the ropes. "It has never entered my mind that I can't nail Kennedy."[659]

One of his punching dummies was his old pal, Frankie Muskie. They and their wives had become fast friends up north. It was the first time the fighters had been in a ring together since their two slug fests in the Bay Area over five years earlier. Despite their friendship, neither held anything back once they started trading blows. Muskie had sparred with Gene Tunney when he trained for both fights with Jack Dempsey, and was amazed at his friend's progress.

As the two men climbed down from the ring, Muskie noted earnestly to Stub that Frankie didn't try to box as much as before, but thought he didn't need to now. Due to Frankie's new fighting style and increased musculature, he now hit twice as hard as he did when the two had fought before. "He's another Dempsey now," he remarked. Frankie slugged his shoulder but his grin belayed his pleasure at the comment. Muskie continued with conviction, "Tunney never did hit me as hard as Campbell." He looked at Frankie to drive home his point. "If Dempsey had the pep and snap that Campbell has now, he would still be the world's champion."[660]

Local sports scribes as well were impressed with Frankie's work. Stub Nelson enthused that he was looking more and more like a new Dempsey these days in the gymnasium. Because he was heavier following his layoff, he appeared more like a solid heavyweight, not a blown-up light-heavy. Stub mused that there was no "phonus bolonus" about comparing Frankie to Jack Dempsey. He considered him the nearest carbon copy in style and effectiveness the game had produced; that he was far more entitled to be called the "Italian Dempsey," than Max Schmeling was to be called the "German Dempsey." "Schmeling only resembles Dempsey in the face. Campbell resembles Dempsey in the fist. Fists win championships—not faces."[661]

During breaks at the Manhattan, reporters pressed Frankie about a fight with Max Baer. Frankie said he was agreeable, especially after having watched Max's recent performances. He thought Baer's peacock display when he fought Ernie Owens had lowered his stock considerably. Fans attended a fight to see blood and brawling; they could see a vaudeville act at the theater.

The *San Francisco Examiner's* sports editor A.T. Baum remarked, that Max's odd attempts at showmanship in the ring were not popular with Bay Area fans either. In a recent fight against Tom Toner at the Oakland Civic Auditorium, not only was Max hopelessly outclassed in the early rounds, before he managed to wallop Toner in the sixth, it was his opinion that Baer would never be popular with the crowds unless he changed his tactics. "No doubt he is confident of his ability, but he greatly overplays that part of the game. Again, he shows signs of childish peevishness. He snarls and sneers, makes faces at his opponent and stoops to actual cursing. A big part of the auditorium was against him last night if the noise meant anything."[662]

Frankie continued to drape the hired help all over the canvas at the Manhattan as he trained for the Kennedy bout. Before a packed house, he sparred with 200-pound veteran fighter Tony Randolph, who had helped Jack Sharkey train for his fight with Vigo Doman. After Frankie knocked Tony down, he helped him back up, only to flatten him again. Tony boasted that Frankie hit a lot harder than Sharkey. "They clout harder than any two men living—and I ain't kidding because I get five dollars a day working with Frankie."[663]

One morning at the gym, Frankie honestly addressed why it took so long to arrange a fight with Kennedy. He keenly resented being called a fighter who avoided opponents, or one who had built up a reputation on pushovers. But despite the fact Tom Maloney's tactics had raked his integrity over the coals, he remained quietly diplomatic.

He apologized if people got the idea that he was afraid to fight Kennedy. If it had been up to him, he would have taken Les on the week after he beat K.O. Christner. "I have a different viewpoint than my managers, but I'm strictly the fighter. Dempsey never used to question plans made by Jack Kearns, and Doc took him into a championship." Frankie later admitted despite intense public pressure, his handlers ducked Kennedy on purpose, for no other reason than to drive up the gate receipts.

Frankie goes for 13 KOs (12 May 1930)
Courtesy Los Angeles Examiner

But Cal Working and Tom Maloney failed to read the room; not only had the integrity and gameness of their fighter been ridiculed because of their avarice, his further development had suffered. When asked whether he thought two thirteens—the May 13 date of the upcoming bout, and the number of his next possible knockout—was a double jinx, Frankie beamed; he considered thirteen a lucky number as it was the day of his birth.

While Frankie devoted his hours to hard sparring at the Manhattan Gym, Tom Maloney slithered off to play middleman in a meeting at a local hotel suite. Before he left the south to head home to Oakland, Tom introduced Jack Kearns to Max Baer. Word had reached Doc that Max was as malleable as cookie dough if the price was right. Kearns wanted to buy a morsel while it was hot. Max's manager Ham Lorimer had no intention of parting with so much as a crumb. The going rate for a promising heavyweight at the time was around $10,000. Ham flippantly told Kearns that he could have 100% of Max's contract for $60,000. Reportedly Kearns took two hours to recover from sticker shock. But Doc was a patient baker.[664]

****

About a week before Frankie's fight with Les Kennedy, promoter Jack Doyle decided to add a layer to his own fistic cake to attract attention. He would hold a double-header, known as a "gigantic," a day earlier on May 12 at Wrigley Field, as the opener of the outdoor boxing season. There were now two main events. Frankie Campbell vs Les Kennedy and Armand Emanuel vs Jim Maloney. The latter fight was a rematch. Armand wanted to avenge those low blows he claimed Jim had administered in Boston which put him in the hospital.[665]

PRINCIPALS IN WRIGLEY FIELD GIGANTIC

On this side we have the San Francisco Barrister and the Boston Fish-monger, otherwise Armand Emanuel (left) and Jimmy Maloney (right) who meet in one half of the Wrigley field contest tonight.

And over here you see the San Francisco "socker" and the Long Beach longshoreman, otherwise Frankie Campbell (left) and Les Kennedy (right) who furnish the other feature fireworks.

Armand Emanuel v Jim Maloney/Frankie Campbell v Les Kennedy
in the double-header at Wrigley Field, Los Angeles (12 May 1930)

The afternoon of May 12, the fighters were announced on an elevated ring in the open-air of Wrigley Field before a crowd of over 12,000. Frankie received a welcome back of thunderous applause that reverberated through the air. Friends had motored down from San Francisco to see him dish out the thirteenth straight knockout of his comeback tour.

Les had a large contingent of fans in the audience from his adopted town of Long Beach. It stuck in the craws of his waterfront fans, that Tom Maloney had wanted Kennedy to fight for what they viewed as a mere sniff of the gate receipts. But the local crowd was with Frankie. A loud chorus of good-natured boos echoed through the warm spring air to greet Les. His blue eyes twinkling, his blonde hair shining in the sun, he raised a glove from his corner in acknowledgement. Frankie had slimmed down to a svelte 179 1/2 pounds, while Les carried a sturdier 188 1/2.[666]

****

Both men left caution in the locker room along with their street clothes and went out for the kill from the opening gong. It made the Jim Maloney–Armand Emanuel tiff that followed look like a boardwalk stroll of two loving brothers. Right from the opening bell, the two stood jaw-to-jaw in the center of the ring and traded swift, hard punches. Kennedy had been expected to fight his usual game, counter-punching with his guard high. He fooled everyone. He met Frankie at his own racket and started slugging with both hands. He took to infighting and showed an aggression that was unusual. The new strategy caught the Campbell team completely off guard.

Les immediately gained the lead as he launched a terrific barrage of hard rights to the head and body that twirled Frankie about like a Maypole Queen. Frankie replied back with brutal hook after hook to the jaw. The two fought so furiously, several times they almost went over the ropes. As the bell sounded, both fighters had a touch of crimson on their faces. Les took the round.[667] [668]

The fighters were evenly matched in the second round. Les missed with a haymaker but connected with a second one. Frankie put over a hard left hook and drove in with a furious assault of rights and lefts which almost floored Les. Frankie ducked under two wild swings and concentrated on repeated body blows that slowed Les up. Les was cautioned for hitting low. Frankie missed a left lead and took a hard right to the chin. Les landed a right uppercut and Frankie snapped over a left hook and a hard right to the heart. Les landed a straight right to the chin then missed with a repeat. Both fighters' nostrils sported a rim of claret at round's end. Frankie had an edge on the round.[669]

Frankie walked into a short right uppercut in the third, followed by an unintentional head butt which cut his left eye. When Les crossed him with a right to the chin, Frankie responded in close fighting with repeated short blows to the body and uppercuts to the face. Les' nose began to bleed steadily. Frankie's eye became progressively swollen. Les concentrated his shots there until it was completely closed and he had a gash across his nose. They wrestled frequently, yet kept such a dizzy pace, the low blows were endless. Both men were bleeding as the bell sounded. Kennedy took the round.

Kennedy crowded Frankie toward the ropes in the fourth round. As Frankie went into a weave, Les hooked a stunning left on his jaw and came right back with a pip of a right hook. Frankie was out on his feet, separated from his senses, yet he kept coming on like an over-wound toy. The Long Beach fans were in an uproar and bellowed at Kennedy to finish him. The San Francisco fans rose to their feet in abject horror. The Campbell crew was near cardiac arrest as their moneymaker seemed about to drop his last gold coin. [670]

But Les made his one big mistake of the night; he left himself open for a fraction of a second, and Frankie wasn't nearly done. Like an errant bolt of lightning had streaked down from a clear sky, he struck Kennedy with a hard jolting right full on the chin. For a suspended moment Les teetered on his toes as if to defy gravity. But still, he did not go down. Frankie's wrecking ball left hook came winging in, and landed so deep into the body, it lifted Les off the floor, sent him flying through the air, and dropped him flat on his back, as if Wrigley Field's baseball stands had fallen on him.[671]

"Teetering like a drunken man walking a tightrope, but still carrying dynamite packed snugly in each shoulder," wrote Robert Cronin for the *Los Angeles Daily News*, "Frankie Campbell touched off the fuse in the fourth round last night, and knocked Les Kennedy as cold as a polar bear's toenails. And a great, prolonged cheer went up for the ending of what had been a great fight." [672]

The roar of the crowd was like an out-of-control freight train. Battered and bleeding, Frankie watched coolly from a neutral corner as Les was given the count. Blood streamed from his nose and mouth. He looked up in a daze as the referee bent over to give him a ten-finger salute. After Les was counted out, a broad grin spread across Frankie's besmeared face. As his hand was raised high, he gazed out at an endless sea of smiles. Then he walked calmly to center ring, lifted Les from the canvas, and helped him to his corner. [673]

Les Kennedy comes in for a landing
Wrigley Field, Los Angeles (12 May 1930)

Right after the fight, Tom Maloney, a 50-cent cigar clenched in his teeth, bellowed challenges all over Wrigley Field. Unaware that Tom Kennedy, manager to Ace Hudkins, stood right behind him, Maloney chirped to all and sundry; "Watch that Hudkins run out on us!" Kennedy stepped up to tap Tom on the shoulder, and said, "Be around with pen in hand and some appearance money and you'll be accommodated tomorrow morning." Maloney gave his cigar a vigorous chew, claimed someone was calling to him and vanished into the night.[674]

Frankie came back from what had seemed certain defeat. He never backed down, he had absorbed every punch, and given just as good as he got. Les Kennedy had fought a surprisingly aggressive fight. The press thought it had been one of his finest performances. Kennedy may have been booed when he first entered the ring, but he was given sustained applause when he left it. And unlike his last grand entrance, Max Baer had slipped quietly into town, and was among the crowd to observe the battle between two of his future opponents.[675]

CHAPTER 24

A TIGER ON HIS TAIL

TALL MEN COME DOWN TO MY HEIGHT WHEN I HIT 'EM IN THE BODY
- JACK DEMPSEY

Offers poured in the next morning from New York and Chicago. Local matchmakers pressed Cal and Tom to seal the deal at a lighter weight for a fight with Ace Hudkins; but Ace had already set his sights set on Mickey Walker. Tom Gallery at the Hollywood Legion wired a better offer to Paulino Uzcudun's handlers for a night bout in June or July at Wrigley Field. In response to waning attendance due to the Depression, Wrigley's was about to join other baseball fields across the nation, with installation of lights for events after dark to attract larger crowds.

Yet the demand for a Baer–Campbell fight continued to gain traction. Barely three weeks had passed since Baer's song and dance against Ernie Owens, and since his handlers had refused promoter Ancil Hoffman's attempts at a Campbell match. However, Max was reported to have his eye on a new $7,600 16-cylinder sedan. He kept three sparring partners and a masseuse on retainer. A retinue of camp followers, dressed in "Palm Beach raiment," trailed in his wake, who needed to be entertained. He spent money like a giddy lottery winner. His creditors' cries were a constant cacophony. He needed more cash and quick.[676]

In an attempt to force a contract, on May 15 promoters Jack Doyle for the Olympic Auditorium and Tom Gallery for the Hollywood Legion Stadium, accused Cal and Tom of running out on matches. Doyle told the press he had offered $7,500 to each fighter for a Frankie Campbell–Max Baer bout. Kay Owe of the *Los Angeles Times* reported Wad, "hung up this attractive bait—sweet pickings in perilous times—for the match, but has had only one bite; this from Baer, and a full gobble." Kay Owe claimed Frankie's handlers had suggested Baer fight Les Kennedy "to prove he is worthy of a Campbell fight." Tom Gallery said he had offered Tom Maloney 27 1/2% for Frankie to fight Paulino Uzcudun. Both offers were refused.[677]

Tom Maloney was offended that Tom Gallery had offered an even split to both fighters; he believed Frankie deserved the larger purse. He also thought a match with Baer would draw better in the San Franciso Bay Area. The local press reluctantly agreed. He remarked that given Uzcudun drew $100,000 gates, they wanted more of a percentage to fight him. When Armand Emanuel's father Charlie heard the Baer match was declined, he jumped in to accept it. "Give me that $7,500 and Armand will take on Baer at the Olympic or on a barge in the Pacific Ocean!"[678]

While Frankie's perseverance in the face of certain defeat against Kennedy had largely redeemed him with the skeptics, and he had once again established himself as the knockout king in the south, Max Baer was clearing a path before him of his northern brethren like Moses parting the Red Sea. By the late spring of 1930, while Frankie packed them in and turned them away at the Hollywood Legion and the Olympic Auditorium, Max's fights filled the bleachers at the Oakland Auditorium and the Arcadia Pavilion. While the press called Frankie "sensational" and "aggressive," Max was termed "dangerous" and "vicious."

Despite the growing clamor for Frankie to fight either Armand Emanuel or Max Baer, on May 17 he accepted 35% of the gate to meet Tom Kirby in a June 3rd main event at the Olympic Auditorium. The bout was Kirby's second start in California. Kirby was a Boston boy, fighting at the top of his game, who had gone the distance with several of the most experienced East Coast fighters. He had twice each fought Will "Young" Stribling, Tony Galento, and Light-Heavyweight Champion Tommy Loughran. He had a sneaky left hook that had floored more than a few of his opponents. If Frankie could stop Tom Kirby, who had a better record, and had fought more top-tier opponents than anyone Frankie had so far faced in the south, it would be a terrific boost for his reputation.[679]

Tom Kirby was a stable mate of hammer-fisted heavyweight Jim Maloney, who had fought Armand Emanuel in the Wrigley Field double-header. He had come west with four other fighters under Dan Carroll for an extended stay in the south. Kirby was said to be a better fighter than Maloney, and though the two ate at the same table, they shared a terrific rivalry. They never held punches in training. During a workout at the Main Street Gym in Los Angeles just days earlier, Kirby had let loose with a stiff right that brought Maloney to his knees. When Jim recovered, he picked Tom up and threw him through the ropes into a row of chairs.[680]

****

When Dave Shade's long-time manager Leo Flynn—who had trained Jack Dempsey for his title bouts with Gene Tunney and Jack Sharkey, and had been a matchmaker alongside promoter Tex Richard at Madison Square Garden—died suddenly of flu-related pneumonia at the age of 50, as a distraction Frankie took Dave on the ferry out to Catalina Island off the Los Angeles coast. Later he motored them up to Soper's Ranch to train together before they headed back to Los Angeles. After Leo's death, Dave Shade agreed to be looked after by Cal Working. Tom Maloney and Larry Morrison would be in Dave's corner for his upcoming fight against the "Nebraska Wildcat" Ace Hudkins. Dave and Frankie were now not only solid pals but stable mates.

When the boys arrived at Soper's, Frankie's fight against Tom Kirby was about a week out. Dave Shade had his bout the week following against Hudkins at the Olympic Auditorium. Shade had chased the "Kitty" for almost three years. When Ace found himself in dire straits with the Federal tax man, and amidst rumors he had gambled away his purses, he finally agreed to a match for some quick cash. Dave figured a win would get him the nod to finally lift the crown from Middleweight Champ Mickey Walker.[681] [682] [683] [684]

Any training camp with Dave Shade present was guaranteed to be a combination of hard work, endless practical jokes, and bets on just about anything. Unless he was part of the shenanigans it made their trainer Larry Morrison's head explode. No challenge was too great for Dave to accept; the more hazardous and bizarre the better. He would tackle a brick wall if somebody dared him. Shade firmly embraced the old proverb that "all work and no play makes [Dave] a dull boy" at every opportunity, and it didn't take much for him to gather a crowd of willing participants.[685]

After a full morning of work at the ranch, which began at dawn and ended before the desert heat began to hard boil the leather of their headgear, the boys broke for the day. To toughen their hands, Dave swore by a beef brine recipe used by Jack Dempsey. He and his stablemates lounged with unshaven cheeks as their sore

Dave Shade fishes near Soper's Ranch
Courtesy author's collection

paws soaked, while they idly discussed technique and swapped ring war stories.[686]

But the boys lived and breathed for those bets and dares. Dave was happy to be their ringleader, but Frankie was front and center slyly egging him on. They bet on who could catch the most fish, rattlesnakes, raccoons, or skunks to roast over a crackling fire for variety in their diets. Or who could throw a lariat from the farthest distance around a stable mate, while he jogged the dusty back roads as the tree boughs danced in the dry wind. Challenges to horse races, horseshoes, and shooting contests, were daily rituals. There was a lot riding on the outcomes of the upcoming battles they trained for, but in the end, they were young men whose boyhoods were still a faint squint in their recent past.[687]

When Ace Hudkins heard what the boys were eating at Soper's he smirked his Beechnut cud to the other cheek; "Them stories about Shade eating rattlesnakes and raccoons gives me a laugh. I don't have to eat freak meat to plaster him." But Ace evidently felt that a special diet might give him an edge over an opponent; last October he brought along a personal chef when he trained in Southern California to fight Mickey Walker.[688]

Unfortunately for Ace, those freak meats may have done the trick. Despite warnings in most every round by the referee, that he would stop the fight when Ace repeatedly fouled his opponent, Dave Shade toyed with the Kitty, and went on to decisively win all ten rounds. Now with 415 combined smokers and professional fights under his belt, Dave was deemed a great piece of fighting machinery.

Frankie Campbell (June 1930)
Courtesy Los Angeles Public Library

Announced as next week's headliner, Frankie was coaxed into the ring, during the pre-fight introductions before Dave's bout, to take a bow and wave to the crowd. He was met with mingled boos and applause. [689] [690] [691]

Days after his own victory, Dave became supervisor for Frankie's morning and afternoon sparring sessions at the Manhattan Gym. Frankie was superstitious about training there. He believed the gym was lucky; he had notched ten of his thirteen southern knockouts with the Manhattan as his training grounds. He insisted part of conditioning for all his fights be held there. Anticipation of a fight with

Max Baer was also on his mind. His handlers may have ignored his continued lack of defensive skills to favor the quick knockouts, but Frankie was openly honest that he still needed work.[692]

"I learned from my fight with Kennedy, that I must improve my defense work or be in line for a knockout at the hands of a good puncher. I believe that a Baer fight would prove me the stiffer puncher and a kayo winner, but I admit that with my present ignorance of a good defense, I might be a kayo victim myself." Frankie also said he was "none too frisky" when he entered the ring against Kennedy, because he had still not recovered from his surgeries; he admitted he had been on the verge of collapse in the fourth round, and was thankful he tagged Les when he did.[693]

When Frankie touched gloves with Tom Kirby at the Olympic Auditorium on June 3, 1930, he weighed in at 179 1/2 pounds to Kirby's 182. Dave Shade was crouched in his corner. Jack Dempsey had flown in from Minnesota after a month's recovery from another surgery at the Mayo Clinic to sit ringside. Jack Kearns sat on the opposite side of the ropes and glared at him. He was purported to be in discussion with Jack Doyle for a Dave Shade–Mickey Walker middleweight title match.[694] [695]

In the first round, Kirby threw some wild swings that Frankie easily ducked. He scored repeatedly with several hard body blows and stinging left hooks to Tom's head. Kirby started to backpedal as Frankie kept weaving in, throwing two-fisted punches. Frankie opened the second round by jarring Kirby with a hard right that knocked him to the canvas for a two count. Kirby leapt up and shot over a hard left hook to the eye as Frankie was coming in that floored him. He went down in a heap but was up in a flash with a no-count. His right eye began to swell. Undaunted he tore in with both hands flying. But as his eye closed his sense of direction was shot and his punches were wild. [696]

He continued to weave and managed to stay on top of Kirby, until Tom shot over a short right cross to the chin that stunned him. Frankie swayed forward and Tom scored heavily with left hook after left hook. Frankie was up against the ropes, dizzy as a Tijuana bar fly. Tom Maloney lumbered to his feet; his face falling faster than the stock market. Spectators jumped up and down in their seats howling like monkeys sighting a lion. The gong of the bell was a relief to his handlers.

While a couple of bellicose fellows engaged in drunken fisticuffs outside the north end of the ring, Frankie recovered under his corner's ministrations. When the bell rang for the third frame, he stalked from his corner in long, leggy strides, determined to end this while he could still see. For the better part of a minute Frankie caught Kirby with sharp rights and lefts to the head. But Kirby peppered him with stiff left jabs and short rights which again forced Frankie to the ropes.[697]

As they fought out of a clinch, Frankie squinted for range with his one good eye, and flashed a brutal right cross. It packed such speed and power it connected solidly on Kirby's jaw before inertia whistled it past his ear. Kirby's nose led his descent as he dropped face down, out cold to the canvas. It looked bad. He was dragged to the corner by his seconds. Frankie rushed to his unconscious foe, and stood looking down anxiously at his still form, his fists clenching helplessly. It was several minutes before his corner men were able to bring him to.[698]

While Frankie had certainly redeemed himself as he eked out a win, for a fighter purported to have a title on his horizon, he had suffered poorly at the hands of a veteran some considered was not much of a challenge. He knew that a fight with Max Baer, would erase any doubt with the press and the public that his southern knockout record was a gift from setups and trial horses, and that he belonged with the select group of fighters who had a solid chance at a title run. He would come to stake his entire career, on what became his last, and greatest, final battle in the ring.

CHAPTER 25

MAKES NO NEVER MINDS

Early June 1930, was off to a busy start. Wad Wadhams announced a Campbell–Kennedy rematch sometime in July. A bout with either Paulino Uzcudun or Ace Hudkins was still in the mix. And through the press, Max Baer challenged Frankie Campbell to fight for the unofficial title of Heavyweight Champion of the Pacific Coast; it was merely a marketing ploy. No challenge was filed through the boxing commission. But the shrill cry for a Baer–Campbell brawl had crescendoed to a constant screech.

Oakland promoter Lou Parente had driven down to Los Angeles to watch the Campbell–Kirby bout. He attempted to sign Frankie to fight Max at the infield of the popular Emeryville Arena, home field for the Oakland Oaks, which was about to get lighting for night events. The Dreamland Auditorium's promoter Frank Schuler, had thrown his hat into the ring of what he saw as the start of a bidding war. He tendered a flat fee of $10,000 each for the duo to fight outdoors at Ewing Field. But the northern press gave the raspberry to the location. Not only had Cal Ewing forbidden alcohol to be sold at his San Francisco baseball park, it was built below Lone Mountain, a bare sand dune which towered over the field. The wind that whistled around the hill and down on to the green made the spectators shiver. The fog was often so thick a baseball would disappear from view for suspenseful intervals. During one ball game, Pete Daly of the Oakland Oaks actually built a fire in the outfield to stay warm.[699] [700] [701]

Promoter Ancil Hoffman had also made the journey south to watch the Campbell–Kirby fight. He made another offer to Cal and Tom. In a hint that he had begun to focus his long-term sights on Max, either for his own benefit or at the behest of others, Hoffman speculated that Baer needed one more big local fight on his resume to present to East Coast promoters as a bridge to the big money. He expected a Baer–Campbell bout to easily draw over $50,000 at Recreation Park in

San Francisco. Before he left town, Ancil informed Frankie's trainer Tom Maloney, that he would top any offer made by either Schuler or Parente, to secure the event. When Ancil thought he could throw a "natural," he picked up the dice and shot the works. Tom grinned with satisfaction; "To the highest bidder goes the Max Baer–Frankie Campbell pugilistic contest!"[702] [703] [704]

Upon hearing word of the northern usurpers' intentions, Wad Wadhams peevishly reminded the press that Frankie had agreed in principle to a rematch with Les Kennedy at the Olympic. Tom Gallery piped up that Frankie was obligated to make his next start at the Hollywood Legion Stadium. The "Boxing Barrister" Armand Emanuel's father Charley offered a personal guarantee of $10,000 and 30% of the gate for Frankie to fight his son at either venue. Everyone seemed to view Armand as a confused fellow who couldn't decide whether to fight or practice law; they ignored his father's histrionics altogether. Promoters in the south weren't keen to engage in a bidding war to host the Baer–Campbell setto, but they did like to throw their weight around as a matter of principle against the northern promoters. In the end both Lou Parente and Ancil Hoffman returned home without an agreement. [705]

Doc Kearns watched from afar and was tickled with the shuffling of the deck. "When you've got a couple of promoters angling for your fighter," he crowed, "the best thing is to hold out as long as you can. One of them is certain to offer more money than the other."[706]

Tom Maloney made note of his words and clasped them to his heart, while a conga line of dollar signs danced through his big greedy head. He was content to play both sides against the middle. In an attempt to get Lou Parente to up his ante—rumored to be a flat fee of $8,500 per fighter—he told Lou that Frankie wanted to fight Max Baer for him, but he was indebted to Jack Doyle. Tom Gallery had abandoned negotiations for a Campbell–Uzcudun bout, so Doyle had jumped in to dangle a fight at Wrigley Field. While Baer was a hot up-and-comer, Uzcudun was internationally known. Frankie admitted his heart was set on the fight. Tom and Cal still viewed it as a bigger shot than one with Baer.[707]

****

By the first week of June however, rumors indicated Cal and Tom were just about ready to accept a Baer match. They could stay in the south for rematches with either Kirby or Kennedy, but they wouldn't mean nearly as much as a Baer match. Baer vs. Campbell was a smoking hot "natural" for California—and much hotter around the San Francisco Bay Area. Even Jack Doyle admitted it would sell better in up north. Louis Parente of Oakland and Ancil Hoffman of San Francisco were both ready to offer real money for the bout in their cities. Hoffman was considered more of a big leaguer than Parente, so was the expected favorite to land it.[708]

Despite continued disgust with Baer's incessant clowning in the ring, despite his insufferable ego, and a thorough personal dislike by boxing fans, spectators and the press just couldn't stay away. Stub Nelson mused "He packs 'em in fighting the rankest kind of a setup." Half the crowd at his fights wanted to see his amazing knockout rights in action, while the other half wanted to see the smug grin knocked off his face.

Many thought that Frankie had shown skill and heart to come back after poundings by Kennedy and Kirby to beat them both convincingly. That he had redeemed himself and was in his most formidable fighting form. Others thought the damage inflicted on him before he rallied, had put a dent in his fistic reputation. [709]

Los Angeles Times scribe Paul Lowry considered the promoters' efforts to arrange a Baer–Campbell bout a waste of time. He thought what Tom Kirby, who had no reputation as a hitter, did to Frankie at the Olympic must have thoroughly convinced his handlers, their boy had no business in the same ring with Baer. Two fights in a row, Frankie had been all but stopped by fighters who were not considered punchers. Baer was a puncher of "the murderous type." It was Paul's opinion that Frankie had a chin of glass and couldn't shed punches. He didn't think the bout would ever be made, until Frankie's team decided he had come to the end of the trail, and they wanted the dough. [710]

Though claims Frankie had a weak chin, ignored the fact he always came up off the floor after punches on the button to knock his opponents out, the Campbell faction wasn't the only one that wanted the dough. Max Baer was desperate for it. He not only spent his purse money in advance, he had learned about the miracle of installment plans. Max had developed the charm of a snake handler when he wanted something; he offered meaningless handshakes to assemble a wardrobe, then reneged on the bills. He made promises and purchases on future earnings with no intent to follow through.

He bought his parents a $37,500 palatial home on St. James Drive in the exclusive Piedmont Hills neighborhood above Oakland (equivalent to $686,000 today). He filled it with $10,000 of furniture and a $3,000 grand piano, then was unable or simply neglected to make timely payments on the mortgage. Max once informed his manager Ham Lorimer that he needed $5,000 to pay toward the mortgage, but instead spent every cent during a three-day trip to Reno, Nevada. He presented his parents with a luxury vehicle, and then gifted himself with another L-29 Cord town car; $7,500 for the limited-edition, 16-cylinder model (equivalent to $130,000 today). He entered into a contract with the Jacklich brothers, four Oakland boys with boxing interests in the Bay Area, for an easy $15,000 and "other considerations" in order to have immediate spending money. [711] [712] [713]

Barely a year into his professional career, Max Baer happily whored himself to anyone who fanned a stack of greenbacks under his nose. He had developed into a manipulative, out-of-control, expensive hobby for his manager Ham Lorimer, who would eventually be hospitalized for a nervous breakdown before the two parted ways. Ham wearily remarked that the fight against Frankie hopefully should take care of all Max's financial obligations, and then he might look into several offers he had received for a cut of Baer's contract. East Coast promoters had already dangled a shot at Madison Square Garden against named fighters if Max got past Frankie. His eyes glittered at the thought of the luxurious lifestyle he could lead with the huge purses discussed.[714] [715]

Frankie flew up north in early June to watch his brother Dolph Camilli play first base for the Sacramento Senators in several night games against the Oakland Oaks. The two didn't know it then of course, but it would be the last time they ever saw each other in this life. When cornered by sports writers, Frankie was again asked the same tired questions, different day. "It's all up to Tom and Cal," he replied with an eye roll at Dolph. "If they want me to box Baer it's alright with me." He was fed up chinning with reporters, and tired of reminding them, it was he who had repeatedly pressed for the fight.

Frankie and Dolph in Sacramento CA (June 1930)
Courtesy UC Davis - Shields Library; Archives and Special Collections

By mid-June, the pot of pugilistic soup, which had simmered down to a mild glow, was again bubbling for a Baer–Campbell bout. Lou Parente upped his offer to a flat fee of $10,000 per fighter. Doc Kearns had advised Tom Maloney to deal only with promoter Ancil Hoffman for the best offer, that from him he could expect a flat fee, plus a percentage of the gate receipts. Ancil met with Ham, Cal, and Tom to discuss the fight. After he had satisfied both sides, an option on the services of both fighters was signed. Ancil said he hoped to hold the match at

202

Recreation Park in late July, but that articles of agreement couldn't be completed until it was determined when Frankie would be in condition to fight.[716]

He went into his bouts against Kennedy and Kirby with bruised ribs. A doctor's examination now indicated two ribs were cracked. His eye still sported rainbow-hues from Kirby's ministrations. A month to heal was expected before he could engage in hard training. In addition, an out-of-weight fight between Welterweight Champion Jack Thompson and Young Corbett III, was expected to be held at Ewing Field over the Fourth of July holiday. Ancil wanted the smoke to clear from that event so it wouldn't interfere with his gate receipts.[717]

****

On June 25th, Max Baer fought a long-anticipated rematch against Ernie Owens at the Oakland Civic Auditorium. This time he left his clowning back in the dressing room. It could not possibly have gone worse for Owens. Baer knocked him down seven times. His manager Dutch Meyers was relieved when Owens finally stayed down. "I don't want to be a party to a murder. One more clout and Ernie might have passed out, and it's easier to ship them live than dead to Los Angeles." Owens admitted he threw his hardest punches only to have Max grin at him. He shook his head ruefully, "that Baer ain't human."[718]

The following morning found the Bay Area press in high dither. They claimed Frankie's handlers had given promoter Ancil Hoffman the run-around on an agreeable date for the Baer fight. Tom Maloney floated the suggestion that an August date was preferable. Reporters scoffed that next week, he would declare Frankie would be ready by September, but might counter with a correction that he actually meant August of 1950.[719]

When Cal Working failed to appear at Ancil's offices that afternoon to nail down a date, by the evening edition, the press was apoplectic. With a satisfied smile, Hoffman immediately called a presser for the next morning to put the kibosh on their pearl clutching. Before a gaggle of reporters, he dropped the bomb everyone had waited for. Two weeks earlier when he had met with Frankie, Ancil had not only walked out with a secured option for his services, Frankie had also scratched a pen on a contract for one fight, against Max Baer at Recreation Park.[720]

Ancil's option on Frankie specified he was forbidden from any further engagements. Unless they were held under the auspices of the Monarch Athletic Club, where Ancil was both promoter and matchmaker, he could not fight any other opponent until he fulfilled the contract to touch gloves with Baer.

Frankie was frustrated with his handlers and with the sports scribes as well. He hated being roped into the endless melodramas played out in the press. In the end, he just wanted to support his family, fight well, and give the fans their money's worth. In retrospect, the first time he purposefully side-stepped his team, he managed to place himself squarely into the lion's den. [721]

Ancil had pleaded his case when Frankie ran into him on the golf links in San Francisco. Frankie had fumed with frustration. A reporter once compared his long hard shots off the tee to golfing great Gene Sarazen. As he cursed, Frankie almost rivaled Gene's 235-yard "shot heard round the world" which won him the Masters Tournament. "I want the fight!" he barked to Ancil. "Maloney is putting me in bad in my home city with his actions!" He swung his club with a crack. "You get Working on the telephone and tell him I want the match!" [722]

Frankie trains at Manhattan Gym, Los Angeles (1930)
Courtesy Harry E. Winkler Collection, University of Notre Dame

Frankie was still incensed the next day. His finger jabbed the air repeatedly, as he reiterated to reporters that Tom Maloney was not authorized to legally do business on his behalf; he was officially his trainer and press agent, not his manager. Tom had intimated for over a year that his was the last word on contracts. Frankie was advised to go on record with the boxing commission to that effect, and that "Silent Cal" Working should step forward and assert himself as Frankie's manager.'" [723] [724]

While Cal's signature was still needed to officially seal the deal for the Baer fight, Frankie was home with his family, content to let the circus roll on by without him. He was surrounded by everyone he loved and the simplicity of that was enough. When a reporter managed to waylay him for a quote on Max Baer, as he and his wife pushed their son's baby carriage along the sidewalk, his response was uncharacteristically terse. "Max Baer makes no never minds in my life," he snapped.

Then he gently placed his hand in the small of Elsie's back and proceeded up the block.

On July 5, 1930, the official announcement everyone had impatiently waited for was finally made; the Baer–Campbell match would be held on August 25th at Recreation Park. Both fighters were guaranteed $5,000 with the privilege of 27 1/2 percent of the gross receipts. If Ancil Hoffman's prediction of a $50,000 gate came true, each fighter could expect the largest purse of their respective careers: over $18,000 (equivalent to over $333,000 today).

A week later, Frankie and his handlers were back in Los Angeles. When Frankie dropped by the Manhattan Gym, he had to push his way through a crush of people crowded around the training ring. Max Baer was holding court to a multitude of fighters, managers, fans, and the curious as he trained for what was expected to be an easy build up fight, against Les Kennedy on July 15 at the Olympic Auditorium. Max assured those gathered he would win handily. "I'm going to be a serious boy tonight, out to knock Kennedy flat in a hurry so that Frankie Campbell will have nothing to shout about. I want to knock Kennedy out a round earlier than Campbell did."[725]

His lofty predictions got knocked right into a cocked hat. When Max Baer touched gloves with Les Kennedy, he entered the ring a 5-to-1 favorite. With a bemused grin, Frankie watched from ringside as over the course of ten rounds, Kennedy battered Baer around at will. Les turned in a near perfect performance, taking all but the first round. He was easily awarded the decision on points.

Baer was reduced to wild swings that missed, squawks to the referee and snarls at Kennedy. By the tenth round he couldn't even keep his hands up. When Les became bored with body blows, he flashed around like a featherweight and hit Max at will about the head. Max swept a look to his corner several times, as if for divine intervention. He became a resigned punching bag to Kennedy's tactically relentless onslaught.[726]

It was considered the biggest upset of the year. It was Baer's first loss in twenty-four bouts. It shattered his string of fourteen knockouts. The gold on the northern K.O. King's crown had developed a touch of tarnish. The press gleefully took to calling him the "Butterfly Butcher Boy," and claimed he ate dainty fruit salads with plenty of whipped cream. The United Press remarked that Les soon found Max was not pleased with body punches and concentrated his attack on the midriff with devastating aim. "During the melee Baer showed the fans more facial expressions than Lon Chaney, but most of them were of mingled pain and surprise."[727]

Max couldn't understand why his attempts to entertain the crowd were met with derision. "They don't like me. They wanted to see me punched around. They razzed me from start to finish." Les Kennedy had achieved such a devastating and decisive upset, and made Max Baer look so amateurish, the expectation was that he would replace him in the bout with Frankie at Recreation Park. [728]

To nurse his hurt feelings, Max promptly went out and bought a new Cadillac 16-cylinder phaeton. He perked up considerably upon hearing the words of Commissioner Charles Traung, who had recently returned to San Francisco from the Jack Sharkey–Max Schmeling title fight in New York. In an incredibly unprofessional display of partiality by a supposedly objective state commissioner, Traung crowed like a proud father, "Max Baer could lick all those palookas I saw box in the east." [729] [730] [731]

Press coverage after Max's bout against Les Kennedy, verses Frankie's fight with him, presents not only how spectacularly Tom Maloney's tactics to build up his fighter had back-fired, but offers an interesting dichotomy of how Frankie's abilities were presented by some southern sports editors. Les Kennedy was seen as a plodding unexciting fighter. In reality, he was a technically savvy boxer who fought two wide-open sluggers. Frankie went into their bout at 2-to-1 odds, kept coming and gave as good as he got in every round, to win the fight with a devastating knockout. Max went in at 5-to-1 odds, lost nine of ten rounds, cursed and berated his opponent in between being beaten with ease, then simply gave up. Yet some in the press claimed Frankie was an outclassed bum, and insinuated his meeting with Kennedy may have been fixed. Others claimed Baer had color and was good material, he just needed more training and an attitude adjustment.

By the spring of 1930, no matter who Frankie matched with, or how hard or well he fought, comments by the local press seldom spoke of his ring savvy, or of his heart and determination. They sneered that his face had been rearranged, but were silent on the fact that he ultimately had persevered. They ignored his proven ability to win when the odds seemed against him. They disregarded the waves of applause that confirmed he was a thrill to watch in action, that he was the very definition of a game warrior. Instead, they made meritless claims that he had a glass chin and his opponents were suckers.

Frankie arguably should have stayed a light-heavyweight; he excelled comfortably under 175 pounds. He became a blown-up heavyweight as the most likely path to big money, in a weight division that not only enjoyed greater popularity among fight fans, but which still cried out for an exciting fighter to replace Jack Dempsey. Cal and Tom knew it, and Frankie knew it. He was often considered too small for a heavyweight, even though he had easily and often sparred with, fought, and won against men who greatly outweighed him. To some scribes he appeared fragile or weak next to bigger men. As a result, they searched for pejoratives that reflected their opinions, and projected that vulnerability with their words, when it didn't exist.

Regardless of perceptions, the stage was now set for one of the most highly anticipated fights ever presented on the West Coast. The winner was at the precipice of a solid path expected to place the crown of Heavyweight Champion of the World within his grasp. And one of them would make a deal with the devil to ensure he emerged the victor.

CHAPTER 26

BRILLIANT YOUNG LUMINARIES

UNDER THE BLUDGEONING OF CHANCE, MY HEAD IS BLOODY
BUT UNBOWED - "INVICTUS" BY WILLIAM ERNEST HENLEY

When word reached Tom Maloney that Max Baer had decided to box a tune-up fight against 36-year-old Meyer "K.O." Christner at the Oaks Ball Park, he trumpeted if Max suffered another loss right after his recent disaster against Kennedy, it would ruin the financial success of the match with Frankie. He intimated cancellation of the Baer–Campbell fight was a possibility. The fight's promoter Ancil Hoffman, gave public assurances before the contract was signed, that the bout with Frankie would be cancelled if Max lost to Christner.

Christner was a dirty fighter whose best days were behind him. His manager Suey Welch admitted in 1949 that Christner was "approaching his pugilistic dotage" when the two touched gloves, but that K.O. needed the money. Sports editor Bob Shand, by then with the *Oakland Post-Inquirer,* claimed in 1947 that Christner was paid to take a dive for this bout, to boost Max Baer's then-shaky reputation before his fight with Frankie Campbell. Christner freely admitted he engaged in fixed fights; an opponent need only wave a glove at him and he flopped to the canvas. Just a year earlier, he travelled the nation with a salaried, hand-picked opponent who fought under a succession of different names to build up his back-country knockout record.[732] [733] [734]

On fight night, while Max initially followed his trainer's carefully laid plans to stand off and box, Christner had agreed to no such thing. He went off-script immediately. In the first round, he cracked Max with a terrific right hand as he held him around the neck, then rubbed the palm of his glove in Baer's face. Fixed fight or not, despite the frantic shouts from his trainer, Max launched himself at Christner like a hawk upon a field mouse. Christner was knocked down five times; then Max kayoed him for good measure in the second round. But while he had restored the faith among Bay Area reporters, the match had elicited little interest with fans; only two-thirds of the seats at the ball park were filled to see it happen.[735] [736]

In late July and the first week of August 1930, Frankie did his initial training for the bout with Max out at Soper's Ranch with stable mate Dave Shade. Frankie was introduced to applause when the boys attended fights one evening at the nearby Ventura Athletic Club. In mid-August, Dave left for a three-fight contract in England, while Frankie and his crew drove north to San Francisco.

Frankie trains for the Baer bout (Aug 1930)
Courtesy Harry E. Winkler Collection,
University of Notre Dame

Along with crowd-pleaser appearances across the bay at Jimmy Duffy's new gym on Eleventh Street in uptown Oakland, Frankie continued conditioning at his old haunt, the Royal Athletic Club in the Mission District. Every day the place was packed to the rafters. An extra set of bleacher seats was built to accommodate the large crowds. Floor manager "Shorty" Brady was forced to put the "No More Room" sign on the door more than once.

Frankie was happy to be home. Contentment was to curl up every night with his wife, and roll around on the floor to play with his son. He was kissed-bronzed by the sun and in superb condition from his training in the hills above Soper's Ranch. He appeared relaxed and smiled continuously as if without a care in the world. He danced easily through multiple rounds of lively sparring. He bobbed and weaved away from sparring mate Tom Toner's long leads, coming up in a crouch with two-fisted body attacks that left the Irishman dizzy. He slipped and crouched against stable mate Don Burchard, and heavyweight Jack Petric, effortlessly slinging his punches with accuracy.[737] [738]

After one workout, Alex McCausland with the *San Francisco Examiner* asked Frankie what he thought his chances were against Baer. He was confidence personified. "I suppose Max Baer's knockout of K.O. Christner in Oakland the other night has convinced a lot of fans that I don't stand a chance of winning," he shrugged while he pulled off his gloves with his teeth. "They are using Baer's victory over Christner as a basis of comparison."

As he dragged off his headgear he continued, "while I believe that if Kennedy beat both Baer and Christner with ease, and I stopped Kennedy in sensational fashion, then that is a pretty good argument for me. I have flattened a fighter that neither Baer nor Christner came close to stopping." With a wink he turned away for a shower.[739]

Frankie trains in Oakland CA
Oakland Post-Enquirer
(22 Aug 1930)

Max Baer drove a shiny new 8-cylinder vehicle out of Oakland to do his initial training up in the North Bay at Lou Parente's boxing camp, located west of the town of El Verano in Sonoma County's Valley of the Moon. He had dented the 16-cylinder phaeton's fender; he figured a shorter ride might prevent future mishaps.

On his 10-acre property, Parente had built a hotel with a brothel hidden behind trick walls next to a casino. He also had a lucrative sideline of bootleg liquor production and distribution with his cousin Joe Parente, known as "the King of the Pacific Coast rumrunners." To protect the operation, the hotel windows were fitted with machine gun saddles enabling 'trigger men' to cover all approaches to the place. When gangster Lester "Baby Face" Nelson used a smuggled gun to force his guard to release him, while on a train headed to Illinois State Prison after conviction for jewel theft, he and his family fled to California. Nelson was one of the Parente's gunmen when he ran trucks of booze to a fleet of ferry boats on the coast. After Max had thoroughly and enthusiastically "trained" at the camp, he returned south to spar at Taussig & Ryan's Gym in San Francisco, and then moved over to Duffy's Gym in Oakland as the bout with Frankie neared.[740] [741] [742]

Everywhere the two boxers appeared they were mobbed by fans. Hundreds watched their daily progress. Hundreds more were turned away. They spilled out into the streets and up alleyways, hopes high to catch just a glimpse of either fighter.

When he upped his game to six-round sparring sessions, Frankie was reported to have hit his old foe, sparring partner Racehorse Roberts, so hard he dislocated his shoulder, but gallantly helped him slip it back into place. He was credited with knocking Tom Toner and Jack Petric out cold, but assisted them both to their stools when they came to. Frankie appeared to onlookers to be in perfect shape as he began to taper off his training regimen. After a sparring session with Tom Toner, who had recently fought and lost to Max Baer, Tom picked Frankie to win the bout. The two had never touched gloves before, but Toner expressed astonishment at the strength of his punches.[743]

Max's handlers issued an open invitation of $15 for two rounds, $5 over the going rate, to all area heavyweights to spar with Max at Taussig's. But word had spread Max hit too hard. "The fifteen looks good," said one old pug from the bleachers, "especially with the room rent due and the landlady getting peevish. But I gotta lot of bridgework that set me back plenty of jack and I can't take any chances with it."[744]

Five days before the fight, Dynamite Jackson's manager Wirt Ross got together with the Disabled War Veteran's Club. They offered Max $6,000 if he emerged the victor against Campbell, for a fight to be held in Stockton where Max had gotten his start. He was turned down. When John J. Peri, sports editor of the *Stockton Record* cornered Max's manager just before the fight at Recreation Park, he pressed for a reason behind the decline. Ham Lorimer told him Max had drawn the color line. Not only did he refuse to meet any "negroes," Max believed a law should be passed forbidding mixed bouts. This became an issue again in late 1931 when black fighters were suggested as opponents for Max in California. Oakland promoter Lou Parente was told that Baer had a "poison list" of black fighters he refused to fight.[745] [746]

Interest in the Baer–Campbell match reached nuclear proportions, when three days before the fight, promoter Ancil Hoffman announced he had asked Jack Dempsey to act as referee. Dempsey's minimum fee as third man however was $2,500. Ancil didn't feel he should be saddled with the entire amount and appealed to the rival camps for monetary assistance. The managers offered Dempsey $500 each and Hoffman ponied up $1,000. He asked Jack to "shave his remuneration a trifle." Word came back from Jack that while he "admitted the pair of G's looked good, he hated to cheapen himself."[747]

Later that day, Commissioner Traung announced a variation of the "no-foul" rule for the bout. "Should one of the boys shoot in more than one foul blow and should the punches appear to be intentional then the referee will immediately award the fight to the fouled boxer and the commission will attend to the case of the other gentlemen later," he sniffed importantly. "If one of the boys is accidentally hit low, he will be given plenty of time to recuperate." Traung, promoter Ancil Hoffman, fight managers Cal Working and Ham Lorimer, and both fighters all signed the agreement.[748] [749] [750]

Traung stated several other State Boxing Commissioners had adopted the revised no-foul rule in recent months, in an effort to head off a rash of faked fouls in the ring, and reported positive results. New York had recently enacted the rule, in response to a night last June, when Jack Sharkey swung an uppercut from the knees, and dropped Max Schmeling with an accidentally or otherwise aimed stiff one to the nether regions, which had copped Schmeling the Heavyweight Champion title on a foul, his right hand raised, while his left cupped his crotch. Another outcome of that decision, was advancement in groin protection. All through the 1920s, protection consisted of an elastic jockstrap with a floating pocket for a metal insert. It was largely used in training not in actual fights. The popularity of Brooklyn shoe sole manufacturer James P. Taylor's invention of the first full groin protector, gained traction after a 1931 patent approval, in professional bouts across the country.[751]

That night, Max and Frankie were introduced from the ring before a slate of fights at Dreamland Auditorium, and were given a standing ovation by a massive crowd. When asked about their upcoming battle, Max boasted he would do to Frankie what he had done to K.O. Christner. Frankie shot back that he would be right there to meet Max toe-to-toe, and that unlike Christner he wasn't an old man.[752]

Two days before the fight, Max's former manager Ray Pelkey, who was said to have been nursing a peeve ever since Max signed on with Ham Lorimer, joined Frankie's camp as an advisor. Ray said he had just one ambition, and that was to see Baer get licked. In a private exhibition Ray was reported to have shown Frankie how to defeat Max Baer.[753]

"I'm sure glad Pelkey went over to aid Campbell," Baer said when he heard about the matter, "for Frankie will need all the help he can get Monday night, and it won't be the first time that Pelkey has helped drag one of my opponents to his corner."[754]

The *Oakland Tribune's* Bob Shand asked Frankie what he thought his chances were. He continued to display confidence in his victory. "If Kennedy could beat Baer, I know that I can take him. Max doubled up every time Kennedy hit him in the stomach. He'll fold up when I smack him there too."[755]

Max and Frankie wound up their pre-fight work outs. Both were trained as fine as Derby Day blue bloods. Both had assumed that irritable air that typically afflicts a well-trained fighter itching for battle. But while Frankie had quietly tuned out the crowd reactions, and head down with pent-up determination, easily plowed through three sparring partners as he trained for the final time, Max's savage attack of one of his sparring partners so shocked the crowd of onlookers, he snarled at their disapproval, wrapped both arms around his opponent's body to keep him upright and continued the beating. [756] [757]

Jack Dempsey had yet to accept terms to referee. He refused an even $2,000. Commissioner Traung declared the choice of referee was between Jack Dempsey, Toby Irwin, Jim Griffin and Willie Ritchie. Preference still sided with Dempsey as the Manassa Mauler was guaranteed to encourage good windows sales.

Tillie "Kid" Herman (1926)
Courtesy author's collection

Former boxer Tillie "Kid" Herman, who had been chief second for Baer's fight against K. O. Christner, had been hired by Ham as a sparring partner at Max's request. Within days however, Tillie was advised to do some boxing if he wanted to remain on the payroll. Without approval, Tillie had recently assumed the role of trainer and instructor and refused to spar with Max. Frankie Burns the official trainer, who had been so usurped by Tillie he was lucky to be allowed to hold the stopwatch, told Tillie to get to work or get out.[758] [759]

Fighting under the ring name of "Kid" Herman, George Ernest "Tillie" Herman had led a tumultuous life full of bad decisions. Now in his mid-thirties, a decade earlier he was convicted and jailed for attempted murder down in the South Bay.

When the woman he loved resisted his advances, he stalked her mercilessly. What started out as earnest cajoling to change her mind, escalated to threats on her life. He followed her one night to the train station as she attempted to flee town. Herman assaulted her, pulled out a gun, and shot her. The bullet went through her hand, and then entered her stomach. Surgeons could not locate the round and feared septicemia. Her survival was questionable for several days. Herman was sentenced to six months in jail for the crime.[760] [761]

****

One day before the fight, newspapers across the North American continent remarked with excitement upon the event to come. The local papers gushed that the clamor over the 'big shot' at the local ball park Monday night, had reached the proportions of a mild tornado!! *San Francisco Examiner* sports columnist Alex

McCausland noted, it had been more than a decade since San Francisco had, "been so wrought up over a gloved combat featuring two brilliant young luminaries of the ring." [762] [763]

The odds of who was favored to win went back and forth like a metronome. Max had opened at 10-to-6 but the evening beforehand it was reported wise money had him at 2-to-1. Rumors abound that gamblers had heavily bet even money Frankie would not come out for the sixth round.

Stub Nelson of the *Los Angeles Record* reminded fans that Frankie had more dynamite in one punch than Baer. He predicted that since Max's fight with Les Kennedy had shown he had a weak stomach, "if Campbell should happen to land that beautiful left hook in Maxie's 'darby,' there may be a celebration in the Glen Park district." Stub mused that while Max was younger, bigger and could take a punch as well as give one, and Frankie could more easily be staggered by a punch, he also thrived under pressure and unerringly came back with a knockout win.

John C. Argens illustration
San Francisco Chronicle (25 Aug 1930)

213

Stub thought the betting odds appeared out of line, considering Frankie kayoed Les, while Kennedy took an easy decision over Baer. But despite the impression K.O. Christner was an easy mark, spectators had cheered when Max knocked him out colder than any mackerel that ever came out of Monterey Bay. He had looked good doing so, which had boosted his stock considerably. [764] [765]

When Tillie Herman refused that morning to don the gloves to spar with Max, and then rumors suggested that he had actually been a plant by Jack Kearns to report on Max's progress, he was officially taken off the Baer payroll by Ham Lorimer. Tillie was heard to smirk as he left camp; "No hard feelings Ham. Doc will take care of me." When Cal and Tom heard Tillie had been fired, they promptly hired him as Frankie's chief second. Tillie said he would accept the position if Frankie and his crew obeyed his decisions without question, and his word was the final word. [766]

Now there were two former Baer camp members on the Campbell team: Ray Pelkey and Tillie Herman. Frankie was confident in his abilities, but Cal and Tom wanted to hedge their bets. Yet any edge they felt they could get by bringing in men with knowledge of Max's strategies and weaknesses, potentially blinded them to where those men's loyalties lay.

Tillie Herman's sudden presence had gained him incredible power, and therein lies a conundrum. Certainly, the Campbell gang hired him for inside intelligence—perhaps he had intimated at injuries or explosive insight on Max's battle plan. But why he was given such an important position as that of chief second for the most pivotal fight of Frankie's career is baffling. The role of a competent second generally requires him to analyze the performance of both fighters, give a quick recap of the round, provide solid guidance on actions for the next round, do what he can in the minute rest between rounds to restore his fighter in both mind and body, and protect his fighter's interests during rounds.

Frankie had people in his camp that already knew what made him tick, who had successfully developed his game plans, who knew how to encourage and advise him between rounds. As his new chief second, Tillie lacked that familiarity. What potentially false guidance and misleading assurances might he have whispered into Frankie's ear during the fight against his old pal Max Baer? A pal that Max, along with Jack Dempsey, would soon forgive after the fight, for any past transgressions or perceived disloyalty. By late 1931 and into early 1932, the primary sparring partner for Jack's barnstorming tour was his old friend Tillie Herman. By 1934, Tillie was picked to be one of Baer's sparring partners as he trained to fight Primo Carnera for the title; an opportunity that disappeared only because in April of that year, a judge ordered Tillie to serve almost one year in jail for assault and public intoxication. [767] [768] [769]

While Ray Pelkey's role with the team was relatively minor, for months he had angrily bellowed to all and sundry a truth that was ignored or ridiculed by the press—he had been the man who worked diligently to develop and give Max Baer his start. Max had dropped Ray in 1929 to grab for the key to the kingdom that

Ham Lorimer had dangled before his eyes. Yet just like Tillie Herman, after Ray Pelkey's role in the Baer–Campbell fight was complete, all the past subterfuges and bad blood were miraculously forgotten. For Jack Dempsey's first event as a West Coast promoter, Ray was one of Baer's sparring partners as Max trained for a Fourth of July 1931 fight in Reno, Nevada with Paulino Uzcudun. Ray was back again in June 1932. As chief sparring partner, he trained Max for a rematch against King Levinsky, fought at a venue built in the middle of Reno's racetrack known as Dempsey's Arena.

Back on the home front, Frankie's fans and friends from Sunnyside, Glen Park, Bernal Heights, and virtually all of North Beach, went into holiday mode with elaborate plans to amass the next day at the ballpark to root him on. Max's supporters from his many Bay Area "hometowns" of Livermore, Galt, Hayward, and Oakland, would be there with fedoras, cowboy hats, overalls, and bells on.

Former Heavyweight Champ Jim Jeffries was expected at ringside. World Light Welterweight Champ Mushy Callahan and Los Angeles middleweight Benny Miller both threw their support behind Frankie. Jack Kearns and his retinue of scouts, who had done everything short of attempted kidnapping to secure Baer's contract, would be watching the fight closely. Kearns' theory was that if Baer lost, a disgusted Ham Lorimer would peddle Max's contract for a small sum. Wad Wadhams, Si Masters, Jack Doyle and other prominent Los Angeles managers, promoters and matchmakers would be present. Fighters of every weight division appeared in town en masse. Reporters and sports editors from across the nation secured ringside seats. [770]

Two o'clock the day of the fight, found both fighters atop the rooftop garden of the Whitcomb Hotel. A great crowd had gathered around Frankie. He had a reputation as a likeable fellow who patiently answered reporters' questions, and graciously received the well wishes of fans with a smile. A physician examined both fighters and declared them fit. The rivals weighed in. Frankie was expected to scale at 184 pounds, with Baer at 194. Max hit his mark, but when Frankie stepped up and the needle stopped quivering, a gasp rose from those gathered around the scale. He weighed only 179 pounds. Now, in addition to a height advantage of four inches, a reach advantage of five inches, and a youth advantage of five years, Max had a fifteen-pound weight advantage. [771]

Critics later blamed Max for fighting a smaller man. But Frankie had fought often against opponents with greater height and reach. He had easily won against boxers who outweighed him. A fifteen-pound weight difference wasn't excessive for heavyweight matches of the era. Sports columnist Bob Edgren later noted that Jack Dempsey gave Jess Willard an eighty-two-pound advantage and a fine beating to boot. Bob Fitzsimmons was twenty-eight pounds lighter than Jim Corbett and he took the title. Tom Sharkey weighed 183 pounds when he gave the 220-pound giant Jim Jeffries the fight of his life. [772]

Promoter Ancil Hoffman intimated he had tried to locate Dempsey to act as referee, but that Jack was somewhere between San Diego and Ensenada in

Southern California. The rumor was that he had stopped over at Agua Caliente Racetrack for some horse racing. "Even if I don't referee," Jack told the press, "I will be there to see the fight." [773] [774]

Jack never made it to ringside. With Dempsey's failure to appear, Toby Irwin was selected by Commissioner Traung as third man in the ring. As a former boxer, and the regular ring referee at the Dreamland, he was considered one of the most experienced men in the state. He had refereed Frankie twice and Max four times in the past. In those instances, he had let Frankie's opponent beat him unnecessarily, but ignored Max's repeated fouls against his.

Frankie and Cal vehemently objected to the choice. He was Charles Traung's paid pawn, and like Traung, Toby Irwin had been an early and excessively vocal supporter of Max Baer. His objectivity was questionable. Events would shortly prove their fears warranted.[775]

Campbell vs Baer Fight Poster (25 Aug 1930)
Courtesy The Printing Corporation, SF

216

CHAPTER 27

PUNCHING, PUNCHING, PUNCHING

IT PROMISED TO BE A BITTER FIGHT. THERE WAS NO CHIVALRY
OR GOOD WILL IN IT - JACK LONDON

A few hours before the fight, Frankie ruffled his son's soft curls as he gurgled in his arms. He embraced Elsie to give her a warm kiss, and promised to "bring home the bacon." As they watched from the parlor window, he flashed his family a dazzling confident smile. Elsie heard the car horn give an exuberant toot before it drove out of sight.

Frankie dropped by one of his favorite haunts, Aasland's Pool Hall on 22nd Street. He looked like a cinema star in a tailored suit, with a camel hair overcoat draped across his shoulders. His hair was beautifully cut and styled. The glimmer of his gold cufflinks winked in the light. His butter soft, leather shoes were buffed to a high shine.

Relaxed and confident, Frankie told the boys his punches tonight would concentrate on Baer's mid-section. It was well-known he didn't like them in the elly-bay. As everyone wished him good luck, he crossed the street to The Coffee Pot Restaurant, and slid onto a stool for a slice of apple pie. He had promised one of his teenage fans from the pool hall an autographed photo of himself, taken just the day before. But he had forgotten it.

"I'll call Elsie and have her remind me," he winked, as he playfully popped the kid's arm with a light left hook and walked out the door. Later that afternoon, Frankie's old schoolmates organized a band and a parade that brought out the Mission District and virtually all of North Beach. Frankie's smile was a brilliant thing, as he waved to the cheers of the huge crowds which lined his hometown streets, the jaunty Grand Marshal once more as he stood in the flower-festooned lead car, while the festivities rolled up Guerrero and Valencia Streets to Recreation Park.

To my Brother
Dolph Camilli
Best Wishes
Frank Campbell

Debonair gent at the gym (May 1930)
Courtesy Camilli family

Recreation Park (c1920s) Courtesy of San Francisco Public Library,
San Francisco History Center

The "Old Rec" was a wildly popular, centrally-located ballpark in the heart of the Mission District. Dominating one-square block with the main entrance on Valencia at Fifteenth Street, the old girl had started to show her age. Erected on the site of the former Woodward's Gardens amusement resort, the park had been hastily constructed of warped old lumber and chicken wire a year after the Great Quake, which had destroyed the Seal's Stadium on Eighth and Harrison Streets. When the fog blew in, the walls creaked like a rusty fence gate in the wind.[776]

The baseball and boxing spectators in the park were a noisy, hard-drinking crowd of working-class folks. Along the third base line to home plate, an eight-row section of the bleachers under the grandstand was surrounded with chicken wire and had been dubbed the "Booze Cage."

Fans who frequented the cage could bring their own liquor; they were said to be knowledgeable, loud and verbally abusive of players on the field. Along with suggestive remarks and bad language, fans often squirted their beverages at players. The players were known to respond with well-aimed spits of tobacco.[777]

Admission price to the park for a sporting event in the early days, entitled patrons to a choice of either a ham and cheese sandwich or two bottles of beer and a shot of whiskey. But fans also had their choice of several watering holes on the streets which surrounded the park. They often arrived three sheets to the wind, yet failed to choose the sandwich to soak up the effects of their libations. As a result, drunken profanity and fists flew regularly in the spectator seating. When a boxing ring wasn't erected over home plate, the ball park was home to both the San

Francisco Seals and the Mission Reds, minor league teams with the Pacific Coast League. [778] [779] [780]

The Monday evening of the fight, over 15,000 fans, who had paid over $35,000, jammed every seat in the park. It was one of the largest crowds in San Francisco history. The seating layout offered every spectator a clear view of the ring. The weather was typical for a late summer night in San Francisco; 57 degrees and dry, with a light breeze pushed by the ever-encroaching fog, as it began to crawl into the bay, and across the span where the Golden Gate Bridge was still seven years from being built, to roll like ghostly tumbleweeds into the park. [781]

The last rays of the sun dipped behind the high wall of the park as Frankie's auto parade pulled up to the park entrance. The rumbling noise of the swelling crowd could be heard, a low cacophony which rippled across the field, like a series of small earthquakes that registered low on the Richter scale.

Recreation Park front entry (10 Aug 1928)
Courtesy of Paul Ayers. Image by Ray Ayers

As the smell of hot dogs and popcorn drifted on the air and moths flitted against the ring lights, the semi-windups began around 8:30 p.m. While they aroused some interest, as the main event drew near, fans milled about like cows scenting a pack of coyotes. One full section of the park was occupied by the Glen Park contingent, who brought along a band, and row upon row of cheer leaders. Finally, just after 10:00 p.m., wearing six-ounce gloves and striped silk robes that absorbed the sweat of their anticipation, Frankie and Max walked from the center field clubhouse and down the aisles of a packed house. The crowd chanted "Frankie! Frankie! Frankie!" as he cut a swath through their back slaps and well wishes, his name trailing behind

220

him like the billowing cape of a super hero, as he approached the ring perched up high over home plate.[782]

They entered the squared circle to a palpable enthusiasm that seemed to make the ring ropes sway. Frankie raised an assured hand in salute as his name was announced, and the hometown crowd went absolutely wild with sustained cheers. Max was booed and hissed to the skies. With a sneering conceited grin, he gave fans a deep mocking bow, before he peacocked about the ring with an egotistical strut. Pictures were snapped. Robes were doffed. The fighters touched gloves. Still Frankie maintained that poised calm. Still Max childishly kept his gazed averted and refused to look at the man he was about to fight. As the boxers took their places, Frankie smiled with bemused confidence from his corner as he gazed across the canvas at his opponent.[783] [784]

(l-r) Larry Morrison, Tom Maloney, Tillie Herman, Frankie Campbell,
Toby Irwin, Max Baer, Frankie Burns, Ray Carlin, Abe Humphries
Courtesy author's collection

The crowd silenced. Everything seemed to hang suspended on the edge of the moment. When the gong sounded, they broke away to the middle of the ring like ponies at the starting gate. Frankie pressed in immediately, letting his punches go fast and hard, a left hook to the body, followed by a short right. Max let loose with looping lefts and rights at Frankie's jaw. Frankie clinched. Max fought his way out of the clinch with a left to the head and a hard right to the body. He missed a right to the chin, and Frankie came back inside to score heavily with rights and lefts to the body. By the sheer energy of his attack, he rushed Max to the ropes time and again. A left hook thudded against Max's body, then a stinging right to the head. Max sneered, but Frankie wiped it right off his face with a hard left to the chin and a right to the head until Max clinched. Frankie had the better of the fight, rushing fast and landing more punches. He was far out in front for most of the first round.

Whenever Max strayed near Frankie's corner, chief second Tillie Herman taunted him viciously. As a former member of Baer's training camp, he knew exactly what buttons to push. If they could get inside Baer's head, they might create some mistakes on which to capitalize. An angry Max was potentially more dangerous. The gamble was that Frankie, as the smaller man, could interrupt Max's rhythm and never let him gain momentum. His corner banked on Frankie's speed advantage as the lighter, more compact opponent to keep him out of harm's way. The question lingers however, as to who exactly Tillie Herman was beholden to during this fight. Did he truly berate Max to break his concentration, or as someone who had cornered Max before, did Tillie amp him up to inflict damage at just the right moments in just the right rounds? [785]

Frankie down in the first round (26 Aug 1930)
Courtesy San Francisco Examiner

As Tillie's jeers echoed in his ears, Max suddenly whipped over a left hook to the back of Frankie's ear which dropped him to the canvas. He calmly took a full nine-count and then got up strong and unhurt to attack again. The bell rang to end the first. Max was awarded the round by a hair.

At the start of the second—one of the most speculative in historical and contemporary discussion—the two furiously traded punches at close range. Max scored with a left to the head and spun Frankie against the ropes. Frankie responded with a left to the jaw, but Max caught him coming with a stiff left to the face and Frankie's knees sagged for a moment. Max lashed out with a straight left to the jaw. Frankie clinched, then fought out of it and winged a hard left hook to the jaw. Max dug a hard right into Frankie's body. He was cautioned to elevate his sights. Max went wide with a haymaker. Frankie slipped under it and retaliated with three hard rights to the body. Max danced away.

Frankie bull-rushed Max, fists flying to get on the inside past his long reach. Some later said Max then became unbalanced after a wild punch, or slipped in a wet patch on the canvas. That the momentum carried him, and he sat down hard, then rolled to his side. The majority of scribes however wrote that Frankie had clearly knocked Max down with a hard left to the jaw.[786] [787] [788] [789]

Frankie proceeds to a neutral corner (26 Aug 1930)
Courtesy San Francisco Call-Bulletin

Toby Irwin later claimed he thought it was as much a slip as a knockdown. Multiple newsmen wrote they saw Irwin rule it a knockdown, and wave Frankie to a neutral corner. But it was the perception that for the first time in his career, Max was out on his feet. Frankie's corner burst into laughter and the crowd joined them. Max was embarrassed and positively furious. Frankie stepped over Max's legs, glanced back, and instinctively started across the ring to wait for resumption of the fight. As he approached the ropes, a sea of shining faces met his and roared its approval.[790] [791]

Procedure called for Irwin to ensure Frankie was firmly in a neutral corner, keep both fighters in his line of sight, check the downed fighter, give a count if warranted, motion him to rise, wipe Max's gloves of any ring debris, wave for action to resume, and as is customary, for the opponents to touch gloves before they resumed battle. Even if Irwin had ruled it a slip, the rules still called for him at a minimum to wipe Max's gloves, and for the fighters to touch gloves. But as Frankie proceeded to a neutral corner, and Irwin motioned for Max to rise, Max ignored all of it. He was hell bent on revenge for being made a fool, and the rules mattered nothing to him.

Max rolled over, leapt to his feet and began to rush after Frankie, who was literally midstride still proceeding to a neutral corner. Irwin later claimed "I hollered to Baer but he kept on rushing." Amidst the roar of the crowd, Frankie didn't realize Max had ignored procedure and raced toward him. A fan yelled "Lookout, Frankie!" As he began to turn, Max knocked him into the ropes with a hard right to his neck and high on the side of his jaw.

The foul almost precipitated a riot among the fans. A barrage of boos and curses, with shouts of "Rat!" and "Dirty Dog!" curled into a sustained wave of displeasure over Max, as Frankie wound his arm around the top rope to save himself from a fall. Irwin made no move to intervene and allowed Max to punch him in the back of, and about the head, seven more times.

John Walbridge illustrations Series Part; Life of Max Baer;
(30 Apr 1934) Courtesy Oakland Post-Enquirer

Max later claimed a flashbulb blinded him as he raced after Frankie, though it's unclear whether this was to excuse the first, the fifth, or the seventh foul punch. [792] [793]

It was at this specific point, that Toby Irwin first showed blatant favoritism toward the fighter that racketeers had bet big to win in the fifth round. He had the power of judge, jury and executioner in his ring and he embraced it. The situation was not as critics say to this day, a matter of "a fighter must protect himself at all times." Irwin had given the signal for a knockdown, and Frankie was giving Max the count. When Baer jumped the count, and Irwin later declared it fair, he effectively said, "I will protect this fallen fighter from further punishment, but I won't protect you while you follow my instructions." It was a blatant violation of procedure and an intentional foul, that broke both the existing state rules and regulations, and the rules for fouls Commissioner Traung had enacted specifically for this fight.

Gregor Duncan illustration (26 Aug 1930)
Courtesy San Francisco Call-Bulletin

Years later, Max shared his own version of round two. "In the second round I started to get desperate. I swung harder but missed by an even greater distance than I had missed in the first round. I threw one right so hard, that when I missed by at least two feet, I lost my balance and slipped to the floor."

"The crowd laughed and I felt like a fool. But that slip turned out to be very important. Frankie thought he had knocked me down, so he immediately turned his back and headed for the nearest neutral corner. I jumped up without taking a count and lunged toward him…. To this day, I still think that the punch which caught him on the jaw when he was partly turned around did the damage."[794]

Irwin stepped between the men and disentangled Frankie's arm from the ropes. As he was in the process of turning him around, Max hit him again. Another foul. The angered insults of the crowd were ear-splitting. Yet Irwin still did nothing. Frankie's chief second Tillie Herman said nothing. It was within Irwin's jurisdiction to disqualify Max for the fouls. Cal Working yelled from ringside while Tom Maloney grasped the ropes, and bellowed at Irwin to award the win to Frankie. Irwin ignored them and barked at Tom to back off.

In 1930 in California, he had that power. Depending upon the state in which a bout occurred, a referee could refuse any request to stop a fight. A fighter's handlers could throw in the towel and have it kicked out. If Toby Irwin was paid by racketeers to keep the fight going through the fifth, and if Tillie Herman played the role of Judas, they had two more rounds to go. Once Frankie was freed from the ropes, he stepped aside, squared off, and just then the bell rang. Max was awarded the round.[795]

As Frankie turned and walked lightly to his corner, he passed veteran sports columnist Robert Edgren, seated at ringside. "I saw that he was laughing. He seemed to be saying to himself, 'Well, well, that was a funny one.' I said to myself, 'What a game guy this is—he'll have a chance yet.'"[796]

As he sat in his corner, a nearby policeman, and ex-boxer Jimmy Dunning, seated in the first row, later claimed they overheard Frankie say to Tillie, "it feels like something snapped in my head." A hemorrhage had begun to develop at the base of his skull from Max's foul punches. Tom Maloney later said after the second round, he noticed swelling on the back of Frankie's head, but he and Tillie denied they heard Frankie make any such claim. *San Francisco Chronicle* editor Harry B. Smith wrote as Frankie later lay stretched on the canvas, Tom had leaned over the ropes, and shouted to him, in reference to the second round, "Didn't you see us working on his head?" Cal Working, who was at the ringside corner, gave Frankie smelling salts during the minute rest of the second round. He later testified that Frankie never said Baer's punches were hurting him, that he repeatedly asked Frankie how he felt, and he responded that he was fine and wanted to continue.[797] [798] [799]

****

A century ago, boxing was unquestionably a more vicious and less-regulated sport. That was part of its allure. Bravery was measured by the amount of punishment a fighter could withstand. To quit was for cowards no matter how bad it got. This mindset was so ingrained, some fighters of the era told their cornermen to never stop a fight under any circumstance. When things go wrong, many an experienced boxer viewed such moments as survival under pressure. This was not a moment to quit, not a moment to let his opponent know how badly he might be injured. To show injury was to toss chum into shark infested water.

If Tillie's loyalties were questionable, he likely assured Frankie he was doing fine, he was just shaken. If he convinced him the pain was manageable, after he weighed his options, Frankie did exactly what he had always done; he got up for another go. But when viewed through the modern lens of head injury awareness, damage to the base of Frankie's neck after the second round was severe enough, that further punishment was life-threatening.

The stakes were excruciatingly high for Frankie to win this fight. He had a wife of two years, an eight-month-old son, and a baby on the way. If he lost, it had been expressed to him his path to the title was likely gone. Negative press had convinced him if he lost, his career as a good draw to fans was effectively finished. In his mind, everything rode on this fight, everything. He became fierce for his future and the care of his loved ones.

Frankie came out in the third with extreme vigor, which lasted through the round. He changed his style and out-boxed his man. As Max measured a punch with his range-finder right, Frankie beat him to it with a jab or a hook, and took away the play before Max could get set. Max had a habit of coming in with his left low at his waist, which left an opening for an opponent to pop his chin. Frankie easily sizzled three stinging rights to the jaw, and then shot a left to the chin. Max clinched. Frankie hooked two lefts to the face and Max backed away. He bored in and sank right after right so deep into the midriff, Max's legs repeatedly lifted from the force of the blows. Max was groggy and on the retreat. He swung a salvo of wild rights that almost carried him out of the ring and into the laps of the cash customers. Frankie nailed him with another flurry of lefts and rights to the jaw until blood poured from Baer's mouth as the bell sounded. Frankie was awarded the round.[800] [801]

Frankie came back even stronger in the fourth round. He ran across the ring to get at Max. He boxed beautifully. He scored easily with a left to the jaw and a right to the body. Max threw a right uppercut but Frankie replied back with a left and right to the head, then whipped three beautiful left hooks to the body. Max shot a right to the head only to be doubled over by Frankie's right to the gut. They exchanged short punches at close range and finally clinched. On the break, Frankie plowed a hard right to the jaw, and then shot two straight lefts to the face. Again, Max clinched. His artfully marcelled hair was now a kinky mop. They traded rights on the break away. Quicker than Houdini's hand, Frankie struck Max with two blazing lefts to the face. Blood now began to stream from Max's nose too.[802] [803]

Somewhere in the depths of the park a lone voice shouted "C'mon Frankie!" The crowd picked it up and the chant grew into a roar. The terrific force of Frankie's punches began to noticeably weaken his opponent. Max threw a left hook to the chin, but it didn't slow Frankie down a bit. He came right back to pummel Max's body. As Frankie bobbed and weaved, Max's swings became progressively wilder. Frankie was cautioned to elevate his sights, but he continued to be the aggressor. The press noted he made a remarkable showing despite the odds against him. He had taken decided control of the fight when so many doubted his abilities. Some scribes thought Max had begun to run out of steam and looked distressed. Others remarked that given the hype and the odds, Max was more or less a disappointment as a prospective champion most of the way. Frankie carried the fight at such a pace, Max was plastered against the ropes and driven back again and again. He had sucked the puff right out of Max's chest and was easily awarded the round. [804] [805] [806]

With honors even, Frankie's seconds sent him out in the fifth round to try for a knockout. Gamblers had waged even money he would not come out for the sixth, so this was the round most anticipated. As he stalked to the center of the ring like a lion in the long grass, Cal Working yelled to friends at ringside, "We've got him, we've got him!! We're going to win now!!" Max's old manager Ray Pelkey, who sat near Frankie's corner, and Tillie Herman, who as chief second commanded it, jeered Max with foul language and personal attacks on his family. [807] [808]

Their well-placed jibes worked. Max's embarrassment and fury were now white hot. Frankie was turning the fight his way. Max's visions of fame and fortune were slipping away. If he was in with gamblers, this was the round he needed to try and end the fight. He left his corner enraged and determined to score a knockout; he now knew his game opponent would not make it easy.

As Frankie moved to slip inside, Max advanced cautiously, his long-left arm out as he slugged with his right. The blows were slow but powerful as Max began to pressure Frankie to a neutral corner. Frankie responded back with a relentless tattoo of vicious body shots. Max threw a wild right but missed. Then he landed. He launched himself forward, hitting with blazing speed and force as he drove Frankie back against the ropes with a left to the stomach. A terrific left hook to the jaw made Frankie's knees buckle. Bill Smith at the *San Francisco Chronicle* noted, Max seemed to have a half hold on Frankie as he pinioned him in the corner, and smashed him on the chin with a lightning right cross. [809]

Many in the press claimed it was that right cross which actually knocked Frankie out cold. But Max was the one in the ring. Max was the one who looked Frankie in the eyes as he inhaled his exhalations. Max knew it was the left hook that had done the job. Max Baer had that half-hold on Frankie Campbell to deliver the right cross which followed, because he had propped the body up, and intentionally begun to punch an unconscious man.

Frankie had collapsed like a bird shot from the air. Several scribes at ringside saw that his eyes had closed, his head flopped to his chest, his guard dropped, his hands dangled loosely at his sides, as though his bones had liquefied. He was clearly unconscious. Shouts arose for Irwin to stop the fight. He refused. He stood behind Max and watched.[810] [811]

Max had completely abandoned the veneer of civilization. He had been humiliated. He was enraged. Frankie had taken the center of attention away from him. Max needed this win to get to Madison Square Garden, and was prepared to do anything to get it. He had toed up against a line between good and evil, and without hesitation he stepped right over it. Rather than back off, he leaned in to continue the slaughter, like a rabid dog that had managed to slip his leash. A sizzling energy seemed to spark up from the floor and crackle in his veins, as he powered punch after punch with his entire body behind it. The ring canvas creaked as he braced his legs wide, and pressed against it to provide more power to his shots.

John Walbridge illustration (30 Apr 1934)
Series Part: Life of Max Baer;
Courtesy Oakland Post-Enquirer

His determined mouth twisted with menace, while he drove in short hard rights and lefts to Frankie's unprotected face and jaw. As all the supportive tissues that held Frankie's brain inside his skull were snapped loose, his head bobbed alarmingly as if his neck was broken. One report claimed Max later said he heard a cracking sound as the tendons in Frankie's head ripped away. His body could not fall down as he was supported on two sides by the ropes. As Max continued his assault, the back of Frankie's head slammed repeatedly against the unpadded turn buckle that joined the ropes to the ring post.[812] [813]

With his face a bleeding mass, Frankie's body started to fall forward, but Max straightened it up again with a brutal left hook to the chin. His knees began to buckle as he sagged down the ropes, but still Max stayed in front of him, still he kept punching, punching, punching, literally keeping Frankie upright with the force of the blows, his head like a puppet with the strings being jerked to and fro. When Max's arms began to tire, Frankie's knees gave way and his body slowly slid like a melting snowman into a sitting position on the canvas.[814]

Yet still Max Baer did not stop. As blood smeared his face and neck, he followed Frankie Campbell down. He bent forward and continued to rain blow after blow on Frankie's unprotected head and chest, and blood began to streak Max's torso and legs. Finally, mercifully, at about 10:20 pm, the Livermore Butcher Boy stepped back from the abattoir he had created, as the carcass slumped onto its side like an ineptly slaughtered lamb.[815] [816] [817] [818]

****

Some claim that in retrospect, the final blows surely occurred more quickly than it took to read the last sentence. That it was all over in a few Olympic-speed milliseconds and Toby Irwin couldn't have possibly stopped the fight any earlier.

No.

Several sports columnists wrote Max threw anywhere from over twenty to at least two dozen punches, while Frankie was clearly unconscious. Others wrote that fully a solid minute ticked by as Max continued his lengthy assault.[819] [820] [821] [822] [823]

Robert Edgren illustration (30 Aug 1930)
Courtesy author's collection

Referee Toby Irwin was positioned ten feet away behind Max. He later tried to claim he could not see the action, and was oblivious to the fact Frankie was out and unable to defend himself. The *Oakland Tribune's* Bob Shand posited, perhaps Irwin had seen Frankie take Max's hardest blows earlier without going down, and believed he was impervious to punishment. But he neglected to judge Frankie's condition based on how he was doing in the moment, not on a past performance. He failed at the first duty of a referee; to always place himself in a position to watch everything as it occurs, and intervene immediately if he sees trouble; unless someone had greased his palm enough to let it happen.[824]

Irwin declared privately to friends; he didn't dare stop the fight after the first punch. He said he had waited until certain Frankie had been knocked out so that gamblers, who had waged he wouldn't come out for the sixth round, would get their dough. An element invested heavily in the outcome of the bout. An element in the city, reported to have a standing offer of up to $1,000 for friendly referees, typically paid $50 per fight. And a man like Toby Irwin, with decades of experience as a crooked referee, who might have been inclined to take an extra chunk of change to react a bit too slowly—because he was in such dire straits financially, after he resigned unexpectedly from the Dreamland Auditorium board of directors, he was forced to sell his shares of company stock, and had pled guilty just weeks earlier, to his second offense for forgery and check fraud.[825] [826] [827] [828]

Al Buescher illustration (16 Jun 1933)
Courtesy Neesha Daily News-Times

Some observed Tillie Herman, as he stood on the steps leading to Frankie's corner in his bright yellow sweater, and did nothing. It was his privilege alone as chief second to enter the ring and stop the bout. He later claimed to a friendly reporter that he entered the ring in back of Irwin to stop the fight as the last six punches were thrown. However, all other scribes noted he did not slip through the ropes until the fight was over and Frankie lay crumbled on the canvas.[829]

Tillie later testified that, "he didn't blame Max for hitting Campbell at any time, that Max was in there to win." The man tasked to take care of Frankie in his corner, favored the actions of the opponent over his own fighter. Cal Working declared that he had screamed at Irwin to "stop the fight, stop the fight!" He said he yelled at a nearby policeman to intervene before he then attempted to climb into the ring. Perhaps so, but in the pandemonium, Irwin just stood and watched as the roar of the crowd filled the air; some yelled with savage glee "kill him!" while others cried "murder!" and pleaded for the whole sordid affair to be halted.[830] [831] [832] [833]

Not until Max tired from his barrage of free shots at Frankie's unconscious body, relentless rights and lefts to the head and jaw, the sound like a skilled butcher methodically swinging his meat-axe, as Max literally pulverized Frankie's brain, did Toby Irwin intervene. When he attempted to pull Baer away, Max fought him. There was a struggle to hold him back, as Max attempted to stalk toward Frankie to administer more punishment. While Frankie lay slumped in the corner, his face turning blue, blood oozing from his eyes, nose and mouth, Irwin stepped over his lifeless body, pushed in between Max and the ropes, and the two paused to pose for several pictures.[834]

As Frankie's life ebbed away on the canvas at their feet, Tom and Tillie were made to wait until the photographers had finished, before they were allowed to rush to his aid. The tips of Frankie's shoes peeked from the bottom of one photo which showed Max's arm raised high in a token of victory.

It was noted as Max posed over and over, he smiled through bloodied lips, his face triumphant, eyes half-closed as he sneered down at the man crumpled on the canvas. Irwin did not even bother with the formality of a count.

Baer and Irwin pose as Frankie lies at their feet
(26 Aug 1930) By Howard Robbins
Courtesy Oakland Post-Enquirer

But as he had raised Baer's hand to proclaim him the winner, an ear-splitting wail of boos rose into the night and echoed across the park, as if the hounds had come to escort them both down to hell.[835] [836] [837] [838]

Irwin finally attempted to lift Frankie up, but he slipped again to the canvas and dropped to one side. He was dragged to his stool, but fell like a neglected rag doll from the seat. He groaned as if in denial and protest, while he struggled to breathe, while blood streamed from his mouth on every exhale, the sound like the gasps of a drowning man before he slipped beneath the waves. His limbs began to convulse as he lay sprawled in the open air. The canvas eagerly drank his blood as if it were a sacrifice, while the cool mist of the fog rolled in on his unfeeling face, head tilted at the indifferent sky. [839] [840]

CHAPTER 28

NOTHING TO BE DONE

LET ME NOT THEN DIE INGLORIOUSLY AND WITHOUT A STRUGGLE, BUT LET ME FIRST DO
SOME GREAT THING THAT SHALL BE TOLD AMONG MEN HEREAFTER - "THE ILIAD" BY HOMER

When "Effervescent Ernie" Smith, the local sports broadcaster for KYA Radio, who provided coverage of the fight at ringside, tried to put into words what he had just witnessed, listeners at home heard several moments of dead air through their speakers.

In an instant, pandemonium reigned. The ring was filled with police, newspapermen, and spectators. Men fell all over each other; some were injured as they toppled off the ring. When several photographers began to take pictures of Frankie sprawled in the corner of the ring, a riot ensued. The smoke and burnt metal stench of their flash powder wafted into the air to mix with the angst and unease of the men who surrounded him.

One intrepid cameraman for the *San Francisco Call-Bulletin* took a chance. But no sooner had he shot his flash, people attempted to smash the camera. Roy Cummings, Assistant Sports Editor for the *Call* later wrote that Frankie's trainer, Larry Morrison kicked him in the eye as he shielded his cameraman. The film of that image survived, and is believed to be the only press photo that still exists to capture Frankie as he lay on the canvas.[841] [842]

Larry managed to punch another photographer in the nose and wreck his camera. Other photographers were tripped or assaulted by several spectators, and even by other members of the press, as they attempted to leave the ring after they had taken their shots. They were escorted through the crowd by the police. Some crying, "this will hurt the game," swarmed them as soon as they stepped outside the ball park, and successfully destroyed their cameras.[843] [844]

As police attempted to clear part of the ring, Dr. Albert H. McNulty, who was promoter Ancil Hoffman's club physician, leapt into the ring, and within moments was bent over the fallen fighter. McNulty had sat in the third row next to Hoffman throughout the fight. The acrid stench of Frankie's sweat, mixed with the piney scent of rosin dust assaulted his nostrils. The sweet metallic pungency of so much blood as it continued to pool onto the canvas was overpowering.

Frankie's crew was heard to yell apprehensively for a doctor, which prompted many in the press to say Frankie was without medical care for half an hour. Cal Working later clarified they sought out the Camilli family physician Dr. Tilton E. Tillman to attend him. They believed him to be in the crowd, but so many spectators had come out of the stands and onto the field like a vast quiet army, it took several minutes for Dr. Tillman to push his way through the mob, and convince a policeman to let him through.[845] [846]

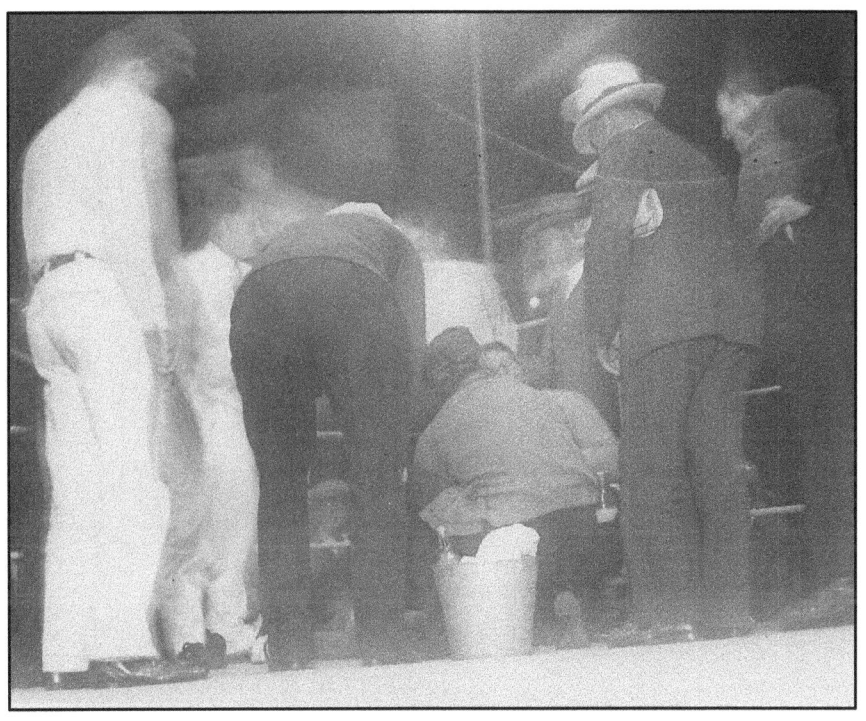

Trainer Larry Morrison (left kneeling), Chief Second Tillie Herman (right kneeling)
Press Agent Tom Maloney (far right) with Frankie on the canvas (26 Aug 1930)
Courtesy San Francisco History Center, San Francisco Public Library

Tom Maloney was next through the ropes with Tillie Herman hot on his heels. Tom's hands shook as he nervously pulled a water bottle from his bucket with the intent to douse Frankie's face to revive him. Toby Irwin told him to leave matters to the doctors. Dr. Frank Sheehy, another ringside spectator, had joined Doctors McNulty and Tillman, in a vain attempt to bring Frankie to consciousness. As the brims of their fedoras cast shadows along their cheekbones, they watched Tom run the blade of a penknife an inch up under the nail of Frankie's thumb; believed to be an effective way to prevent a coma. When Frankie's body convulsed again, Tom noted his left side appeared to be paralyzed. [847] [848] [849] [850]

There was no procedure in place for emergencies such as what occurred. Promoter Ancil Hoffman's pals, State Boxing Commissioners William Hanlon and Charles Traung, were seated less than thirty feet from where Frankie lay unconscious, yet made no move to have the ring cleared or summon an ambulance. Fans were allowed to mill around in and outside of the ring; the outfield grass was trodden flat by thousands of feet, the chalk baselines smudged like panicked bird's tracks. The bolder ones pushed against the crowd that circled Frankie's still form, or shoved toward the corner ring post outside where he lay for a morbidly curious peek. [851] [852]

As time ticked by like a leaden dirge, the majority of spectators continued to stand with hushed hope all across the ballpark. Thousands of eyes from up in the bleachers, on down to the infield, were pinned on Frankie's prone body. Collectively they willed him to rise up, and assure them with his dazzling smile, that he was okay. But he did not rise. A howl of anguish like a wounded beast, suddenly rose up into the night air, and the mood of the crowd turned darker.

Several of Frankie's enraged supporters tried to push through a human barricade that had formed to protect Irwin and Baer. Toby was small in stature; he managed to slip down among the milling thousands in the grassy field and vanish into the night. Max towered above most everyone around him. He presented an easy target. He had to move fast through the hostile mob to his dressing room, which fortunately for him was on the opposite side of the ring from where Frankie's followers had congregated. [853]

Bob Shand of the *Oakland Tribune* noted Max dress hurriedly and left in a panic. He immediately went to his parents' home in the Piedmont Hills above Oakland. Max later wove several elaborate tales about his actions in the immediate aftermath of the bout, which he shared repeatedly, and seemed to enjoy acting out. One oft-repeated fable was that after taking a leisurely shower, he remarked to promoter Ancil Hoffman his intent to visit Frankie for a handshake. He claimed instead, as he emerged from the clubhouse in his robe, he saw Frankie prone on the canvas. He said as fog swirled around the ring like a caress, a ghost-like yellow spotlight highlighted his body, before the fog enveloped it entirely.

Years later, with a fresh crowd of reporters in England to dupe, Max claimed he and Frankie had been good friends, and after their fight, Max dressed quickly, went to Frankie's dressing room for a hearty handshake, only to see Frankie stretched out dead on the table. But it was all just a litany of detestable deception that for years would play well in the papers. Max knew what he had done. He wasn't blind to the frenzied folks in the ring, as they pushed against his handlers in a desperate attempt to get to him. He did not linger unaware with good sportsmanship suddenly on his mind. He fled the scene of his crime. [854] [855] [856] [857] [858]

While some spectators slowly pushed out of the park into the mist of the evening, several others in the horde that packed the field again began to attempt to climb into the ring. As police officers kept them at bay, Frankie was moved from the corner to the middle of the ring while the doctors awaited the ambulance. Twenty-two minutes passed, before heads turned at its faint first wail, when it finally raced down Sixteenth Street and stopped behind the grandstand on Bryant Street. Summoned by a clear-thinking newspaperman via a call through the *San Francisco Chronicle's* special ringside telephone, it had been stalled in traffic as people left the park. All available police formed a pathway through the crowd. Frankie's face was reported to look black from lack of oxygen to his brain. A steady stream of blood flowed from his eyes, from his mouth, and from his nose; spinal fluid dripped from his ears. He was loaded onto a stretcher, and carried from the ring on the shoulders of four husky officers, across the baseball infield, and into the ambulance. [859] [860] [861] [862]

About 10:45 p.m., Frankie was taken up the hill to Mission Emergency Hospital. Dr. Tillman had followed the ambulance, and was soon joined by Doctors Sheehy and McNulty in an attempt to give further assistance. After additional tests were conducted, Dr. Sheehy thought Frankie had a fractured skull, or one or more vertebrae were broken, because of how alarmingly his head had flopped on his neck under Baer's punches. Still unconscious, and non-responsive to any aid given, Frankie was then taken down to St. Joseph's Hospital for a more thorough examination. Dr. Sheehy was a Staff Surgeon there in case surgery was a possibility. Brain specialist Dr. Edmond Morrissey was called in for a consultation. The invention of CT scans and MRIs was still four decades away, but after x-rays and a lengthy examination, he determined Frankie suffered from multiple brain bruises and hemorrhages. [863] [864]

Someone finally thought to call Frankie's wife Elsie to break the news. She left their son with her mother and took a taxi to St. Joseph's. Her heels echoed in the quiet corridor as she raced breathlessly down the halls of the hospital. When she saw the full extent of what Max Baer had done to husband, she whimpered in horror as she slowly approached his bed.

Hundreds of phone calls were made throughout the evening to all nearby hospitals, and all local newspaper switchboards, as fans inquired after Frankie's condition. Hundreds more, who discovered where he had been taken, huddled on benches across the street in Buena Vista Park or congregated about St. Joseph's hospital grounds, to await any news. A mood of grim reflection enveloped them like burial shrouds as all eyes faced the entrance.

Dr. Sheehy finally emerged out the front door. For a moment, his eyes touched on the many anguished faces in the crowd. Then he shook his head regretfully and began to speak. "The prognosis is poor and the outlook is very dark. There will be no operation." He raised his voice to be heard over the distressed murmurs. "The critical stage will continue for twenty-four hours." Of note is that in 1930, an "operation" meant to remove the top of Frankie's skull, or perform exploratory "woodpecker surgery" to release pressure build-up caused by his brain swollen within his skull. Privately, the doctors knew that surgery was useless. Max's fists had reduced Frankie's brain to pulp. [865] [866] [867]

****

Max was still up in the Oakland Hills. He received a phone call that Frankie remained unconscious, and likely would not survive. The police requested that he return to San Francisco and stay at the Whitcomb Hotel on Market Street, where promoter Ancil Hoffman kept a suite. "He just stood there," a family member later claimed, "tears as big as golf balls rolling down his cheeks" before he drove back to the city. [868] [869]

Retired veteran sports editor Ed Orman of the *Fresno Bee*, recalled Baer's demeanor quite differently soon after the fight. He and a group which included future Welterweight Champ Young Corbett III's manager Ralph Manfredo, had gathered in the lobby of the Whitcomb Hotel to discuss the fight. Around midnight, he observed Max as he drove up in his luxury convertible, parked it illegally on Market Street and "swaggered into the lobby, smiling and happy as if nothing had happened."[870]

As Max proudly recounted the glorious victory to his rapt audience, Frankie slipped into a coma. Elsie became progressively more hysterical as her husband's condition deteriorated, and it dawned on her death was the likely outcome. At 1:00 a.m. she was sent home and ordered into a physician's care. Frankie's sister Florence and Elsie's sister Bernice remained by his bedside. In the reception area, a row of chairs was filled with waiting figures, shoulders heaved in sorrow over their bent heads. [871]

Frankie's mother lived a hundred miles away in Sacramento with her son Dolph. She knew nothing of the tragic finale of the bout until she read it at dawn the next day in the early morning newspaper. Albina finally arrived at the hospital some three hours later. As she entered the room where her son lay, Elsie stood up and their anguished eyes met and held. After a moment of restraint, they fell into each other's arms and sobbed out their heartache for the boy they loved. [872] [873] [874]

Oxygen was administered to aid Frankie's respiration, but it was effectively a cheap parlor trick. There was no coming back from this. Realistically the man he had been died on the canvas the night before. The effervescent everyman with the crooked smile and the body beautiful was now just a memory.

Following an examination at 9:00 a.m. on the morning of August 26, 1930, which included x-rays and a withdrawal of fluids, all three physicians in attendance gave an update. "We have just made a test of Campbell's brain fluid and found he is in worse condition than last night. We doubt very much whether he will ever regain consciousness, and he is liable to die at any moment."[875]

Elsie hovered in the hospital room where her husband's life ebbed away. Time passed on tiptoes, as she held his body while it convulsed in waves of agony, as she wiped the fluids that dripped from his ears and eyes, from his nose and mouth; as she took care not to reopen the grievous wounds that covered his battered face.

Now and then her thumb slid over the wedding band on her finger, before it returned to caress her rosary beads as she whispered words to God; as if she could piece back together the broken parts of the man she adored, with the force of her faith. She prayed he came to consciousness just one more time, so she could profess her love. But she couldn't make him come back to her any more than she could capture the wind in a jar. [876]

Max arrived at the hospital, and advanced hesitantly toward the room where Frankie lay. He offered Elsie Camilli the hand that hit her husband. Resignedly she took that hand as the press hovered like vultures. With baited breath they strained to hear the interaction. The two stood speechless for a moment. "It was unfortunate. I'm awfully sorry," Max muttered nervously. Elsie looked up from that hand, and whispered the words every family member murmurs, after the ring death of a loved one, "It was not your fault. The same thing might have happened to you."[877] [878] [879] [880]

As Max quickly departed, reporters asked of her feelings toward him. She sighed at their continued intrusion, before she softly replied, "I have no room for bitterness in my heart today, only sorrow." She had been given firsthand accounts of Max Baer's determined slaughter of her husband. She also knew how the papers might skew her words around; she was careful to say nothing incendiary. As she sat beside her husband, she caressed her gently rounded belly and murmured to Cal, "I've got to keep up for the baby's sake." [881] [882]

Baer headed back to the Whitcomb Hotel, where Joe Custer of the *San Jose Mercury Herald* pressed him about the bout. "I can't let this interfere with my career," Max snapped, as he wore the carpet out in his room, "I was in there to win fair and square and I did my best. I pray that Frankie recovers."[883]

At mid-morning, while a massive crowd continued to stand outside the hospital, last rites of the Catholic Church were administered by the hospital's chaplain. With a lit candle laced between his crossed fingers, Elsie's hand lightly resting on his, Frankie Campbell's last breath quietly drifted from his lips. He was pronounced dead at 11:35 a.m., barely thirteen hours after the fight that was supposed to provide a better life for his family, and clear a path toward a title as Heavyweight Champion of the World.[884]

As the last tendrils of Elsie's hopes slipped away with him, she sobbed, "It's over. I can't believe he's really gone." Her vision blurred as a future without him loomed long before her. She dreaded having to let his mother know. Finally, she let go of his hand. She felt a longing as her fingers slipped away from its lingering warmth one last time. With a leveling breath, she turned and slowly approached the anteroom down the hall where the family waited. Upon hearing the news from

Elsie's lips, Albina Camilli made an unearthly noise that sounded only vaguely human and fainted to the floor.[885]

Frankie's brother Dolph Camilli, now first baseman with the Sacramento Senators, was on a late train north that night, to play a series the next day against the Beavers in Portland, Oregon. At a depot stop, a messenger boy located his seat and handed him a telegram that Frankie had been injured. Though he rushed to the next southbound train, he did not get back in time to be at his brother's side in his final moments.[886]

"I didn't think I could keep on playing after Frankie's death," Dolph would admit years later, "but somehow, I did. Frankie and I were that close. Yes, I was a great boxing fan then. But I haven't seen a bout since." [887]

Front page Oakland Post-Enquirer
(26 Aug 1930)

CHAPTER 29

IT WAS ALL SO UNCALLED FOR

THE ONLY DIFFERENCE BETWEEN STREET FIGHTING AND BOXING IS
THERE'S A REF THERE SUPPOSED TO STOP ME FROM KILLING YOU - MARVIN HAGLER

One hour after Frankie Campbell's death, Max Baer's arrest for manslaughter was ordered by Chief of Police William G. Quinn. Frankie's wife and mother declined to press charges. They were private women with an inclination to pacify not provoke. They had already witnessed the firestorm of threats and anger which had developed and wanted no part in it. Quinn directed the referee, the promoter, the managers, and the fighters' seconds, to make themselves available for questioning. A city-wide search was underway to locate referee Toby Irwin, who police had been unable to find, either at his home or in his usual haunts.

Two hours after Frankie's death, the fight's promoter Ancil Hoffman and Max Baer's lawyer Allen C. Cunha, accompanied Max as he surrendered to Detective Sergeant Otto Frederickson. They left immediately for the Hall of Justice. His face swollen from Frankie's punches Max posed for several photos as he was booked at the Central Prison. Stating he viewed the fight as one of the most brutal affairs in the history of boxing, bail was set by Superior Court Judge George H. Cabaniss in the amount of $10,000, the highest amount ever seen in the city for a manslaughter charge.[888]

Frankie's death was the second ring fatality in a week in San Francisco. Johnny Anderson, a nineteen-year-old novice in his second professional bout, fighting for a $20 purse at National Hall, had died the previous Thursday after being beaten over four rounds in a bout with Reinhardt "Red" Kuehl. The public outrage over Johnny's death had yet to settle down when Frankie was killed. It was suspected that in a temporary outburst of moral piety, Judge Cabaniss' record-breaking bail against Max Baer, was an attempt to somehow assure the city's citizens that authorities were taking the situation seriously.[889]

Ham Lorimer had flatly refused to bail out his fighter. While Max had left the ring as the mood of the crowd turned ugly, Ham had remained inside the ropes. While Max had made a quick appearance at the hospital for press coverage, Ham had accompanied the ambulances to both hospitals and waited outside Frankie's rooms all night and into the morning. Promoter Ancil Hoffman happily stepped up and took charge of obtaining Baer's freedom. Some have claimed Max spent all day in a jail cell. Despite the fact August 26 was a statewide primary election day, his wait was short; most of the time was spent being booked, posing for pictures, and waiting for completion of the process of counting out the bail money.[890]

Max Baer (left) booked for manslaughter by Judge Fritz (right)
Courtesy San Francisco Public Library, San Francisco History Center

Accompanying Max and Ancil to the Hall of Justice were several of Hoffman's assistants. They had arrived to pay Max's bail carrying large sacks which contained $33,351, the receipts of the fight taken in at the entrance wickets the night before. Of this, each fighter was to receive 27 1/2 % percent, or $9,171.63. The sacks were carried into the Bond and Warrant Office. Clerks laboriously counted out $10,000, approximately $900 more than Baer's share of the receipts, for the required bail in bills, dollars, halves, and quarters. [891] [892] [893] [894]

Accusations and censure by the press swirled like a raging wildfire around the parties involved. Contemporary works unceasingly repeat the words of one or two sports editors who sat ringside, or the opinions of people who were not at the fight, that claimed Baer was vilified or made an example of, that he threw a couple punches and Frankie suddenly collapsed, that he was well within his rights to do what he did, that it was all just an unfortunate accident.

No.

Never brought to light until now, are the dozens more sports writers, fighters, and spectators who sat ringside, and were not only thoroughly disgusted by Baer's actions in the ring, but slack-jawed as they tried to make sense of any fighter engaging in such a determined and lengthy slaughter upon an opponent.

A *San Francisco Chronicle* editorial piece written by sports columnist Prescott Sullivan, echoed the angered sadness which permeated the city. "It is difficult to find words sufficiently strong to condemn the episode at Recreation Park Monday night, when a young fighter, Frankie Campbell, was virtually beaten to death by his opponent.... Was there any sportsmanship on the part of his opponent? None! Not indeed for a moment! Although it was apparent to all that the boy was unconscious and was upright only because the ropes held him so, the unmerciful tattoo of his opponent's fist on his face went on, blow after blow.... Was there any action by the referee? Not a move! While the brutal work was at its worst, this official stood by without raising a hand to stop it. The fight was obviously over, but the referee calmly let the slaughter proceed without interruption.... And what did the police do? Nothing! Nothing whatsoever."[895]

Frankie had dropped within arm's reach of *Sacramento Union* sports editor Steve George, who described what he saw. "His upturned face showed the mutilation of a countenance carved by an artist's knife. His lips were torn, his eyes split, his nose battered, and blood flowed profusely from every wound. It was a pitiful sight, and one this writer will not forget, in all his days of living." [896]

Associated Press sports writer Russell Newland was six feet from the corner during the fight. Where, he asked, was the referee during this unnecessary beating? Why was Toby Irwin in back of the fighters, on the other side of the ring ten feet away? Why was he not a jump away, as any good referee would be, especially when fighters are on the ropes or in the corners? Newland described how for the first time in all his years sitting ringside, he lost his objective composure, stood up along with three other newspapermen in the same row, and shouted, "stop it!!" After the first two or three punches, Newland lamented, "it was all so uncalled for." [897]

Nat Fleischer, founder and editor of The Ring Magazine, regarded as one of the foremost authorities on the sport, was equally disgusted with how the fight was conducted. "His opponent was permitted by the referee, Toby Irwin ... to stand directly over the helpless creature and batter away." Nat stated that a referee's job was "to see that the rules are obeyed, that the men fight fairly and above all, to offer his protection to the man who is so helplessly beaten, that a continuation of the contest might prove fatal."[898]

Paul Lowry of the *Los Angeles Times* wrote, "Regulations say 'any physical actions which may injure a contestant, except by fair sportsmanlike boxing, are considered fouls.'" Lowry reasoned he could see no valid excuse, why the referee said such a blow as in the second round, was "fair sportsmanlike boxing" and if the rules supported it, then the rules needed amendment. He decried how after Max slugged Frankie in the head when the latter's back was turned, "Nothing was done about it. The state rules say this was a foul. Later Baer knocked Campbell unconscious on the ropes and continued to rain blows on the slumping body. Nothing was done about it, not until Campbell sagged to the floor, never to regain his senses." [899] [900]

Referee Toby Irwin confirmed to the press his actions favored racketeers. Asked the reason why he failed to act when it was obvious Frankie was in distress, Irwin said, "much money had been wagered by professional gamblers that Campbell would not be able to last five rounds.... I would not care to antagonize those gamblers."[901] [902]

The *Pomona Progress* sports editor was disgusted by such a statement. "Irwin was not thinking of the regulations when he saw Baer punching Campbell's brains away from his skull ... his mind was concentrated on keeping Campbell going, if he could, without any interference on his part to avoid the howls of the 'big money.'" [903]

One North Bay scribe wrote the fight would "no doubt go down in pugilistic history as one of the most brutal, most unsportsmanlike, and most inefficiently refereed boxing matches on record anywhere." San Francisco fight fans, he said, finally got what they had been clamoring for, "a bloody fistic battle to the death."[904]

The city's Italian newspaper sports editors were beside themselves over the appalling loss of one of their most promising sons. "There are two corpses here!!" they cried with shocked disbelief at yet another death in a San Francisco ring. They put to words what so many across the city were thinking. "BARBARIE!! BARBARIE!! BARBARIE!!" They denounced the unnecessary violence Max had exhibited against Frankie, as barbaric savagery on the level of cannibalism, and equal to the work of headhunters.[905] [906]

Frankie's manager "Silent Cal" Working was inconsolable and finally found his voice. He focused first on the fact that Max had ignored what little refereeing Toby Irwin had engaged in, and repeatedly fouled his opponent during the second round. He took the regulations and rules book from his pocket, and for a moment held it aloft before the press like a cross against the devil. Under the section for "Fouls," he quoted Rule #13. "The failure to obey the referee, or any physical actions which may injure a contestant except by fair, sportsmanlike boxing" constituted a foul. He might also have read aloud the next section, paragraph B, on when a fighter was considered "Down," which said: "A contestant shall be deemed 'down' when he is hanging helplessly over the ropes," and must not be struck.[907] [908]

Cal next excoriated Irwin, for his repeated failure to enforce the rules, and for allowing Baer to do as he wished. "He should have stopped the contest before he did. After my boy was out on his feet, he took enough punches to have done for ten other men." Then he went after the commissioner. "Yesterday morning I asked Traung not to appoint Irwin referee," he cried. "The commissioner paid no attention to me, although I asked him again at the weighing-in to name either Willie Ritchie or Jim Griffin."[909] [910]

Bob Shand of the *Oakland Tribune* had a curious take on the rules. While he said they specifically call for the men to protect themselves at all times; he used a moment in 1927, which didn't resemble the present circumstances one whit, to prove his point. When Jack Sharkey had turned his head for a split second in appeal to the referee, over Dempsey's numerous fouls in their title contender bout, Jack's left knocked him down for the ten-count. Bob claimed, "they lauded Dempsey for his smartness." He might have instead used the example of the Jack Sharkey–Tommy Loughran bout of just a year earlier, in pursuit of Gene Tunney's vacated heavyweight crown. An utterly dazed Loughran rose and turned his back as he wobbled against the ropes. Sharkey flew across the ring for another punch, but the referee pushed him off to protect Tommy. A referee doing his job didn't fit Bob's narrative.[911]

"Baer simply followed the code of the ring," Bob continued, "and the natural impulse of the born fighter. He punched and punched until his opponent was unconscious. That was his unwritten contract despite altruistic allusions to 'boxing' in the written contract. The 15,000 people who attended the fight came to see a knockout. They were warned that the fight could go the limit as the principals were the hardest hitters in the game. But even the most hardened men in the 'racket' wanted the affair over after that first punch in the fifth round."[912] [913]

****

Multiple contemporary arguments pull quotes from Ron Fimrite's 1978 article for *Sports Illustrated,* titled "Send in the Clown," which includes a discussion of the fight. But Fimrite's work is light on sources and incorrect on supposition. One such quote states, "at the weigh-in, both fighters were admonished by the State Athletic Commission to 'keep fighting as long as the other man is on his feet.'"

While Fimrite quotes *Oakland Tribune* retired sports editor Alan Ward by name in other areas of his article, he doesn't offer a single source for this particular statement. Ward was a human interest and "ladies who lunch" correspondent in 1930. He didn't pen his first sports article until June 1932, so it certainly didn't come from him. Realistically though, what commissioner would make such an amateur comment to two professional fighters with a combined sixty-seven fights under their belts?

The only remotely similar admonishment, stated for an entirely different reason—that the Baer-Campbell fight was "in the bag"—was relayed by *Oakland Post-Enquirer* sports editor Al Santoro in 1933. Santoro claimed rumors that the fight was fixed were so persistent, the commissioners had "hurried to the dressing rooms of each before the fight, shook a finger in the face of each, told both that they must make the best fight of their career or be banished from the ring."[914]

Ron Fimrite also states in his article that Frankie's "favorite tactic was playing possum," which was supposedly why Max continued to throw punches. That is a lie. No sports article which covered Frankie during the six years he actively fought, comments that he ever adopted tactics of faked injury or faked exhaustion, to lure his opponent into carelessness. He consistently waded in with both fists. He rarely backed up.

If anyone "played possum" it was Max Baer. An examination of press coverage of Max's early fights shows that if he didn't score an early kayo, he used the tactic to absorb punches until his opponent had exhausted himself, before he suddenly found his right and scored a knockout. After he saw Baer's first fight with Ernie Schaaf, Damon Runyon remarked on the tactic in disgust. "No one ever saw Dempsey fold his arms around his head and let his opponent pound away at his elbows."[915] [916]

Sports editor Harry B. Smith of the *San Francisco Chronicle*, focused on the viciousness of Baer's attack of Campbell. "Perhaps it was inexperience that caused Baer to batter a helpless opponent as he did in the fifth. That is a most charitable way of looking at the situation—far too charitable, I would say. Jeffries wouldn't do such a thing, and I've seen Joe Gans, in the old days, turn appealingly to a referee to stop a one-sided fight in which the Old Master was winning. Experience or no experience, there was too much cold-bloodedness in the spectacle we had to watch, and which sent so many away to their homes sick at heart."[917]

Harry offered an alternative possibility—where that word *anxious* crops up again—which was eerily almost word for word the same comments made ten months earlier, by Baer's friend Louis Lippi, about the first Tiny Abbott fixed fight. Lippi said, "Baer knew he could not disappoint his friend Larry Doyle, who bet every cent he had that Max would win in three rounds. This I believe caused Max to get very *anxious* in the third round" and commit the foul.

Harry noted in his own column, "even money offered that Campbell would not last five rounds. He didn't last five rounds, and possibly that is why Baer was so *anxious* to end the encounter." What gambler did Max hook up with this time to win in a specific round, only for Frankie to interrupt his plans, and make him *anxious* at the thought of lost money? [918] [919]

A spectator at the fight that night, told columnist Annie Laurie of the *San Francisco Examiner*, "I'll bet that seven out of ten of the men who saw Campbell beaten to death right before their eyes Monday night are tickled to death to think they were there to see it." Laurie herself, who enjoyed a well-fought bout, and was friendly with many of the great fighters of the past thirty years, was horrified. "This thing of throwing a man up against the ropes and crushing his head to jelly after he is unable to lift a finger to help himself—this thing of making an exhibit of plain brutal murder—isn't it just about time to put a stop to it?" [920] [921]

Former Heavyweight Champion James J. Jeffries, appears to be the only man interviewed by the press, who had both fought in a ring, and was ringside at the event. Jeffries had been beaten to a bloody pulp in 1910 by Jack Johnson, during the racially charged "Fight of the Century." He was one of the men to post bail for Jess Willard after Bull Young's death in 1913. Jeffries unequivocally wasn't buying the excuses of the pundits, or of Max Baer.

"No man ever had his brains beaten out in a boxing match in my day. No referee would have ever permitted such a thing to happen, nor were the fighters bloodthirsty enough to beat a helpless man as Baer did Campbell. Mashed his brains, the doctors say—and the boy out on his feet! The referee should have stopped it. He says he couldn't see Campbell. The crowd saw, didn't they? Why didn't he see it? That's what he's paid to do!"

"I would have given the fight to Campbell on a foul in the second round, when Max hit him from behind. I don't know whether it is a foul or not to hit a man like that, but it was a cowardly, unsportsmanlike thing to do, and I would have stopped it. Campbell was walking to his corner, giving Baer the count! There weren't any boxers in my day who had such a 'will to win' that they would resort to such tactics as that to do it. I don't think many of the boys in the ring today would hit a man who wasn't looking. I don't believe Campbell would have pulled a stunt like that. He would have touched gloves with his opponent before continuing. Any clean boxer would; that's the sporting thing to do."

"In my opinion the law which compels a man to walk to a neutral corner after a knockdown is a foolish one. When I was fighting, a fighter scoring a knockdown was required to move away a reasonable distance, and if he didn't the referee wouldn't start the count. But since there is such a law, the fighter should be protected from such attacks by the referee. A warning shout wouldn't have hurt anything, and in this case probably would have saved the life of a game young man."

"I am satisfied from all accounts that it was that cowardly blow which snapped something inside Campbell's head. Frankie was following the rules as well as he could; the rules state that a man must protect himself at all times, but with that law how is it possible to always be facing an opponent? A man can't back into his corner! That was ten times as brutal a fight as any ever staged during my boxing career. Campbell's seconds could have saved their man when he told them something in his head had snapped. It was butchery to allow it to go on in that fifth round; Baer was simply hammering a dying man. Exhibitions like that disgust a true sportsman."

Jim Jeffries and Frankie Campbell at Jim's Burbank CA ranch (Nov 1929)
Courtesy Harry E. Winkler Collection, University of Notre Dame

Beloved veteran San Francisco sports editor Art Rosenbaum, shared a story in the 1960s, how as a teenager he and his pals snuck to a locally known spot at Recreation Park's left field, where you could climb over the fence, drop down several feet, and get in for free. During the fifth round of the Baer–Campbell bout, thinking the yelling was enthusiasm for a good fight, they crept to seats emptied because fans were in a crush around the ring.

Some stood rooted in place completely captivated, others thoroughly aghast by the scene. Some jumped up and down, arms waving wildly with enthusiasm, others in horror and disgust. As the boys got nearer, they could hear the shouts of, "Stop it! Stop it! It's murder!" Art declared after what he saw Max do to Frankie, the "Old Rec" ceased to ever again be a friendly haven to him and his pals. When months later it was demolished to build Seal's Stadium, he applauded its destruction.[922]

In the midst of the tumult and the shouting, sports writer Sid Ziff fondly remembered the Frankie Campbell he knew, during his successful comeback in Los Angeles. "He took a keen pleasure in his ring success. But he was never boastful or arrogant about his conquests."

Sid once asked Frankie whether he thought he could beat Armand Emanuel. "I don't know," he replied, with a flash of his crooked smile, "but I'd like to try."

One night after a particularly easy fight at the Hollywood Legion he rushed to the radio broadcast microphone and addressed remarks to his mother, "Don't worry mother, I'm alright."[923]

Stub Nelson of the *Los Angeles Record* remarked on the man he remembered, and on Frankie's thoughts about his upcoming fight with Baer. "Campbell was an extremely pleasant young man—a good mixer who had the knack of making friends. He was just as natural and unaffected as a grammar school kid—and eager to please." Frankie, he said, had staked all on the fight. "It was do-or-die with him. If he lost, he wanted to lose gallantly."

"I'll give him all I got and if I win, I'll continue fighting." Frankie vowed. "If he stops me, I'll go down fighting and take that nice chunk of money as a starter in some business."[924]

Mark Kelly of the *Los Angeles Examiner* had spoken to Frankie on several occasions, and tabbed him as a genuine person, a determined fighter not given to arrogance, and utterly devoted to his family. "So often is the term 'fine fellow' applied indiscriminately and undeservedly, that it loses its punch. But Campbell was a gentlemanly chap, quiet, reserved, loyal to family ties and friends ... his life was wrapped up in his family to such an extent, that he had promised his wife should he lose to Baer decisively, he would quit the game and go into business."[925]

"I met Campbell three or four times and was impressed with his belief in himself, his desire to get to the top of the heavyweight heap." Kelly continued, "I asked him why, and he said that fighting was the quickest road to comfort for his wife and youngster—that's why he wanted to absorb so much of it before someone better than he belted him out of the picture." [926]

EAGLE SOUP

Two days after Frankie's death, accompanied by his lawyers Allen C. Cunha and John J. Allen Jr., Max Baer appeared in court to be arraigned on a criminal charge of manslaughter before Municipal Judge Albert J. Fritz. Max had tried in vain to arrange it so he need not be present at the proceedings. When this was denied, he was nearly an hour late and was harshly reprimanded by the judge. Before a packed courtroom, the judge announced *Case #13; the State of California vs. Max Baer.* [927] [928]

After the charges were read, and Max pled not guilty, his lawyers immediately asked that the $10,000 bail set by Superior Court Judge Cabaniss be reduced to $1,000. Judge Fritz denied the request. He wasn't familiar with the circumstances of the fight and he was not the one who had set the amount. Baer's attorneys asked for a continuance to September 12 for the preliminary hearing—where a prosecutor presents evidence to show probable cause a crime was committed and a defendant should face trial—which the judge approved. The D.A.'s office wanted to wait until the coroner had conducted his inquest, as required by law to determine cause for violent deaths. [929] [930]

Max was observed to be nervous and white-faced by some scribes as he answered Judge Fritz' questions. Though not too nervous that he didn't pose for some suitably dramatic press photos with the judge during the encounter. "I went into the ring to do my best," he said before the packed courtroom. "I can't express how sorry I am that the fight ended as it did." As soon as he cleared the court house doors after the proceedings, reporters surrounded him on the front steps. He was pressed further about his actions in the ring, until he blew his stack.

Forty-eight hours after Frankie's death, Max shrugged off his contriteness like a snake sheds its skin. The coroner had barely stitched up Frankie's ruined head a few floors below the courtroom—and Max's handlers had already reached out to

New York matchmakers to arrange his next fight, because the East Coast clamored to sign a killer—when Max spun toward the newshawks who hovered around him in front of City Hall, and dared to question him.

"I have my career to think of!" he growled, "This whole thing is terrible, but I can't let it ruin my life! It was only a boxing match, and although I tried hard to win, I couldn't foresee such a result!" And there he was. Gone was the charmer, the jokester, the good time fellow. Jekyll had turned into Hyde. He angrily insisted he had played the game according to the rules, and refused to reply to questions about fouls and sportsmanship. [931] [932] [933]

****

Then like the first sporadic drops of a rainstorm, a whisper campaign began to take shape. It started to appear by dribs and drabs in the press. Max and his handlers figured, why not direct fault away from him and place it squarely on a dead man who couldn't tell his side of the story? Why not question Frankie's suitability, not only as an opponent, but to insinuate his condition was questionable? And why not present Max as a dumb kid fresh off the farm, as a novice who didn't know any better? It was the beginning of a crusade of lies that endures to this day, which successfully gained traction and rolled through the decades, without a care for the truth.

Max claimed he did not realize that Frankie was limp and 'out' when he kept up his bombardment. But Max Baer was hardly a novice. This had been his twenty-seventh professional fight. James J. Jeffries engaged in only twenty-one fights during his entire boxing career, seven of which were title defenses. Recall what Sid Ziff noted just six months earlier after the first Baer-Owens bout: "Whatever you say about Baer, he has guts and a cool knowledge of his own capabilities." After Max had knocked Owens senseless to the canvas in the eighth, he "walked nonchalantly over to the other side of the ring. He knew his man was out." As far back as December 1929, seven months into Max's professional career, veteran *San Francisco Examiner* sports editor A.T. Baum noted that, "his ring generalship is remarkable." [934] [935]

When Ancil Hoffman tried to blame Frankie's death on the weight difference, the press eagerly took the bit and ran with that for a while. But with very few exceptions over his career, especially once he entered the heavyweight ranks, it was rare for Frankie to have height and weight advantages. More often than not, he gave away ten or more pounds and won handily. Next Ancil pondered perhaps his mind was troubled going into the fight and he was scared of the coming encounter. He indicated his ring physician Dr. McNulty, who examined both principals before the fight, told him "Campbell was in better physical condition than Baer. I had been told that Campbell weighed well over 180 pounds, and his advisers are inclined to believe he worried off many pounds the night before the fight."[936]

Frankie's manager Cal Working hotly repudiated such claims. "There is much a about who made the match," he said. "I can tell you. It was Frankie Campbell who insisted. I had not been too anxious for the bout until after I saw the Baer–Kennedy fight. But before that, Frankie had watched Baer box Owens and sent word to me that he wanted the Baer fight. He was confident from start to finish and not worried in the slightest degree."[937] [938]

Finally Max and his handlers landed a first blow in the court of public opinion. Rumors were floated it had been kept secret that a hit by a baseball bat had fractured Frankie's skull as a child, that he may have even had some kind of mysterious medical condition, and he had no business being in the ring.

Frankie's wife Elsie Camilli deflected the claims immediately. She had grown up with her husband. She confirmed he had never fractured his skull, and that the only time Frankie had ever landed in a hospital was mere months ago for his nose, his tonsils, and his teeth. But by as early as 1932, variations of the claims had stuck and were taken as gospel among the press. Columnist Frank Menke for the *International News Service* airily claimed Frankie was poorly conditioned, that Max draped him all over the ropes, and that Max even pleaded with Toby Irwin to stop the fight. By 1941, syndicated columnist Bill Cunningham stated with authority, but without a source, that Frankie "was known to have a skull like a paper shelled pecan." In 1949, Santa Rosa, California *Evening Press* sports editor Howard Smith claimed after a recent ring death, that an unnamed doctor indicated Frankie had an exceptionally "thin brain pan."[939] [940] [941]

San Francisco County Coroner Dr. Thomas Byers Woods Leland had specifically instructed Autopsy Surgeon Augustus A. Berger, to look for prior health conditions during the autopsy. Nowhere in his report or in pathology results did he allude to any such aberrations or prior injuries to Frankie's skull. None of the doctors who were present at the post-mortem exam, ever remarked publicly or in scholarly works, that Frankie's skull, his brain, or its supporting parts, were anything other than normal and healthy, prior to Max Baer obliterating them.[942] [943] [944]

Max's family hurried to speak to the press in an attempt to polish his image. "Nobody feels sorrier over the tragic ending of the bout than Baer. The big kid is heartbroken and ready to quit the racket," said his father, Jacob Baer. "He worked himself into a frenzy when Tillie Herman and Ray Pelkey shouted at him from Campbell's corner. Herman had trained Max for the bout and then appeared as chief second for Max's opponent. The taunts from the opposite corner hurt my boy and he lost his head. We are all sick and disgusted with the whole affair. His mother is confined to her bed and his sister is on the verge of a breakdown. It is all too terrible. Of course, we want to do everything we can for Frankie's widow. She is the one who is suffering the most."[945]

While heartfelt, if after this statement, Jacob Baer or his wife Dora, two retirees who loved chattering incessantly to reporters, or if any of Max's siblings ever reached out to, or lifted a single finger to help or comfort Elsie Camilli and her son, it was never remarked upon by either family or by the press.

Less than twenty-four hours after Max had indicated on the courthouse steps, that he wouldn't let Frankie's death ruin his boxing career, his manager Ham Lorimer entered the fray for some damage control. Max's heartless words had made the city and its citizens livid with anger. The Mission District was a tinderbox just waiting for one more match to set it off. Ham did an adroit pivot; he now claimed Baer misspoke; he thought he might quit the game after all. "Max is heart sick. He can't sleep and he can't eat. He tells me he doesn't want to fight again, and the only thing that might persuade him back into the ring would be in the event of a benefit show to aid the widow of Frankie Campbell and her child."[946]

Yet when Ed Lynch, the Dreamland's promoter, reached out to Max and his handlers with an offer to put on a boxing card, and donate half the proceeds to Elsie and her son, if Max gave half of his purse from the fight, Ed's calls went unreturned. Max later claimed he visited Elsie soon after he killed her husband, to tell her the only inducement to fight again, was if he gave her part of all his future purses, but that she said it was not necessary. Max made this claim repeatedly through the years; contemporary works treat it as truthful. If Max had actually made such an offer, then why refuse to do exactly that when Ed Lynch made his proposal? Other than one single benefit in 1935, heavily covered in the press, why are there zero feel-good stories in the years which followed, that Max ever gave Elsie one nickel from his "future purses?"[947] [948] [949]

****

Later that day, Dr. Tilton E. Tillman—speaking for the Camilli family and his fellow colleagues, Dr. Frank Sheehy and Dr. Edmund Morrissey, who had worked over Frankie all night—declared that "death had been caused by a succession of blows on the jaw, and not by any struck on the rear of the head," and that "Campbell's brain was knocked completely loose from his skull. If it had been a case of one cerebral hemorrhage, or two, or even three, we might have saved his life. But his brain tissue literally was one huge mass of bruises. There was nothing to be done."[950]

The mechanics of a punch to the head and jaw, and the angles from which they are thrown—especially at an unconscious man pinned in a corner—are worth noting when discussing the extensive damage Max inflicted to Frankie's brain and brainstem. Recall also that mouth guards were still of simple design. If they were even worn in the fight, they would have protected Frankie's teeth and gums, but offered no protection from Max's blows to his unprotected jaw, nor reduced impact and shock to his jaw, brain, skull and spine. [951]

Upon receipt of a single straight punch to Frankie's face, the motion of his head halted abruptly and inertia came into play. His brain rapidly sloshed around inside his skull like the yolk when shaken inside a raw egg. Such blows would have momentarily deformed his skull. A single punch to Frankie's jaw, added further trauma to the base of his skull and spine. The rotational force of a punch like a hook to the side of his head or jaw, caused a rapid outward rotation of his skull and violent twisting force to his brain.[952] [953]

253

As Max continued his uninterrupted assault, the arteries, nerve cells and blood vessels in Frankie's head were twisted, stretched, and ruptured. They were cut by bony protrusions in his skull from his brain slamming against it. The damage to the base of Frankie's brain was so severe, all the protective barriers in his brain and his spinal cord which kept his blood within its vessels burst like collective balloons. His own blood turned deadly, because blood carries waste products away from cells and transports them to the lungs, liver, and kidneys to be detoxified. Allowed to flow freely throughout his body, his blood attacked, permanently damaged, and killed his arteries, cells, and vessels.[954] [955]

Max's punch force could have been mitigated so long as Frankie could bob and weave; he could not only have slipped punches, but let his head and neck go with the blows. Pinned unconscious in a corner, he was helpless as he received the full force of Max's punches at least twenty times. The fact Max was allowed to throw repeated sub-concussive blows virtually guaranteed Frankie's death; he was in a battle from which he would never emerge victorious.[956] [957] [958]

Dr. Tillman's press statement was further corroborated by Dr. Berger—who not only conducted the autopsy, but was a close eye-witness to the fight—when he released his results. In his report summary, Dr. Berger noted there was extensive internal hemorrhage to tissue across the entire left side of Frankie's brain, the membrane covering the brain, and deep throughout the brain stem (the pons and medulla). Damage to the back of Frankie's head, and the base of his skull, was partially caused by trauma from the eight foul blows to the back of Frankie's head, that Toby Irwin allowed in the second round, and further exacerbated because he was unconscious, as Frankie's head repeatedly slammed against the turn buckle in the fifth round. [959] [960]

If by some miracle Frankie had survived, doctors told the press chances were high he would remain in a vegetative state, blind in one or both eyes, deaf, paralyzed, and prisoner to an iron long, the precursor to the modern ventilator, to breathe. But Frankie was a Camilli. He descended from shockingly strong stock. After such a merciless beating, virtually any other boxer would have breathed his last in that ring. Instead, he suffered through thirteen excruciating hours, suffering seizures, and gasping for breath while blood and spinal fluid leaked in a steady stream from every orifice, while hemorrhagic pressure caused his eyes to bleed, until his ravaged broken body slowly gave up its final fight. His transition was not peaceful and his final journey was not light. In the end, death was a mercy to him and to his loved ones who helplessly watched his struggle.

Cal Working later testified he had given Frankie smelling salts only after the second round. But more rumors were fed to the press that he had been given an injected stimulant prior to and during the fight. Baer and his supporters were desperate to lay the blame for Frankie's death on poor physical condition or artificial means gone wrong. The autopsy was an insult to a body already desecrated, yet they held no qualms to encourage further violations. Frankie's stomach was sent to be tested to determine whether he had been "doped or pepped up with poison." He tested negative for alcohol and strychnine. [961]

In the first half of the twentieth century, rudimentary performance-enhancing drugs were used by some corner men on their fighters, either before a fight or in the one-minute rest period between rounds. Strychnine, commonly used as rat poison, but also a popular drug to kill dogs, commit suicide, murder your enemies, and dope up race horses, was used by handlers in small doses to stimulate their fighter's central nervous system. Contents in a corner man's bag of tricks might include an array of concoctions for a burst of energy. "Eagle soup" consisted of strychnine, spirits of ammonia and either digitalis or nitroglycerin. A mixture of brandy and cocaine, or wine and spirits of ammonia, (smelling salts) were other popular options.

It was curious that Max and his supporters suggested Frankie used illegal stimulants, when in actuality he was the one who used them. Max garnered headlines nationwide at an August 1934 testimonial dinner in Oakland before 300 attendees, when he stated "Carnera's gloves looked big because of the strychnine given me before the fight." Though the audience clearly heard him use the words, when later informed that his title might be stripped from him for illegal drug use, he claimed it was a slip of the tongue. He said he meant to say he was given cherry wine and spirits of ammonia. [962]

In the days just before Max Baer lost his title to Jim Braddock in June 1935, Jim's manager Joe Gould dominated headlines when he reported Mike Cantwell, Max's former trainer and then Braddock's current trainer, confirmed Max was "hopped up on a load of strychnine" in a glass of wine before the Carnera bout. Gould said he would direct the boxing commission to monitor Max and his handlers to prevent such a repeat when Max defended his title.[963]

The rumors were persistent enough that in September 1935, Joe Louis' co-manager Joe Roxborough made an unprecedented request; "We will ask that the commissioners do something to prevent use of strychnine, hypodermic needles or any artificial stimulant" to ensure a fair contest.[964]

Mike Cantwell told a Buffalo, New York sports editor days before the Baer–Louis bout that "Max cannot fight unless he is all hopped up. The commission found that out and has put its foot down on his handlers giving him any dope in his stimulants." The reporter later noted Max's marked indifference in both the Braddock and Louis bouts. That his "inclination to be aggressive, to carry the fight to his man and to swing desperately and determinedly, as he did in the Carnera and Schmeling bouts, and the Levinsky affair, was conspicuous by its absence."[965]

Many of these elixirs were later found to be not only addicting, but damaging to a fighter's heart. Though his death certificate indicates an autopsy was not performed after his death, and his demise was likely hastened from genetics and the usual effects of the trifecta of smoking, noted obesity, and high cholesterol, Max Baer died of a heart attack at 50 years of age.

CHAPTER 31

APOLOGETIC WHITEWASHING

HELL IS EMPTY AND ALL THE DEVILS ARE HERE
- WILLIAM SHAKESPEARE

As Elsie Camilli reached up to the top shelf in search of her ebony hat, her son Frankie Junior's head bumped into her leg. He had started to crawl early and walking seemed but a short victory away. He wobbled up on his sturdy legs to clutch her darkly-hosed calf as he peered into the depths of the closet. He was already a strong and bold boy ready to challenge the world. He was so much like his father some days, she pondered how her heart continued to beat, so many pieces of it had been torn away.

She drew a raven coat with a fur collar around her charcoal dress, just as his curious eyes saw a familiar satchel on the floor. His eager fingers spilled its contents around him like hidden gifts. The familiar scent of her husband's hard-earned sweat wafted up from it to assault her wounded senses.

Her son smiled up at her with a familiar crooked grin. His new teeth gave him the look of a happy, drooling jack o'lantern. He dragged the pair of boxing gloves to his mouth and began to gnaw on the worn leather. As she pinned the hat with care upon her head, she looked down at their son. A tear dropped onto his dear inky curls. He was so much like his father.

On the same day final plans were approved to build the Golden Gate Bridge, the people of San Francisco buried one of their dead gladiators. A viewing of Frankie's remains was held in the chapel of McBrearty & McCormick Funeral Parlor on Seventeenth and Valencia streets.

Some members of the press, who observed the Camilli family seated in resigned silence near the casket as thousands of people filed by for a glimpse of the body, remarked that commercial fistiana, who's financial interests were bound up in the fight game, had taken command of the affair, and saw to it that Frankie's last public appearance was a gaudy one. It was suggested perhaps his family might have preferred a quiet setting to say goodbye to their boy. [966] [967]

A large procession then proceeded to St. Paul's Catholic Church, where the family members were congregants, for the funeral. It was attended by thousands of mourners. It brought the Mission District to a standstill. The streets for blocks on either side of the church were jammed. It was one of the largest and most elaborate funerals San Francisco had ever witnessed.

The funeral was an especially somber affair. There were no jokes or banter to break the tension. The multitudes filed in silently. Row after row of heads were bent over knuckles clenched white with anguish. Subdued weeping was layered with the murmurs of those reciting the rosary. Hundreds acted as honorary pallbearers, friends and relatives of Frankie, sports editors and writers, notables and ex-notables of the ring, and followers of pugilism who had known Frankie well. Dignitaries included soon-to-be Governor, San Francisco Mayor James Rolph, former State Senator Samuel C. Murphy, and Dolph's old boss San Francisco Seals ball club manager Nick Williams.

Frankie's Funeral (28 Aug 1930)
Courtesy San Francisco Public Library
San Francisco History Center

The casket was covered from end to end under a massive cascade of flowers. The words "Good-by Old Pal" were inscribed in roses on the top of the casket, sent by Mickey Walker and Jack Kearns. A cross of red carnations was the farewell of the Mission District boys with whom Frankie had grown up. The *San Francisco Examiner* noted "there were flowers in such abundance that Campbell might have been one of California's most conspicuous citizens, dead after a life of useful service to his state." To his family, his friends, and his fans, he was unquestionably worthy of the honors. [968] [969]

"Throughout the ceremonial of death," wrote Bob Shand of the *Oakland Tribune*, "the fighter's widow, Mrs. Elsie Camilli bore herself with the same air of tragic calm which has marked her since she first learned her husband might die. His mother, Mrs. Eliza Camilli, broke down during the singing of the mass."[970]

As she had proceeded up the steps into the church, photos captured Elsie as she stumbled to remain upright from the tears that flooded her eyes, her hand pressed tight against the ruin of her mouth, while she walked next to Frankie's father. She later collapsed when she returned home, and their son toddled into her arms, peering behind her in search of his father.

Alessio Camilli abandoned all pretense of stoicism; in every photo he mopped copious tears from his eyes, his hair disheveled from finger plows of anguish. Elsie's hand clung desperately to Dolph, who appeared thunderstruck as he clutched his mother's arm, guiding the two women along. The scent of flowers was overpowering as they dropped from the magnificent floral blanket that adorned the casket, to be trampled underfoot by the massive crowd.[971] [972]

(l-r) Albina, Dolph, Elsie, Alessio Camilli
(28 Aug 1930) Courtesy San Francisco Public Library
San Francisco History Center

Among the mourners at the church was Max Baer. He had not visited the chapel to view Frankie's body. He was observed as someone dropped him off moments before service began at the church. He arrived with protection. Agitation over what he had done to Frankie was so high, he had two armed men shadow his movements and peruse the throng of mourners.

Vehement curses were uttered in his wake, and so many spectators' eyes threw daggers at him, he largely remained on the periphery of the crowd. He was the cause of this funeral. He was not wanted nor welcome. Max did not attend the burial at the cemetery, though in 1932 he claimed he stood beside Elsie before Frankie's open grave as dirt was shoveled over the coffin. As mourners had proceeded to the cemetery, Max and his lawyers went downtown to appear before Judge Fritz to request a reduction in bail. It was denied. [973] [974] [975]

With a handkerchief pressed to his face, Max was observed to lean on Ham Lorimer when the crowd left the church. As they passed the press photographers, several requested some pictures of him. He carefully arranged his breast pocket square to a fine point, walked away from the crowds, and paused to lean dramatically against a pillar while the shutters clicked.

Strike the pose (28 Aug 1930)
Courtesy Oakland Post-Enquirer

With a quick switch in character, he cried out dramatically, "If this is the fight game, I want no more of it. I'd be happier back in the Livermore hills tending pigs. I'm sorry I ever drew on a glove.... I could never forget what *I've* gone through since poor Frankie went down."[976]

But as Ham and Max repeatedly declared that Baer thought he might quit the game, it was just more public spin, tossed into the current ambiguity of the situation. Three days after Frankie's death, word got back to local newsmen that Ham had confirmed with East Coast promoters Max could still expect to fight there.

In 1951, Max told a reporter that prior to the bout, he had already been promised big money for fights in New York if he won against Frankie. "I had to win that fight," he confirmed. "When he went down, I knew he was done." [977]

Some claim it was over one year before Max fought again; it was less than four months. New York approved Max to fight Ernie Schaaf in December 1930, Tom Heeney in January 1931, and Tommy Loughran in February 1931.[978]

Frankie's burial place at
Holy Cross Cemetery in Colma, CA
Courtesy findagrave.com

As St. Paul's church bells tolled the conclusion of the funeral mass, a line of automobiles over a mile in length proceeded to Holy Cross Cemetery in nearby Colma for burial. Final rites were delayed nearly thirty minutes for the procession of vehicles to draw up. Hundreds of floral arrangements, from massive displays to simple bouquets surrounded the gravesite.[979]

Jack Dempsey did not attend the funeral. Los Angeles scribes reported he slipped quietly out of town on the 27th via a train headed east, where he intimated, he expected to get "close to 50 g's" for an appearance and referee tour. He sent a telegram of condolences and a floral arrangement to the family.

The only known public comment Jack ever made about his dead protégé was before he refereed the Max Baer–Paulino Uzcudun bout in 1931.

"For my part I will try as referee to do things properly. What happened with Campbell and Baer was wrong and should never have happened."[980]

With Frankie's passing, Dempsey soon pivoted to become personally involved in assurances that Max became a success; he had privately bought a 7.5% cut of Baer's contract just before the Uzcudun fight. By 1933, Jack was often referred to by the press as Max's co-manager. He confirmed in 1935 just prior to the fight with Joe Louis, that he had a financial interest in Baer.[981] [982]

****

In the days that followed Frankie's death, before the commencement of boxing events across the state, the lights were dimmed, the crowd stood, and with bowed heads the ring bell was tolled ten times. The day after his death, ring announcer Dan Tobey paid "sterling tribute" to Frankie's memory before the Ace Hudkins–Jack McVey main event down south at the Olympic Auditorium.

Three days after Frankie's death, nine men were indefinitely suspended from further activities by the State Boxing Commission pending investigation of the situation: Max Baer, referee Toby Irwin, Baer's manager J. Hamilton Lorimer,

Frankie's manager Cal Working, Frankie's seconds Tom Maloney, Tillie Herman, and Larry Morrison, and Max's seconds Ray Carlin and Frankie Burns.

Max was given a special dispensation regarding use of his boxing license until the investigations played out. He could fight only if it was to stage a benefit for Elsie Camilli and her son. But a benefit wouldn't result in a payday for the perpetually in debt fighter.

Ancil Hoffman was actively working to finalize a fight in New York, but California also remained on the table. Ancil snorted indignantly that he had friends in all the right places, and was personally unaffected by the outcome. He stated his intentions to promote the next big fight in California that he could sign. "My conscience is clear and I see no reason why I should not keep right on promoting." 983 984

The local papers breathlessly reported the same day that gangsters were hunting down Max Baer. Four men, "reportedly from the San Francisco underworld," had knocked on Papa Baer's door. They issued threats when he declared Max was not home, and that he had to bar them from entry. Armed police purportedly patrolled the home's perimeter. But it was just a made-up story. The next day, the family denied any such thing ever happened.985

While the boxing commission promised a thorough investigation, their first meeting was behind closed doors. No witnesses were called, and no statements were issued afterwards. The press, who in the past had repeatedly watched fistiana unerringly circle the wagons, didn't expect in the end that much would be done, stating "the usual apologetic white-washing was anticipated."986 987

Sports editor Buddy Leitch of the *San Jose Evening News* compared the already negligible actions by the boxing commissioners to ringmasters of a three-ring circus, who's clowning stunts to make any effort to investigate Frankie's death should have taken place under a gaudy striped tent, instead of in a suite at the Whitcomb Hotel. After a three-hour session, in which no witnesses were called, "the three ringmasters brushed the ashes off their cigars, emerged from their secret confab, and postponed any further action." It was Buddy's opinion that their confusing silence provided no assurances to the public that any changes would be made, or that the racketeers would be routed from the game. 988

"Why not admit the truth, tell what little they do know about it, and start the ball rolling toward the betterment of the game, instead of marking time and allowing grass to grow under their feet? The state commission is the only body that can clean these undesirables from its ranks. Why not act and act fast to expose the underhanded work, if any, connected with the death of Frankie Campbell?"989

The state commission realistically could not objectively investigate the failures of the few laws it had set, but repeatedly refused to enforce. They didn't dare enact new regulations to address racketeers. Promoters, matchmakers, politicians, venue owners, the commission, and the press had a symbiotic relationship to keep the gravy train rolling. Sports editors were not investigative reporters, their job was to engage, entertain, and encourage sales of their papers. Control would not be given up and fault would not be admitted, so pockets would continue to be lined. Then as now, the main purpose of a State Boxing Commission is to oversee the tax that comes to the state. It's not to protect the fighters. It's about the money first. Next, it's to protect the politicians who oversee the state, and those politicians are the men who appoint the commissioners in the first place. The fighters come last.[990]

The county grand jury announced they planned to step in, since the boxing commission appeared to have washed its hands of the affair. Jury foreman John P. Murphy stated several members had demanded that the entire body get to the bottom of the tragedy. In the past, it has not been their policy to conduct investigations with a view toward criminal prosecution where sport matters are concerned. They preferred to leave that procedure to the regular county and state officers. However, several members of the jury believed that crimes had been committed, and insisted upon jury action.[991]

The movers and shakers of boxiana all across the state had valid reason to expect that the sport might again become illegal. The *San Francisco Examiner* led a drive to repeal the state boxing law that had been in place since 1925. There was discussion of enactment of a local city ordinance, but the state law was framed not to permit such restrictions. An attempt to place a repeal on the ballot couldn't occur until the next election cycle, which was two years away. Anti-boxing groups pressured the state legislature to issue a referendum for a general member vote which would produce an immediate decision. But just as many wealthy men involved in the game had friends in the legislature, and the efforts were ultimately unsuccessful.[992]

Mark Kelly of the *Los Angeles Examiner* held scant hope that anything would change. "The clamor that follows any sport tragedy will die down and Baer will go on to bigger and more lucrative slaughters elsewhere."[993]

****

On August 30, four days after Frankie's death, Commissioner Charles Traung approved a permit for promoter Al Young to resume the Wednesday Night Fights at National Hall. It was under the guise of a benefit event for Frankie's pregnant widow and child, and the family of young Johnny Anderson. Frank Schuler at the Dreamland Auditorium announced plans to host a benefit as well.

The press was outraged. The front page of the *San Francisco Examiner* called it a flimsy pretext of a benefit and a "shocking announcement of a new fight, made only 24 hours after the last rites had been said over Frankie Campbell." They thought to grant such permits was the most flagrant abuse of power yet exhibited, and said "the rank commercialization of two recent killings was final proof of the sordidness and degradation of this 'sport.'"[994]

Some claim the *Examiner*, under publisher William Randolph Hearst, was the sole arbiter of a determined campaign to end boxing in the state after Frankie's death. But many in the press, in the boxing industry, and especially fight fans, were similarly appalled. They voiced the opinion that no new rules to protect fighters had been enacted, and any proposed benefits to aid the families of two dead fighters, were nothing more than subterfuge by promoters and racketeers, to determine whether box office receipts would suffer.

Spectators said it with empty seats the night of the first benefit; they stayed away in droves from National Hall; less than half the seats were filled. Instead of the usual shouts of "kill him," whenever a fighter was knocked to the canvas, the hall erupted with cries of, "stop it!" After Frank Schuler at the Dreamland heard what happened at the National, he abandoned the idea of his benefit altogether. [995]

That evening, Police Captain Fred Lemon, who was lead investigator for the Homicide Squad, announced that, "Max Baer, Oakland fighter, continued to punch Frankie Campbell, his opponent in a prize fight last Monday night, after it was clearly evident to all concerned that Campbell had been knocked unconscious—and it was these blows that caused Campbell's death." Lemon said these accusations were among other charges he planned to lay before the District Attorney's office during Baer's preliminary hearing.[996]

While the various factions in San Francisco fought like wildcats in a burlap bag over boxing's future in the state, Max Baer had left town. He later stated on numerous occasions he was so distraught, that for weeks he could barely function.

In actuality, five days after the fight he drove to Reno, Nevada to escape the endless questions and accusations by the public, and the constant hounding by the local press. He later claimed it was the first week of October, a full five weeks, before he left the Bay Area, but this was a lie. Local newspapers reported on his activities in Reno as soon as he hit town. [997] [998]

In one of countless 'Life Stories" Max gave in 1934 to multiple newspapers, before his June title fight with Heavyweight Champ Primo Carnera, he claimed after his suspension by the commission, he was still so crushed that he "didn't much care whether they made it a month, a year, ten years. I had lost my enthusiasm for the game. I felt afraid to try to fight again—afraid I might kill somebody else."

However, the Nevada papers reported as soon as Max had arrived in Reno, and during trips between court appearances, he attended local fights, was sparring partners with fighters Madison Dix and Red McDonald, who were matched at the Reno Arena, trained at the local boxing gym to keep trim in anticipation of his next bout, stayed at a luxurious private bath house, located over a mineral bath at Reno Hot Springs, and partook of all that Reno offered in the way of carousing, gambling, and dancing at the nightclubs. [999] [1000] [1001] [1002] [1003] [1004]

****

On August 31, five days after Frankie's death, a reporter in Reno sat down with Max for an interview. He casually admitted to the reporter he knew the exact punch which had knocked Frankie unconscious. It was his opinion that it was not the right cross, as much of the press had supposed, but the left hook just before it, which knocked him out and put him on the ropes. Max "believed at the time, he said, that Campbell was holding himself up" but that "subsequent examination convinced him that Campbell had been knocked out with the first blow and it was the middle rope that held him up." [1005]

Max slipped up in several areas of this one interview. In the Bay Area, he had embraced his fresh-off-the-farm shtick, and he simply didn't know Frankie was out. He was quoted in multiple papers during this timeframe with claims that, "I was pretty much out of my head and didn't know all that happened." His Father said he "worked himself into a frenzy," and "lost his head."

Away from the circus in San Francisco, and sitting before a comforting ear, he states in the Reno interview he was aware of the exact punch which did the deed. He inadvertently admitted he was aware enough in the moment to decide Frankie held himself upright, and it was not the ropes that kept him off the canvas.

He was thinking in there. He had made note of Frankie's actions and reactions. Like any experienced fighter, he had conscious split-second thoughts and predictions, weighed his options, and made decisions. Since the fight wasn't filmed, one wonders who provided a "subsequent examination" of the event to arrive at such "new conclusions." [1006]

Max Baer may not have had good defense techniques, or been elegant in his delivery, but he was not by any means even remotely a novice when he entered the ring that night. Ask any professional fighter with even half the number of the twenty-seven fights Max had under his belt, and they will tell you they literally feel when they land that kind of shot. Ask anyone who works with journeyman amateur fighters and they will support the same premise. [1007] [1008]

A fighter knows how deeply they have their opponent in trouble. If the spectator in the back row of the ballpark knew the exact moment Frankie Campbell was knocked unconscious, then Max Baer, as the one inches from his opponent, certainly knew too. Yet he made a conscious decision to throw at least twenty more unanswered punches at an opponent he knew was out cold.

264

The Reno reporter, who had not seen the fight, innocently pivoted subjects and delicately asked Max what he thought about "the [fight] situation in San Francisco." For weeks after this interview, even as Ancil Hoffman was dickering in New York for his next fight, Max insisted he was too affected by Frankie's death and would never box again. Yet he nonchalantly replied back, just over one-hundred hours after the fight, that he didn't think Frankie's death and his hand in it would affect prizefighting much in California, and unless the unforeseen occurred, he expected to fight Otto von Porat at Recreation Park in about six weeks.[1009] [1010] [1011]

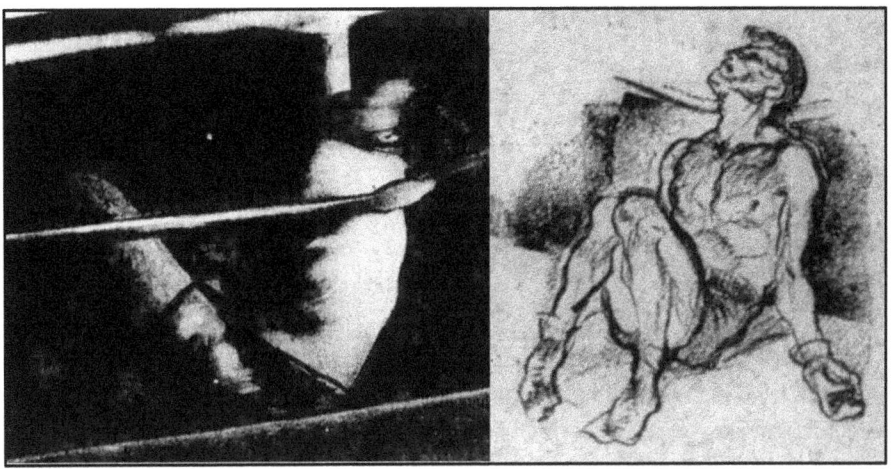

Photo (left) / Illustration (right) of Frankie down (25 Aug 1930)
Howard Robbins / Gregor Duncan

CHAPTER 32

TOSSED TOWELS

BOXING IS THE ONLY JUNGLE WHERE THE LIONS ARE AFRAID OF THE RATS
- JACK NEWFIELD

The men in control of boxing were desperate for the story to die down so they could return to business as usual. It was wishful thinking. This was a tsunami after an earthquake; it was just getting started and it was going to come at them from every direction. The outrage and opinions from several sources, in the days before official inquiries were anticipated to begin in earnest, came in waves that spread across the state.

Speaking from the pulpit one Sunday, the Rev. Dr. Daniel William Stevens, a Spanish-American War veteran who was among the calvary which stormed San Juan Hill with Teddy Roosevelt's "Rough Riders," gave a passionate sermon on the "legalized butchery known as boxing." The Reverend decried the interests who profited from the prize ring, and said they would not lightly relinquish their hold, merely because two human pawns had been sacrificed.[1012] [1013] [1014]

In a slam against Commissioner Charles Traung's erratic behavior during his tenure, Mark Kelly with the *Los Angeles Examiner*, blamed his regular and repeated failures for boxing's deplorable condition. "The percentage of connivers in the racket runs very, very high," he noted. Known fixers had been allowed to go their merry way polluting the sport. Yet when the commissioner was asked why a cleanup against certain men was not affected, "we have no evidence," was usually the excuse used. "Give us men who rout the connivers without waiting for flagrant evidence," he encouraged. Yet Kelly held out scant hope that the new incoming Governor, former San Francisco Mayor "Mission Jim" Rolph, would appoint a commission based on fitness, instead of one solely related to politics.[1015]

Even the American Legion, who's members had a hand in drafting, and had enthusiastically sponsored, the bill which made prizefighting legal again in 1925, washed their hands of the sport. A leading editorial in their monthly magazine for

September, demanded that prizefighting be cleaned up or wiped off the statute books. They declared that fighting in the state had degenerated into a "bloodthirsty Roman holiday" and accused gamblers of being responsible.[1016] [1017]

Curmudgeonly Oakland sports editor John J. Connolly later recalled a moment two weeks after Frankie's death that broke his gruff heart. It occurred over the Labor Day weekend in 1930. He was down in Los Angeles to cover the Oaks' game against the Sacramento Senators at Wrigley Field. He ran into the Senator's manager Buddy Ryan, and after they caught up for a bit, he looked around the near-empty field for someone he had become quite fond of. "Where's Dolph?" he asked. Buddy's face fell as he pointed wordlessly to a dark corner of the dugout. Dolph Camilli sat alone with his head in his hands as he quietly continued to mourn his brother.

"He'll never get over it," Buddy whispered as he removed his hat to run a weary hand through his hair. "But see if you can cheer him up," he said with an encouraging shoulder bump. "We need him, and I want to keep on playing him to keep him from falling to pieces."

For fully half an hour in the quiet of that warm summer day, John sat next to his young friend and gave him a shoulder to lean on. While the Camillis had not publicly voiced their feelings about the fight, to avoid adding gasoline to a bonfire, privately it was a different story. Dolph was intensely bitter and angry toward Max Baer for what he had done to his brother, and toward referee Toby Irwin for doing nothing while it happened. He blamed both men for Frankie's death. Dolph's son Rich, later confirmed to author and boxing historian Glen Sharp when the two worked together, that the family felt Max intentionally hurt Frankie. The Camillis keenly resented Max's enduring legacy as a loveable, gentle giant, when they viewed his actions as murder.[1018]

"Frankie should have stayed a ball player," Dolph cried to John as he dashed tears from his eyes. "He was a better hitter, a better fielder, and faster than me. WHY didn't he stay in baseball?" he asked as he looked helplessly to John for answers. John had no reply. He could only shake his head in sorrow at a life cut short and the heartrending grief of his pal.[1019]

****

On September 5, Coroner Dr. Leland announced his intentions to convene a coroner's inquest on the 16th, to review evidence of Frankie's death and question all individuals involved in the Baer–Campbell fight. District Attorney Matthew Brady continued Max's preliminary hearing to the following day, and stated the grand jury would shortly be empaneled to begin an investigation into prizefighting in general, and the recent deaths of Frankie Campbell and Johnny Anderson in particular.[1020]

Matthew Brady had quite a sordid history during his tenure as a District Attorney. During the 1921-1922 rape and murder trials of film star Roscoe "Fatty"

Arbuckle, Brady's pursuit of a guilty plea for Arbuckle in the death of Virginia Rappe, was said to have gone well beyond prosecutorial zeal, and become a largely self-serving hunt for a sensational win that promised to catapult him into the Governor's office. Witness intimidation, suppressed evidence, and encouragement to lie under oath was rampant.

It later emerged that Arbuckle's boss at Paramount Pictures, Adolph Zukor, having determined his star's public persona was utterly destroyed, decided to cut his losses. Two checks totaling $20,000 and dated during Arbuckle's trials, were made out to Matthew Brady to ensure a conviction.[1021]

After a third jury in a third trial again found Arbuckle not guilty, all twelve jurors and both alternates wrote Roscoe a heartfelt note of apology, and stated he was unequivocally innocent.[1022] [1023]

District Attorney Matthew Brady (1925)
Courtesy Bancroft Library, University
of California, Berkeley

Brady hid his ambitions behind rosy cheeks, a fatherly demeanor, and a voice said to be soothing and beguiling. But a corrupt smiled bloomed easily on his lips. And he liked to help his pals. Recall that his golfing partners and personal friends were Commissioner Charles Traung, Baer–Campbell promoter Ancil Hoffman, and Assemblymen William Hornblower and Harry Morrison. Just as Traung and Irwin ruled their corner boxing fiefdom, Brady operated under his own agenda. He could persecute or protect at his leisure.

Ultimately, he kowtowed to his friends in the state legislator. Prizefighting put too much coin into state coffers, and into the hands of its profiteers, who whispered into the right ears of politicians, judges, and prosecutors like Brady. Money was proffered by the men who controlled boxing, ostensibly as donations to political pet projects and campaign funds. In reality, they were bribes to insure they had friends in all the right places, which included the courts.

Matthew Brady's bias to taint the jury pool, was both subtle and overt. After Toby Irwin gave Max Baer a clean bill of health and proclaimed he had broken no rules, Commissioner Charles Traung then absolved Irwin of any blame. He expressed the opinion that "Irwin had performed his duties well." In turn, Brady declared that since it was Irwin and Traung's opinion that no regulations had been broken, his case was weak. He told the press, "The fact that the state boxing law was not violated, has important bearing upon the manslaughter charge."[1024] [1025] [1026] [1027]

Brady even indicated how he planned to direct any court proceedings, because he already knew the outcome. After he publicly downplayed Baer's savagery, he focused on a person the press and the public wanted to punish: referee Toby Irwin. Then he made it the problem of the boxing commission, who had thrown their support behind their referee. Brady already knew no action would be taken against Toby Irwin.

"Sport is not murder, neither is murder sport," he piously declared. "If we can't have honest boxing bouts in San Francisco—if we can't have bouts that stop short of public executions—we would be better off without any.... In the case of Frankie Campbell, the man appears to have been gradually murdered on his feet. I do not blame Max Baer so much. He was in the ring solely for the purpose of knocking out his opponent if he could. He had been getting the worst of the bout and I can readily imagine that in his pain and fury he reverted to savagery and became a killer. But there is one other man in that ring who was neither in pain nor in fury and who should have stopped the fight long before it stopped itself—that was the referee."[1028]

Brady tapped Assistant District Attorney John Roland Tyrrell to participate at the coroner's inquest, and then to lead the grand jury proceedings. Requests to testify at both investigations had been issued to all direct participants at the fight. An angry public was assured an indictment of Max Baer by a grand jury was possible, and the results of the coroner's inquiry would be telling. If the grand jury confirmed Max had committed a crime, his case would proceed directly to the State Superior Court.[1029] [1030]

****

It became a matter of public record on September 14, when Elsie Camilli filed Letters of Administration because Frankie had left no will. Newspapers across the nation reported on a statement released to the press by Elsie's attorney to clear Frankie's probate, State Assemblyman William B. Hornblower. His services were reportedly paid for by Baer's manager Ham Lorimer, which doesn't seem sketchy at all.[1031]

Hornblower accused Frankie's handlers, Cal Working and Tom Maloney, of being prizefight racketeers. In the last year, he figured Frankie had earned nearly $30,000 prior to his fatal match. Yet when Frankie entered the ring against Baer, he had $1,800 cash in hand, a car worth $750, and a land lot valued at $1,500. Hornblower said Cal told him he took a manager's cut of 25%, but that Elsie stated it was 33%. He said Elsie told him she went to Los Angeles trying to find out where Frankie's money went, but nobody would tell her a thing. Hornblower said when he asked Cal for an accounting of Frankie's earnings, Cal was said to have replied he kept no books; that he and Frankie "had a perfect understanding on that matter."

Out of the remaining two-thirds of his earnings, Frankie paid Tom Maloney's trainer salary and all expenses incidental to his fights. Hornblower estimated more than $10,000 was still unaccounted for. When he asked Cal where the money went, he said Cal claimed it had been used to exploit Frankie as a "fistic attraction," but had refused to provide details. Hornblower threatened a civil suit, but cautioned that just as Elsie had been against involvement in the manslaughter trial, she was against participation in this suit. She wanted neither the public attention, nor to "create a fuss" that further shined a spotlight on her family. [1032] [1033]

Hornblower warned when he filed the papers that granted Elsie as Administratix of Frankie's estate, he would turn Frankie's last purse over to the estate. He informed Cal and Tom if they attempted to sue Elsie to claim any of Frankie's last purse, he would effectively tie them up in court until they were old men.[1034]

But somebody got to Hornblower. They told him public use of the word "racketeer" was inadvisable while the sport of boxing was under a magnifying glass. The following day he ate his words, every damn one of them. He pulled up his stool, tucked in his napkin, sprinkled a seasoning of crow on each tiny bite, and methodically cleaned his plate. Though the press had quoted him word for word, because he sent them a statement of his findings, he denied he ever issued any such thing.

He now claimed Elsie was not robbed by racketeer. She was perfectly satisfied with the accounting rendered by Frankie's managers. He said Frankie did not make $30,000 as published yesterday, he made $20,000 of which he received $13,333. He asserted Elsie was able to account for all of Frankie's other expenses. The costs of living expenses in two cities, numerous airplane trips between households, money sent to his relatives, and what he loaned to friends, was accounted for. Given the detail in the initial bombshell report, which was even carried by the Associated Press, amazingly the press once again let it go without question.[1035]

****

On September 16, the coroner's jury assembled for an inquest at San Francisco City Hall. County Coroner Dr. Leland was to have led the proceedings, but he was at home sick. He had been adamant that he would personally conduct the inquest. Leland believed laymen should not guide nor render verdicts on such cases. That people with more than a modicum of education would better understand the nuance of the autopsy findings. But since state law stipulated such juries be comprised of laymen, he wanted to make clear to the jury the physics involved, the sheer force required, to administer such extensive damage to Frankie's head. It had not been a matter of a fighter who punched exceptionally hard; it was a matter of determined effort by an experienced fighter to inflict severe injury or death on his opponent.

Along with Autopsy Surgeon Berger, Coroner Leland was an early advocate of a recently emerging study of the short- and long-term damage caused by repeated punches to prizefighters' heads and jaws known then as punch-drunk-syndrome. In 1931, Frankie's brain was among several others whose examination of findings was presented by city pathologist Dr. Adelbert M. Moody in a lecture titled "Contusion Hemorrhages of the Brain" before a panel at the California Medical Association. The results of Dr. Moody's findings, and the new discoveries made from the uniquely horrifying damage to Frankie's brain, were quoted in medical treatises for years.[1036]

****

The day the coroner's jury convened, Municipal Judge Alfred J. Fritz, who largely presided over general crimes cases, hastily took Dr. Leland's place. As Leland had feared, a layman would oversee the case against Max Baer before laymen. Max was subpoenaed to appear, but upon the advice of his attorneys, he took the fifth and declined to testify under the grounds he might incriminate himself. Before proceedings began however, he did make sure to pose for several photos with Police Chief Lemon and Judge Fritz.[1037] [1038]

When Baer's handlers began to beat the same tired drum that Frankie was sick or injured prior to the fight, Elsie Camilli, who sat in the courtroom, had finally had enough. She stood up and shakily made her way to the front of the court. The press noted she "appeared in obvious emotional freefall" and was "observed to be on the verge of collapse." The idea of facing a room full of strangers terrified her. But she would be damned if she allowed false claims to be her husband's legacy. A ripple of murmurs in the court gallery trailed in her wake when she quietly asked to speak.[1039]

Before a packed courtroom who hushed in anticipation of her words, she took a breath to steady herself. In a firm unwavering voice, she stated that Frankie was not sick, not poorly trained, and that "he was never as healthy as he was the night of the fight." She testified that Frankie objected strenuously to having Irwin as the referee. He told her Irwin would never give him a square deal, and that he "might as well swing" if he was third man in the ring.[1040] [1041] [1042]

Curiously just weeks earlier, sports columnist Bob Edgren, who later become a member of the California State Boxing Commission, wrote an opinion piece on boxing commissioners and their relationships with referees. He noted commissions had become extremely lax in enforcement of the rules. That in the past, referees had worked independently, and their standing depended upon fairness, rigid enforcement of the rules, and not playing favorites. Today, Edgren noted, a referee's actions and decisions were nothing more than a rubber stamp by the commission, which had allowed boxing to become a business instead of a sport.

Favored fighters were allowed to use foul methods to win. Add in the gambling element, and the actions of referees were suspect.[1043]

Figures directly involved in the fight began to point fingers at each other. When Frankie's seconds took the stand, a shocking revelation emerged during questioning, which added to the many excuses why the fight wasn't stopped sooner. Months earlier, Toby Irwin was referee for a fight between Primo Carnera and Leon Chevalier at the Oaks Ballpark. The fight was fixed; Carnera was ignorant that his early bouts in America for the most part had their outcomes prearranged by gangsters.

The fight's promoter Frank Churchill, whom the press had labelled "a contaminating influence to clean boxing," was bad news. He was a lieutenant of a consortium of gangsters which operated at the direction of East Coast underworld mob boss Owney Madden, said to have "set the blueprint for mob control of the fight game." Churchill was seen whispering into the ear of Leon's second, Bob Perry, between rounds. Despite his own corner rubbing his eyes with a towel embedded with pepper between rounds to give Carnera the advantage, Leon hadn't read the gambler's script, and the sheep was killing the butcher.

In the sixth round, the white flag of truce came fluttering into the ring. Not from Carnera's corner, but from Chevalier's own second, Bob Perry. The ploy was so blatant, that after he left ringside, Bob was bludgeoned to the ground by an infuriated crowd. He later admitted he had met with Churchill and Madden's chief aide, Billy Duffy, in a local hotel room to plan the fix. Mrs. Chevalier testified before the commission that her husband had been offered $900 to fake the fight or be killed. Chevalier stated he had directed the gamblers to his manager Tim McGrath, but Tim claimed ignorance of the entire affair.[1044] [1045]

As a result of the Carnera–Chevalier bout, the state boxing regulations were changed. The chief second was the only one of a fighter's team able to demand a fight be stopped. He must enter the ring to do so. Tossed towels would be ignored. A rule which had been in place for years was gone, and resulted in confusion that proved to be deadly.

Tom testified that during the frantic moments as Frankie was being beaten to death, he and Tillie couldn't agree which one of them was actually chief second. Tom said he argued away precious time with Tillie over who could legally make the request to stop the fight. Tillie may have even prolonged this conflict, to prevent Tom from an early fight stoppage in the exact round gamblers had bet Frankie would be put down. Realistically though, they both effectively decided to be among a growing group of men who chose to save themselves with attempts to shift the blame. Any hope of justice for Frankie was further abandoned without a backward glance.[1046] [1047]

Years later, promoter Ancil Hoffman was still remolding the story about the night Max killed Frankie. He had something curious to say about tossed towels, which were legally not allowed in the ring that night. In 1970 he told a Sacramento paper, that "Frankie's manager threw in the towel but the referee kicked it out and forced Max to keep hitting him until Frankie went down in the fifth."[1048]

When referee Toby Irwin took the stand, he audaciously claimed Frankie was not helpless on the ropes. He claimed his arms were on guard in front of him until the last four or five blows were struck. "I reached him before his body slumped to the floor. That was all I could do." At least five other witnesses, chiefly sports writers assigned to the fight who sat ringside, vehemently disagreed. To a man, they stated Irwin did not have control over the action, and Frankie was quite obviously unconscious and completely incapacitated as Baer bludgeoned him.[1049]

Detective Police Captain Fred Lemon was next in the hot seat. Though he had been with the police force for over twenty years, eight of them as a captain, and had monitored fights in the city for decades, he testified he thought he had no right to interfere in the bout. After the day's testimony, a copy of the rules book was slapped into his hand, which indicated a peace officer could have stepped in at any time to stop the fight.[1050]

In his concluding remarks to jurors at the coroner's inquest, Assistant D.A. Tyrrell echoed his boss Mathew Brady's words almost to the letter. He stated that "the evidence against him [Baer] is weak, and I don't think the case will get far either before the Superior Court or the Grand Jury." Then he unaccountably startled the courtroom when he turned suddenly to pound his fist repeatedly on the lectern.

"Although Baer may be accused by some of unsportsmanlike conduct for the blows he struck Campbell from behind in the second round," he shouted into the stunned silence as he struck the wood again, "I feel, and the coroner's inquest testimony shows, that the fight was carried out according to the regulations of the State Boxing Commission!!" A weak rendition as performance art goes, but he got it into the record.[1051]

At the end of the proceedings, the jury for the coroner's inquest deliberated for thirty-five minutes. They issued a non-committal verdict. They stated Frankie Campbell died of injuries received in the fight with Max Baer three weeks prior, but because of the way current boxing commission regulations were written, they were legally unable to place responsibility for Frankie's death on Max.

Spectators who filled the courtroom seats, and the large crowd who milled outside City Hall were livid. Heated words rumbled through the air that nobody possessed the morality and bravery to do the right thing. Police caressed their batons in anticipation of a riot. A cacophony of voices was heard to declare with disgust, that such avoidance indicated not only a lack of the effectiveness of the boxing rules and regulations, but complete failure to enforce the few laws that did exist.[1052]

CHAPTER 33

ROTTEN TO THE CORE

WHEN A FIGHTER KILLS IN THE RING HE DOES NOT GO TO JAIL: INSTEAD, HE GAINS
A STRANGE NEW RESPECT FROM SOME PEOPLE - FLOYD PATTERSON

The public outcry for answers continued unabated. The prosecutor's office was deluged with demands for action; this was not a mess to be tossed over someone else's fence. Frankie's death was like a boulder heaved into still waters. The news rippled through the Mission District and across the city. The man, Frank Camilli, and the fighter, Frankie Campbell, had been an immensely well-liked and popular fellow; the pride of the Mission District, a beloved son of the city, and a fan favorite in the ring. If a negative word was said or written against his character, or that portrayed him as anything but a genuinely decent person, it remains elusive.

Word leaked on September 19, that Assistant D.A. John Tyrrell had quietly assigned three men to investigate Toby Irwin. Informants claimed when he still sat on the Dreamland Auditorium board of directors, Irwin regularly made bets on the outcome of fights which he refereed. This came as no surprise to sports reporters who for years had heard him choreograph the action in local rings.

Numerous people in the sport had privately begged Tyrrell to hold a grand jury trial to expose the rot in the game. Yet they refused to sign complaints, or give voluntary testimony, in fear for their lives if they appeared publicly. On the same day, *Oakland Tribune* sports editor Bob Shand noted, his sources said informants confirmed what reporters had always known; the Dreamland and its associates, which included their head referee Toby Irwin, was consistently favored above other clubs by Commissioner Traung.[1053] [1054]

As the press printed one salacious detail after another, the rising discord from all directions finally became too loud to ignore. The empaneled grand jury publicly stated they believed Max Baer had committed a crime. When they demanded official action, since the jury for the coroner's inquest had refused to place blame, the D.A.'s office was finally backed into a corner. District Attorney Brady requested a third postponement of Max's preliminary hearing to October 1 due to imminent action by the grand jury. In a move that was a rarity for a county D.A., he also announced plans to take charge of the grand jury investigation. Word was that informants continued to come forward with damning claims. Brady said he wanted to personally study their testimony before the grand jury was seated; those who shielded Max Baer and the fight game from harm needed to get their ducks in a row.[1055] [1056] [1057] [1058]

Ham Lorimer shocked the public and the press the next day, when he threw Max Baer's five-year contract onto the market to the highest bidder. Despite Baer's fat purses, Ham was in the red. "I have met with nothing but grief since I broke into the boxing game as a manager … I can't get out soon enough." [1059]

Baer was so irresponsible with his winnings, he once bought forty-nine pairs of silk socks in one crack. He acquired a new silk fedora every week because his hair grease stained the liners. Sports columnist Russell Newland reported in October, Max bragged that his monthly haberdashery bill was over $150 and his monthly tailor bill was almost $500. In the last year, Max had made over $50,000, (equivalent to $875,000 today), and it was all gone. Lawyers' fees for collection agency liens, and defense for the manslaughter charge, had eaten into profits at an alarming rate. Despite the fact virtually everyone expected that Max was on his way to a heavyweight title, Ham wanted out.[1060] [1061]

The last of Max's claims that he would never fight again did a vanishing act. Three weeks after Frankie's death, he eagerly indicated he hoped to go under Jack "Doc" Kearns' management and finally head east to fight in New York. Not only Kearns, but Frank Churchill wanted a cut of Max's contract on behalf of his boss, mobster Owney Madden. Churchill was a close associate of promoter Ancil Hoffman. Whenever Churchill, based down in Los Angeles, wanted to hold fights, or match his fighters, up in San Francisco, it was Ancil as his advance man, who arrived with a smile and a roll of benjamins to close the deal.

Frank Churchill was still under indefinite suspension for his part in the Carnera–Chevalier fix. Three fighters had died under his watch; Dencio Cabanela in 1921, Pancho Villa in 1925 and Clever Sencio in 1926. Churchill's western representative for Pancho Villa, which included the Jimmy McLarnin fight—a bout Villa fought in San Francisco while suffering an improperly treated bacterial infection from wisdom tooth extractions that killed him ten days later—was Ancil Hoffman.

As the mob's liaison, Ancil bought a quarter interest of Max Baer's contract from Ham Lorimer on a six-month option; the gang wanted a test run before they committed. Ancil claimed publicly to be simply an adviser; it was prohibited in most states for fighters to have two managers. He denied a reporter's point-blank query whether Frank Churchill was part of the sale. But within three days of Ancil's signature, Churchill was heard to brag down in Los Angeles that he now owned a piece of Max Baer.[1062] [1063] [1064] [1065] [1066] [1067]

Bob Shand at the *Oakland Tribune* rightly smelled a rat. "It is something new when a fight promoter takes an option on a fighter for six months, as in Baer's case, agreeing to pay $25,000 for the contract if the fighter makes good ... the boxing commission wants to know more about the circumstances surrounding such an agreement and just what Frank Churchill had to do with it ... too much money is involved in a heavyweight title."[1068] [1069] [1070]

Max was given $5,000 from the sale. He told Ham Lorimer he needed the money to pay toward the mortgage on the Piedmont Hills mansion he had bought his parents. The money lasted three days and not a dime of it went toward the loan. In between court appearances, Max had made repeated trips to Reno, Nevada. While there, the 21-year-old had successfully wooed 37-year-old married socialite Dorothy Dunbar-Maurice-Wells-de Garcon, who was in town from New York to divorce her third husband.

Max's parents were shocked. His father sputtered, "she's old enough to be his mother!" Though Max had professed his love to all and sundry, given her pending divorce, Dorothy was more circumspect. Nevertheless, the pair had taken Reno by storm, with photos and loving quotes of their burgeoning romance appearing in the newspapers. Max confessed to "a knockout at the hands of King Cupid." He had bought a large diamond ring in the hopes Dorothy accepted his proposal of marriage. [1071] [1072] [1073] [1074]

****

Back in San Francisco, the first blades of grass had begun to peep from the ground before Frankie's headstone. Elsie Camilli was finally able to emerge from under the weight of her sadness, and gather her thoughts together enough to function. She made a visit to Aasland's Pool Hall. A young man was pointed out to her, and she walked over to him as he made a bank shot.

"Frankie called me before the fight that he had promised you one of these." With a haunted smile, she handed over a print of the last publicity photo ever taken of her husband. As the widow and the boy bent their heads over the image, she murmured softly, "But he didn't get a chance to sign it."[1075]

Still across the pond, Frankie's old pal Dave Shade had engaged in a fight with England's Len Harvey at Royal Albert Hall. Dave lost a bout he should have won easily, simply because he did the right thing. The *London Daily Herald* noted one moment behind why that might have been. "He fought a clean and sportsmanlike match. Once, when Harvey slipped down, Shade, who was in a position to flash home his right glove, drew it back and allowed Harvey to rise. It was an act of grace which pleased the big crowd."[1076]

Frankie's former opponent, Tony Stabenau, wrote to his hometown pal in Buffalo, New York that week, and the letter somehow made it into the local paper.

"This Max Baer took an unfair advantage of Frankie, hit him while his back was turned.... Frankie had scored a knockdown and was walking over to a neutral corner. Baer jumped up and hit him in the back of the head.... Campbell thought Baer was taking a long count ... of course, [in the fifth] Campbell was knocked out standing from the first punch, and the referee was afraid to stop the fight because of gambler's influence."

"You see the gamblers were betting on Campbell to last a certain number of rounds, so that was just another case of a poor boy going to his death to satisfy a bunch of gamblers and grifters. That is all the fight racket amounts to out here in California. It is the worst, most crooked, corrupted, dishonest, dishonorable racket any place in the world, and I for one am glad to be out of it ... since the deaths, the fight racket in 'Frisco is absolutely shot, the last couple of shows drawing nothing but flies."[1077]

****

In an evening session at City Hall on September 22, the grand jury finally began its investigation into the Baer–Campbell fight, and the sport of boxing in the city in general. It's important to note, a 1930 county grand jury operated under certain limitations not then found at state-level hearings and criminal trials. Their job was not to find guilt or innocence. It was to determine whether Max should be criminally indicted and stand trial before the State Superior Court. A judge monitored, but didn't control or decide, the direction of the proceedings; that was District Attorney Matthew Brady's purview.

Jurors could only evaluate evidence and hear witnesses the prosecutor chose to present. Brady could guide the trial in a direction guaranteed to either ensure or prevent an indictment. The jury could request a subpoena for a witness, but the D.A.'s office made the final decision whether to allow witnesses to be subpoenaed to appear. Witnesses were not subject to vigorous truth testing under cross-examination. Unlike today, where grand juries conduct their queries in secret, proceedings were open to the public and the press. Brady could have asked that some or all witness testimony remain secret, but chose to keep most of it public, which discouraged many people from coming forward voluntarily. Individuals with pertinent stories to corroborate other witness testimony, or to offer damning or clarifying information, were not heard from.[1078] [1079]

One state history of grand juries noted that for criminal prosecutions, although the grand jury originally was conceived as a protector of ordinary citizens by other ordinary citizens, "the fairness of its criminal operations has been questioned by various commentators and judges." U.S. Supreme Court Justice William Douglas stated, "It is, indeed, common knowledge that the Grand Jury, having been conceived as a bulwark between the citizen and the Government, is now a tool of the Executive. Some even have referred to it as a 'rubber stamp' for prosecutors." District Attorney Matthew Brady was about to use that power to adroitly do a favor for friends, and protect the fighter certain to make them a mint on his way to a Heavyweight title.[1080]

In the tense atmosphere the day the grand jury convened, the halls outside the courtroom were patrolled by a special detail of police large enough to wipe out a crime wave. A huge crowd jammed the room; more spectators gathered in the hallways, and streamed outside the front doors. Max's lawyers had submitted in advance a written affidavit to Commissioner Traung, which purportedly contained Max's version of the fight. Max had been subpoenaed to appear for questioning. But he once again took the fifth, and declined to testify under the grounds he might incriminate himself. His lawyers worried after all the subterfuge to insulate him, that he would nervously blurt out something which would irrevocably condemn him.

Frankie's manager Cal Working had waited for this trial. If he could take any one of them down, he would. Right out of the gate he dropped a bomb of such nuclear proportions it sucked the air clear out of the room. He stated Ham Lorimer had come to him and said to the effect that, "Listen, Baer wants me to cut Traung in on his purse." [1081]

He finally got it on the record, that Commissioner Charles Traung named Toby Irwin as referee, despite his and Frankie's vigorous protests that Irwin was so crooked, they'd have to screw him into the ground when he died. Cal had precedence to support his claims. Instances where fighters and their managers repeatedly and vehemently objected to, and threatened to call off a bout, if a specific referee was third man in the ring, was upon the assignation of Toby Irwin.

Irwin was so blatant with favoritism and fixed fights, one veteran local reporter observed that he literally directed the ring action, making promises to the "loser" of a fight that he could be the "winner" next time. Under Charles Traung's commission, Irwin was often sent to Southern California to act as referee for bouts later determined to be shady. He was so unpopular with fans that a chorus of jeers greeted him when he stepped into the ring.

No such universal dislike or blatant chicanery existed for virtually any other referee in the state on such a regular basis. Cal had attended fights with Toby Irwin as referee, and when grievous fouls were committed by fighters he favored, he ignored them. Irwin had stood by back in 1926, as Jim Woods beat Frankie cock-eyed while he was defenseless in a ring corner, until Jim paused in consternation, and Irwin was effectively forced to stop the fight. [1082] [1083] [1084] [1085]

Cal testified when he was in Traung's office before the fight, with promoter Ancil Hoffman and Baer's handlers present, he tricked Max into showing him how he had fouled Tom Toner in their bout, and that Toby Irwin was the referee. Max demonstrated how he held with one hand and slugged with the other; a move some scribes noted was the same illegal tactic Max used against Frankie in the fatal fifth round. [1086]

Cal later met privately with Traung, and reminded him that Irwin was the referee for the Baer–Toner bout and paid no attention to Baer's foul tactics. He reiterated he didn't want Irwin as the referee for Frankie's fight with Baer. But Traung wouldn't listen. "I'll pick whomever I like," he said with an irritated wave, as if Cal were a pesky fly. Cal begged Traung on five separate occasions to pick a referee other than Irwin, but Traung was unmoved. Cal condemned the fight game in the city. "All Irwin had to do [in the second round] was come between the fighters and stop the fight. The fight game in San Francisco is rotten to the core. Traung, Irwin and others all stand together to run the fight racket to suit themselves." [1087] [1088]

Cal then turned to Traung in the courtroom to remind him of these protests. His voice was a terrible thing, cracked and broken as he pointed at Traung, and cried out bitterly, "Now see what you have done! You are responsible for Frankie Campbell's death!"[1089] [1090]

Toby Irwin testified again to repeat the same lies he told at the coroner's inquest. Once again, he claimed Frankie covered up his face with his hands. And once again, all other witnesses vehemently and directly refuted his story. They declared Frankie was quite obviously unconscious as Baer continued to punch him; more than one called it "the slaughter." Irwin denied reports that he had a financial interest in athletic clubs and in certain local fighters whom he refereed. Grand jury foreman John Murphy said after adjournment, it was very obvious Irwin continued to lie in an attempt to protect himself.[1091]

****

A surprise witness testified next, to explain a letter she sent to Frankie's widow Elsie Camilli. Its implications were so horrifying, Elsie promptly handed it over to the court. Mrs. Anna Byrnes DeLiso was described as a "motherly woman," who brought her two young children with her to court. Her husband Gaetano worked at a cigar store on Telegraph Avenue in Oakland. She had never attended a prizefight, but alleged a few days before the bout, she was witness to a heated spat among six men, which occurred in a parking lot on Telegraph and Seventeenth Street, as she walked from the lot to her husband's cigar store. From photos in the newspaper, she identified one of the men as a central figure in the argument. The man was Max's father, Jacob Baer.[1092] [1093]

The conversation she overheard followed a comment by one member of the group, that high betting on Max Baer, for Frankie Campbell not to make it to the sixth round, "looked queer." To which another remarked, "Baer must be going to foul Campbell as Toby Irwin is referee." When one of the men mused, "Campbell might just whip Baer." Jacob Baer replied with a confident wink, "Maxie will get him in the fifth round if he has to cripple or kill Campbell."

His lips curved into a wide grin as he continued. "Tillie Herman's going as second to take Campbell's attention so Max can get him. It's safe money to bet on Baer." Jacob openly boasted that, "Traung was bound to back him up, because Traung had been making money out of Baer's fights and fixing referees." He patted a fellow's lapel in reassurance. "Take my word for it, there will be no trouble because Traung is in on it." When Commissioner Traung was later asked for an explanation by reporters, he declined to comment. [1094] [1095] [1096]

Mrs. DeLiso's testimony was eerily spot on in its support of Cal Working's claims, that Commissioner Traung profited from Max's fights. Papa Baer immediately issued someone's carefully worded blanket denial to the press.

"These charges that I argued with a group of men in a parking station on Seventeenth Street and Telegraph Ave, and told them that it was all fixed with Traung so Max could win against Campbell in the fifth round by fouling, crippling or killing him are a pack of lies. I never saw nor heard of this woman. I never was in a parking station at 17th and Telegraph. I didn't know until today there was one there. And I never, at any time or to any person, made such statements as I am accused of making."[1097]

Seventeenth and Telegraph however, were in the same blocks as Max's rooms at the Harrison Hotel, and the Imperial Gym where he trained. When Jacob Baer drove the four-mile trip down from the family's Piedmont Hills home to visit his son, the likelihood is high that more than a time or two he used that specific parking lot.

Some ridiculed Mrs. DeLiso as an attention seeker. Others suggested Max should sue her for defamation. He and his handlers often made regular threats to sue people, but never threatened to do so here—almost as if they already knew the outcome of the trial, or didn't want anyone to delve further into the truth behind her testimony.

But Anna Byrnes DeLiso received threats from someone. Within weeks of her testimony, she and her children were on a boat to Ireland for an extended stay with family. She even enrolled the children in a local school. They did not return to America for a full six months. She and her family went on to live quiet, uneventful lives in California and faded into obscurity.[1098]

As Ham came out of the courtroom after Mrs. DeLiso's testimony, he was observed to be flushed and flustered. Given Max's past involvement in fixed fights, he had been asked by a juror if Baer was approached for the purpose of fixing the Campbell match. Lorimer's voice was husky as he whispered uneasily, "He may have been. I don't know." When asked if he himself had been approached, he denied he had.[1099]

When Max was questioned by reporters outside the courtroom about Mrs. DeLiso's testimony, he scoffed, "of course, she made it up!" As he adjusted his silk fedora onto his marcelled curls, his eyes flashed angrily at the assembled press. He barked that he didn't intend to "let this accident ruin his ring career." He shot his diamond cuffs and turned toward his waiting limousine. His lips quirked into a satisfied smile. "Why should I go back to the pick and shovel just when I'm going good? Jack Kearns has been after me to take on some of the big shots back east!"[1100]

When later asked about Max's miraculous change of heart, Ham stated with tongue firmly in cheek, "You know how it is with a fighter. It's just a hand to mouth existence, and Max has been out of work for several weeks now." With a dark twinkle in his eye he smirked, "He is having a tough time of keeping up his sixteen-cylinder car with a chauffeur and paying for a home for his folks over in Piedmont. He bought them a sixteen-cylinder car too."[1101]

****

On September 26, the grand jury presented the results of its findings and submitted its recommendations to outgoing Governor Clement Calhoun "C.C." Young, who had lost his reelection bid to San Francisco Mayor "Mission Jim" Rolph. Over the course of five days of testimony they had heard from twenty-two witnesses. Before jurors issued their recommendations however, they issued a warning; the grand jury made public the fact that several of its members had been intimidated by racketeers during the trial. If it continued, they would act as a committee, and take the lead to end boxing in the state by a ballot initiative.

The grand jury found "unsportsmanlike conduct on the part of Baer, a professional fighter, who is alleged to have boasted repeatedly of the viciousness of which he is charged," and which were contributing factors in the death of Frankie Campbell.[1102] [1103]

They accused Toby Irwin of being in league with racketeers for the Baer–Campbell fight. They asserted he was a puppet who took orders from higher-ups to keep a lucrative job. Jurors asked for the permanent and perpetual suspension of his license to referee. They stated by a preponderance of evidence, he was "guilty in our eyes of carelessness and inefficiency—deliberate or otherwise—on the night in question, and his sworn testimony is at variance with all other testimony heard."[1104] [1105]

The jury asked for the removal from office of Commissioner Charles Traung. They declared based upon his own testimony—which among other things included the fact he was financially obligated to one of the Dreamland's owners—that he was wholly unfit to hold his position. Their list of Traung's transgressions, which they found to be highly suspect, not satisfactorily explained, or unsubstantiated, included: 1) His allowance of fight promoters like Ancil Hoffman to request appointment of specific referees. 2) His appointment of Toby Irwin as referee over legitimate protest by Frankie and his handlers. 3) His clear favoritism of Irwin, especially for major fights, many of which ultimately were considered fixed. 4) His bogus claim that referee appointments were made by rotation. 5) His arbitrary change of the no-foul rule at Ancil Hoffman's request for the Baer–Campbell fight to boost box office receipts.[1106]

The jury declared the fight game in the Bay Area under Traung's erratic and suspicious hand, "reeks to high heaven." That the evidence presented justified the following conclusions: 1) The professional boxing 'racket' so-called, is not cleanly conducted and does not merit the support of adherents of clean sportsmanship. 2) The conduct of boxing matches is prostituted by the alliance therewith of gambling cliques, the gamblers have their influence and are, without doubt, the silent controlling influence over many fight clubs, fighters, managers, seconds and referees. 3) The selection of certain referees is subject to severe criticism, and their decisions may be said to be based more upon the desire to increase gate receipts for the clubs involved and profits for gamblers, than to do strict justice to the fighters themselves. 4) Sports writers and boxing clubs engaged in an entirely too cozy racket to boost box office receipts through publicity.[1107] [1108]

In the end, the grand jury's hands were tied. They lacked the power, jurisdiction, or authority to act, if in the boxing commission's eyes, none of their rules had been broken. Foreman John Murphy remarked angrily that the further the jury went into not only the situation in San Francisco, but across the bay in Oakland, the rottener it got. The grand jury was instructed to turn over their transcripts and their discoveries of corruption in Oakland to Earl Warren, the District Attorney for Alameda County. Yet even Warren's hands were tied.

As he had informed Traung during the Baer–Abbott fixed fight fiasco, unless the commission's regulations had specific written rules to address instances of bribery, fixed fights, and racketeers, he couldn't investigate or indict anyone. In a reminder that Traung had failed back then to file a complaint with Oakland police, he remarked, "I told Traung I was convinced there was crookedness in the prize fight business in Alameda County. He took no action and made no investigation."[1109]

Declaring the evidence presented, did not permit the return of indictments under existing laws against any of the principals involved, the grand jury put forth recommendations in an attempt to clean up the sport, which included: 1) The commission must not be permitted to change the rules governing fouls to bolster up a promoter's ticket sales. 2) The state should have nine commissioners, three to each division, to prevent any one man being invested with too much power or authority. 3) Referees should not be vested with the full power to make a fight's decision. Instead, three competent judges should be selected after fighters entered the ring. This would remove power from bought referees, and leave the third man in the ring the freedom to focus his attention on the fighters and see that all rules and regulations were carried out.[1110] [1111] [1112]

Before Max Baer's preliminary hearing began on October 1, where the prosecutor would present evidence to show probable cause a crime was committed, and the defendant should face a trial in Superior Court, Police Captain Fred Lemon asserted he planned to call witnesses who would prove that Baer was "guilty of unjustified brutality." He never got the chance. Because the grand jury could not indict him, the D.A.'s office directed the court to dismiss charges against Max Baer that very day. Assistant District Attorney John Tyrell stated the grand jury had made a complete and comprehensive investigation and had found, under the current rules and regulations of the State Boxing Commission, that no evidence of a crime was committed.[1113]

Five weeks after Frankie's death, when he learned he would not be charged with a crime, rather than say something meaningful about the man he killed, rather than have a thought for the woman he made a widow, or the boy he made fatherless,

Max Baer stood on the courthouse steps, and thought only of himself. Grinning from ear to ear, and full of so much energy he almost danced a jig, he crowed, "Now I'll step out and win the Heavyweight Championship of the World!"[1114]

Upon receipt of the grand jury's findings, Governor Young admitted one or more of the commissioners had privately told him that gamblers had a throttle-hold on the sport, but they were too cowardly to take any action. Part of the investigation was said to involve, "a reported huge betting coup by professional gamblers and fixers," in connection with the Baer–Campbell fight. But since the commission's regulations didn't address such things, nothing could be done.[1115]

****

To assuage the public, and so it appeared he was taking some action, Governor Young announced a Board of Inquiry to conduct a statewide probe into the condition of boxing. He tasked Allen Bigelow Bixby, State Director of Military and Veterans Affairs, whose jurisdiction included the State Boxing Commission, to lead the investigation.[1116]

Bixby however had already shown his hand on his opinion of the situation. In his monthly cabinet report, submitted the end of September 1930, he stated he viewed Frankie's death as an "unavoidable, unfortunate accident." He absolved Commissioner Traung and Toby Irwin too. "Neither members of the athletic commission, nor officials acting under their authority, can be justly criticized for inefficiency or lack of proper precautions."

Bixby hand-selected a panel of prominent "sporting men" to continue the farce. From the beginning, it was clear the inquiry had no teeth. Rudy Hickey of the *Sacramento Bee* even claimed Commissioner Charles Traung was in back of Bixby orchestrating the action. Bixby said the probe would be strictly an invitational affair. Subpoenas would only be a last-ditch effort to obtain information. It was expected requests to appear would simply be ignored, and ultimately, many were ignored. [1117] [1118] [1119] [1120]

While parts of the investigation, which the press dubbed "Bixby's Inquiry," were conducted publicly, numerous witnesses testified before the group in private. They named names, and purportedly told stories so damaging to the sport as conducted, Allen Bixby abruptly declared his final report would remain confidential; only Governor Young and members of the boxing commission would see it. The public and the press howled to the moon and stars, that yet again, it was a whitewash. There would be no justice for Frankie Campbell.[1121]

Young declined to grant the grand jury's request for the resignation of Commissioner Traung, until Bixby's inquiry demonstrated it was a fair and reasonable mandate. As predicted, he referred their demand for the permanent suspension of referee Toby Irwin's license to the State Boxing Commission, who would protect him from consequence.[1122]

In the weeks that followed, as Allen Bixby conducted his inquiry in cities across the state, the board was hammered from all sides to hurry to a conclusion. The combination of disgusted California fight fans, and a Depression being felt in earnest, had resulted in gate receipts that were a fraction of what they had been before Frankie's death. Some reports claimed fully 75% of San Francisco area fights had lost money in the months after his death; in Los Angeles the numbers were down over 50%.[1123] [1124]

On October 27, having squeaked by his manslaughter charge, the commission lifted the indefinite suspension of Max Baer's license to box in California. They continued to have one stipulation. His first fight must be a benefit bout for Elsie Camilli and Frankie Junior; there would be no purse.

The *San Francisco Examiner* was outraged. They declared Governor Young must make a clean sweep of the boxing commission before he left office; a group of beholden men had rewarded a killer. The paper chided Max for his reversal of pious proclamations. "Baer's announced determination to 'quit the ring' made with a show of remorse after Campbell's death, proved yet another prizefight myth yesterday."[1125] [1126]

One shocked North Bay sports editor remarked "If someone would only hand him a medal for quick and painless killing, the sporting world would no doubt then consider everything hotsy-totsy."[1127]

In a desperate effort to restore the sport to public favor, the clown commission stumbled over its outsized shoes once more. They announced Max would box a benefit for Frankie's family at Recreation Park, the very location he had died just weeks earlier. Ancil Hoffman claimed Jack Dempsey had offered to referee, and he hoped the benefit allowed the sport to "do a comeback." The location was met with disgust. Once again, the public let Max know in no uncertain terms they had not forgiven him. The benefit was abandoned. Ancil and Max were unperturbed; they thought they didn't need California. Ancil boasted he had received over fifty offers from eastern promoters for Max to fight there. [1128] [1129] [1130]

****

Bixby's Inquiry set up shop at the State Building to begin hearings in San Francisco in early November 1930. Max nervously offered one denial after another when asked about his associations with various shady characters. Though he wore a bespoke suit and hand-crafted shoes, during testimony he launched into a twang worthy of a hillbilly. In an attempt to improve himself, and to convince Dorothy Dunbar that he was no ham-and-egger, he was a sophisticated fellow she should marry, Max had been avidly putting into practice tips from *"Emily Post's Etiquette"*— a reference book about proper behavior and decorum in any situation. Before a room full of men who controlled his future however, he slipped into country bumpkin mode during his testimony, as if he was just a greenhorn being hoodwinked by some city slickers. "It's quite a jump from pitchin' hay to this here business," he declared, "I can't keep up with these here racketeer fellows."[1131]

While Ancil Hoffman was in negotiations with Madison Square Garden to arrange Max's next fight, his friends had Max covered. When Commissioner Charles Traung was questioned about the Baer–Abbott fixed fights, he finally admitted he thought Max was approached by gamblers, and "failing to realize the seriousness of it, mixed with the gamblers. But," he tutted, "I'm sure he is all right now." Commissioner William Hanlon was asked, "When Max wanted to be reinstated after he killed Campbell, didn't the fact he was supposed to have been bribed to carry Tiny Abbott have any weight?" "No." Hanlon replied airily, "We felt the fine and suspension had closed that incident." One member of the inquiry was heard to ask John Clute, head of the boxing inspectors, how Max could be mixed up in so many suspicious fights, and socialize with so many unsavory individuals, and claim innocence. Clute had no reply. [1132] [1133] [1134] [1135]

The commission's Secretary Joseph Genshlea, who would hold the position for three decades and was beholden to nobody, bucked the trend of his compatriots; he was honest about the state of boxing in California. He admitted boxing laws had so many loopholes they had lost every case taken to court but one. This was well-known to racketeers and boxing interests. He proffered a list of several major fights it was felt were crooked. None of them were made public, but the majority of major fights held under suspicious circumstances in the last five years were promoted by one man: Ancil Hoffman. The majority of fighters involved were owned in part by one man: mobster Owney Madden. Genshlea urged stricter oversight of referees. He testified that "smart and honest referees would put prizefight gamblers out of business." It was his opinion the affairs of the commission were handled in a haphazard, unbusinesslike, and inefficient manner, and commissioners were not sufficiently familiar with boxing because they were political appointees. [1136] [1137]

Commissioner Traung testified that since Frankie's death, racketeers had made threats against him and his family. The maid had once called his wife to the telephone, where a menacing voice threatened, "the next time you see your husband he'll be on a slab at the morgue." Traung received letters in the mail that warned he "would be taken for a ride." Notes were pushed under his door which told him he "was marked for death." Traung claimed to be mystified at the anger. "I don't know why anyone should blame me for that fight, but apparently some did."[1138]

Veteran promoter Ed Lynch thought any scandals that had developed were due to "fly-by-night promoters." He said interlopers like Ancil Hoffman had never belonged in the city. He hadn't joined the area's boxing fraternity; he had simply bribed his way to profits and prominence with a little help from highly-placed pals. Lynch and reporter Bob Shand both noted Ancil was entirely too cozy with Commissioner William Hanlon. Rumors abounded that Hanlon owned an interest in Ancil's Monarch Athletic Club. The two were old "sporting" pals since before the First World War; both operated saloons on K Street before Ancil became a Sacramento fight promoter. Along with State Senator Jack Inman, Hanlon had been an investor in Ancil's old Sacramento Athletic Club. Back in 1926, it was Hanlon who greased the skids for Hoffman to jump over several other local promoters angling for a license in San Francisco. It was Inman who campaigned in

1928, for Ancil to be given sole use of the State Armory to hold prizefights. Ancil was viewed then as a carpet bagger who rode into town on his one-trick pony, and that opinion had not changed.[1139] [1140] [1141] [1142] [1143] [1144]

Bixby's Inquiry discussed implementation of a boxing czar, which had vocal support by Assemblyman William Hornblower and promoter Ancil Hoffman, because it took power away from the commissioners. Ed Lynch piped up again that Commissioner Traung effectively *was* the state's boxing czar. Commissioner Hanlon had largely "lost interest" in boxing unless it was to help his friends along, and Commissioner Woods was often incapacitated by illness. With a thumb in the eye at how blatant control of the game was interconnected, Toby Irwin, whose license to referee was still suspended, was called as an expert witness on the subject. Ancil Hoffman, whose promoter's license was also suspended, and who was effectively the middlemen for mobsters, was invited too. Asked whether gamblers influenced fight results, he answered with a straight face, "Absolutely not!"[1145] [1146] [1147]

****

Ancil continued to negotiate through mid-November with Tom McArdle at Madison Square Garden for Max to fight there. When both Jack Kearns and Frank Churchill bragged to East Coast reporters that they each owned a cut of Baer's contract, given Churchill's mob ties to Owney Madden, the New York State Athletic Commission hesitated initially to even match Baer in the state. When McArdle proposed a December bout between Max Baer and James J. Braddock, commissioners denied it, stating "this match will not be approved by the commission in view of the alleged entangling alliances existing between Eastern representatives of Baer and the present recognized and unrecognized managers of Braddock." It was common knowledge among sports editors that Braddock's manager Joe Gould, was a managerial front for Owney Madden. Not only did Madden hold part of Jim's contract, Gould was there with a ride and a smile when Madden had emerged from Sing Sing Prison, after serving eight years of a twenty-year sentence for murder.[1148] [1149] [1150] [1151]

Lt. Jack Kennedy, beloved Navy veteran and colorful ring arbiter in Los Angeles, asked aloud to reporters in mid-December 1930, the question many had long pondered. "It has been about four months since the death of Frankie Campbell and what has been done about it ... exactly nothing!?" he boomed to himself in response. "There have been investigations and speeches but not one constructive step has been taken to lose the chances of further fatal ring accidents." Nor did he expect anything would come of the inquiry. "All these investigations that follow the Campbell death will come to the usual end and nothing will be done. We need action, not investigations."[1152]

Fans across the state echoed his sentiments. Large numbers of them continued to stay away in protest that nothing had changed, and nobody had paid for Frankie's death. Those few promoters that still held events lost money with every card. Many local boxing venues in the city and across the bay had largely closed down to wait it out.[1153]

Ancil Hoffman reached out in the last weeks of 1930 to fighter's managers across the state to arrange a benefit bout with Max as an opponent. He experienced the same reactions by the press and the public as that of the promoters at the National and the Dreamland. *Oakland Tribune* scribe Bob Shand reported, that "while Baer was now finally willing to appear in a benefit show … so far there has been no demand for such a thing." Shand suggested there were plenty of other fighters whose appearance on the proposed benefit card "would not antagonize good taste." [1154] [1155] [1156]

On December 30, the Governor's Board of Inquiry submitted their report. As the press had predicted, it was a whitewash. Allen Bixby said they had made a serious effort to verify rumors that fights were fixed, and racketeers controlled the sport. With tongues firmly planted in cheeks, the board declared these were simply isolated incidents. They held up Commissioner Traung as a bastion of fisticuffdom. Traung likely wrote one sentence of the report himself, which claimed he had, "devoted more of his time and energy to his duties as a commissioner and under greater sacrifice than any other member of the State Athletic Commission," period!!

Out at the State Capitol, Rudy Hickey of the *Sacramento Bee* was scathing in his denouncement of the entire affair. He said the report was not worth the paper it was written on, the investigation had proved to be just as big a joke as the thing they investigated, and that the law-breakers were effectively allowed to investigate themselves. "If ever the state's money was poured down a rat hole, it was that which was used by and for Bixby's famous picnic."[1157] [1158]

San Francisco grand jury foreman John Murphy remarked after the report was issued, that despite the damning discoveries and damaging testimony in the transcripts the jury had provided to the Governor's investigators, he had expected a whitewash. He reiterated again that commissioner Charles Traung's obvious favoritism to ensure Toby Irwin was referee at big dollar bouts controlled by racketeers, was one of the main reasons the jury had asked for Traung's removal from office, and for Irwin's permanent suspension.[1159]

Governor Young said he hadn't decided what to do with the Board of Inquiry's recommendations. In fact, before he handed over the keys of the state of California to incoming Governor "Mission Jim" Rolph at the end of January 1931, he acted on exactly none of it.[1160]

On the same day Bixby's report was released, Max Baer was in New York City, as he trained for a bout at Madison Square Garden against Ernie Schaaf. Though he had shipped one of his limousines east on the train, the fighter soon added a third car to his fleet. He also brought along a chauffeur, a footman and a private social secretary, all of whom were owed back pay. He later had the interior of his most luxurious model fitted with rose-colored lighting, so everyone could see him in the limelight as he swept down Broadway after dark, waving to passersby like a queen to the commoners.

When he had arrived by luxury Pullman rail car in the Big Apple the month before, Max brought ten trunks of clothing, filled with forty custom-tailored suits, twenty overcoats, a dozen hats, and all the accoutrements. Eighteen more trunks would arrive on a later train. Max bragged that though he had never met fashion dandy Beau Brummel, "he was a cinch to run no better than second to me." As his entourage made its way to the Plaza Hotel on Central Park South, they passed by bread lines that ran for blocks; the number of Gotham's Depression-weary homeless and hungry consumed 50,000 meals a day.[1161] [1162] [1163] [1164]

As one of his last acts before he was termed out, Commissioner Charles Traung reinstated Toby Irwin's license to referee. When Frankie's former manager Cal Working asked that his license be reinstated, Traung personally informed him he denied it specifically because of Cal's grand jury testimony against him. Before he left office, Traung decried his position as a thankless job, "The way some folks acted you would have thought it was me who killed Campbell," he sniffed haughtily, "I was giving it more time than I was devoting to my private business and my golf and hunting combined."[1165] [1166]

Sometime during the tumultuous last months of 1930, Elsie Camilli suffered a miscarriage of Frankie's second child.

And in the way of things, then the world moved on, as if nothing had ever happened. And the relentless rewrite of the truth inexorably ground on through the decades. Until now.

CHAPTER 34

MAN WITHOUT A COUNTRY

I WOULD RATHER DIE ON MY FEET THAN LIVE ON MY KNEES
- EMPEROR CONSTANTINE

Six months after Frankie's death, Max Baer had fought three times in New York City. He lost bouts to both Ernie Schaaf and Tommy Loughran. He won through a counting error by referee Jack Dempsey against trial horse Tom Heeney. He lost not because the specter of Frankie Campbell haunted him. In between bellowing to all and sundry that he was the Great I Am, he neglected any serious training to juggle all the shiny baubles the Big Apple had to offer. He actually gained weight in camp because he shunned roadwork. He lacked the stamina necessary for ten rounds of hard fighting, and was outclassed by more experienced fighters. Despite claims that he held back in his first fights after he killed Frankie, his ring brutality continued unabated. After the Schaaf bout, one ringside reporter noted he was "a fiery youngster with a destructive spirit" and "the man in front of him is not merely an opponent, but an enemy to be destroyed." Another that he "started aggressively, swung hard and tired fast ... as he is today Baer is hopelessly inadequate in spite of his wallop."[1167] [1168]

Many on the East Coast initially appreciated this crude new scrapper in the heavyweight ranks, who was game and fast, with a carefree manner that was enticing. After his losses, the claims of superior fighting prowess which vomited unceasingly from Max's mouth, was viewed as a feeble bid for heavyweight importance that had been thoroughly debunked. His performances were labeled largely such a disappointment, it was suggested he was a flash in the pan no longer considered a top contender. He had lost the interest of a majority of fans in Gotham. As had been the case on the West Coast, many also found his clowning tactics unnerving and offensive. [1169]

"There is something wrong with that Baer grin." remarked Sid Ziff who had been ringside of a disappointingly small crowd at Madison Square Garden for the Ernie Schaaf bout. "It seems imbecilic, sort of registering somebody half off his top.... It was a novelty in New York last night. But all novelties wear off." Si Burick of the *Dayton Daily News* noted, "his taunting laughs and his clowning tactics incites a sort of repulsion in many persons." [1170] [1171]

His eastern invasion under Ancil Hoffman's guidance had also been a financial flop. Not because he wasn't paid well. Max had waded through his purses so quickly, that he was already in the hole for advance money to his manager Ham Lorimer. "Baer is an expensive luxury," said Ham, "Too expensive for me to maintain unless he is fighting all the time." His disinterest in the sweet science as anything other than a means to a lavish lifestyle was already apparent. Back home, the *Oakland Tribune's* Bob Shand later noted, "his eastern campaigns had been joyrides with the fighting a more or less necessary evil." [1172] [1173]

Ancil Hoffman had failed in his attempts to land any other matches. Then the New York Boxing Commission began a probe into whether Ancil's professed 'advisory' role, was in fact a shared management with Max's actual manager, which was forbidden in most states. Ancil abruptly announced they had set their sights back home in California. Max was not interested in fighting anywhere however; he wanted to stay in New York to close down the night clubs. When Ham refused to give Max any more money, he finally relented. Ham spent almost $2,000 of his own money to get the team back home. As Ancil, Max, and Dorothy Dunbar prepared to board a steam ship for home via the Panama Canal, Max indicated that upon his return, he planned to apply for his 1931 annual state license to fight in California. [1174] [1175] [1176]

But while Max and Dorothy had spent the slow trip in bed before she departed in Cuba, the State Boxing Commission deemed Max a "boxing undesirable," and a detriment to clean boxing; if he applied for a license, it would be denied. Appointed by the new Governor, the three new commission members indicated the ban would last two years. Ham's manager's license and Ancil's promoter's license applications were also tabled. The commissioners also sought a working agreement so that suspensions in one state were enforced in all others. Because New York already recognized such bans in other states, Max could become virtually a man without a country to earn a living as a fighter. When he heard the news, Max threatened to sue the commissioners. "Why they continue to harp on that fight with Frankie Campbell is more than I can understand."[1177] [1178] [1179]

The new commissioners were indeed not ready to let go of Frankie's death and Max's part in it. The existing state boxing laws at the time of the 1930 fight may have saved him from consequences. Moving forward, the new board was determined to do what they could to enact appropriate punishment in the event of a ring death under suspicious circumstances. New rules they enacted in 1931 would result in a forfeited purse, a permanent suspension, and a conviction for manslaughter if Max repeated the actions he had taken against Frankie. Toby Irwin would permanently lose his license to referee and be drummed out of boxing.[1180]

Many of the new rules were enacted specifically due to Frankie's death. They seem almost quaint today, but at the time, the Associated Press labeled them "extensive and radical." Holding and hitting, as Max had done in the fatal fifth, was barred. Any unsportsmanlike act which caused serious injury, such as punching a helpless opponent over the ropes, and striking a fighter whose back is turned, was regarded as a foul, with the bout forfeited, the purse held, and an investigation conducted. Specific new rules suspended any referee who ignored unsportsmanlike acts causing injury, and dictated actions referees must take for fouls, slips, knockdowns, and for when a fighter is on the ropes. Commission-appointed physicians were finally stationed ringside at all fights, and fighters were examined every six months to determine their physical and mental fitness.[1181] [1182] [1183] [1184]

"He's a great prospect," said Central California Commissioner Robert Edgren about Baer, "but his fatal bout with Frankie Campbell last August showed he lacked intelligence and good sportsmanship, and it would be detrimental to boxing here to issue him a license." He clarified, "I think his absence from California rings will help revive the sport.... We have no objections to Max boxing in other states, but we don't want him here." Northern California Commissioner Reverend Father Leslie C. Kelley, dubbed "the Fighting Padre," intimated word reached him that Baer and his handlers had not only boasted in New York that he killed Frankie, but encouraged being labeled a killer to promote ticket sales. Kelly stated there was such a strong distaste on the part of the public against Max, he was not welcome in the state. [1185] [1186] [1187] [1188]

Ancil Hoffman placed the blame for denial of all three licenses squarely on Father Kelley. "I expect to make the fight of my life. I know where the nigger in the woodpile is and I'll chase him out in the open. I'll even take the case to court if necessary."[1189]

Perhaps because Ham was the only one in Baer's camp, that had expressed personal concern over the seriousness of Frankie's situation as he lay in the ring, his manager's license was approved in mid-February. But he had no fighter to manage. Max's application was again tabled, and it was going to stay tabled with plenty of furniture piled on top. Ham cornered Father Kelley in a sparse crowd at the Dreamland one night with another appeal to reinstate Baer. Kelley told him he was wasting his time, that Max was a beast—a former butcher boy whom the sight of blood incited to fury. He said his fellow commissioner Robert Edgren had been at the Baer–Campbell fight and declared it the most brutal thing he ever saw.[1190] [1191]

As a veteran sports columnist and illustrator, Robert Edgren had been ringside at over 1,500 fights in his career. He had witnessed the Ad Wolgast–Battling Nelson rematch in 1910; an almost three-hour, 40-round slaughter said to be so barbaric, that blood and gore splattered onto reporter's hats and across several rows of the ringside seats. At the battle's end, Nelson barely clung to life and was battered beyond recognition. One spectator later said he "looked like a great chunk of round steak down as far as the belt.... Whenever a Wolgast punch landed on Nelson's gory face, "it was almost like a child pushing his fists into a moist mud pie." Yet Edgren said what he had watched Max do to Frankie was much worse.[1192]

The Baer–Campbell fight seemed to endlessly haunt Robert Edgren. He wrote in 1932 it "was a terrible thing to see—a giant of a man who had been outboxed and plastered against the ropes by a man much smaller, suddenly going berserk, smashing his opponent into a corner, hanging him on the ropes and battering his head from side to side in blind fury."[1193]

Though he wrote objectively and often enthusiastically about Max Baer's future victories, in 1934 for an article on deaths he had witnessed ringside, Edgren appears to suggest Max deliberately killed Frankie. He wrote that another ring death "was a real accident." But for his next recollection, that of Baer–Campbell, he wrote, with the quotes, "that was by far the worst *'accident'* I ever saw in the ring and in my judgment the greatest piece of brutality."[1194]

Robert Edgren was equally as adamant as Father Kelley that he would not grant Max a license for 1931. He declared Frankie's death at Baer's hand could not be forgotten. The third member of the commission, Dr. Harry Martin, who oversaw Southern California, indicated a license would not be issued to Max again, "for a long time, if ever." Some intimated the commissioners had "the goods" on Max. Bob Shand of the *Oakland Tribune* confirmed Allen Bixby had kept secret the intimate details of many fights and fighters contained in his final report to the Governor because, he admitted, they "contained much dynamite" which included "pages and pages of testimony" concerning the two Baer–Abbott fights. Confidential testimony from Max's depositions during the Bixby Inquiry was said to be highly incriminating.[1195 1196 1197 1198 1199 1200]

Ancil Hoffman and his friend, attorney and State Assemblyman William Hornblower, induced the aid of San Francisco native, former Heavyweight Champ James J. Corbett while he was in town, to sway public opinion. Corbett had a popular radio show, and penned a syndicated opinion column read by millions. Jim voiced support for Hornblower's threat of a boxing czar to get the commissioners in line. He wrote a piece that attacked Father Kelley's "butcher" and "beast" comments about Max. The article was replete with lies and innuendos that had already taken root about Frankie's fitness as an opponent. Corbett wrote Frankie was "not in good fighting condition," that Max battered him around the ring with ease, and Frankie was "poorly trained." Corbett lived in New York at the time; he was nowhere near the fight; Hoffman and Hornblower obviously guided his pen. Six months after Frankie's death, the campaign to denigrate him had worked wonders. The reverence and respect by fight fans that surrounded Corbett's opinion gave it the weight of the world.[1201]

****

While Ancil Hoffman campaigned on his behalf to get his license approved, Max was with his manager Ham in Portland, Oregon, to fight Ernie Owens for a third time. He was not welcomed by the folks in Portland. The boys in the $3 seats at ringside, hurled "raucous raspberry horns mingled with boos" after what many felt was a fixed fight. [1202]

To see what resonated with the press and the public, Max repeatedly tried out various tales on the night he fought Frankie. He gave an extensive interview to *The Oregonian's* William Hill Lair "H.L." Gregory. Max initially claimed he was down on the canvas in the second round "more from a shove than a punch," only to pivot and admit "Frankie did sock him." Then he threw out a whopper; he said they were both down at the same time. He erased the moment when he repeatedly fouled Frankie, to replace it with the fantasy they were both rolling around in the rosin dust. "I just didn't realize he was already out," Max said earnestly as the lie rolled easily off his tongue, "and I don't think anyone else did." With the exception of tens of thousands of spectators and virtually every member of the press at ringside. [1203] [1204]

The boxing commissioners in California continued to deny Baer's application for a license. Ancil dangled a benefit fight for Frankie's widow Elsie Camilli and her son Frankie Junior, but it was seen as an obvious ploy. Assemblyman Hornblower used his political position throughout the spring and summer to press for action. He played dirty. He charged that Father Kelley diverted funds from a charity. He lassoed the State Attorney General and a State Senator onto his side. He failed spectacularly to get the Governor involved; he publicly sided with Father Kelley. He did manage to further alienate the other two commissioners. [1205]

As State Assemblyman, Hornblower introduced a bill through the Legislature, to put the boxing commission into the hands of the State Assembly, and install a boxing czar of his choosing, with the implicit threat that he would withdraw the bill if Baer and Hoffman's licenses were reinstated. Father Kelley declared that if Hornblower thought he could use coercive tactics to change the boxing laws to make himself dictator over the sport, he was badly mistaken. [1206]

On a parallel course beginning in May 1931, several state assemblymen, all long-time personal friends with fellow Assemblyman Hornblower and with Ancil Hoffman, announced another new committee to conduct their own investigation into boxing, because of course they did. It had very vocal backing of Assemblyman Don Shields, who at the time was personal secretary to Ancil Hoffman. The committee reached out to San Francisco Superior Court for a copy of the grand jury's transcripts from *Case #13; the State of California vs. Max Baer.* They remarked in their final report that the paperwork had disappeared. The last known tie to any chain of custody for the transcripts, was when the grand jury was ordered to turn everything over to Bixby's Inquiry. All contemporary attempts to locate the trial transcripts at the county, state and federal levels have proved fruitless. [1207] [1208] [1209]

Father Kelley was pressed in early July 1931, for the reasons behind his stance on tabling Ancil's promoter's license. He stated content in Bixby's Inquiry included private testimony from Willie Ritchie, former partner with Ancil at his Monarch Athletic Club. Ritchie confirmed that virtually every big match Ancil promoted had something rotten about it. Kelley ticked off a list of transgressions, which included bribery, fixed fights, and a major ticket scandal. He offered proof Ancil fabricated broad press support for Max to be a part of a benefit bout for Elsie Camilli and Frankie's son, and for reinstatement of Baer's license; claims newsmen adamantly denied ever existed. "I don't propose to be a commissioner to the racket," Kelley declared, "I would be derelict in my sworn duty were I to vote contrary to such evidence." [1210] [1211]

Ancil certainly didn't further his case after he bragged to Kelley, "When I was a promoter, I had the political power back of me, and I could do as I pleased, and did." He added he still had that power and planned to promote fights with or without a license. In 1933 during a corruption investigation, Governor James Rolph handed Ancil's old pal, State Senator Jack Inman, a $1,000 cancelled check, signed by Ancil Hoffman in February 1928, and asked him to explain reports it was a bribe, so that Ancil could leapfrog over other local promoters, to lease the State Armory on Mission Street in San Francisco to hold prizefights. [1212] [1213]

As Max had awaited potential reinstatement of his boxing license in California, he fought and lost a 20-round Fourth of July 1931 bout against Paulino Uzcudun in Reno, Nevada, at Jack Dempsey's new boxing arena. The arena was financed by notorious Reno mobsters James McKay and William Graham, who had the police in their pockets, and got a cut of all action in the city. Ancil Hoffman was purported to be one of the venue's financial backers. [1214] [1215]

When Max announced right after the Reno fight, that plans were imminent to marry Dorothy Dunbar, his parents were horrified. "Neither I nor his mother are in favor of this marriage," his father Jacob sputtered. "He's a young fellow with a career ahead of him. He's heavily in debt." (he had just received an $18,000 purse, equivalent to $360,000 today). "That woman is too old for him. It's like a woman taking a child to raise as a husband," Jacob blurted. "We told him he's just a kid and to forget it. If he gets married, we're not going to the wedding." [1216] [1217]

After what the press intimated was a desperate appeal by Jack Dempsey to commissioner Robert Edgren in late July, Max Baer's license to fight in California was finally reinstated. Robert had motored down to Reno to cover Max's fight against Uzcudun; a performance so poor, Max was knocked from boxing critics favored top ten list. Dempsey called him a bum as he left the ring. West Coast scribes called him "the fistic flop from the butcher shop". It later emerged why Dempsey was so disgruntled; he had recently bought a 7.5% cut of Max's contract. [1218] [1219]

Max continued to dig up Frankie's corpse and parade it around with proclamations that his death still affected him. But a pal from the past begged to differ. When he touched gloves in a November 1931 rematch against a shopworn Les Kennedy at Oakland Civic Auditorium, where less than half the 8,000 seats were filled, none other than his old trainer Bob McAllister was back in the fold. Bob boasted Max had returned to his old killer ways. "Max is using his right hand as he did before the Campbell fight and if he connects with Kennedy's chin the fight will be over." Over two rounds, Max stalked his former foe and gave him a vicious beating, before a savage right uppercut in the third round knocked Les out cold." [1220] [1221] [1222]

Just before a January 1932 Reno battle against King Levinsky, Baer said he had conquered his fear of killing an opponent. He concluded that not holding his punches was "all part of the game. I feel now that Campbell's death was just an accident as if I had hit him unavoidably with an automobile. It doesn't bother me anymore, and I'll knock out Levinsky without any worry at all." During his rematch with Levinsky less than six months later, which put him in line for his most important bout to date, against Max Schmeling, *Cinderella Man* author Jeremy Schaap remarked, "If Baer was still thinking about Frankie Campbell, it didn't show. He enjoyed hurting Levinsky."[1223] [1224] [1225]

The end of August 1932, Max arguably contributed to another ring death, when he fought a rematch with Ernie Schaaf. Baer knocked Schaaf cold in the last round and it took several minutes for Ernie to come to. While Ernie went on to fight beautifully in two more fights, when he touched gloves with Primo Carnera in February 1933, he was noticeably sluggish as Carnera easily pounded on him through thirteen rounds. A light tap knocked Ernie out cold. He died three days later of a cerebral hemorrhage.

An autopsy later revealed Schaaf had meningitis, a swelling of the brain, brought on by a severe case of influenza. He was still recovering when he touched gloves with Carnera. Syndicated sports columnist Grantland Rice suggested it was Max Baer's punches five months earlier that had softened up Schaaf's brain. Viewed through a modern medical lens, with knowledge of the effects of cumulative blows over time to the head, we now know that Max's punches were among those which likely contributed to Schaaf's early demise. Baer himself vacillated whether it was his punches that had done the deed. He alternately claimed either that he didn't know, or that he *had* contributed to Schaaf's death; he was known to boast and pointedly refer to the deaths of two fighters by his hands.

****

Despite claims that Baer was a tenderhearted tiger, and it pained him to injure his opponents, nothing revved up his blood lust more, than to be given an excuse to hate or ridicule. Psychological warfare disguised as a joke, of Max just being Max, was actually an outlier in the era. A certain level of respect was the norm. But there was a special brutishness to Baer's bullying taunts, and never was that vicious streak more apparent than on a June evening in 1933; the night he fought Max Schmeling of Germany at Yankee Stadium.

Mere months before the Schmeling fight, Adolph Hitler had become Chancellor of Germany. His Third Reich had assumed control of the country. Jews already were under the burden of laws and decrees that restricted all aspects of their public and private lives. Ticket sales for the "Battle of the Maxes" were concerningly lackluster. A large portion of New York's boxing fans were Jewish. There were calls for a boycott because Schmeling was German and therefore must be a Nazi.

From his publicity headquarters at the Ritz Hotel, the fight's promoter Jack Dempsey and Schmeling's co-manager Bill McCarney dreamed up a wicked idea. "Baer was made into a Jew overnight," Bill later chuckled in 1938 to a Canadian reporter. He figured Jews would "delight in seeing a Nazi walloped by one of their own." Numerous Wehrmacht officers, personally approved to serve under Hitler, possessed more Jewish blood than Max Baer, but he was suddenly seen wearing the six-pointed Jewish Star of David on his trunks. He was encouraged to toss around a few hundred "schmucks" and "oi veys." Ticket sales to the fight exploded almost overnight.[1226] [1227] [1228]

Syndicated sports columnist Paul Gallico later wrote he was "but a synthetic Jew, a Hebrew ordained overnight for box-office appeal." That such a scheme so blithely proceeded, becomes even more dreadful, after Max Baer's manager Ancil Hoffman later boasted repeatedly, that in the 1930s he had dined with the Führer Adolph Hitler, the Nazi Minister of Propaganda Joseph Goebbels, and Hermann Goering, who authorized implementation of the Final Solution: the mass murder of Europe's Jews.[1229] [1230] [1231]

Max Baer claimed at various times to be half-Jewish or German-Jewish; he was one-quarter-Jewish and that's being generous. In his lifetime Judaism was determined through the matrilineal bloodline. Intermarriage between a Jew and a non-Jew was not recognized as a valid Jewish marriage. His mother Dora Bales descended from Scots-Irish Catholics. His parents were joined in "the holy bonds of matrimony" in Nebraska in December 1904. His German grandfather and Hebrew grandmother, were joined by a Justice of the Peace in Laramie, Wyoming Territory in August 1869.[1232] [1233]

After marriage to his second wife, Mary Ellen Sullivan, who was staunchly Roman Catholic, the newlyweds split over religious differences two weeks after they exchanged rings. Mary said she'd "never viewed Max as anything but a German." She expected he would convert to Catholicism. Max said he wasn't sure whether he was Jewish or whether he'd been baptized, and couldn't say whether he'd become Catholic. When reporters queried whether he was a member of any Jewish synagogue he remained silent. When asked once during training whether he would observe Yom Kippur, he replied, "Yeah I'll fight him next." In the end, Max appears to have drifted into the Catholic faith. His children attended Catholic schools, and opposite the pair of boxing gloves on the mausoleum name plaque where he is buried, is a Christian cross. [1234]

By ever after wearing the Star of David on his trunks, did Max Baer give hope to Jews during utterly dark days? Absolutely. But it was at the expense of Max Schmeling's reputation, who later wrote the change in attitude by fans was difficult to endure. Schmeling was apolitical. He had a Jewish manager. Holocaust survivors Werner and Henry Lewin confirmed he hid them in his hotel room during Kristallnacht. Schmeling was such a failure as a marketing tool to promote Hitler's "Master Race," when he lost the Joe Louis rematch in 1938, with minimal training as a paratrooper, Hitler had him dropped out of a plane over Crete.

But Baer happily joined in to label Schmeling a Nazi. His vitriol shocked columnist David J. Walsh when in April 1933, Max roared over the phone, "I've never wanted to hurt a man. But that's off in this fight.... I'm going to hurt him. I'm going to keep on hurting him." Simply because Schmeling was German, Baer said he'd have to suffer what he "would like to give personally to some of those leaders persecuting Jews."[1235] [1236] [1237]

He was merciless in the ring. Visions of Frankie Campbell did not haunt him. As he threw each brutal round-house right, he snarled in Schmeling's face, "this one's for Hitler." No punches were pulled. Fouls were abundant. Tennis matches had fewer vicious backhands. Holding, rabbit punches, headlocks, forearms to the face, low blows, shoves into the ropes, all got a touch to his forelock, or a bow of insincere contrition to referee Arthur Donovan's warnings. He lost four rounds on fouls and was behind on points going into the tenth.

After a knockdown in the round, Baer swarmed Schmeling into the ropes, where he cringed, utterly dazed and helpless. Schmeling turned away as he grasped the ropes. Baer then used one of his favorite tactics; he slugged Schmeling on the back of the neck. As Baer drew back to inflict further punishment, Donovan threw his arms around Schmeling, fearful for his life, to end the fight. If Arthur Donovan had not acted at that moment, Max Baer appeared perfectly willing to add another death to his belt. Schmeling's manager realized one more punch might have killed his fighter. His face was observed to be "white and horrified" as he led his fighter from the ring, while spectators spat at Max Schmeling and called him a Nazi.[1238]

After the bout, David Egan of *The Boston Globe* wrote that, "cruelty is Baer's stock in trade." He observed that the world "loves a killer. And it has found one who would put Al Capone, the famous government guest to shame…. It has been our luck never to have seen a fighter killed in action. I was afraid, for a few seconds tonight, that I was to see one. And that, more than paragraphs and columns of words, describes the terrific beating which Schmeling took in 1 minute 51 seconds of a round which will go down through the corridors of boxing time for its sheer brutality."[1239]

****

It is possible what also fed Max Baer's fury as the Schmeling fight approached, had to do with a woman named Olive Beck. As Max prepared for the bout, Olive named Max in a $250,000 breach of promise suit. She claimed to be his fiancé, and that they had been in an intimate relationship for two years, which ended when the 21-year-old fighter jilted her to become the fourth husband of 37-year-old wealthy socialite, Dorothy Dunbar. Max denied all of it. His manager Ancil Hoffman intimated Olive was another gold digger, chasing Max's newfound fame and fortune.

Reporters and modern historians considered it all a lark, with a certain admiration that Max seemed to gather energy from such conquests, shoving hearts into his mouth like a plate of unattended pastries. But Olive said she had first loved him when he was collecting garbage in Livermore for his father's hog ranch, well before he took up prizefighting. She claimed they were to marry right after the Campbell bout, and that she would accompany him on his Eastern invasion.[1240] [1241] [1242] [1243]

When Olive later demanded a trial, Max ran from process servers. She produced proof that he had paid for an illegal abortion. She presented doctor's bills from when he "knocked her over a chair with his fist, cutting her face and scalp so severely it was necessary to call a doctor." His lawyers tried to get the documents struck from court records. In the midst of the imbroglio, Dorothy Dunbar filed for divorce. She charged that her husband used her "somewhat like a sparring partner," often beat her severely, became violently angered without provocation, and frequently stayed away from home nights with other women. Dorothy disclosed she had loaned Max $20,000 and demanded he pay her back or she would seek alimony.[1244] [1245] [1246] [1247]

After Max's continued denials of a relationship with Olive Beck, she produced an engagement ring, personal letters, and intimate photos of the two together. She was adamant that her suit go to trial. Max admitted he bought Olive the ring with proceeds from his first fight. When newspapers helpfully printed them in their entertainment sections, he admitted the letters and photos came from him too.

In his February 1933 boxing newsletter, Bob Shand wrote how the boys who used to hang around Oakland's Bash Boulevard regularly attended parties at a hotel up in Sonoma County, and out at the beaches of Alameda, which involved numerous Baer conquests of which he boasted, and "which took considerable fixing," of cash payments to shut up any "misled" or abused women. Eventually Max got smart. He assembled a list of men whom he knew to call when he wanted to order a woman for the night. Shand thought Baer was in a real pickle for Olive Beck's suit, which would be decided by an Alameda County jury, because he was no longer welcome in Oakland. "He threw down everybody who ever helped him, and those who made it possible for him to succeed in the boxing game were ruthlessly tossed overboard when he became a big shot."[1248] [1249]

Max threw the folks in Livermore under the bus as well. Among his personal letters to Olive Beck made public, was this gem. "As to the trip to the [Livermore] Rodeo. Just forget it. I wouldn't be seen at another. Too much dust and it's all right for weak-minded people. I wouldn't have boxed at Livermore if it wasn't for the support they gave me when I first got my start."[1250]

At a pre-trial deposition in November 1933, just as he had done at the two investigations into Frankie Campbell's death, when he was guilty as charged, Max's favorite Constitutional Amendment unerringly was the 5th. He repeatedly pled it on the grounds his answers would incriminate him. One day before the trial, his lawyers settled out of court with Olive for an unspecified amount.[1251] [1252]

The number of sirens who tried to lure Max onto the rocks, with the intent to later make him pay for the privilege, are numerous. But not all of the women were opportunists. A month after he settled with Olive, Max travelled to New York City, where he was soon implicated in a rape case. In 1938, at the conclusion of four years of appeals and counter-appeals, after his accuser was hounded, harassed, intimidated, and offered jobs out of state by numerous individuals acting on behalf of Max Baer, just as he had done with Olive Beck, one day before a public trial, Max settled out of court with Shirley LaBelle.

Enticed with promises of a job, LaBelle testified that Max asked the 105-pound stage performer to a Park Central Hotel room in December 1933, and that when she refused his advances, "thereupon the defendant, Max Baer, who is a pugilist, attacked the plaintiff, who was a virgin before said attack, and then and there, with force and violence, the defendant made an indecent assault upon the plaintiff, and then and there forcibly debauched and ravished and carnally knew her." [1253] [1254] [1255]

****

In the lead up to, and just after he won the Heavyweight Champion title, in June 1934 from Primo Carnera, Max gave numerous interviews and wrote endless "Life Stories" for the press. Once again, his recollections about the fight with Frankie Campbell changed from week to week.

He wrote in one opener, which contemporary works quote repeatedly; "Nothing that ever happened to me—nothing that can happen to me—affected me like the death of Frankie Campbell." Then he proceeded to lie shamelessly throughout the article. He brazenly declared Frankie was still conscious in the fifth round; "The volley I fired at Campbell in the final round violated no rules of the ring. He was backed against the ropes, free to hit me if he willed." [1256]

In a January 1934 interview, the final death blows had moved again up to the second round, not the fatal fifth. Frankie being unconscious and trapped on the ropes, and Max slugging Frankie in the back of the head, had disappeared from the narrative. Despite his continued shuffling around of the truth, Max did appear to admit he punched a defenseless man. "During a furious exchange we both slipped and fell. Frankie scrambled to his feet, thinking he had kayoed me. He did not see me rise, and when I struck him, he started to fall. He seemed to settle in his corner slowly as I pounded away at him." [1257]

Frankie's widow Elsie Camilli purportedly made repeat appearances in Max's life. If you believed Max, she practically seemed to follow him around, to events, to trials, maybe even a phone call or five, to repeatedly reassure him, in quotes that grew in length and detail over the years, that she held no malice toward him. [1258]

Similar to how he had publicly denigrated Schmeling, Max's contempt of Primo Carnera—once again excused by the premise he was just joking around—was relentless before he fought for Primo's title in 1934. The year before, the two had agreed to appear as screen opponents in the movie "The Prizefighter and the Lady." Where Max was naturally gregarious in a group, Primo was painfully shy and awkward. On the film set, Max coaxed the film crew to play endless practical jokes and belittle him for amusement. Primo was a native of Italy, so Max repeatedly mocked his thick accent and gave him the Fascist salute.

Max certainly had no plans to pull his punches as faux visions of Frankie Campbell danced in his head, in the days leading up to the fight. Two days beforehand, he told the *Buffalo Daily News*, "when I blast away, every ounce that belongs to me goes into that punch ... he knows I can do more damage with my fists than anybody he's ever faced." [1259] [1260]

The night the two men fought, as Carnera hobbled on torn ligaments and a right ankle fractured from a first-round tumble, numerous sports editors from major newspapers who had sat ringside, noted that over the course of the fight, Max spat in Primo's face, spat on his chest, and spat at his feet. Many of the same reporters noted after round five, Max knew he could stop Primo any time he wished. Instead, he mocked and humiliated an injured man for six more rounds to entertain the crowd and for his own perverse pleasure. From his dressing room after the fight, Max bragged to the *Liverpool Evening Express*, "If I had trained really seriously, I could be in jail right now for killing Carnera."[1261] [1262] [1263] [1264] [1265] [1266][1267] [1268]

As Max settled the heavyweight crown into place, sports columnist Paul Gallico remarked that in the tenth round, referee Arthur Donovan may have prevented a repetition of the terrible death of Frankie Campbell. Carnera was propped up against the ropes, out on his feet, hands down, chin out, exactly as Frankie had been. Fortunately, Primo had a square referee on top of the action to swiftly step in.[1269]

Max later claimed he told friends that "the ghost of Frankie Campbell swept before his eyes," when he had both Schmeling and Carnera on the ropes, which he said caused him to beg Donovan to stop the fights. Edward Burns at the *Chicago Tribune* called him out for the lie. He noted the similarities of attack between Campbell, Schmeling and Carnera, and how Baer brutalized all three opponents when their backs were turned as they dazed on the ropes. There was no hesitation, and no begging involved. The "killer instinct" Max had supposedly lost was amply in evidence, and it was fortunate Arthur Donovan was the referee of the latter two fights, there to save Baer's opponents from fatal injury, but that Toby Irwin had failed to save Frankie.[1270]

In July 1934, as Max Baer admired recent purchases from a New York City Park Avenue tailor—which included twenty-five new suits, a mink-lined auto robe, and multiple new additions to a necktie collection that within a year approached over 250—the new champ announced he planned to hold a benefit fight, to repay his long overdue debt to Elsie Camilli and her now five-year-old son. Over the next seven months he had to be shamed into actually following through on his promise.[1271]

By August with no set date, the press inquired when the promised benefit for Frankie's widow and child would occur. Some ridiculed Baer's gesture about putting on a benefit as just that, simply a gesture. Others suggested he had simply forgotten in between posing for pictures and chatting on radio shows. Ancil Hoffman said the benefit couldn't proceed until civil litigation over whether he or Ham Lorimer had managerial control of Max's contract was settled in court. But this made no sense since the benefit, which most scribes viewed as simply another four-round barnstorming exhibition, had no purse, therefore no need to determine a manager's cut.

When local scribes pressed Max about his promise during a banquet in Oakland, he said instead of a benefit he might just send a check as a Christmas present. In September, commissioner Claire Goodwin, who had replaced Rev. Kelley when his term expired in 1934, wired Max to request a date for the benefit. Max replied from Hollywood that he was in production of the film "Kids on the Cuff" until mid-November. Goodwin suggested the benefit should be followed through, as it might "make friends for the new champ in his district." The ghost of Frankie Campbell still lingered mightily in the minds of Bay Area fight fans.[1272] [1273] [1274]

In late October, production of "Kids on the Cuff" was put on hold for several months. Max blamed script issues, but sources claimed the content of his "wisecracks" to ring spectators, radio hosts, and reporters during and after his fights, had started to offend so many people, the studio thought movie patrons would stay away from any film that included him. When the state's commissioners requested a meeting about the benefit, Max said he had obligations as champ and couldn't "drop everything and rush into training for a benefit match." That a suitable opponent needed to be found, because "fans aren't going to pay money to see me against a pushover." He said he had big expenses, and couldn't afford to spend weeks getting into shape for an event in which he volunteered his purse. Max's claim to be cash poor was curious; his father had just boasted that his son made $8,000 a week on stage appearances alone ($185,000 a week today) and could expect a "truckload of cash for movie work." [1275] [1276] [1277] [1278] [1279]

In early November, as Max refereed a benefit fight, scribes pressed him again. Max replied testily he might instead make a donation of $1,000 to Elsie Camilli. His grand gesture back in July had played well in the press, but any follow-through had become tedious; maybe if he bought her off, reporters would get off his case. The press continued to suggest appearance at a benefit would demonstrate his sincerity better than a check. Claire Goodwin went to Los Angeles in mid-November to attempt a meeting. Goodwin returned home in defeat. Harry B. Smith of the *San Francisco Chronicle* stated he couldn't see any reason why Baer wouldn't make more of an effort. That he had made the promise in New York and needed to honor it.[1280] [1281] [1282]

CHAPTER 35

DAMN BASTARD

YOU TAKE THE LIES OUT OF HIM, AND HE'LL SHRINK TO THE SIZE OF YOUR HAT.
YOU TAKE THE MALICE OUT OF HIM, AND HE'LL DISAPPEAR - MARK TWAIN

As 1934 turned to 1935, Max said in one breath that he intended to hold the benefit shortly, then in the next breath that he had no time for a benefit. While in Los Angeles before he went on a jaunt to Mexico, he boasted he had plans to shove off on a lengthy trip to Europe for personal appearances. A benefit for Frankie's widow and son wasn't even on his radar. His manager Ancil Hoffman attempted to smooth it over. He said he had belated a response on a date for a benefit until their return to California by mid-January. Now-former boxing commissioner Robert Edgren, back to his work as a sports columnist, observed that Max had promised a benefit for four years, but noted the team had absolutely no plans to head home. Ancil had just announced Max would go barn-storming through the Mid-West until it was time to go back to Hollywood in the spring; "Which may be more of a benefit for Maxie Baer."[1283] [1284] [1285] [1286]

By the end of January, with no sight of the Baer entourage, Bill Leiser of the *San Francisco Chronicle* declared that nobody had asked Max to make any promises in the first place. That it had been months now with no results. He said Max seemed to have time for fights all over the country, and that in itself was fine and dandy. But it was time for Max either to come back home and make his promise good or tell the folks he wasn't going to do it. And it wasn't time for the latter." [1287] [1288] [1289]

The first week of February, the persistence of Commissioner Claire Goodwin and seven months of public pressure finally backed the Baer team into a corner. An agreement to a benefit in mid-February was finalized, and Goodwin set the wheels in motion. Because Max was now the heavyweight champ, an agreement was drawn up for a non-title exhibition. Without such a stipulation, some ambitious fellow could potentially knock him out and become the new champ. A list of potential fighters from across the country was submitted to Baer's team. The local press agreed the best choice, was a fighter who largely fought in California; Leroy Haynes of Los Angeles. His manager said Leroy would fight for free. [1290]

But there was one problem. Leroy was black. Max and Ancil continued to draw the color line. They reiterated he would "not meet a negro unless it was a title bout." From New Jersey, they shipped out Stanley Poreda. Poreda was a white heavyweight who looked like he hadn't trained since Hoover was President. The quest for a suitable opponent who wasn't a pushover had evidently been abandoned.[1291] [1292]

Elsie Camilli and Frankie Junior were persuaded to be part of the marketing campaign to sell tickets to the event. They sold like hot cakes.

On February 16, 1935 the benefit was held at Frankie's old haunt, the Dreamland Auditorium. His legions of friends and fans came out to honor the boy they loved; they did not let his widow and son down. The house was a sellout crowd of over 12,000. More than 500 tickets were sold for standing room only. The Fire Marshall would have stroked out. Spectators, which included sports

Frankie Junior and Elsie Camilli discuss the show (Feb 1935) Courtesy of The Bancroft Library, University of California, Berkeley

greats Ty Cobb, Slip Madigan and Lefty O'Doul, occupied every available seat, spilled into the aisles, and jostled for any decent vantage point. It was the largest attendance ever recorded at the Dreamland.

Elsie was led through the ropes before the bout. She was too shy to make a speech. From the center of the ring, as relayed through the announcer, she said with tears in her eyes, and a thousand memories in her heart, that she could only repeat the words of William Howard Taft and say, "San Francisco knows how," as she thanked everyone for attending. She received tumultuous applause that brought the house down.

On his way to the ring, clad in the boxing robe from his starring role as fighter 'Steve Morgan' opposite Myrna Loy in *"The Prizefighter and the Lady,"* Max crouched down to chat with Elsie. As was expected by the press, Elsie grasped the hands that had killed her husband and graciously wished Max 'good luck.'

Once in the ring, Max sincerely thanked the thousands of attendees and expressed his pleasure that the profits would go to Mrs. Campbell. He closed by saying, "If in the future there is anything that I can do for her, I'll be glad to do so. Thank you all." The remarks brought an ovation for Baer as the crowd approved his evident depth of feeling.[1293]

Elsie Camilli and Max Baer (Feb 1935)
Courtesy of The Bancroft Library,
University of California, Berkeley

While the benefit was a huge financial success—over $15,000 was raised, $10,600 of which went into two $5,300 trust funds for Frankie's son—it left something to be desired in the thrills department. Referee Fred "Babe" Bottaro laughed so hard at times he almost split a seam. Max did everything but stick out his tongue at his washed-up opponent. He could have knocked Poreda out at any stage of the fight, but preferred to play at being groggy, threw in a few rubber chicken legs and demonstrated a bit of everything he had in the way of wild swings and clowning. In return, he received Elsie's thanks and a bloody nose, compliments of Poreda's one effective contribution to the proceedings.[1294]

Max then hurled his ring worn gloves into the crowd and waved goodbye. In a contemplative mood as he showered afterward, Max addressed the storm of hoots and boos that had arisen from all parts of the arena after the lack of activity in the ring. "Sure, they wanted blood. They wanted a knockout. Maybe I'd have killed the fellow, and wouldn't that have been a swell note at a benefit for the family of a fighter who died at my hands in a San Francisco ring?"[1295]

A month later Max was back in a San Francisco court, attempting to sever his contract with his manager Ham Lorimer. During proceedings, it came to light that in the last eighteen months, going back to September 1932, Max Baer had earned over $500,000 (equivalent to $11 million dollars today). He declared he did not have a dime to his name. As his attorney argued before the judge on his behalf, Max repeatedly gave his lawyer a "hot foot"—a lit match placed in the sole of his shoe.

When attorney Clifford Russell plowed his fingers through his hair in frustration, he discovered Max had put a wad of chewed gum in his locks.[1296] [1297]

Despite modern claims to the contrary, Max Baer did engage in a fear campaign prior to a June 1935 defense of his title against James J. Braddock, and he used the death of Frankie Campbell to do it. National headlines that Mae Braddock couldn't possibly have missed blared, "Baer Afraid He'll Kill Braddock." He requested an ambulance be nearby and hinted that the damage to Jim would be severe. Max told the *New York Daily News,* "I'm scared stiff I'll kill Braddock. I dreamed last night I hurt the boy.... I hate to hurt him because he has a wife and three fine kids—but I'll never forget what happened to poor Frankie Campbell."

Two days later, Max was quoted again; "When that bell rings I forget everything and go wild. I just naturally punch to the head and I put everything I've got on my blows. Sometimes I hurt somebody. When I bring him down, I hope they'll take Jim to a hospital and have his head x-rayed. If they'd done that with poor Frankie Campbell, they might have saved his life."[1298] [1299]

Max's veiled threats worked. As predicted, reporters helpfully rehashed Baer's hand in the death of Frankie Campbell and Ernie Schaaf. One scribe mused, "Would you want to fight a bloke like Mr. Baer who confessed he had dreamed just how he murdered you?" His words hit their mark with Jim's family. As Mae Braddock shredded a handkerchief and bit the polish off her nails while she listened to the fight on the radio at home, a family member turned to Mary Elizabeth Plummer with the Associated Press to say, "She's heard Max Baer is a killer, and she's afraid." [1300] [1301]

Rightly or wrongly, Max continued to use the death of his ring opponents to intimidate people. In 1948, as he left an appearance in Porterville, California, he observed a trucker force a car off the road. He motioned the driver to stop. Once the trucker exited his cab, Max punched his right fist into his left palm, and threatened, "See this right—I've killed two men with it. If you ever do that again, I'm coming after you." To drive the point home, he picked the trucker up by his collar and shook him in mid-air.[1302]

****

Perhaps no story lines Max Baer floated have been more comically inventive than the excuses surrounding his losses to James J. Braddock and Joe Louis.

Directly after Max clowned away his title to Jim Braddock—a bout so apathetic the odor of a fix still lingers, a fight one boxing historian deemed, "The most lackluster snoozefest I've ever wasted time to watch. If they fought on the front lawn, I'd close the curtains," a fight where rumors persisted that Baer bet big *against* himself—Baer told Tommy Manning of NBC radio he was happy for Jim's win; Braddock needed the money because he had a wife and kids. Then Max oddly segued that he likely had a string of illegitimate children across the country; a comment that not only disgusted fans, but one which several sports editors refused to quote in their papers. It lost him a popular radio program, several advertising campaigns, and literally the last shred of any respect still held by his dwindling admirers.[1303] [1304]

Baer then offered an alibi for his loss to Braddock that is still believed today; he had "broken hands" going into the bout which hadn't healed from prior injury. He claimed from his dressing room that they were broken during the fifth round, or maybe it was the third round, the round kept changing. As the crowd had applauded Braddock's victory, Baer's manager Ancil Hoffman made sure to announce from the ring apron that Max "broke both hands early in the fight."

Amidst the snickers, because Max had spent most of the fight adjusting his shorts, and had hardly thrown any effective punches, someone quipped back, "How did he do that? Between rounds with a hammer?" Associated Press sports writer Edward J. Neil noted the nakedly pleading look in Max's eyes as he leaned toward his own physician in the dressing room after the bout to query, "Broken aren't they, Doc?" The quiet reply was, "Just bruised." A condition to be expected after weeks of training and a 15-round fight.[1305]

The following day, Max persuaded his good pal Dr. Leo Michel, known as "Doctor Broadway"—said to be an "unctuous fellow of middle years with a celebrity complex and a gusto for headlines"—to declare upon physical examination, that Max had a chip fracture of his left thumb and two small fractures in his right hand. Alas a dozen x-rays taken the next day at John Hopkins Hospital, and examined by Dr. William Reinhoff, and a group of physicians large enough to fill an operating theater, confirmed Max had only inflamed tendons, similar to tennis elbow. They noted x-rays revealed old dislocations but no signs of recent injury; the old injury was likely one that occurred around 1931, which Max later stated was when he "hit that coon on the head." It was suggested Max's malady might be elsewhere, and that he should get an x-ray of his head. [1306] [1307] [1308] [1309]

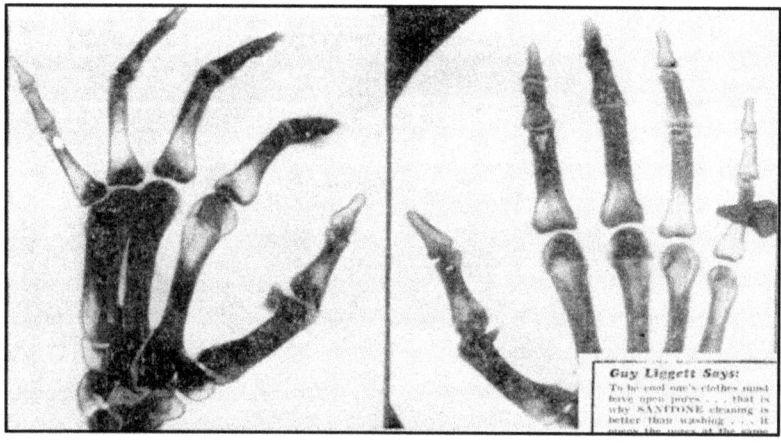

Max Baer's hand x-rays (01 Jun 1935)
Courtesy Omaha World Herald
306

Max was now a virtual maestro however at public perceptions and short memories. As soon as fans moved on, he went right back to claims his hands had been fractured before or during the Braddock fight. Max even claimed he bravely entered the Braddock fight despite doctors' warnings that his hands required surgery. Dr. Reinhoff declared at the time however that surgery was unnecessary; he advised rest and simple hand exercises.[1310] [1311]

In the weeks leading up to the fight against Joe Louis, Max yammered on about his broken hands so often, that New York's boxing commissioner finally stepped in. Bill Brown growled the excuse was, "just one of the guy's dodges." That Max needed an alibi for his poor performance against Braddock, but he wouldn't get away with it a second time. Brown had a doctor repeatedly examine and x-ray Baer's hands during training. Max's pinkie ring was the only aberration on every single film. His hands were again declared fit.[1312] [1313]

One contemporary article states Baer wrote a letter to his fiancé (by then she was his wife), to say, "I hope to God my hand heals before the fight." However, Mary Ellen Baer resided in a house a block away from Max's training camp for the Louis fight. He could have walked over to her; the letter writing story was invented. As the Louis bout neared, Max changed tactics. On September 16, he bragged his hands "never were better." The day before the fight on the 24th, Max told the press his hands were in perfect condition and that he was going to chase Louis out of the ring and down Lenox Avenue in Harlem.[1314] [1315] [1316]

Near the end of the fourth round on a late September night in 1935 at Yankee Stadium, Max Baer was a pitiful sight. Bloody, blank-eyed and trembling, he groggily peered up from the canvas. His face a ruin, his chest streaked with blood, he gazed to the corner of the ring, as if he watched the man about to spring the trap at his hanging. Splatters of Baer's blood smeared the chest of Joe Louis as he gazed coolly across the ring with his back firmly against the ropes, ready and able to throw the lever.[1317]

Joe's trainer Jack Blackburn told reporters he had reiterated repeatedly to Louis not to ever turn his back on Baer. "He'll hit you from behind just as quickly as he will from in front." The move Max had used on Frankie Campbell, Max Schmeling, and Primo Carnera had become a well-known part of his illicit bag of tricks.[1318]

When Max began the battle with Joe, it was noted he wore a derisive grin; he patted Joe condescendingly on the shoulder at the end of the first round. Four rounds later, as Max sat there, groggy, battered and thoroughly dismantled by Louis, having put up no more defense than a cow under the mallet at a slaughterhouse, perhaps he considered the possibility he could die if he absorbed further punishment. That his much-touted jaw of iron might be the death of him.

But rather than follow his own oft-repeated advice—to trust in the referee to intervene—in this moment he conveniently didn't have faith in the referee. Now that he was the prey not the pursuer, now that he didn't have a crooked third man in the ring, rather than rise and muster the courage of a game gladiator, while a chorus of boos resounded through the crowd of over 90,000, Max Baer quit on one knee. Then he announced his retirement from the ring.

His cornerman Jack Dempsey, who during the fight had covered his face with his hands and muttered repeatedly, "This is awful. This is awful," later wrote with disgust, "It is hard to believe a fellow could slip as far as Baer did in a year. He had absolutely nothing.... Baer's all washed up and I advised him to quit the ring." Max himself admitted a year later that, "I was on my way downhill against Carnera and worse against Braddock and Louis. Much worse." The loss to Louis appears to have been the final straw with Jack. He had advised, cajoled and threatened Max for five years. Though the two remained friends, Jack sold his 7.5% interest in Max's contract, and washed his hands of any direct involvement with his career once and for all.[1319] [1320] [1321]

Baer left the ring to curses and jeers as Joe Louis' hand was raised in victory. For a moment Joe's normally stone-faced expression developed a crack. The corner of his mouth quirked in a fleeting smile of recognition at former champ Jack Johnson, who wore a beaming grin as he applauded him from ringside.[1322] [1323] [1324]

As he sat in his dressing room after the fight, Baer unwisely flashed a needle mark to a room full of reporters. He said he attempted to inject cocaine into his right hand, but "made a mess of it." Later the story of his drug of choice and even who had injected him changed. Sources known variously as "a man who telephoned with the story as told to him by Baer's bookkeeper," and "I heard it from a fella," claimed myriad unnamed doctors administered the shot. Dr. Max Stern was often suggested as the man with the needle, but at the time he was the ring physician for the New Jersey boxing commission, not for New York.

By 1948, the cocaine injection had become Novocain, which had worn off when the fight was supposedly delayed for rain. Promoter Mike Jacobs had however checked the forecast and at the time was pleased to announce no rain would mar the event. New York weather had been exceptionally fine and clear that week; the stars had twinkled merrily down upon Yankee Stadium. [1325] [1326]

Despite the fact Joe Louis' team had conceded the allowance of not only specially padded gloves, but extra lengths of wrap and tape, when Max immediately picked up his "broken hands" excuse for his loss, Jack Dempsey remarked in disgust, that if Max's hands were broken, it was because referee Arthur Donovan must have stepped on them for as many times as Louis knocked Baer to the canvas.[1327] [1328] [1329]

If x-rays were taken by a legitimate doctor after the Louis fight, they were not made public. Dr. Broadway seems not to have been consulted for a second time. Max Baer's hands may have been bruised or swollen, as would be expected from the rigors of training and six years of fighting in the ring, but they were never chipped, fractured or broken just before, during, or after, both the Braddock and the Louis fight. No future reports exist that Max ever had surgery to repair his many supposed maladies.[1330]

The fact Max quit after the Louis bout, was yet one more unforgiveable arrow among many embedded into the tattered target of his reputation. Writer Ernest Hemingway famously deemed his performance that night, "the most disgusting public spectacle outside of a hanging." A quote Max was supposed to have made directly after the loss to Louis, "When people want to see me executed, they're going to have to pay more than twenty-five bucks a seat for the privilege," has had more variations of its origins than a bulldog has wrinkles. It was said a whole three years later, in an aisle at Yankee Stadium to United Press columnist Henry McLemore, before the 1938 Joe Louis–Max Schmeling rematch. It was in response to Max's remark that top ticket prices for a rematch with Joe Louis weren't high enough. If he was going to get beaten up again, somebody needed to pay him a lot more money.[1331] [1332]

Today, the "execution" comment is considered a great one-liner. At the time, it was a shameful thing for a fighter to say. Max was labeled a coward. He was said to "lack sheer decent principles," and that he had some nerve demanding more money for a Louis rematch after his miserable performance the first time. Several scribes noted he landed but one effective punch in the Louis fight; after the bell, and to the back of the head—just like he had hit Frankie Campbell in the second round—as Louis was on the ropes with his hands down. Others suggested Max purposefully threw punches after the bell in an attempt to foul out, so he wouldn't have to fight anymore. From his dressing room, Joe Louis confirmed, "the only punches that hurt me at all were those he landed after the bell rang in the second round."[1333] [1334]

Even the folks in Livermore, California, where Max came of age, were done with him. A Livermorean who compiled a family history of his local ancestors wrote, "admiration for Max waned following his losses to Braddock and Louis. Baer had a tendency toward being a 'play-boy' and that did not set too well with his local followers."[1335]

The *Fort Collins Express Courier* printed a derisive rebuke of Max Baer's fight career after he quit. He "brought something new and refreshing to the prize ring. He brought contempt to it.... He recognized the fight fans as suckers and never uttered a single word about the 'character building qualities' of boxing. The ring was not a field of glory for him. It was a rostrum for heaping contempt upon his opponent and ridicule upon the assembled fans.... He laughed when Joe Louis knocked him to the floor two times within a few minutes.... He could afford to laugh, for while babies starve for lack of milk and our national leaders prate about soaking the rich, 95,000 of the 'well to do' paid Max over $300,000 for less than fifteen minutes of punishment."[1336]

When Max later professed a desire to fight again, one sports editor wearily asked, "Wouldn't it be worthwhile for the long-suffering fight fans to chip in a dime apiece and turn the purse over to the Baer bust just to keep him quiet and keep him out of the ring?"[1337]

Jim Braddock called him crazy for even thinking about it. "That guy can't fight anymore. He hasn't got anything left to fight with. He didn't have much to start with, you know. A concrete chin and a steel head, that's all."[1338]

****

By the late 1930s, even the casual fight fan's tolerance of his clowning performances—ever hopeful for a glimpse of his sledgehammer right, which when it appeared was still a wonder to behold—had waned. To pay his ever-mounting bills, lawyer's fees for court cases that never seemed to end, and to keep happy the crowd with cuts of his contract, throughout 1936, Max fought 20 four- to six-round bouts on a barn-storming tour for a few thousand dollars a fight. Curiously, those 20 fights pad his professional fight record. In Toronto, Canada, after three and a half minutes of what was effectively a half-hearted sparring session, deemed "a fake, a fiasco, and a disgrace to sport," by the Province's Premier, spectators threw a pack of cigarettes and a half-empty whiskey bottle at Max's head in protest of such a sham fight. He leaned over the ropes to sneer at the crowd, "you paid to get in, suckers."[1339] [1340]

To fierce devotees of the sweet science, Max's continued thumb of the nose at the sport had become sacrilegious. His almost non-existent training regimen, his physical condition—so poor that reporters repeatedly remarked he was only able to fight in 30-second fits and starts and clowned the rest of each round—his lackluster ring work before fans who had contributed liberally to his bank roll, his disrespect for a profession that had amassed him a fortune which he blithely squandered away, assured that the damage to his reputation was nearly complete. The crowds got smaller. The boos became louder and longer. His own father said in 1937 that he was either washed-up, or his hands were gone, and he should quit. [1341] [1342] [1343] [1344]

"Baer didn't just stroll down the primrose path," said columnist Harry McLemore in 1938, "he used starting blocks for a quick getaway and ran the whole distance ... all the training he wanted was a brisk trot behind the milk wagons as dawn and a hangover came up like thunder over Central Park."[1345]

No matter how often he professed, that he had turned over a new leaf, that he was serious about clawing his way back to the top, that he would annihilate Joe Louis in a rematch—the fact that he quit against Louis when it got too hard in the ring, followed him everywhere. Jeers at public events, in endless newspaper columns, and catcalls from passersby that he was a quitter and a second-rater, continued to ring incessantly in his ears, Max jumped on an offer to fight in England. Perhaps the British suckers would love him.

He had mixed success across the pond. There were flashes of the old gamester to thrill the crowds. In the ring, it was apparent his condition was abysmal; he continued to fight in fits and spurts because his wind and his legs were both long gone. After viewing his tactics in London rings against their island sons, one veteran fight commentator declared disgustedly, it was "incredible that Baer ever had held the world's champion title." His own manager Ancil Hoffman admitted in 1939, that even marriage and the birth of his first son, had only tempered by 50-percent his "drinking, smoking and general hell-raising."[1346] [1347]

The curtain finally closed on Max Baer's boxing career in a 1941 rematch with a young and hungry Lou Nova. The two fought a brawl like the days of old before a sellout crowd at Madison Square Garden. But unlike past ring wars, Baer entered the ropes as the trial horse to a title-contender. The crowd came to see Nova put the finishing touches on Baer's career. After he was counted out in the eighth round, his face a gory swollen mess, in between gasps like a fish landed on a pier, Max's last words as a pro fighter inside the ring, oddly came full circle, "In my time, I could have knocked this guy's brains out."[1348] [1349]

****

After a stint as a physical conditioning instructor for the U.S. Air Force during the Second World War, Max returned to one of his favorite pastimes; creation of one imaginary tale after another about his interactions with the Camilli family. On through the 1940s and 1950s, there are literally not enough negative adjectives in existence to convey just how appallingly he lied about the subject.

One atrocious claim is that Max helped put Frankie's children through college. There was only one child, Frank Junior. Elsie Camilli's distress in the aftermath of her husband's death was so profound, she suffered a miscarriage of their second baby. Max's claims to have helped Frankie's son financially from grade school to college are lies. His son attended public schools, prepared for years to look good on college applications at the school of his choice, and passed the entry exams on his own merits, which gained him a full scholarship.

Max intimated that he and the Camillis were friends who kept in regular contact; why he and Dolph were practically best buddies. He was there with a paternal smile for major milestones in Frank Junior's life too. In fact, he was never again in contact with Frankie's widow and son. Not for other mythical benefits which never occurred, not for made up encounters on city streets.

He lied repeatedly about the number of boxing benefits he held for Frankie's family, he lied that he gave parts of all future purses to the family, and he lied about the amount of money raised for the family. The one benefit in 1935 was the first and last held, and he had to be shamed into it. No press accounts remark on any other benefit. That one benefit raised $10,500, but he even managed to balloon the final amount to anywhere from $12,000 to $21,000.

He told Tony Cordaro of the *Des Moines Tribune* in 1949, that fifteen years earlier, just after he had won the title in 1934, Frankie's then five-year-old son, miraculously appeared before him one day as he strutted down Broadway in New York City—presumably with his mother Elsie and perhaps even his favorite Uncle Dolph looking on with admiration, hands clasped to their hearts at a glimpse of their hero. The story went that a cheeky little fellow who looked vaguely familiar, tugged on his coat sleeve, and peered up at Max to chirp, "My mother and uncle talk about you a lot. They say you're a great guy."

Yet another delusional lie. Frankie's widow and son were not in a financial position to take a pleasure trip to New York City. There is no indication that Max Baer *ever* met Frankie's son. Frank Junior never left California until he attended college in 1948. Elsie Camilli never left the state of California, much less travelled outside the San Francisco Bay Area, in her lifetime.[1350]

Max had the gall to again make Frankie's son the center of his delusional fantasies, when he told a teary-eyed, horrifically fictional story in July 1951. He said that he couldn't have been prouder if Frank Junior was his own son, when he watched him graduate from the Military Academy at West Point. Frank Junior never graduated because he *died* six months before graduation—covered in the Epilogue. Alas Max now had two bodies to dig up and parade around, and for a time he even tried to make it three. He invented out of whole cloth, another son named John Camilli, who was supposedly an Army pilot that died in South Carolina! He even claimed he had set up two trust funds for these two sons.[1351] [1352]

At sports luncheons and awards events, Max would drunkenly corner Dolph Camilli to apologize for accidently taking his brother's life. But Dolph and the family read the newspapers and heard of the lies. They never forgave Max for killing Frankie; in their minds what he did was not an accident, it was intentional. Dolph later remarked that every time he saw Baer weaving unsteadily through the crowd toward him, how he wished wholeheartedly that the "damn bastard would just go away." The "damn bastard" was the same nomenclature Dolph used to describe the abusive father he despised.[1353]

Modern works and a posthumous documentary, present Baer as a gentle giant, and his wife claimed he hated to hurt people. However, in an apparent case of road rage over a parking spot in 1948, Max forced a car off the road, emerged cursing from his own vehicle, and slugged a man in the face, while his wife and six-year-old child looked on in horror. Max settled the case out of court for an undisclosed amount.[1354]

Max's wife was purported to have claimed he often bolted awake at night, sweating and muttering, "You're okay! Please be okay!" That he had a dream which always ended the same; Frankie lied prone on the canvas as Max tried in vain to revive him. People pay their dues owed the devil in their dreams. If such nightmares even occurred, perhaps they weren't about sorrow and regret. Perhaps Max was held hostage in his dreams, because it was the one place he was held responsible for what he had done, the one place he couldn't control the narrative with his lies.

∗∗∗∗

Some ask why attack Max Baer now, when he is not alive to defend himself? He had three decades to defend himself. Three decades to tell the truth. Three decades to just…stop…talking…about…it. Instead, he spun reality around like a roulette wheel with his own version of events, and blithely selected a ball to suit a given situation. The press didn't repeatedly try to drag Max back into the story; he continued to voluntarily bring it up. He left a newspaper trail of ever-changing remolded stories to present himself as the innocent, as an object of pity for how *he* suffered, as a shining example of what a benevolent benefactor he was to the Camilli family. And the lies worked spectacularly.

Over time, Max became the one the press and the public felt sorrow for. After his death in 1959, one of his obituaries claimed he suffered a cruel blow in the ring in 1930. What of Frankie Campbell, a husband and a father who was killed for fame and fortune? What of Elsie Camilli, who sat beside the utter horror that was now her husband for almost thirteen hours, as he died hour by agonizing hour while their second child grew within her? What of Frankie's only child, who grew up with a handful of elusive memories of his father, that shifted like a wind beholden to the slipstream of his mother's memories? What of Frankie's parents and siblings, who to their dying days, never got over his death, who suffered in silence to avoid the resultant uproar if they voiced their true beliefs, while their boy's killer lied through his teeth?[1355]

There are thousands of stories where an older and perhaps wiser Max Baer went on to do extraordinary things for his fellow man. He donated a phenomenal amount of his time to help others less fortunate; he handed out coins and his own clothing to the homeless, donated countless hours to benefits and TV telethons, was especially involved in sports programs for children, made ice cream runs with the neighborhood kids and even bought a sports car for the son of a friend.

But his generosity did not wipe his sins away. Being benevolent isn't always just a personality trait. It can also be a strategy. The night that set him on the path to the successes he enjoyed, and the luxurious life he led on the road, the night he knowingly knocked a man unconscious and intentionally beat him to death, that night he made a deal with the devil for his own benefit.

I was once a great admirer of Max Baer. When the heartwarming Depression-era film "Cinderella Man," about Jimmy Braddock and the night he took the title from Max Baer, debut in 2005, an uproar followed the release of the movie. As an endlessly curious historian, and a veteran genealogist, I did what I do best: research to get to the truth. As my knowledge via contemporary sources grew and became known, my fellow historians, and documentarians, reached out for rare photos and little-known stories of his life.

How utterly naive I was. I'm ashamed of myself now that I failed to dig deeper then to discover the real truth. Like most everyone, I was so thoroughly entertained and enthralled by Max's charm, his humor, his lust for life. I even named one of my dogs after him. A relentless years-long dig into primary source materials however, has now utterly destroyed the myths and exposed the truth. While some scenes in "Cinderella Man" were Hollywood illusions, the movie rightly portrayed Max Baer as exactly what he was. A sadistic lout in a bespoke suit, who fought dirty, bragged he was a killer, was abusive to women, and threatened to knock his opponents into the grave. Needless to say, it has been horrifying to discover such malevolence and deceit in a man you once considered your hero.

Do not damn me for the thousands of hours it took to ferret out the truth and piece it all together. Hold Max Baer, who effectively was the Venn diagram of a narcissistic sociopath, accountable for the lifelong lies he perpetuated about Frankie Campbell and the Camilli family, to have a good life, to be seen as the victim, and to feed his bottomless need for attention. Hold the endless parade of people who enabled this man-child, while he created one catastrophe after another, content with the knowledge that someone else would always clean up his mess, and shield him from taking even one iota of responsibility.

Max Baer lied. He lied about all of it. If he drew breath, he lied. Constantly. Repulsively. Cavalierly. Horrifically. And the lies are perpetuated and rehashed and explained away to this day.

Sacramento Union reporter Dick Edmonds once mused that on Baer's tombstone should be the epitaph: "Here lies Max Baer. While he was alive, he lived." He most certainly did. But he not only stepped over the dead body he created to get there, he repeatedly yanked Frankie Campbell up out of his grave to use as a public relations tactic.[1356]

Before Frankie Campbell slipped through the ropes that night, he had everything in life that mattered. Everything. The future lay bright and uncomplicated at his feet. He had success and respect as a result of diligent hard work at his craft. He was a moral and decent man, who had the love of a good woman, a son he adored, and a baby was about to make three. Max Baer took that all away.

Frankie Campbell embodied the word courage as he entered the ring to fight Max Baer. Almost everyone expected him to lose, and a virtual den of thieves worked to make it a reality. That expectation certainly must have seeded doubt in his heart of hearts. But he stepped through the ropes with the belief and the determination that he would win, for his fans, for his hometown, and for his family. Frankie Campbell did not fight a perfect last fight. But he fought his very best fight. And there's a certain kind of gallant nobility in the gesture that should never be forgotten.

EPILOGUE

FRANKIE CAMPBELL CAMILLI

By all accounts Frankie Campbell Camilli was an outgoing, effervescent, well-liked young man. He was the apple of his mother's eye and the spitting image of his father. While a student of Saint Ignatius High School in San Francisco, he was Colonel of the Reserve Officers Training Corps (ROTC), the largest unit in the city. For his leadership skills, military science and tactics proficiency, he was twice awarded the ROTC Efficiency Medal.

He was solid, strong, well-muscled, and avid in a variety of sports, just like his father. He was a four-year member of the Sodality. He was one of the stars of the varsity baseball and varsity football teams, the boxing club, and a medal winning shot putter with the track team. He was a member of the Block Club as a result of his outstanding achievements in sports.[1357]

Frankie Campbell Camilli
Saint Ignatius High School Senior
(1947)

A graduate with the Class of 1947, in May 1948 after week-long qualifying examinations at The Presidio U.S. Army post in San Francisco, he was formally accepted by the U.S. Military Academy at West Point in New York for the Class of 1952.

He was an ideal candidate for West Point. Not because someone had a hand in it—he was given $15 a year from the trust fund set up due to Max Baer's benefit

315

fight—but because he had diligently worked for years to earn it. As a Cadet, his acceptance included a fully funded tuition, a small salary, healthcare, room and board. He showed an aptitude for Physics, the Russian language, Topography, and Military Leadership. He was a tackle with the Army football team and took part in intramural basketball, soccer, and boxing. [1358] [1359] [1360] [1361]

In his senior year at West Point, Frank Junior went home to San Francisco on Christmas leave to see his family. On Sunday, December 30, 1951, he boarded a bus near home with an intended destination of Hamilton Field Air Force Base (AFB), in nearby Novato. As a Cadet, he could hitch a free ride on a Douglas C-47 transport plane bound for West Point, which would make a stop to refuel at Goodfellow Air Force Bases in Texas. Frankie almost missed the flight. Pranksters pointed him to the bus they said would take him to Hamilton AFB, but he discovered the bus was instead headed to Las Vegas. With a good-natured grumble, he hopped off and walked back to base. Eventually he and eighteen other military Cadets boarded the C-47.[1362] [1363]

Cadet Sergeant Francis Campbell Camilli (1951) Courtesy of U.S. Military Academy Library Archives & Special Collections

At 2:38 p.m. Mountain Standard Time, as the C-47 approached the Arizona-California border, the plane's pilot, Major Lester G. Carlson requested a change of destination to nearby Williams AFB in Chandler Arizona for insufficient fuel. In an interaction with Phoenix Approach Control, he seemed confused as to his location, yet was instructed to reduce altitude for approach. A stormy southwest wind was blowing, visibility was low, and it was later presumed the plane was blown off course into a rough, mountainous section of central Arizona. [1364] [1365]

When the plane went quiet on radio just after 3:34 p.m., eventual search and rescue efforts were coordinated out of March AFB. The Air Rescue Squadron and two divisions numbering more than sixty aircraft from half a dozen Air Force Bases took off to comb the mountains. A ground rescue team on horseback plodded into rough terrain where it was believed the plane went down.[1366]

A team of parachutists trained in medical and rescue work stood ready at Sky Harbor Airport out of Phoenix, to jump to the scene once the craft was located. A second ground rescue team from nearby Williams AFB also was placed on alert. The resulting search was later termed, "The greatest air search in the history of Arizona," with pilots making more than seventy flights over a 24,000 square mile grid, hoping to locate survivors. [1367] [1368]

Bad weather hampered the search on Monday the 31st. About noon on New Year's Day 1952, aerial searchers in a B-52 bomber spotted the wreck at an elevation of 7,000 feet, against a sheer slate cliff a mere 100 feet from the crest of Armer Mountain. On the ground, when Edna Johnson heard the piercing screech of the B-52s engines and caught sight of the wreck through her field glasses, she informed her husband Arnold, a local cattle ranch foreman. Johnson immediately guided his horse up the mountain, arriving at sundown to confirm it was the C-47.

Early Wednesday morning, Johnson led thirty-five men from the Williams AFB Ground Rescue Crew, some on horseback and some on foot, out to the site. The crews were supplied via parachuted boxes dropped from low flying planes as they trudged the steep, icy, snow-covered mountainside.

Front page crash announcement (2 Jan 1952)
Courtesy The Arizona Republic

The plane had exploded upon impact, showering debris over half a mile's distance. An upturned section of the tail stood like a tombstone at the scene. Several parachutes had deployed, cast in ghostly fashion over snow-covered rocks and trees, their silk waving gently in the wind on the hillside. All twenty-eight passengers died instantly. [1369]

A board of investigators initially determined that both propellers were in motion and the engines were operational at the time of impact, which indicated the crash was not due to mechanical failure. When it came to light that the plane's compass

317

had caused problems in the past, the board concluded navigational error compounded by faulty equipment as the cause of the crash. [1370]

Due to the remoteness of the crash site, and the depth of the snowpack, arrangements were made to remove the bodies from the mountain via horse pack. No plans were made to remove the wreckage. The fuselage was painted with yellow crosses to signify a known crash site. More than five decades later, hikers who make the grueling trek to visit the site today, still occasionally touch up the paint on the crosses that adorn the rusted and disintegrating metal fuselage. The odd and old mementos and memorials still dot the landscape along the steep trail to the crash site.[1371]

Headstone Francis Campbell Camilli
San Francisco National Cemetery
at the Presidio

Twenty-two-year-old Francis Campbell Camilli's entire bright future lay before him his last Christmas of 1951. When his plane crashed on December 30, he was six months shy of graduation. Instead of throwing his white cap into the air at West Point in June 1952, as his mother's bitter tears dropped onto yet another flower-bedecked casket, Cadet Sergeant Camilli was laid to rest just after the New Year in the hallowed grounds of The Presidio in San Francisco's National Cemetery.

DOLPH CAMILLI

After almost eight years in the minor leagues, Frankie's brother entered major league baseball in the summer of 1933. His contract as first basemen with the semi-pro Pacific Coast League team, the Sacramento Senators, was sold for $24,000 to the Chicago Cubs. His stint with the Cubs lasted barely a year.

An astute reporter later ferreted out the likely reason behind Dolph's abrupt sale to the Philadelphia Phillies. He remarked in his column on a story that had circulated just before Max Baer was to fight Primo Carnera for the Heavyweight title in June 1934. One of the Cub's hottest veteran pitchers had gone around the locker room in early June with a baseball cap held out. He wanted to pool a chunk of dough to bet on Baer to win the title.

When he approached Dolph, he was told in no uncertain terms that Dolph would never place any money, ever, on Max Baer to win anything. Heated words were exchanged. Fists were thrown before the two were separated. When the veteran pitcher informed management he would not play on the same team with the then-rookie first baseman, Dolph was traded to Philadelphia just three days before the title fight.

Dolph Camilli with the Logan Collegians,
Utah (1926) Courtesy Camilli family

During his stint with the Phillies, Dolph came into his own as a player with the team. He changed his stance, and credited playing plenty of right-handed golf in the off-season, for his marked success as a southpaw home run menace in the spring of 1935. He was an integral part of Phillies' successes, while ironically his sudden trade from the Cubs saw that team experience one of its worst seasons in memory. It was Dolph's hand that recorded the now famous film of Babe Ruth's last out before retirement, now held at the Baseball Half of Fame in Cooperstown, New York.

Dolph was sold for $50,000 to the Brooklyn Dodgers in 1938. His assocation with the Dodgers was a heady time for him, his team, and New York baseball fans. He hit the first-ever televised homerun on NBC when he slugged a two-run homer for the Dodgers against the Cincinnati Reds in 1939. He was named the National League's Most Valuable Player in 1941, after hitting .285 with 34 home runs and 120 runs batted in. Along with Pee Wee Reese and Pete Reiser, as part of the "Dodgers Renaissance," he swept the team to their first World Series in twenty-one years.

"Camilli was a quiet, gentle man, but he was strong as an ox," Dodgers Manager Leo Durocher later recalled. "He had a ferocious swing and would swat balls over Ebbets Field's right-field screen clear onto Bedford Avenue."

During his stint with the Dodgers, sports editor Keith Topping wrote; "there isn't a finer fielding first sacker in either league than the taciturn Italian ... for a big man—a muscular 200-pounder—Camilli covers an incredible amount of ground between first and second. He traps balls that would go for hits against almost any other first baseman in the major leagues; he makes difficult plays look graceful and easy; he keeps the infield buttoned up tight and practically impregnable at its axis terminal—first base." [1372]

In 1943, Dolph was traded to the New York Giants, but refused to report to the Dodgers' despised rivals. Years later he explained his decision. "I hated the Giants. This was real serious; this was no put-on stuff. Their fans hated us, and our fans hated them. I said nuts to them, and I quit."

After a short stint with the Boston Red Sox, he retired as a professional ball player in 1945. He had played twelve years in the major leagues. During the decade

1935-1945, he hit 219 home runs. Only one other National League player ever hit more home runs during the time period. He went on to manage the Oakland Oaks and the Sacramento Senators with the Pacific Coast League. He was a spring training instructor for the California Angels, a farm club manager of the Spokane Indians for the Cleveland Indians, and a scout for the New York Yankees. He was inducted into the Dodgers Hall of Fame in 1984 and recalled of his fans, "All they cared about was their family, their job and the Dodgers. And I don't know which one was the most important."

Dolph swims the Russian River (c1920s)
Courtesy Camilli family

Dolph had seven children by his lovely first wife Ruth Wallace. The couple's offspring emerged to be a remarkably talented and passionate sports family. Dolph lived for ninety glorious years and was incredibly active almost to the end. He lived an exceptionally rich and full life. Almost as if he lived a life enough for two.

ELSIE ANA MCGUIRE CAMILLI TOICH
Frankie's wife lived in San Francisco for the rest of her life. She remained a quietly feisty woman. She never forgave Max Baer for killing her husband. In 1931, after Max lost to Paulino Uzcudun in a 20-round fight at Reno Nevada she sent a pointed telegram to Paulino wishing him, "Congratulations and further success."

For over fifteen years after her husband's death, she and her son lived above her mother's grocery store on Randall Street in the Glen Park neighborhood. She continued to wear the delicate gold band Frankie had placed upon her finger in 1928. [1373]

Above all else, Elsie was a mother. That was how she defined herself. She raised her son with love, devotion, and stories of his father. When he went away to school, the first path on his journey to independence, only then did she allow herself to fall in love again. Given the heartbreak that had marred her young life, the man she entered into a union with had to be exceptional. She picked well. She found someone who offered stability, a slice of competitiveness that matched her own, and a sly sense of humor.

Elsie remarried about 1948 to Nicholas Marion "Nick" Toich. After his service in the Second World War, Nick succeeded his father to run one of the family's gas station/auto body shops. Located at 1100 Potrero Avenue in San Francisco, as of this writing, miraculously the old shop still stands, though yet another ubiquitous multi-story dwelling rises behind it. The original 1925 building still has an old wood sign with "N. Toich" written on the arch.

The couple lived in a home next to the shop, directly across from St. Joseph's Hospital, now the Zuckerberg San Francisco General Hospital. The building where Frankie breathed his last after that fateful night still stands on the Zuckerberg campus. The number of memories Elsie relived by simply looking out her parlor window must have been incalculable. Nick died in July 1989. Elsie followed him in death five months later in December. Married for over forty years, after Elsie's miscarriage of Frankie's second child, they were unable to conceive children. But they were active in their community, avid tournament-level bowlers, and loved nothing better than to sip cocktails and bet on the ponies at the old Bay Meadows Racetrack. They are buried together, not far away from Frankie and from Elsie's parents, at Holy Cross Cemetery in Colma, California.[1374]

ALBINA ELIZA TASSI CAMILLI

Despite the abuse she suffered as a young woman, Frankie's mother retained and passed on to her boys, her never-ending sense of humor and playfulness.

She died at age 95 on August 26, 1980 in San Mateo, California, 50 years to the day after she lost her son. She was surrounded by her loved ones in her final moments as she finally went to join her dearly missed boy.

Her recipe for Thanksgiving dinner gravy is said to be a winner at family holidays.

Albina Camilli (c1930s)
Courtesy Camilli family

ALESSIO CAMILLI

Frankie's father Alessio Camilli remodeled, built, and sold homes across the San Francisco Bay Area. He died from the effects of long-term alcohol abuse in March 1966 in San Jose,

California. No obituary was posted. No funeral was held. To the present day he is referred to by the family as "that damn bastard."

ALBERT CAMILLI

Frankie and Dolph's eldest brother Albert created a wonderful life in Humboldt County, California. In every family video and photo his beaming smile, and a wise-cracking, War. After he earned his pilot's license, in time he became manager of the Eureka Airport on the Samoa Peninsula. He owned Camilli's Flying Service, which offered rentals, sales and flying courses. He was a member of the Humboldt County Sheriff's Marine Posse, which engages in search and rescue emergencies. He was also a popular referee for local boxing matches. He died at age 73 from the long-term effects of the lead in the paints he used.

FRANKIE THOMAS CAMILLI

In 1958, twenty-five-year-old Francis Thomas Camilli, son of Frankie's eldest brother Albert, died in a horrendous automobile accident in Samoa, California, near Eureka. He left behind a wife and three children. Dolph Camilli's second wife asked members of the Camilli family to please stop naming their sons Frank.[1375]

CAROLLE "CAL" WORKING

After Cal's license to manage fighters was reinstated in 1932, he and Tom Maloney took up with Armand Emanuel after Pop Emanuel's retirement. It was a disastrous short-lived comeback. In 1933, Cal then bought part of the contract and became co-Manager of Alberto "Baby" Arizmendi. Cal guided him to California Featherweight and Welterweight titles. Their association ended when Arizmendi retired and served overseas during the Second World War. In the 1940s Cal bought the contract of Al "Turkey" Thompson, who fought Bob Pastor in two sensational bouts, and then guided him to a California Heavyweight Title. He then opened what was described as a "poor man's Stork Club," known as The California Club, on lower Sunset Boulevard in Los Angeles. He had stints in the 1950s as matchmaker for the Hollywood Legion and the Olympic Auditorium. He retired from the boxing game to devote his time to what became a well-known Mexican and Spanish restaurant on Restaurant Row on South La Cienega, known as Casa Cienega. He died at age 70 in 1965 of a brain tumor.

TOM MALONEY

Tom became a bail bondsman in Los Angeles after Frankie's death. In 1932, he was arrested for extortion after it was asserted, he took money to 'fix' morals charges on two ladies of the evening. When his license to manage fighters was reinstated in 1933, he wasted no time giving the State Boxing Commission cause to regret it.

He was repeatedly suspended, often for months at a time. He once changed a contract after it was signed. Another time he tried to raise ticket prices after sales opened. In the mid-1930s, he owned a cigar store in San Francisco before he drifted to the Pacific Northwest. For a time, he managed local Seattle, Washington boxers, and later trained a promising heavyweight, "Wild Bill" Boyd, until Jack Dempsey coaxed Boyd to the East Coast. [1376]

322

He eventually engaged in questionable employment at card rooms and race tracks in Seattle and Portland, Oregon. In 1957, he was among 116 grand jury indictments as the result of a massive vice investigation in Portland. Maloney was charged with conspiracy and corruption and sent to trial. He was said to be in league with top officials of the Teamsters Union in Portland Oregon, with Seattle and Spokane, Washington mob-backed gambling figures, and with a former D.A. engaged in illicit activities with Portland's self-proclaimed "Vice Czar" James B. Elkins. Elkins had county politicians, members of the judiciary and law enforcement in his pocket.

Tom Maloney (c1920s)
Courtesy author's collection

Tom Maloney's association with Elkins made him a peripheral part of the United States Senate's McClellan Committee on labor racketeering, which included Robert F. Kennedy as Special Counsel, and Senator John F. Kennedy as a committee member. In ill health and playing the hapless victim before the jury, Tom was acquitted of all charges. He happily married late in life, and in 1946 had one child. He named his son Frank.[1377]

ALBERT YOUNG

National Hall's owner Al Young's devotion to the game was complete; he lived just over 100 feet away from the National on Adair Street. On a July evening in 1940, he collapsed dead right on the floor of the hall that held his heart. For many years, he had been engaged in a hard-fought battle of complications from anemia and bleeding ulcers. When doctors suggested a succession of blood transfusions, fighters he had promoted through the years were first in line among those who donated blood, though ultimately all efforts to save his life were unsuccessful.

After Al's death, the National struggled along. William P. Kyne, the patriarch of Bay Meadows Racetrack, financially backed a major remodel of the hall in early 1949. He installed North Beach native Louis Beaux, who in the 1940s had cornered fights with legendary trainer Dolph Thomas, as the National's matchmaker.

But the advent of fans content to watch fights on television was the death knell for the venerable old club. By year's end, after mixed financial returns, Kyne withdrew his support. Louis promised fans he had plans to again run Friday night cards early in 1950. When he encountered issues with the lease, the haven that had given Frankie Campbell his first chance in the ring quietly closed its doors without fanfare for the final time.

JACK DOYLE

Despite his acumen as promoter for the Olympic Auditorium, by the mid-1930s with the Depression at its height, the Olympic, as with all other venues in the state, consistently and profusely bled red ink. Many a night the Olympic sat dark rather than lose more money. Doyle largely abandoned the fight game and devoted all his efforts to other endeavors.

He had been an early investor in what was known as the Signal Hill oil fields, where a wildcatter for Shell Oil struck a gusher in 1921. Located above the coastal town of Long Beach, so many oil derricks soon littered the little town that one rise was nicknamed Porcupine Hill, and eventually derricks extended down to the edge of the Pacific Ocean.

Within two years, Southern California became the source of one-quarter of the world's entire output of oil. With his profits from Signal Hill, Jack bought more oil fields, and developed land in the rapidly growing Los Angeles Basin. When he died in 1944 at the age of 66, Jack Doyle would have made King Midas envious.

WAD WADHAMS

Life was not so kind to matchmaker Hayden "Wad" Wadhams. After he parted ways with Jack Doyle, Wad fought tooth and nail to arrange profitable fights for the Olympic Auditorium. The Great Depression had other plans. Wad left his position with the Olympic in 1933. He was among several backers to promote boxing events through various small athletic clubs throughout Southern California. His efforts were unsuccessful due to pressure on the State Boxing Commission by the Olympic and the Legion to snuff out competition for the few event dollars available. He turned to management of several boxers who showed promise, but the endeavors eventually fizzled.

In the summer of 1937, when he read about the sudden death of his old friend Robert Cronin, sports editor of the *Los Angeles Illustrated Daily News*, Wad suffered a stroke, and became partially paralyzed. Earning a living was now impossible. He then contracted Valley Fever; one of the side effects of which resulted in hallucinations. After he began to fly into violent rages, with threats to kill his wife and son, in October, 1937, a Superior Court Judge granted his wife's request that he be ruled insane, and committed to a mental hospital.

The Hollywood American Legion held a benefit to help pay Wad's mortgage and medical bills. They reached out to their members, boxing fans, and fighters, to ensure the event was a financial success. In 1941, the man who along with Jack Doyle, was responsible for keeping Southern California boxing alive through the Four-Round Era; the man who easily arranged over 10,000 fights, raked in millions for the Vernon Arena, the Olympic Auditorium and Wrigley Field, and brought the finest fights and fighters to the area; died destitute at the age of fifty-six. He left a widow and three children. Jack Doyle and Cal Working were among the pallbearers at his funeral.

TOBY IRWIN

Toby Irwin remained a habitually shady and sadistic referee who picked and chose which ring rules to follow. He was consistently despised by fans, many of whom never forgave his role in Frankie's death. In professional, amateur, and inter-collegiate rings across the state, a resounding chorus of boos greeted him every time he slipped between the ropes. Upon the occasion in 1942 wherein Toby Irwin "muffed the verdict" by giving the decision under suspicious circumstances to the wrong man at the Ray Lunny–Richie Lemos State Featherweight title bout, *Oakland Tribune* sports writer Art Cohn listed all five recommendations put forth by the grand jury back in 1930 to clean up boxing, and noted that none of them was ever adopted. For his questionable work, predictably, the State Boxing Commission later made him a fight judge.[1378]

Despite how close he came to being convicted of a crime in 1930, Irwin went on to repeat his questionable actions in the future. Former fight manager and assistant at Newman's Gym, Joe Herman, recalled a preliminary fight in the 1930s when he managed Eddie Halligan as he touched gloves in a rematch with Kid Ray at the Dreamland. Toby Irwin was referee. The fight ended up with Eddie sitting on Ray's chest and beating the crap out of him. The police entered the ring, handcuffed them both, and carried them out of the ring. "And that cold-blooded Toby Irwin—he never even moved," remarked Herman, "He wouldn't break 'em if they killed each other."[1379]

ALLEN BIGELOW BIXBY

Just over a decade after he submitted the results of his sham investigation into the death of Frankie Campbell, Allen Bigelow Bixby, married scion of a wealthy pioneering Long Beach family, died from a blow to the head as a result of a parking lot brawl. In November 1941, Bixby, along with his friend Charles Weyland Sizemore of Arizona, both of whom had already frequented several bars earlier in the evening, decided to do a bit of slumming. They were on their sixth drink since their midnight arrival at a cocktail lounge on 3rd Street in downtown Pasadena. After closing time, as the lounge's organist Velma Williams Salich, estranged wife of Hafis Salich—a former Naval intelligence Officer, who was convicted in 1939 on an espionage charge—tried to get past Bixby to slide into her car to drive home, Bixby grabbed her inappropriately and tried to get her to leave with him. The lounge bartender Howard Crooks intervened on her behalf. Bixby knocked Crooks against Velma's car, whereupon the men exchanged blows. Bixby slipped, fell, and struck his head on the sidewalk. Though Crooks was later absolved of the charges, he spent several days in jail for attempted murder after Bixby suffered a basal skull fracture, lapsed into a coma, and died from his injuries.[1380]

****

Frankie Campbell's family members take great pride in their fistic uncle's story. Frankie's niece, Joanne once remarked with pride in her voice; "We fight back when challenged, even the girls. We Camillis are all strong-boned people, though none of us are tall or look very big.... We have large hands. My father Dolph's fingers were like cigars.... My father was a wonderful man. He truly lived in the 'now.' He had such a presence; he was adventurous, but dignified and almost bashful. Oh, and he was so ingenious. He even taught himself how to build houses.... I tend to think Frankie and my father were quite alike.... I've often thought we must be descendants of a warrior-class."[1381]

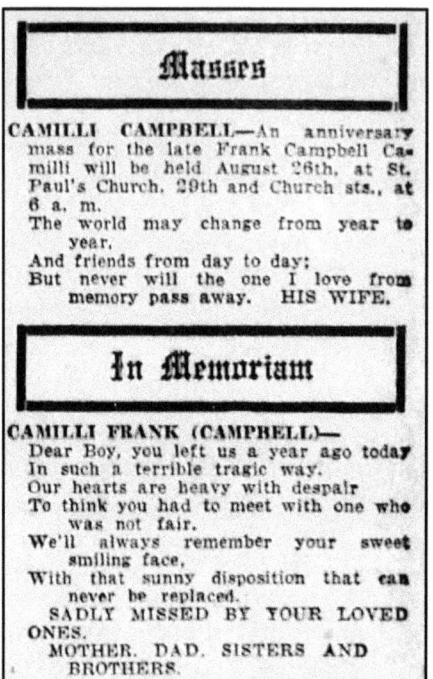

One of ten "In Memoriam" ads
placed over ten years
by Frank's family on the
anniversary of his death

Though she doesn't know it, a pained wistfulness crosses the lovely face of Frankie's niece Diane, when the subject of her uncle's death comes up. She said it was a tragedy too difficult to discuss in the family, and was rarely spoken of. As young children, she and her siblings once inquired who the fighter was in photos autographed to her father, in pride of place on the walls of home. When she once asked about Frankie, in the last year of his life, her proud ninety-year-old father broke down. The pall cast from Frankie's death has literally spanned generations.[1382]

In his eulogy to Frankie Campbell, *Oakland Tribune* sports writer Bob Shand wrote in 1930, "Frankie Campbell went to his death fighting, and as long as the 'racket' endures they will tell of the last stand of Frankie Campbell, gentleman and sportsman and the gamest boxer that ever drew on a glove."[1383]

ACKNOWLEDGMENTS

ALWAYS GO TOO FAR, BECAUSE THAT'S WHERE YOU'LL FIND THE TRUTH
- ALBERT CAMUS

Just as history doesn't occur in a vacuum, no biography is written alone. My sincerest thanks to the following people for sharing their time, care, support, thoughts, expertise, documentation, photos, and experience with me:

Amy O'Hair: Words cannot express my deep appreciation for your infinite support, kind encouragement, and blunt honesty every step of the way. Thank you for your boundless kindness as my mentor, as a richly gifted historian, as a researcher extraordinaire, and as a generous editor of my manuscript.

Jim "Kid Daylight" Stinson: Instant connections are a rarity. I'm so grateful to have found one with you. Thank you for being a dear and true friend, for the endless belly laughs, all those moments you talked me off the ledge, the woo-woo stuff nobody else gets, the smoky (hack, cough) sexiness of your voice, and your ever-wise council. Stahhhhhpit, I'm so done with you. =)~

Tony Hood: For so long I was intensely alone with this nightmare. Then some stoopid head came along and shouldered a bit of my burden. Thank you for once being my most encouraging supporter, and an endlessly patient sounding board. So much of your exacting eye and insatiable curiosity for the truth lies within these pages. We sure did thaw a million frozen chickens on Mars.

Jeff Bumpus: This book would have never approached what I envisioned without you, wonderful you. For the countless times we went over the second and fifth rounds. For how often I pestered you about the mind and motivations of a fighter and their handlers. And for being among the first to tell me I wasn't crazy, the truth really was as awful as I thought, I can only say, thank you endlessly, dearest pal o' mine.

Diane Camilli Abraham: Dear Lady Di, how Frank would have adored you, as do I, you have been so lovely to me. Thank you for the many joyful moments spent in your company, the phone calls that lasted for hours, the endless stories of your family, the incredible home movies, and the photos, oh the photos. Without the remembrances by you and Joanne, your uncle would have remained a forgotten tragic sports figure, and not the still very much missed son of a true tribe of warriors.

Bill Dettloff, Michael Kronenberg, and Nigel Collins: That you reached out to some wacky broad, keyboard-pounding out facts on classic boxing groups, which banned me for telling the truth, that you believed in my research, that you took a chance, that you consistently gave me legitimacy every step of the way, will always mean the world to me. Thank you, gents.

M.L. Zambrana: Bix!! Your mad research skills, and your tireless efforts as historian of the Hollywood American Legion Stadium, brings boxing history alive every day on Facebook. Bottomless thank-youse, wonderful, amazing you that I get to call friend.

Gary Todd: Your painting of "Perdition" was always there to motivate me, to anger me, to push me harder to seek the truth. Still honored every day at your generosity, your thoughtful creativity, those writer-to-writer chats, and a deep dive into the mindset of butchery and animal husbandry. Thank you, mister.

Doug Cavanaugh: For allowing me to borrow so many good lines that seem to flow endlessly from your creative tongue, thank you, pal.

Edo, Steve, Paul and Michael: Hand on heart, for all the days your memes and words and wisecracks were a wonderful and welcome break from the mental gymnastics of this journey. The only thing that exceeds an Australian sense of humor are your huge and thoughtful hearts. Thank you, fellas, you are true princes, and I'm grateful to know each one of you.

Eternal appreciation to the truly unsung heroes that are librarians, archivists and historians; from the History Center at the San Francisco Public Library, the Doe Library at University of California, Berkeley, the Shields Library at UC Davis Special Collections, the California State Archives, the Witkin State Law Library, the University of Notre Dame Hesburgh Libraries Rare Books & Special Collections, the New York State Library, and the San Francisco Municipal Transportation Agency for every prompt, thorough, and friendly interaction.

Many of my book's images come from digital history archives lovingly preserved and stewarded by the fine folks at Western Neighborhoods Project outsidelands.org, OpenSFHistory opensfhistory.org, and FoundSF foundsf.org.

As a San Francisco Bay Area native, with family who once lived in the same neighborhoods, and were congregants of the same parish as the Camillis, Tassis, and McGuires, to discover as a child I unknowingly walked the exact same streets which knew Frank's feet, and passed the houses he called home, will always be still my heart. It was excruciatingly hard to let you go, fella. To truth. To justice. To you.

ABOUT THE AUTHOR

Catherine Johnson parlayed her four-decade long experience as a genealogist and historic researcher, five-decade long interest in boxing, and a six-decade long insatiable curiosity that drove her parents bonkers, into this, her first non-fiction biography.

Any factual mistakes, errors of omission, or faulty analysis are the authors alone. While the author has made every reasonable effort to trace the copyright owners for any and all of the photographs and illustrations in this book, there may be some errors or omissions of credits.

Fascinated by the first Golden Age of Boxing?

Follow Catherine on Twitter/X @BoxingGoldenAge for random and rare boxing photos and facts from circa 1900-1940.

Visit Catherine's new blog page at https://brownglovebooks.substack.com/ for stories and facts that didn't make the book's final edit, and for posts and photos about boxing circa 1900-1940.

INDEX

ENDNOTES

1 Charlotte Observer 28 Jul 1934 p18

2 Nevada State Journal 31 Aug 1930 p1

3 Verbal confirmation of full name and DOB via Blessed Sacrament Parish of Hibbing MN 12 May 2022

4 Michigan, U.S., Marriage Records, 1867-1952; Film; 68; Page 528

5 The Gilded Age, directed by Sarah Colt. (2018; Boston, MA: WGBH Educational Foundation for PBS); Season 30 Episode 3, PBS

6 1899; Arrival; New York, New York, USA; Microfilm Serial; T715, 1897-1957; Line; 1; Page Number; 326

7 1899; Arrival; New York, New York, USA; Microfilm Serial; T715, 1897-1957; Line; 1; Page Number; 326

8 Born From Iron; Iron Mountain, Michigan, 1879-1979 by Mary Louise Dulan, pp. 138-150

9 familysearch.org/ark;/61903/1;1;KD4Y-9V7; Italians to America Passenger Data File, 1855-1900

10 New York, U.S., Arriving Passenger and Crew Lists 1820-1957

11 Michigan, U.S., Marriage Records, 1867-1952; Dickinson County; Film 68; Page 582; Record 1130.

12 National Archives WWII Draft Registration Cards for California, 10/16/1940-03/31/1947; Record Group; 147; Box; 265

13 U.S., Social Security Death Index, 1935-2014

14 Minnesota Territorial Census Schedules, 1849-1855; 10 Jun 1905; ED 42, Hibbing, Stuntz, St Louis, MN, Sheet 36

15 August 2008 Phone Interview Joanne Camilli Griggs

16 Frank Blatnik, "Culture Conflict; A Study of the Slovenes in Chisholm, Minnesota" (Master's thesis, University of Minnesota, 1942) 184

17 Duluth and St Louis County MN Their Story and People, Walter Van Brunt; p559

18 Duluth and St Louis County MN Their Story and People, Walter Van Brunt; p559

19 1905 MN U.S. State and Territory census

20 06 Jun 1903 Duluth Evening Herald p11

21 Sanborn Fire Insurance Map; Hibbing, Saint Louis County, Minnesota. Dec 1908

22 Labor World - Duluth, MN; 06 Aug 1904 p2

23 Duluth News-Tribune 07 Oct 1904 p3

24 The Labor World 15 Apr 1905

25 Duluth News-Tribune 20 Oct 1904 p10

26 Duluth News-Tribune 20 Oct 1904 p10

27 Town of Hibbing arrest record #182266; Vol 1, Page 66, Line 11; 28 Nov 1904

28 Duluth News-Tribune 29 Aug 1907

29 archives.gov/legislative/features/sf

30 San Francisco Examiner 20 Apr 1906 p5

31 sunnysidehistory.org/2015/11/08/cows-in-sunnyside-2/

32 sunnysidehistory.org/2018/10/12/high-on-a-hillside-the-sunnyside-sign/

33 Sunnyside Oral History Project Transcripts (SFH 467), San Francisco History Center, San Francisco Public Library

34 sunnysidehistory.org/2019/01/04/1911-snapshot-of-life-on-monterey-boulevard/

35 sunnysidehistory.org/2023/01/24/of-goats-and-groceries-some-italians-in-early-sunnyside/

36 sunnysidehistory.org/histories-of-sunnyside/

37 The Recorder, San Francisco 24 Nov 1904 p1

38 San Francisco City Directory 1909 p357

39 Phone interview Diane Camilli Abraham April 2023

40 Email conversation with Amy O'Hair August 2022

41 Email conversation with Amy O'Hair January 2022

42 sunnysidehistory.org/2016/11/04/the-sunnyside-crossing/

43 sunnysidehistory.org/2016/02/29/the-ballad-of-ellen-furey/

44 Sunnyside Oral History Project Transcripts (SFH 467), San Francisco History Center, San Francisco Public Library

45 sunnysidehistory.org/2015/11/08/cows-in-sunnyside-2/

46 Sunnyside Oral History Project Transcripts (SFH 467), San Francisco History Center, San Francisco Public Library

47 San Francisco Bulletin 21 Aug 1913 p2

48 mtfca.com/encyclo/1918.htm

49 1921 CA Vehicle Registration Vol 1-2

50 Horatio's Drive. Directed by Ken Burns. Walpole; Florentine Films, 2003

51 Weinberg, S. Kirson and Arond, Henry, The Occupational Culture of the Boxer: American Journal of Sociology. Vol. 57, No. 5, The Sociological Study of Work (Mar 1952), pp. 460-469.

52 Phone Interview Joanne Camilli Griggs Jul 2008

53 Phone interview Diane Camilli Abraham 25 October 2022

54 The Recorder; San Francisco, CA; 19 May 1922; Page 5

55 National Center for Health Statistics: Marriage & Divorce 1920

56 Phone Interview Joanne Camilli Griggs Jul 2008

57 Phone Interview Joanne Camilli Griggs Aug 2008

58 Giant's Magazine "Sandlot Stars; Dolph Camilli" p154, Le Pacini

59 April 2022 email Sacred Heart Preparatory Cathedral

60 Phone interview Diane Camilli Abraham 21 Oct 2022

61 Giant's Magazine "Sandlot Stars; Dolph Camilli" p154, Le Pacini

62 Phone Interview Joanne Camilli Griggs Sep 2008

63 Phone Interview Joanne Camilli Griggs Sep 2008

64 Los Angeles Times 17 Nov 1929 p87

65 Los Angeles Times 17 Nov 1929 p87

66 Philadelphia Inquirer 08 Jul 1934 p34

67 Interview Diane Camilli Abraham 25 October 2022

68 "SF Baseball; A Walk Down Memory Lane" Jimmy Custodio; Good Old Sandlot Days website

69 San Francisco Chronicle 14 Feb. 1944 p15 - Will Connolly

70 Hometown San Francisco, Jerry Flamm p68

71 Los Angeles Times 17 Nov 1929 p87

72 San Francisco Bulletin 11 Mar 1924 p18

73 Los Angeles Examiner 01 Jun 1930 p86

74 San Francisco Chronicle 28 Feb 1928

75 San Francisco Bulletin 24 Sep 1925 p24

76 Philadelphia Inquirer 08 Jul 1934 p34

77 Jewish Boxers Hall of Famers, Ken Blady p26 1988 Shapolsky Publishers New York

78 Los Angeles Times 24 Apr 1899

79 San Francisco Examiner 01 Nov 1881 p2

80 Twitter post reply by Ray Esten 21 Jun 2024

81 The Truth About Toledo's Day in the Sun, Jul 3, 2019, Tedd Long, holytoledohistory.com.

82 Indianapolis Star 05 Jul 1919 p10/11

83 Evansville Journal 20 May 1919 p6

84 Empire of the Air; The Men Who Made Radio; Ken Burns Florentine Films Walpole, NH; 1992.

85 Empire of the Air; The Men Who Made Radio; Ken Burns Florentine Films Walpole, NH; 1992.

86 Los Angeles Times 23 Aug 1913 p21

87 Los Angeles Times 24 Aug 1913 p83

88 Los Angeles Evening Post-Record 23 Aug 1913 p11

89 Los Angeles Evening Post-Record 23 Aug 1913 p1

90 San Bernardino County Sun 09 Sep 1913 p15

91 ballotpedia.org/California_Proposition_20,_Prize_Fights_Initiative_(1914)

92 Jerry Flamm, Hometown San Francisco (San Francisco: Scottwell Associates, 1994) p80-81

93 boxrec.com/media/index.php/USA;_California_Laws

94 Jerry Flamm, Hometown San Francisco (San Francisco: Scottwell Associates, 1994) p70

95 Jerry Flamm, Hometown San Francisco (San Francisco: Scottwell Associates, 1994) p70

96 100 years ago; The Law That Gave Birth to the Modern Era of Boxing - Mike Silver 28 May 2020 BoxingOverBroadway

97 ballotpedia.org/California_Proposition_7,_Boxing_and_Wrestling_Contests_Initiative_(1924)

98 100 years ago; The Law That Gave Birth to the Modern Era of Boxing - Mike Silver 28 May 2020 BoxingOverBroadway

99 boxrec.com/media/index.php/USA;_California_Laws

100 100 years ago; The Law That Gave Birth to the Modern Era of Boxing - Mike Silver 28 May 2020 BoxingOverBroadway

101 City Journal "The Ghost Sport" Paul Beston; Summer 2011

102 New York Times 01 Feb 1981, Section 5, P3

103 Oakland Post Enquirer 28 Aug 1935 p14

104 Los Angeles Evening Express 22 Oct 1929 p23

105 San Francisco, California, City Directory, 1924 p1406

106 San Francisco Examiner 27 Apr 1907 p2

107 San Francisco Examiner 18 Jul 1907 p10

108 Family Search ID M1CR-L7V, Albert Bartholomew Valerga (1878-1947)

109 Santa Rosa Republican 18 Dec 1924 p1

110 Ft Bragg Advocate 22 Jul 1925 p1

111 San Francisco Bulletin 25 Jun 1925 p22

112 San Francisco Chronicle 19 Apr 1929 p28

113 La Voce Del Popolo 19 Feb 1925 p5

114 San Francisco Examiner 28 Aug 1924 p27

115 boxrec.com/en/proboxer/191532

116 October 2022 interview Diane Camilli Abraham

117 boxrec.com/media/index.php/National_Hall

118 San Francisco Chronicle 8 Feb 1923 p1

119 King, Osric S. "Infectious disease and boxing." Clinics in sports medicine vol. 28,4 (2009): 545-60

120 Richmond News Leader 05 Feb 1940 p12

121 City Within a City; Historic Context Statement for
San Francisco's Mission District; Nov 2007; p58

122 Germany, Births and Baptisms, 1558-1898, FHL Film #415948 FamilySearch.org

123 H.F. Suhr Company, Case #16983, San Francisco Area Funeral Home Records, 1895-1985.

124 San Francisco Chronicle 08 Feb 1923 p1

125 San Francisco Newsletter 18 Feb 1911 p3

126 Jerry Flamm, Hometown San Francisco (San Francisco: Scottwell Associates, 1994) p87

127 San Francisco Bulletin 07 Feb 1923 p11

128 San Francisco Examiner 03 Feb 1923 p30

129 San Francisco Examiner 15 Apr 1972 p29

130 History of Wages in the US; Construction labor wages in San Francisco for 1924.

131 Our Navy, the Standard Publication of the U.S. Navy, Volume 19; Page 22; 01 May 1925.

132 Gallimore, Andrew; Babyface Goes to Hollywood, The O'Brien Press; Dublin, Ireland; 2013

133 Higgins, Brian Patrick; Alameda's Pugilistic Heyday, Alameda Magazine

134 Oakland Tribune 06 Mar 1923 p25

135 Oakland Tribune 30 May 1925 p10

136 Kisliuk, Bill. Tenderloin Times. April 1990. Vol. 14, No. 4, p1.

137 San Francisco Bulletin 01 Feb, 1917 p14

138 San Francisco Bulletin 16 Jul, 1917 p11

139 San Francisco Bulletin 06 Sep 1916 p11

140 San Francisco Bulletin 15 Jul 1919 p16

141 San Francisco Chronicle 16 Jan 1923 p3

142 Hayward Daily Review 12 Oct 1960 p11

143 Jerry Flamm, Hometown San Francisco (San Francisco: Scottwell Associates, 1994) p69

144 Find Box Rec or articles on next few fights

145 U.S. Department of Labor, Bureau of Labor Statistics, All Industries, 1924

146 Interview Diane Camilli Abraham 5 April 2023

147 San Francisco Examiner 11 Dec 1924 p33

148 San Francisco Bulletin 11 Dec 1924 p20

149 The San Francisco Examiner 8 Jan 1925 p29

150 San Francisco Examiner 1 Feb 1925 p101

151 Tacoma Daily Ledger 16 Jan 1925 p8

152 San Francisco Bulletin 24 Jan 1925 p16

153 The San Francisco Examiner 7 Feb 1925 p30

154 San Francisco Examiner 18 Feb 1925 p30

155 San Francisco Bulletin 19 Feb 1925 p21

156 San Francisco Examiner - 22 Feb 1925 p100

157 Oakland Tribune 05 Feb 1925

158 San Francisco Chronicle 25 Feb 1925 p27

159 Los Angeles Evening Post-Records 12 Nov 1929 p8

160 Wisconsin Rapids Daily Tribune 30 Nov 1929 p7

161 The Marysville Appeal 19 Apr 1925 p7

162 San Francisco Chronicle 16 Apr 1925 p23

163 The Marysville Appeal 12 Apr 1925 p8

164 The Marysville Appeal - 12 Apr 1925 p8

165 San Francisco Chronicle 11 Jun 1925 p23

166 San Francisco Chronicle 22 Jul 1925 p24

167 Ogden Standard Examiner 31 Jul 1925 p17

168 Fort Worth Star Telegram 31 Jul 1925 p16

169 San Francisco Examiner 01 Aug 1925 p29

170 San Francisco Call 16 Oct 1906 p7

171 San Francisco Chronicle 19 Aug 1906 p38

172 2-0 Police Journal; Nov 1928; A Temple of Happiness; p21

173 2-0 Police Journal; Nov 1928; A Temple of Happiness; p21

174 Don't Call Me Babyface, Maclean's Magazine, 01 Nov 1950 p17

175 Oakland Post Enquirer 21 Dec 1925 p22

176 Byington, Lewis Francis, "History of San Francisco 3 Vols", S. J. Clarke Publishing Co., Chicago, 1931. Vol. 3 Pages 140-142

177 San Francisco Call 26 Apr 1905 p10

178 San Francisco Examiner 26 May 1964 p58

179 Byington, Lewis Francis, "History of San Francisco 3 Vols", S. J. Clarke Publishing Co., Chicago, 1931. Vol. 3 Pages 84

180 Byington, Lewis Francis, "History of San Francisco 3 Vols", S. J. Clarke Publishing Co., Chicago, 1931. Vol. 3 Pages 140-142

181 Petitions For Naturalization, U.S. District Court for Central District of California (Los Angeles), 1940-1991; NAI Number: 594890.

182 San Francisco Examiner 19 Jul 1925 pP2

183 San Francisco Examiner 25 Sep 1925 p33/35

184 San Francisco Chronicle 29 Sep 1925 p25

185 San Francisco Chronicle 29 Aug 1925 p33

186 San Francisco Bulletin 25 Sep 1925 p28

187 San Francisco Chronicle 22 Sep 1925 p2H

188 San Francisco Chronicle 22 Sep 1925 p2H

189 San Francisco Examiner 25 Sep 1925 p33

190 San Francisco Chronicle 26 Sep 1925 p25

191 Los Angeles Daily News 05 Sep 1925 p18

192 San Francisco Chronicle 27 Sep 1925 p28

193 San Francisco Bulletin 26 Sep 1925 p21

194 San Francisco Chronicle 05 Oct 1925 p22

195 San Francisco Chronicle 28 Sep 1925 p20

196 San Francisco Recorder 13 Jul 1925 p8

197 Oakland Tribune 07 Nov 1925 p14

198 San Francisco Examiner 17 Oct 1925 p36

199 The Idaho Statesman 15 Sep 1935, p6

200 U.S., World War II Draft Cards Young Men, 1940-1947; SN 656, ON 11169

201 San Francisco Examiner 12 Nov 1925 p31

202 San Francisco Examiner 14 Nov 1925 p31

203 Oakland Tribune 14 Nov 1925 p9

204 San Francisco Chronicle 14 Dec 1925 p21

205 Tampa Tribune 02 Nov 1925 p10

206 San Francisco Chronicle 05 Jan 1926 p25

207 San Jose Evening News 05 Jan 1926 p8

208 Honolulu Advertiser 28 Feb 1926 p11

209 San Francisco Chronicle 08 Jan 1926 p25

210 San Diego Union 18 Jan 1926 p8

211 San Francisco Chronicle 01 Feb 1926 p21

212 La Voce Del Popolo 28 Jul 1925 p4

213 San Francisco Examiner 02 Mar 1926 p29

214 San Francisco Bulletin 31 Jul 1925 p21

215 Oakland Tribune 29 Mar 1926 p20

216 San Francisco Chronicle 31 Mar 1926 p24

217 Oakland Tribune 31 Mar 1926 p22

218 Denver Post 1 Apr 1926 p24

219 Oakland Post-Enquirer 01 Apr 1926 p10

220 Oakland Post-Enquirer 01 Apr 1926 p10

221 San Francisco Bulletin 02 Apr 1926 p17

222 Fitzgerald, F. Scott. My Lost City: personal essays, 1920-1940, p112. Kiribati: Cambridge University Press, 2005

223 The San Francisco Standard. SF Then/Now: Policing a Vice-Filled San Francisco 100 Years Ago. Lindqwister, Liz. 25 Aug 2022.

224 Prohibition. Directed by Ken Burns and Lynn Novick. Walpole NH; Florentine Films, 2011

225 Oakland Tribune 04 Apr 1926 p34

226 San Francisco Chronicle 04 Apr 04 1926 p80

227 San Francisco Examiner 04 May 1926 p29

228 Oakland Tribune 17 May 1926 p49

229 Oakland Tribune 17 May 1926 p49

230 Los Angeles Times 09 May 1926 p26

231 Calgary Albertan 29 May 1942 p4

232 Oakland Tribune 20 May 1926 p23

233 Los Angeles Post 28 May 1926 p22

234 San Francisco Chronicle 18 Jan 1926 p19

235 San Francisco Examiner 05 Feb 1926 p27

236 San Francisco Examiner 18 Jan 1926 p27

237 San Francisco Chronicle 28 Sep 1926 p2H

238 San Francisco Chronicle 05 Oct 1926 p22

239 San Francisco Examiner 27 Oct 1926 p33

240 San Francisco Examiner 23 Oct 1926 p28

241 Melbourne Sporting Globe 12 Apr 1947 p4

242 San Francisco Chronicle 25 Oct 1926 p23

243 San Francisco Examiner 23 Oct 1926 p28

244 San Francisco Examiner 23 Oct 1926 p28

245 San Francisco Examiner 01 Dec 1926 p33

246 San Francisco Examiner 02 Dec 1926 p29

247 Oakland Tribune 04 Dec 1926 p10

248 San Francisco Examiner 04 Dec 1926 p29

249 Oakland Tribune 04 Dec 1926 p10

250 San Francisco Examiner 04 Dec 1926 p29

251 San Francisco Examiner 04 Dec 1926 p29

252 San Francisco Bulletin 13 Dec 1926 p15

253 California State Library; Sacramento, California; Great Register of Voters, 1900-1968; Roll # 035; 8 Oct 1927

254 San Francisco Examiner 29 Apr 1927 p9

255 San Francisco Chronicle 29 Apr 1927 p12

256 Crocker-Langley San Francisco city directory; R.L. Polk & Co; 1928

257 Sausalito News, Volume XXXXIII, Number 18, 30 April 1927

258 San Francisco Examiner 23 Apr 1927 p32

259 The Kansas City Star 10 Feb 1921 p11

260 New York Daily News 26 Aug 1927 p45

261 San Francisco Bulletin 30 Mar 1928 p21

262 San Francisco Examiner 25 Apr 1928 p29

263 San Francisco Examiner 26 Apr 1928 p35

264 Oakland Tribune 26 Apr 1928 p29

265 San Francisco Bulletin 26 Apr 1928 p21

266 San Francisco Examiner 05 May 1928 p21

267 sfarmory.com/history.html – Chris Carlsson

268 San Francisco Examiner 07 May 1928 p29

269 bayarearadio.org/history-index/timeline_kya-koit

270 San Francisco Chronicle 02 May 1928 p27

271 San Francisco Chronicle 07 May 1929 p25

272 San Francisco Examiner 05 May 1928 p21/23

273 Oakland Tribune 08 May 1928 p26

274 San Francisco Call-Bulletin 08 May 1928 p17

275 Oakland Post-Enquirer 08 May 1928 p25

276 San Francisco Examiner 08 May 1928 p29/32

277 San Francisco Call-Bulletin 08 May 1928 p18

278 Oakland Tribune 08 May 1928 p26

279 San Francisco Chronicle 08 May 1928 p27

280 San Francisco Chronicle 08 May 1928 p27 Harry B Smith

281 San Francisco Bulletin 08 May 1928 p17

282 Winnipeg Free Press 21 Dec 1929 p20

283 San Francisco Bulletin 08 May 1928 p18

284 San Francisco Chronicle 13 Jun 1928 p29

285 San Francisco Examiner 19 Jun 1928 p30

286 San Francisco Bulletin 06 Dec 1928 p23

287 2-0 Police Journal; Nov 1928; A Temple of Happiness; p21

288 San Francisco Examiner 23 Jun 1927 p9

289 Souvenir Program, New Dreamland Auditorium, 29 Jun 1928

290 Police Journal November 1928

291 Souvenir Program, New Dreamland Auditorium, 29 Jun 1928

292 San Francisco Examiner 21 Apr 1927 p31

293 San Francisco Examiner 29 Jun 1928 p33

294 San Francisco Examiner 15 Apr 1972 p29

295 Los Angeles Evening Express 04 Feb 1930 p19

296 San Francisco Examiner 02 Mar 1929 p19

297 Los Angeles Evening Express 22 Mar 1929 p23

298 San Francisco Bulletin 06 Dec 1928 p23

299 San Jose Evening News 01 Jan 1931 p21

300 San Jose Mercury Herald 23 Dec 1928 p28

301 March 2023 phone interview Diane Camilli Abraham

302 Santa Clara County CA Marriage Cert # 2801164

303 San Francisco Chronicle 07 Dec 1923 p1

304 boxrec.com/en/proboxer/85901

305 San Francisco Examiner 01 Feb 1929 p25

306 New Dreamland Auditorium Newsletter 31 Aug 1928 p3

307 Los Angeles Examiner 06 Jan 1930 p86

308 Los Angeles Daily News 13 Jul 1936 p9

309 Oakland Tribune 24 Aug 1930 p30

310 Los Angeles Evening Post-Record 24 May 1930 p5

311 Los Angeles Evening Post-Record 11 Apr 1930 p19

312 Rachel Surls, Judith Gerber. 2016. From Cows to Concrete: The Rise and Fall of Farming in Los Angeles. Angel City Press: Santa Monica.

313 Los Angeles Evening Express 25 Jul 1925 p11

314 Los Angeles Daily News 20 Feb 1925 p23

315 Bakersfield Morning Echo 19 Feb 1928 - p4

316 Los Angeles Daily News 3 Jun 1930 - p14

317 Los Angeles Daily News 20 May 1930 p13

318 Los Angeles Evening Post-Record 18 Nov 1929 p8

319 Los Angeles Record 07 May 1930 p12

320 The Long Beach Sun 31 Jul 1929 p9

321 Los Angeles Evening Post-Record 07 May 1930 p12

322 Los Angeles Evening Post-Record 18 Nov 1929 p8

323 Los Angeles Evening Post-Record 18 Nov 1929 p8

324 Los Angeles Daily News 03 Jun 1930 p14

325 Oakland Tribune 24 Aug 1930 p30

326 Oakland Tribune 04 Mar 1930 p39

327 Los Angeles Evening Post-Record 22 Nov 1929 p18

328 The Spokesman-Review 23 Jan 1939 p25

329 Los Angeles Evening Express 22 Dec 1928 p8

330 Los Angeles Evening Post-Record 16 Jul 1929 p9

331 Los Angeles Evening Post-Record 14 Nov 1929 p11

332 Riverside Daily Press 13 Sep 1926 p9

333 Winona Daily News 26 Jul 1926 p11

334 Los Angeles Times 09 Jan 1925 p38

335 Illustrated Daily News 29 Jul 1925 p11

336 Los Angeles Times 01 Aug 1925 p10

337 Los Angeles Times 01 Aug 1925 p10

338 Los Angeles Times 26 Oct 1924 p3

339 Los Angeles Times 04 Aug 1925 p36

340 Frank Kiki Baltazar Interview 18 Oct 2023

341 Jeff Bumpus Interview 17 May 2022

342 1910 US Fed Census; Bethel, Fairfield, CT; Roll; T624_127; Page; 20B; ED; 0002

343 Larry Harnisch, Mary Mallory / Hollywood Heights: Barney Oldfield Sets Up Shop in Downtown Los Angeles, 26 Sep 2016

344 Los Angeles Evening Post-Record 08 Jul 1916 p3

345 Los Angeles Times 23 Jul 1929 p39

346 Los Angeles Evening Citizen 24 Jul 1929 p11

347 Los Angeles Evening Post-Record 28 Jul 1929 p6

348 Los Angeles Examiner 24 Jul 1929 p13

349 Los Angeles La Opinión 10 Aug 1929 p10

350 Los Angeles Evening Post-Record 08 Aug 1929 p11

351 Los Angeles Evening Post-Record 24 Aug 1929 p6

352 boxrec.com/media/index.php/George_Blake

353 Los Angeles Evening Express 29 Aug 1929 p22

354 Los Angeles Evening Post-Record 30 Aug 1929 p16

355 California Eagle 30 Aug 1929 p8

356 Los Angeles Evening Post-Record 19 Nov 1929 p6

357 Los Angeles Times 17 Nov 1929 p87

358 Los Angeles Examiner 06 Sep 1929 p18; Fane Norton

359 Los Angeles Times 06 Feb 1937 p27

360 Email conversation, Bix Zambrana, July 2023

361 Email conversation, Bix Zambrana, Apr 2022

362 socaluncensored.com/2018/07/12/top-ten-venues-in-socal-history-4-hollywood-legion-stadium/

363 East Liverpool Evening Review 27 Feb 1925 p16

364 Los Angeles Times 01 Oct 1929 p37

365 Nato, William Wrigley Jr – "Father of Chewing Gum," snackhistory.com, accessed 17 Dec 2022

366 Los Angeles Times 15 Oct 2016 pE5

367 New Orleans Item 17 Oct 1929 p26

368 Los Angeles Times 27 Oct 1929 p87

369 Port Arthur New York Daily Item 01 Oct 1923 p2

370 The Chico Enterprise 05 Oct 1923 p5

371 Los Angeles Times 03 Nov 1929 p86

372 San Francisco Examiner 30 Oct 1929 p19

373 Los Angeles Evening Express 01 Nov 1929 p35

374 Los Angeles Evening Post Record - Stub Nelson; 31 Oct 1929 p11

375 California Eagle 25 Oct 1929 p7

376 Los Angeles Times 04 Nov 1929 p12

377 Los Angeles Examiner 07 Nov 1929 p19

378 Los Angeles Evening Citizens News 07 Nov 1929 p18

379 Los Angeles Times 04 Nov 1929 p12

380 myburbank.com/friday-flashback-james-j-jeffries/

381 Holstein-Friesian Herd-Book. United States; Holstein-Friesian Association of America, 1921.

382 Los Angeles Evening Post-Record 18 Nov 1929 p8

383 The Yonkers Herald 28 Nov 1929 p21

384 San Antonio Light 09 Nov 1929 p5

385 Los Angeles Evening Post-Record 12 Nov 1929 p8

386 Walker, Mickey. 1961. Mickey Walker: The Toy Bulldog and His Times. 1st ed. New York City: Random House.

387 Los Angeles Evening Post-Record 19 Nov 1929 p6

388 Phone conversation Diane Camilli Abraham Sept 2022

389 Collyer's Eye; 16 Nov 1929

390 Los Angeles Evening Express 19 Nov 1912 p19 Bill Smith

391 Los Angeles Evening Post-Record 16 Nov 1929 p5

392 Los Angeles Times 19 Nov 1929 p37

393 Los Angeles Evening Post-Record 19 Nov 1929 p6

394 Los Angeles Times 19 Nov 1929 p37

395 Los Angeles Evening Express 16 Nov 1929 p13

396 Los Angeles Times 18 Nov 1929 p10

397 San Jose Mercury Herald 27 Nov 1929 p24

398 Los Angeles Times 18 Nov 1929 p10

399 Los Angeles Evening Post-Record 14 Nov 1929 p11

400 Los Angeles Evening Post-Record 20 Nov 1929 p6

401 Los Angeles Times 20 Nov 1929 p35

402 Los Angeles Evening Post-Record 20 Nov 1929 p6

403 Los Angeles Evening Express 20 Nov 1929 p27

404 Los Angeles Evening Express 22 Nov 1929 p26

405 Los Angeles Evening Express 21 Nov 1929 p22

406 Los Angeles Post 20 Nov 1929 p6

407 Los Angeles Times 02 Dec 1929 p10

408 Wichita Beacon 19 Dec 1899 p8

409 St. Louis Globe-Democrat 19 Mar 1899 p11

410 Los Angeles Times 03 Oct 1903 p11

411 Los Angeles Times 02 Mar 1909, Tue · Page 15/22

412 Los Angeles Herald 22 Oct 1907 p8

413 Tacoma News Tribune 27 Sep 1907 p13

414 Evans, Leslie, How the LA Times After a Hundred-Year Love Affair with the City of Vernon Decided It Really Hated the Place All Along, 01 Dec 2010

415 Meares, Hadley, Vernon: The implausible history of an industrial wasteland. How one unscrupulous landowner spoiled the city's reputation, 19 May 2017

416 Los Angeles Evening Post-Record 18 Jun 1908 p6

417 How the LA Times After a Hundred-Year Love Affair with the City of Vernon Decided It Really Hated the Place All Along, 01 Dec 2010, By Leslie Evans

418 The Furlongs of Vernon and of Van Buren Place. Evans, Leslie, and Charnofsky, Jennifer. West Adams Heritage Association.

419 Nordin, Richard. The Iron Fist. Chapter 10. Xlibris, Bloomington, Indiana, 2017. 1467, 1477.

420 Los Angeles Evening Post-Record 10 May 1915 p6

421 Los Angeles Evening Express 18 May 1921 p22

422 Los Angeles Times 08 Oct 1937 p38

423 Los Angeles Times 08 Oct 1937 p38

424 Los Angeles Times 01 Jan 1924 p228

425 Los Angeles Evening Express 18 May 1921 p22

426 Los Angeles Times 08 Oct 1937 p38

427 A Visit to Old Los Angeles; 6. Spring Street I(Part 2) by Brent C. Dickerson

428 Los Angeles Times 27 Jan 1937 p31

429 Los Angeles Evening Express 10 Feb 1928 p19

430 Los Angeles Times 01 Dec 1929 p88

431 Vancouver Sun 13 Sep 1933 p12

432 Los Angeles Evening Express 06 Dec 1929 p20

433 Los Angeles Times 7 Jan 1930 p33

434 Los Angeles Evening Post-Record 07 Dec 1929 p6

435 Los Angeles Evening Post-Record 09 Dec 1929 p14

436 Los Angeles Times 5 Jan 1930 p85

437 Los Angeles Examiner 09 Dec 1929 p15

438 Oakland Tribune 29 Dec 1929 p38

439 Petaluma Argus-Courier 12 Jan 1935 p4

440 Leicester Evening Mail 03 Apr 1937 p21

441 Douglas County NE Birth Register, Vol 5, p4 (1892-1910)

442 Topical Times magazine 21 Oct 1939 p27 – Leo Fuller

443 Omaha Evening Bee 22 Feb 1909 p5

444 Omaha World Herald 11 Feb 1909 p1

445 Omaha Daily Bee 04 May 1888 p2

446 The Sacramento Union 01 Jul 1934 p8

447 Omaha World Herald 16 Feb 1909 p1

448 New York Daily News 20 Jun 1934 p409 - p38

449 Buddy Baer, Autobiography. New York: Rhino Publishing, 2003, 24.

450 New York Daily News 20 Jun 1934 p409 - p38

451 St. Joseph News-Press 17 Oct 1939 p8

452 Hayward Daily Review 09 Dec 1927 p8

453 New York Daily News 20 Jun 1934 p409 - p38

454 Nat Loubert, The Ring Magazine, February 1960

455 Text conversation with Gary Todd, 17 Sep 2023

456 San Bernardino County Sun 27 Jan 1932 p14

457 Galt Herald 19 Nov 1926 p8

458 Galt Herald 07 Jan 1927 p10

459 London Evening Standard 14 Jun 1935 p7

460 New York Daily News 14 Jun 1934 p60

461 Sacramento Bee 21 Apr 1926 p9

462 Sacramento Bee 17 Aug 1927 p8

463 Galt Herald 13 Apr 1928 p10

464 Oakland Tribune 11 Dec 1930 p30

465 Oakland Tribune 22 Nov 1959 p15

466 Livermore Herald 06 Sep 1940

467 Stockton Evening and Sunday Record 14 Jan 1939 p16

468 Livermore Herald 06 Sep 1940

469 The Foxworthy-Fallon Saga p4 - Donald F. Foxworthy

470 Oakland Tribune 22 Nov 1959 p15

471 Oakland Tribune 03 Jun 1925 p22

472 Oakland Tribune 05 Jul 1926 p14

473 San Francisco Examiner 13 Dec 1959 p14

474 Feather River Bulletin 04 Dec 1985 p13

475 San Francisco Examiner 13 Dec 1959 p14

476 The People, London, England 01 Apr 1934 p5

477 Oakland, California, City Directory, 1930. p238

478 Livermore Herald 06 Sep 1940

479 San Francisco Chronicle 14 Sep 1930 p79 Bob Edgren

480 Livermore Herald 06 Sep 1940

481 San Francisco Examiner 23 Nov 1959 p42

482 Quesnel Cariboo Observer - 11 May 1929 pA3

483 Stockton Independent 10 May 1929 p6

484 Stockton Evening and Sunday Record 11 May 1929 p30

485 Stockton Evening and Sunday Record 17 May 1929 p23

486 Stockton Independent 17 May 1929 p8

487 Oakland Tribune 16 Mar 1930 p29

488 Sacramento Bee 29 Jun 1980 p8

489 San Francisco Chronicle 21 Apr 1941 p4H

490 California State Athletic Commission 1929 Boxer, Manager, Trainer License Book

491 Los Angeles Evening Post-Record 7 Jan 1930 p9

492 Los Angeles Evening Post-Record 07 Jan 1930 p11

493 San Francisco Examiner 18 Jan 1930 p17

494 Los Angeles Evening Post-Record 09 Jan 1930 p13

495 Los Angeles Evening Express 03 Jan 1930 p40

496 San Francisco Examiner 15 Jan 1930 p21

497 Los Angeles Evening Citizen News 03 Jan 1930 p11

498 Oakland Post Enquirer 13 Jan 1930 p21

499 Los Angeles Times 5 Jan 1930 p85

500 Los Angeles Record 10 Jan 1930 p15

501 Los Angeles Evening Post-Record 09 Jan 1930 p13

502 Los Angeles Times 28 Jan 1934 p57

503 Los Angeles Times 19 Jan 1930 p83

504 Los Angeles Times 25 May 1930 p81

505 San Diego Evening Tribune 07 Jan 07 1930 p21

506 San Francisco Examiner 08 Jan 1930 p 19

507 Los Angeles Evening Citizen News 10 Jan 1930 p10

508 Los Angeles Evening Post 11 Jan 1930 p6

509 Los Angeles Evening Post-Record 11 Jan 1930 p6

510 Los Angeles Evening Express 11 Jan 1930 p15

511 Los Angeles Record 11 Jan 1930 p6

512 Los Angeles Record 11 Jan 1930 p6

513 Los Angeles Evening Express 26 Nov 1929 p21 Sid Ziff

514 San Francisco Examiner 17 Jan 1930 p19

515 Wilmington Daily Press Journal 08 Jan 1930 p6

516 San Pedro News-Pilot 08 Jan 1930 p8

517 Los Angeles Examiner 19 Dec 1929 p18

518 Los Angeles Evening Express 20 Jan 1930 p15

519 Oakland Tribune 10 Sep 1940 p18

520 San Francisco Examiner 18 Jan 1930 p17

521 Oakland Tribune 05 Sep 1929 p32

522 Los Angeles Evening Express 04 Feb 1930 p16

523 Los Angeles Times 31 Jan 1930 p19

524 Pasadena Post 31 Jan 1930 p11

525 Hollywood Daily Citizen 01 Feb 1930 p16

526 Los Angeles Evening Express 01 Feb 1930 p19

527 Los Angeles Evening Express 27 Jan 1930 p11

528 Los Angeles Evening Express 01 Feb 1930 p19

529 Los Angeles Evening Express 04 Feb 1930 p16

530 Hollywood Daily Citizen 01 Feb 1930 p16

531 Los Angeles Evening Post-Record 27 Jan 1930 p10

532 Illustrated Daily News 04 Feb 1930 p20

533 Los Angeles Evening Express 06 Feb 1930 p22

534 Stockton Daily Evening Record 19 Jul 1929 p22

535 Hayward Daily Review 13 Jun 1930 p3

536 Oakland Tribune 16 May 1930 p47

537 Oakland Post Enquirer 20 Jun 1930 p25

538 Los Angeles Examiner 31 Jan 1930 p16

539 Riverside Daily Press 31 Jan 1930 p17

540 snopes.com, "Did Early 20th-Century Commercial Airplanes Use Wicker Chairs to Seat Passengers?" 16 Jun 2023

541 San Diego Evening Tribune 07 Jan 1930 p21

542 Los Angeles Examiner 06 Feb 1930 p16

543 San Francisco Examiner 17 Jan 1930 p21

544 Los Angeles Evening Express 05 Feb 1930 p25 - Sid Ziff

545 Los Angeles Evening Post-Record 05 Feb 1930 p11

546 Petaluma Argus-Courier 22 Jan 1930 p3

547 San Francisco Chronicle 21 Jan 1930 p25

548 San Francisco Chronicle 03 Mar 1948 p9

549 San Francisco Examiner 26 Jan 1930 p35

550 San Francisco Examiner 28 Jan 1930 p19

551 San Francisco Chronicle 25 Jan 1930 p25

552 Oakland Tribune 05 Feb 1930 p15

553 San Francisco Examiner 26 Jan 1930 p35

554 Oakland Tribune 23 Jan 1930 p33

555 San Francisco Chronicle 01 Mar 1930 p24

556 Oakland Tribune 26 Jan 1930p37

557 Oakland Tribune 31 Jan 1930 p40

558 Oakland Tribune 06 Feb 1930 p1

559 Oakland Tribune 04 Feb 1930 p34

560 San Francisco Chronicle 30 Jan 1930 p27

561 Oakland Tribune 09 Feb 1930 p25

562 San Francisco Examiner 11 Feb 1930 p27

563 San Francisco Examiner 07 Feb 1930 p17

564 Oakland Post Enquirer 18 Feb 1930 p21

565 Oakland Post Enquirer 11 Nov 1930 p2

566 Oakland Tribune 09 Feb 1930 p25

567 Oakland Post Enquirer 06 Feb 1930 p17

568 Oakland Tribune 28 Feb 1930

569 Oakland Post Enquirer 27 Feb 1930 p1

570 San Jose Mercury Herald 02 Oct 1930 p21

571 Oakland Tribune 06 Feb 1930 p1

572 Oakland Tribune 04 Feb 1930 p34

573 San Francisco Chronicle 04 Feb 1930 p25

574 Brooklyn Daily Eagle 10 Feb 1936 p18

575 San Francisco Examiner 28 Feb 1930 p19

576 Oakland Tribune 28 Feb 1930

577 San Francisco Examiner 28 Feb 1930 p19

578 San Francisco Chronicle 25 Jan 1930 p25

579 Oakland Tribune 28 Feb 1930

580 San Francisco Examiner 28 Feb 1930 p21

581 San Francisco Examiner 28 Mar 1928 p19

582 San Francisco Examiner 24 Jun 1931 p1

583 San Francisco Examiner 12 Oct 1932 p1

584 San Francisco Examiner 28 Feb 1930 p21

585 Oakland Tribune 27 Feb 1930 p26

586 Oakland Post Enquirer 07 Mar 1930 p31

587 San Francisco Chronicle 03 Mar 1948 p9

588 Napa Journal 07 Nov 1930 p7

589 Los Angeles Examiner 12 Feb 1930 p11

590 Long Beach Sun 16 Feb 1930 p10

591 Morning Oregonian 27 Feb 1930 p19

592 Oakland Post Enquirer 21 Mar 1930 p33

593 Los Angeles Times 17 Feb 1930 p13

594 Los Angeles Evening Post-Record 18 Feb 1930 p11

595 Los Angeles Times 18 Feb 1930 p33

596 Los Angeles Evening Express 14 Feb 1930 p25

597 Venice Evening Vanguard 19 Feb 1930 p8

598 Oakland Post Enquirer 07 Mar 1930 p31

599 Indianapolis Star 09 Mar 1930 p30

600 Los Angeles Illustrated Daily News 12 Feb 1930 p13/14

601 Napa Journal 02 Feb 1930 p4

602 San Francisco Examiner 17 Feb 1930 p20

603 San Francisco Examiner 19 Feb 1930 p19

604 Oakland Tribune 19 Feb 1930 p17

605 San Francisco Chronicle 19 Feb 1930 p27

606 Santa Cruz Evening News 21 Feb 1930 p4

607 Pomona Progress Bulletin 03 Mar 1930 p10

608 Fresno Morning Republican 16 Mar 1930 p7

609 San Francisco Examiner 26 Feb 1930 p21

610 Los Angeles Post 12 Mar 1930 p11

611 Oakland Tribune 09 Mar 1930 p36

612 San Diego Evening Tribune 18 Feb 1930 p22

613 Oakland Tribune 09 Mar 1930 p36

614 Oakland Tribune 03 Mar 1930 p14

615 The Pomona Progress Bulletin 04 Mar 1930 p10

616 Oakland Tribune 03 Mar 1930 p14

617 Vallejo Evening News 06 Mar 1930 p2

618 San Jose Mercury Herald 06 Mar 1930 p21

619 Hayward Daily Review 06 Mar 1930 p1

620 San Francisco Examiner 07 Mar 1930 p19

621 Vallejo Evening News 06 Mar 1930 p2

622 Oakland Post Enquirer 07 Mar 1930 p31

623 Long Beach Sun 06 Mar 1930 p10 Tige Clinton

624 Los Angeles Times 11 Mar 1930 p32

625 Los Angeles Times 23 Feb 1930 p93

626 Oakland Tribune 20 Mar 1930 p34

627 Sacramento Bee 25 Jan 1930 p35

628 Los Angeles Record 21 Mar 1930 p18

629 Los Angeles Record 21 Mar 1930 p18

630 California Eagle 21 Mar 1930 p9

631 Long Beach Sun 06 Mar 1930 p10 Tige Clinton

632 Los Angeles Daily Evening Citizen 20 Mar 1930 p10

633 Los Angeles Daily Evening Citizen 20 Mar 1930 p10

634 Los Angeles Daily Evening Citizen 20 Mar 1930 p10

635 Los Angeles Evening Citizen News 29 Mar 1930 p8

636 Los Angeles Evening Post 26 Mar 1930 p8

637 Los Angeles Evening Citizen News 29 Mar 1930 p8

638 Los Angeles Evening Post 26 Mar 1930 p8

639 Hollywood Daily Citizen 01 Apr 1930 p8

640 pubmed.ncbi.nlm.nih.gov/9082784/

641 Los Angeles Evening Citizen News 01 Apr 1930 p8

642 Los Angeles Record 26 Mar 1930 p8

643 Los Angeles Record 22 Apr 1930 p9

644 Los Angeles Evening Express 23 Apr 1930 p23

645 Los Angeles Record 23 Apr 1930 p12

646 Los Angeles Record 23 Apr 1930 p12

647 Los Angeles Evening Express 23 Apr 1930 p25

648 Los Angeles Examiner 23 Apr 1930 p15

649 Oakland Post Enquirer 25 Apr 1930 p34

650 Los Angeles Evening Express 23 Apr 1930 p23

651 Los Angeles Evening Express 23 Apr 1930 p25

652 Oakland Tribune 27 Aug 1930 p14

653 San Francisco Examiner - 25 Apr 1930 p22

654 Oakland Post Enquirer 28 Apr 1930 p24

655 Vallejo Evening News 28 Apr 1930 p6

656 Los Angeles Times 07 May 1930 p31

657 The Helena Independent-Record 01 Oct 1961 p5

658 Los Angeles Times 11 May 1930 part VI-a p3

659 Los Angeles Evening Post-Record 29 Apr 1930 p10

660 Los Angeles Record 03 May 1930 p4

661 Los Angeles Record 05 May 1930 p8

662 San Francisco Examiner 08 May 1930 p19

663 Los Angeles Record 06 May 1930 p8

664 Oakland Tribune 09 May 1930 p48

665 Los Angeles Evening Post-Record 29 Apr 1930 p10

666 Los Angeles Evening Citizen 15 May 1930 p16

667 Los Angeles Examiner 13 May 1930 p17

668 Los Angeles Evening Citizen News 13 May 1930 p8

669 Los Angeles Examiner 13 May 1930 p17

670 Los Angeles Examiner 13 May 1930 p17

671 Los Angeles Daily News 13 May 1930 p16

672 Los Angeles Daily News 13 May 1930 p16

673 Long Beach Sun 13 May 1930 p15

674 Los Angeles Examiner 14 May 1930 p13

675 Oakland Post Enquirer 10 May 1930 p10

676 Oakland Tribune 09 Jun 1930 p15

677 Los Angeles Times 15 May 1930 p38

678 Los Angeles Evening Express 15 May 1930 p24

679 San Francisco Examiner 03 Jun 1930 p23

680 Los Angeles Times 12 May 1930 p10

681 Los Angeles Record 23 May 1930 p20

682 Los Angeles Record 27 May 1930 p12

683 Los Angeles Evening Express 04 Jun 1930 p15

684 Los Angeles Evening Post-Record 21 May 1930 p10

685 Morning Oregonian 26 May 1930 p15

686 Los Angeles Evening Express 22 May 1930 p23

687 Los Angeles Evening Express 22 May 1930 p23

688 Los Angeles Times 01 Oct 1929 p37

689 Los Angeles Record 27 May 1930 p12

690 Los Angeles Record 22 May 1930 p13

691 Los Angeles Record 21 May 1930 p11

692 Los Angeles Times 29 May 1930 p33

693 Los Angeles Examiner 16 May 1930 p17

694 Louisville Courier-Journal 11 May 1930 p59

695 Los Angeles Evening Citizen News 07 Jun 1930 p8

696 Los Angeles Examiner 04 Jun 1930 p13

697 Pasadena Post 04 Jun 1930 p18

698 Pasadena Post 04 Jun 1930 p18

699 Los Angeles Evening Express 04 Jun 1930 p17

700 San Francisco Examiner 14 Jun 1930 p18

701 outsidelands.org/ewing-field.php

702 San Francisco Examiner 05 Jun 1930 p21

703 San Francisco Examiner 14 Jun 1930 p18

704 Los Angeles Evening Post-Record 04 Jun 1930 p10

705 Los Angeles Evening Express 04 Jun 1930 p17

706 San Francisco Examiner 05 Jun 1930 p21

707 San Francisco Examiner 07 Jun 1930 p18

708 Los Angeles Evening Post-Record 06 Jun 1930 p22

709 San Francisco Examiner 05 Jun 1930 p21

710 Los Angeles Times 05 Jun 1930 p37

711 District Court of Appeal, 3rd District, CA; Jacklich et al v Baer; Civ. 6717. 17 Mar 1943.

712 Oakland Tribune 13 Dec 1931 p25

713 Stockton Evening and Sunday Record 19 Sep 1930 p21

714 Oakland Tribune 13 Aug 1930 p13

715 Oakland Tribune 09 Jan 1932 p10

716 San Francisco Examiner 16 Jun 1930 p19

717 San Francisco Chronicle 13 Jun 1930 p27

718 Oakland Tribune 26 Jun 1930 p27

719 Oakland Tribune 25 June 1930 p16

720 San Francisco Examiner 26 Jun 1930 p22

721 San Francisco Examiner 26 Jun 1930 p22

722 San Francisco Chronicle 28 Jun 1930 p26

723 San Francisco Chronicle 27 June 1930 p27

724 San Francisco Chronicle 28 Jun 1930 p26

725 Oakland Tribune 15 Jul 1930 p26

726 Los Angeles Express 16 Jul 1930 p15-16

727 The Montana Standard 17 Jul 1930 p8

728 Los Angeles Evening Post 25 Jul 1930 p16

729 Oakland Tribune 17 Jul 1930 p25

730 Oakland Post Enquirer 26 Jul 1930 p9

731 Oakland Post Enquirer 08 Jul 1930 p25

732 San Francisco Examiner 20 Jul 1930 p29

733 Honolulu Advertiser 25 May 1947 p17

734 Los Angeles Evening Express 24 May 1929 p28

735 Oakland Tribune 12 Aug 1930 p34

736 Honolulu Advertiser 25 May 1947 p17

737 San Francisco Examiner 20 Aug 1930 p16

738 Vallejo Evening News 16 Aug 1930 p3

739 San Francisco Examiner 17 Aug 1839 p15

740 Oakland Tribune 25 Nov 1928 p72

741 Elliott, Jeff; The Village of Vice in the Valley of the Moon; Santa Rosa History; 03 Jul 2016

742 Oakland Post Enquirer 14 Aug 1930 p22

743 Oakland Post Enquirer 20 Aug 1930 p11

744 Oakland Tribune 20 Aug 1930 p15

745 Stockton Record 26 Aug 1930 p15 John J. Peri

746 Oakland Post Enquirer 22 Aug 1931 p9

747 Bob Shand - Oakland Tribune 22 Aug 1930 p29

748 Bob Shand - Oakland Tribune 23 Aug 1930 p10

749 Miami Herald 04 Sep 1930 p11 Bob Edgren

750 Bob Shand - Oakland Tribune 22 Aug 1930 p29

751 Taylor, James P., patent no US1830572A, granted 03 Nov 1931

752 Vallejo Evening News 21 Aug 1930 p2

753 Bob Shand - Oakland Tribune 23 Aug 1930 p10

754 Bob Shand - Oakland Tribune 23 Aug 1930 p10

755 Oakland Tribune 23 Aug 1930 p10

756 San Francisco Examiner 23 Aug 1930 p18

757 San Francisco Examiner 23 Aug 1930 p18

758 Oakland Tribune 21 Aug 1930 p16

759 Oakland Tribune 27 Aug 1930 p14

760 San Jose Mercury Herald 30 Mar 1916 p1

761 San Jose Mercury Herald 16 Apr 1916 p1

762 Modesto Bee 24 Aug 1930 p10

763 San Francisco Examiner 25 Aug 1930 p15

764 Los Angeles Evening Post 23 Aug 1930 p5

765 Los Angeles Evening Post 25 Aug 1930 p4

766 Oakland Tribune 27 Aug 1930 p14

767 Nevada State Journal 14 Jan 1932 p7

768 Reno Gazette-Journal 21 Jan 1932 p9

769 Oakland Tribune 09 Apr 1934 p14

770 Oakland Tribune 25 Aug 1930 p22

771 Oakland Tribune 25 Aug 1930 p22

772 San Francisco Chronicle 14 Sep 1930 p79

773 Hanford Sentinel 25 Aug 1930 p4

774 Oakland Tribune 25 Aug 1930 p22

775 San Francisco Examiner 06 Dec 1929 p26

776 Fimrite, Ron. "Send in the Clown." Sports Illustrated, 20 Mar 1978

777 Flamm, Jerry; Good Life in Hard Times; 1978; Chronicle Books, San Francisco; p62-63

778 City Within a City; Historic Context Statement for San Francisco's Mission District; Nov 2007; p58

779 City Within a City; Historic Context Statement for San Francisco's Mission District - Nov 2007 - p80

780 wikipedia.org/wiki/Recreation_Park_(San_Francisco)

781 The Fresno Morning Republican 24 Aug 1930 p13

782 San Jose Evening News 26 Aug 26, 1930 p8

783 San Francisco Chronicle 14 Sep 1930 p79

784 Sacramento Union 27 Aug 1930 p6

785 Oakland Tribune 26 Aug 1930 p3

786 Nebraska State Journal 11 Jun 1933 p5 Gayle Talbot AP

787 San Francisco Chronicle 26 Aug 1930 p25/26

788 New York Daily News 07 Jun 1933 p8

789 Stockton Evening and Sunday Record 26 Aug 1930 p15

790 San Francisco Chronicle 28 Aug 1930 p25

791 Fresno Bee 11 Jun 1933 p13

792 San Francisco Chronicle 28 Aug 1930 p25

793 San Jose Evening News 26 Aug 26, 1930 p8

794 The All Time Vault 28 Mar 2016, Mike Casey

795 Los Angeles La Opinión 27 Aug, 1930 p11

796 San Francisco Chronicle 14 Sep 1930 p79

797 San Francisco Examiner 27 Aug 1930 p20

798 San Francisco Chronicle 30 Aug 1930 p26

799 San Francisco Call-Bulletin 26 Aug 1930 p1

800 Oakland Tribune 26 Aug 1930 p34

801 San Francisco Chronicle 26 Aug 1930 p25

802 Oakland Tribune 26 Aug 1930 p34

803 San Francisco Chronicle 26 Aug 1930 p25

804 San Francisco Chronicle 26 Aug 1930 p23/25

805 Hayward Review 26 Aug 1930 p1

806 Monroe (Louisiana) News-Star 26 Nov 1934 p7

807 Oakland Tribune 26 Aug 1930 p3

808 San Jose Evening News 01 Sep 1930 p8

809 San Francisco Chronicle 26 Aug 1930 p1

810 Oakland Tribune 26 Aug 1930 p3

811 San Francisco Chronicle 26 Aug 1930 p23

812 Nevada Appeal "Oscar Nominated Film Missed True Story" 08 Feb 2006

813 Oakland Tribune 26 Aug 1930 p3

814 San Francisco Chronicle 27 Aug 1930 p1

815 San Francisco Chronicle 26 Aug 1930 p23

816 Sacramento Bee Rudy Hickey 25 Aug 1930 p14

817 Oakland Tribune 26 Aug 1930 p3

818 Time Magazine 15 Sep 1930; Sport; Ring Death

819 Oakland Tribune 26 Aug 1930 p27

820 San Francisco Examiner 27 Aug 1930 p7

821 Minneapolis Star Tribune 03 Sep 1930 p13

822 San Francisco Examiner 02 Sep 1930 p9

823 Los Angeles Examiner 27 Aug 1930 p11/13

824 Oakland Tribune 26 Aug 1930 p27

825 The Recorder, San Francisco 04 Jun 1930 p8

826 Oakland Tribune 24 Jan 1930 p37

827 San Francisco Examiner 27 Aug 1930 p7

828 Los Angeles Examiner 27 Aug 1930 p11/13

829 San Jose Evening News 01 Sep 1930 p8

830 Oakland Tribune 26 Aug 1930 p27

831 San Jose Evening News 01 Sep 1930 p8

832 Oakland Tribune 26 Aug 1930 p3

833 Oakland Post Enquirer 17 Sep 1930 p4

834 Sacramento Union 27 Aug 1930 p6

835 Oakland Tribune 26 Aug 1930 p3

836 Oakland Tribune 26 Aug 1930 p27

837 Oakland Post Enquirer 29 Aug 1930 p28

838 Oakland Post Enquirer 26 Aug 1930 p4

839 Oakland Tribune 26 Aug 1930 p27

840 Oakland Tribune 26 Aug 1930 p3

841 Los Angeles Evening Express 14 Nov 1931 p12

842 Journal of Sigma Phi Epsilon 01 Oct 1930; 7, No. 3, p155; Roy Cummings San Francisco Call-Bulletin

843 Los Angeles Evening Express 14 Nov 1931 p12

844 Oakland Tribune 26 Aug 1930 p3

845 Oakland Tribune 29 Aug 1930 p29

846 Oakland Tribune 29 Oct 1930 p29

847 Oakland Tribune 29 Aug 1929 p29

848 Stockton Daily Evening Records 26 Aug 1930 p16 John J. Peri

849 The New Yorker; 09 Jun 1934 p22; Paul Gallico

850 San Francisco Chronicle 26 Aug 1930 p23-25

851 Sacramento Bee Rudy Hickey 25 Aug 1930 p14

852 Sacramento Union 27 Aug 1930 p6

853 Oakland Tribune 26 Aug 1930 p3

854 San Francisco Chronicle 26 Aug 1930 p23-25

855 Oakland Tribune 26 Aug 1930 p3

856 Buffalo Evening News 26 Jun 1934 p9

857 The Daily Register 21 Nov 1934 p20

858 Sunday London Mirror 14 Mar 1937 p13

859 Oakland Tribune 26 Aug 1930 p3

860 Stockton Daily Evening Records 26 Aug 1930 p16

861 San Francisco Chronicle 26 Aug 1930 p23/25

862 San Francisco Chronicle 27 Aug 1930 p1

863 San Francisco Chronicle 26 Aug 1930 p23/25

864 San Francisco Chronicle 26 Aug 1930 p23/25

865 San Francisco Chronicle 27 Aug 1930 p25

866 San Francisco Chronicle 26 Aug 1930 p1

867 Lee KS. How to Treat Chronic Subdural Hematoma? Past and Now. J Korean Neurosurg Soc. 2019;62(2);144-152

868 Hayward Review 26 Aug 1930 p1

869 Fimrite, Ron. "Send in the Clown." Sports Illustrated, 20 Mar 1978

870 Fresno Bee 08 Dec 1968 p75

871 Oakland Tribune 26 Aug 1930 p3

872 wikipedia.org/wiki/U.S._Route_50

873 wikipedia.org/wiki/Lincoln_Highway

874 Oakland Tribune 26 Aug 1930 p3

875 Oakland Post Enquirer 26 Aug 1930 p1

876 Santa Ana Register 26 Aug 1930 p28

877 San Francisco Chronicle 27 Aug 1930 p9

878 Los Angeles Times 27 Aug 1930 p6

879 Los Angeles Examiner 24 Jun 1934 p21

880 San Francisco Examiner 09 Jan 1983 p240-241

881 San Francisco Chronicle 27 Aug 1930 p4

882 Los Angeles Times 27 Aug 1930 p1

883 San Jose Mercury Herald 27 Aug 1930 p25

884 California, San Francisco County Records, 1824-1997; familysearch.org/ark;/61903/1;1;Q23Q-SZK8 report #2399

885 San Francisco Chronicle 27 Aug 1930 p9

886 Morning Oregonian 27 Aug 1930 p16

887 The Pittsburgh Press 02 Sep 1935 p15

888 Oakland Tribune 27 Aug 1930 p14-17

889 Oakland Tribune 26 Aug 1930 p3

890 Oakland Tribune 27 Aug 1930 p14/17

891 San Antonio Light 28 Jun 1936 p39

892 Oakland Tribune 27 Aug 1930 p14-17

893 Los Angeles Times 27 Aug 1930 p1

894 San Francisco Chronicle 27 Aug 1930 p9

895 San Francisco Chronicle 27 Aug 1930 p24

896 Sacramento Union 27 Aug 1930 p6

897 Fresno Morning Republican 08 Sep 1930 p8

898 The Ring Magazine, Sep 1930 issue

899 Los Angeles Times 28 Aug 1930 p30

900 Los Angeles Times 28 Aug 1930 p30

901 Omaha World-Herald 30 Aug 1930 p17

902 San Francisco Examiner 27 Aug 1930 p7

903 Pomona Progress Bulletin 30 Aug 1930 p10

904 Santa Rosa Republican 26 Aug 1930 p12

905 Voce Del Popolo 27 Aug 1930 p4

906 Il Corriere del Popolo 28 Aug 1930 p1

907 Oakland Tribune 29 Oct 1930 p29

908 Los Angeles Evening Post-Records 02 Feb 1931 p9

909 The San Diego Union 27 Aug 1930 p12

910 Los Angeles Evening Post-Records 02 Feb 1931 p9

911 New Britain Herald 27 Sep 1929 p26

912 Oakland Tribune 26 Aug 1930 p27

913 Oakland Tribune 26 Aug 1930 p27

914 Oakland Post Enquirer 14 Feb 1933 p17

915 Fimrite, Ron. "Send in the Clown." Sports Illustrated, 20 Mar 1978

916 Nevada State Journal 28 Dec 1930 p7

917 San Francisco Chronicle 27 Sep 1930 p25

918 San Francisco Chronicle 21 Jan 1930 p25

919 San Francisco Chronicle 27 Aug 1930 p5

920 San Francisco Examiner 27 Aug 1930 p7

921 San Francisco Examiner 29 Aug 1930 p6

922 San Francisco Chronicle 15 May 1966 p140

923 Los Angeles Evening Express 27 Aug 1930 p27

924 Los Angeles Times 26 Aug 1930 p27

925 Los Angeles Examiner 27 Aug 1930 p11

926 Los Angeles Examiner 27 Aug 1930 p11

927 San Francisco Chronicle 28 Aug 1930 p5

928 Oakland Tribune 27 Aug 1930 p1

929 San Francisco Chronicle 28 Aug 1930 p5

930 San Francisco Examiner 29 Aug 1930 p6

931 San Francisco Chronicle 28 Aug 1930 p5

932 Riverside Daily Press 28 Aug 1930 p11

933 San Francisco Examiner 27 Aug 1930 p1

934 Los Angeles Evening Express 23 April 1930 p25

935 San Francisco Examiner 06 Dec 1929 p26

936 Los Angeles Times 27 Aug 1930 p6

937 San Francisco Chronicle 28 Aug 1930 p25

938 San Francisco Chronicle 28 Aug 1930 p26

939 Shamokin News-Dispatch 02 Sep 1932 p8

940 Pittsburgh Sun-Telegraph 27 Sep 1941 p11

941 Santa Rosa Evening Press 18 May 1949 p14

942 Santa Rosa Evening Press 18 May 11949 p14

943 San Francisco Examiner 27 Aug 1930 p7

944 Oakland Post Enquirer 17 Sep 1930 p4

945 Oakland Tribune 27 Aug 1930 p14

946 San Francisco Chronicle 29 Aug 1930 p27

947 San Francisco Chronicle 28 Aug 1930 p5

948 Los Angeles Times 27 Aug 1930 p6

949 Long Angeles Daily News 27 Nov 1959 p62

950 San Francisco Examiner 27 Aug 1930 p7

951 Rotational head acceleration and traumatic brain injury in combat sports; a systematic review, British Medical Bulletin, Volume 141, Issue 1, March 2022, Pages 33–46

952 San Francisco Examiner 09 Jan 1983 p240-241

953 "Punch Drunk" Harrison S. Martland; 13 Oct 1928; Journal of American Medical Association; Vol 91, No 15, p1104

954 Study – Why are CTE Symptoms Worse for Boxers vs. Other Athletes?" 11 April 2017 by EMagraken combatsportslaw.com

955 Study – Why are CTE Symptoms Worse for Boxers vs. Other Athletes?" 11 April 2017 by EMagraken combatsportslaw.com

956 "Punch Drunk" Harrison S. Martland; 13 Oct 1928; Journal of American Medical Association; Vol 91, No 15, p1104

957 Intracerebral Hemorrhage; mayfieldclinic.com/pe-ich.htm

958 Kurland, David et al. "Hemorrhagic progression of a contusion after traumatic brain injury; a review." Journal of neurotrauma vol. 29,1 (2012); 19-31

959 Necropsy Report A.A. Berger Coroner's Office, Necropsy Dept. City and County of San Francisco 26 Aug 1930 5;00pm

960 Study – Why are CTE Symptoms Worse for Boxers vs. Other Athletes?" 11 April 2017 by EMagraken combatsportslaw.com

961 San Francisco Chronicle 29 Sep 1930 p12

962 Oakland Tribune 28 Aug 1934 p16

963 Los Angeles Evening Post-Record 11 Jun 1935 p12

964 Brooklyn Times Union 21 Sep 1935 p11

965 Buffalo News 15 Jun 1935 p9; Bob Stedler

966 San Francisco Chronicle 29 Sep 1930 p12

967 San Francisco Examiner 29 Aug 1930 p6

968 San Francisco Chronicle 29 Sep 1930 p12

969 San Francisco Examiner 29 Aug 1930 p6

970 Oakland Tribune 28 Aug 1930 p3

971 San Francisco Examiner 29 Aug 1930 p6

972 Oakland Post Enquirer 29 Aug 1930 p28

973 27 Jan 1932 Nevada State Journal p7

974 Oakland Tribune 28 Aug 1930 p3

975 San Francisco Examiner 29 Aug 1930 p6

976 Oakland Tribune 29 Aug 1930 p28

977 Dayton Daily News 15 Jul 1951 p52

978 New York State Athletic Commission meeting minutes 18 Nov 1930

979 Oakland Post Enquirer 28 Aug 1930 p1

980 Sacramento Union June/July 1931

981 Los Angeles Evening Post Record 28 Aug 1930 p11

982 The Fresno Bee 28 Aug 1930 p13

983 San Francisco Chronicle 29 Aug 1930 p27

984 Oakland Tribune 29 Aug 1930 p29

985 Fresno Morning Republican 30 Aug 1930 p12

986 Los Angeles Times 29 Aug 1930 p29

987 San Francisco Examiner 27 Aug 1930 p7

988 San Jose Evening News 30 Aug 1930 p6

989 San Jose Evening News 30 Aug 1930 p6

990 Dr Margaret Goodman; Tris Dixon, "Ch 10: Chaos," Damage: The Untold Story of Brain Trauma in Boxing, Hamilcar Publications, Boston, 2021, p151

991 Oakland Tribune 29 Aug 1930 p1

992 San Francisco Examiner 29 Aug 1930 p6

993 Los Angeles Examiner 29 Aug 1930 p12

994 San Francisco Examiner 30 Aug 1930 p1

995 San Francisco Examiner 04 Sept 1930 p3

996 Oakland Tribune 30 Aug 1930 p1

997 Nevada State Journal 31 Aug 1930 p1

998 Omaha Evening Bee-News 07 Jul 1934 p8

999 Nevada State Journal 01 Sep 1930 p5

1000 Nevada State Journal 03 Sep 1930 p5

1001 Reno Gazette-Journal 03 Sep 1930 p9

1002 Nevada State Journal 22 Sep 1930 p2

1003 Transcripts Audio Interview W. Wallace White for University of Nevada Oral History Program 1968; p60

1004 The People, London, England 01 Apr 1934 p5

1005 Nevada State Journal 31 Aug 1930 p1

1006 Evansville Courier 27 Aug 1930 p7

1007 Phone conversation Jeff Bumpus 27 Apr 2023

1008 Phone conversation Tony Hood 08 Oct 2023

1009 Transcripts Audio Interview W. Wallace White for University of Nevada Oral History Program 1968; p60

1010 Nevada State Journal 31 Aug 1930 p1

1011 Nevada State Journal 22 Sep 1930 p2

1012 San Francisco Examiner 01 Sep 1930 p3

1013 wikipedia.org/wiki/2nd_Cavalry_Regiment_(United_States)

1014 National Archives and Records Administration (NARA); Washington, D.C.; Returns from U.S. Military Posts, 1800-1916; Microfilm Serial: M617; Microfilm Roll: 756

1015 Las Vegas Review-Journal 29 Aug 1930 p6

1016 Oakland Post Enquirer 09 Sep 1930 p22

1017 American Legion Monthly – Sept 1930

1018 Email conversation Glen Sharp Apr 2024

1019 Oakland Post-Enquirer 01 Dec 1941 p10

1020 Oakland Tribune 12 Sep 1930 p17

1021 Edmonds, Andy; Frame Up: The Untold Story of Roscoe "Fatty" Arbuckle, William Morrow & Co., New York City

1022 The Many Trials of Fatty Arbuckle; 2018; Mark H. Hull, PhD, JD

1023 San Francisco Examiner 13 Apr 1922 p1

1024 San Francisco Bulletin 19 Jan 1927 p18

1025 San Francisco Bulletin 16 Feb 1929 p23

1026 San Francisco Examiner 28 Aug 1930 p6

1027 San Francisco Examiner 14 Nov 1935 p1

1028 San Francisco Chronicle 18 Sep 1930 p4

1029 Oakland Tribune 02 Sep 1930 p29

1030 Oakland Tribune 02 Sep 1930 p29

1031 San Francisco Examiner 14 Sep 1930 p33

1032 San Bernardino County Sun 14 Sep 1930 p3

1033 San Bernardino County Sun 14 Sep 1930 p3

1034 San Bernardino County Sun 14 Sep 1930 p3

1035 San Francisco Chronicle 14 Sep 1930 p77

1036 Contusion Hemorrhages of the Brain. A. M Moody, Read before California Medical Association session, San Francisco, 27 Apr 1931; Vol XXXVI No 3, p166–167.

1037 The Searchlight, Redding CA 23 Sep 1930 p4

1038 San Francisco Chronicle 17 Sep 1930 p2

1039 San Francisco Examiner 17 Sep 1930 p3

1040 San Francisco Examiner 17 Sep 1930 p2

1041 San Francisco Examiner 17 Sep 1930 p3

1042 Oakland Tribune 26 Sep 1930 p2

1043 Los Angeles Evening Express 04 Aug 1930 p18

1044 boxrec.com/en/proboxer/12086

1045 Oakland Tribune 17 Jan 1941 p32

1046 Los Angeles La Opinión 27 Aug, 1930 p11

1047 San Francisco Examiner 17 Sep 1930 p3

1048 Sacramento Bee 10 Feb 1970 p24

1049 San Francisco Examiner 17 Sep 1930 p3

1050 San Francisco Examiner 17 Sep 1930 p3

1051 Oakland Post Enquirer 17 Sep 1930 p1

1052 San Francisco Examiner 17 Sep 1930 p3

1053 Richmond Record Herald 19 Sep 1930 p8

1054 Oakland Tribune 19 Sep 1930 p41

1055 San Francisco Chronicle 17 Sep 1930 p2

1056 San Francisco Examiner 19 Sep 1930 p11

1057 Oakland Tribune 17 Sep 1930 p2

1058 Santa Cruz Evening News 19 Sep 1930 p1

1059 Oakland Tribune 18 Sep 1930 p26

1060 Fresno Morning Republican 10 Oct 1930 p16

1061 Los Angeles Times 15 Nov 1930 p7

1062 Los Angeles Times 15 Nov 1930 p7

1063 Sacramento Bee 21 May 1925 p18

1064 Dayton Daily News 25 Jun 1934 p14

1065 Los Angeles Evening Express 12 Jan 1931 p15

1066 Acevedo, Carlos, "The Duke of the West Side: Owney "The Killer" Madden," Hannibal Boxing, 7 Aug, 2019

1067 Oakland Tribune 09 Oct 1930 p34

1068 Oakland Tribune 30 Nov 1930 p37

1069 Oakland Tribune 13 Dec 1931 p25

1070 Oakland Tribune 31 Oct 1930 p38

1071 Oakland Tribune 04 Nov 1930 p34

1072 Nevada State Journal 06 Nov 1930 p8

1073 Oakland Tribune 18 Sep 1939 p26

1074 The People, London, England 01 Apr 1934 p5

1075 The Most Infamous Fight by Le Pacini, San Francisco magazine, Vol 10, 1968

1076 London Daily Herald 30 Sep 1930 p1

1077 Buffalo Evening News 23 Sep 1930 p31

1078 Superior Court of California, County of Glenn, "The Grand Jury's Role," Criminal Prosecutions, accessed 13 Jul 2022

1079 Journal of Criminal Law and Criminology, Vol 74, Issue 4, Article 15, p1453, Fall 1983, The Admissibility of Grand Jury Testimony under 804(b)(5): A Two-Test Proposal

1080 Superior Court of California, County of Glenn, "The Grand Jury's Role," Criminal Prosecutions, accessed 13 Jul 2022

1081 San Francisco Examiner 26 Sep 1930 p3

1082 Los Angeles Evening Post-Record 04 Feb 1927 p19

1083 Collyer's Eye 26 Apr 1930 p2

1084 Los Angeles Times 03 Feb 1927

1085 Fresno Bee 01 Jul 1930 p15

1086 San Francisco Chronicle 26 Sep 1930 p1

1087 Press Democrat 26 Sep 1930 p1

1088 Richmond Record Herald 27 Sep 1930 p1

1089 San Francisco Examiner 26 Sep 1930 p3

1090 San Francisco Chronicle 26 Sep 1930 p1

1091 San Francisco Examiner 26 Sep 1930 p1

1092 The Press Democrat 26 Sep 1930 p1

1093 San Francisco Examiner 26 Sep 1930 p1

1094 San Francisco Examiner 26 Sep 1930 p1

1095 The Press Democrat 26 Sep 1930 p1

1096 San Francisco Chronicle 26 Sep 1930 p1

1097 Press Democrat 26 Sep 1930 p1

1098 Passagiersregisters, Lijn New York-Rotterdam: 1930, 27 Sep.-31 Dec., 27-09-1930 T/M 31-12-1930 / : 1931, Mei-Juli, 01-05-1931 T/M 31-07-1931

1099 San Francisco Chronicle 26 Sep 1930 p6

1100 San Francisco Examiner 27 Sep 1930 p13

1101 San Francisco Chronicle 02 Oct 1930 p2

1102 Sacramento Bee 27 Sep 1930 p13

1103 The Press Democrat 28 Sep 1930 p18

1104 Sacramento Bee 27 Sep 1930 p13

1105 San Francisco Examiner 27 Sep 1930 p13

1106 The Sacramento Bee 30 Dec 1930 p10

1107 Sacramento Bee 27 Sep 1930 p1

1108 Press Democrat 27 Sep 1930 p1

1109 San Francisco Examiner 03 Oct 1930 p1

1110 Oakland Tribune 27 Sep 1930 p1

1111 San Francisco Chronicle 25 Nov 1930 p2

1112 Oakland Tribune 27 Sep 1930 p1

1113 Oakland Post Enquirer 01 Oct 1930 p1

1114 Modesto Bee 02 Oct 1930 p1

1115 Oakland Post Enquirer 06 Oct 1930 p1/6

1116 San Francisco Examiner 25 Nov 1930 p13

1117 Sacramento Bee 07 Jan 1932 p16

1118 Pasadena Post 03 Oct 1930 p1

1119 Petaluma Argus-Courier 03 Oct 1930 p1

1120 San Francisco Examiner 25 Sep 1930 p3

1121 Richmond Record Herald 16 Sep 1930 p5

1122 Oakland Post Enquirer 03 Oct 1930 p1

1123 Nevada State Journal 17 Feb 1931 p7

1124 Kennebec Journal 17 Feb 1931 p8

1125 San Francisco Examiner 29 Oct 1930 p36

1126 San Francisco Examiner 28 Oct 1930 p1

1127 Santa Rosa Republican 08 Oct 1930 p14

1128 San Francisco Examiner 28 Oct 1930 p1

1129 Oakland Tribune 28 Oct 1930 p27

1130 Nevada State Journal 31 Oct 1930 p6

1131 Los Angeles Times 15 Nov 15 1930 p7

1132 San Francisco Examiner 15 Nov 1930 p19

1133 Los Angeles Evening Express 13 Nov 1930 p1

1134 San Francisco Chronicle 08 Nov 1930 p3

1135 Oakland Tribune 07 Nov 1930 p36

1136 San Francisco Chronicle 15 Nov 1930 p3

1137 Oakland Tribune 18 Nov 1930 p39

1138 San Francisco Chronicle 14 Nov 1930 p4

1139 San Francisco Bulletin 19 Jul 1926 p13

1140 San Francisco Chronicle 29 Nov 1930 p12

1141 San Francisco Chronicle 22 Nov 1930 p12

1142 Sacramento Independent-Leader 18 Apr 1909 p8

1143 Marysville Appeal-Democrat 15 Nov 1930 p14

1144 San Francisco Bulletin 13 Jan 1928 p19

1145 San Francisco Chronicle 14 Nov 1930 p4

1146 Oakland Tribune 14 Nov 1930 p3

1147 Oakland Tribune 22 Nov 1930 p13

1148 New York State Athletic Commission meeting minutes 30 Nov 1930, pg2559-60

1149 Washington D.C. Evening Star 14 Nov 1930 pD-3

1150 Wilkes-Barre Times Leader 05 Jun 1936 p24

1151 Lincoln Star 20 May 1936 p11

1152 Los Angeles Evening Express 18 Dec 1930 p19

1153 Fresno Morning Republican 24 Dec 1930 p10

1154 Santa Rosa Republican 01 Oct 1930 p1

1155 Oakland Tribune 07 Oct 1930 p 40

1156 Oakland Tribune 19 Sep 1930 p41

1157 Sacramento Bee 06 Jan 1931 p20

1158 Sacramento Bee 07 Jan 1932 p16

1159 Sacramento Bee 30 Dec 1930 p10

1160 Fresno Bee 29 Dec 1930

1161 Cinderella Man, Jeremy Schaap, 2005, Houghton-Mifflin; NY p96

1162 The People (London England) Anthony Williamson 29 Dec 1946 p7

1163 Tacoma Daily Ledger 19 Dec 1930 p10

1164 St. Louis Post-Dispatch 23 Jun 1934 p15

1165 San Francisco Chronicle 01 Jan 1931 p24

1166 Oakland Tribune 01 Jan 1931 p22

1167 Kansas City Times 20 Dec 1930 p18; Walter Trumball

1168 San Bernardino County Sun 20 Dec 1930 p20

1169 Wilkes-Barre Times Leader 07 Feb 1931 p19

1170 Los Angeles Evening Express 20 Dec 1930 p15

1171 Dayton Daily News 15 Jun 1934 p32

1172 Los Angeles Express 20 Dec 1930 p15

1173 Oakland Tribune 25 Aug 1932 p18

1174 Oakland Tribune 04 Nov 1930 p34

1175 Burlington Free Press 03 Dec 1930 p13

1176 Oakland Tribune 22 Jan 1931 p20

1177 San Francisco Chronicle 04 Feb 1931 p27

1178 The Erie Times 02 Feb 1931 p15

1179 Oakland Tribune 04 Jan 1931 p21

1180 San Francisco Chronicle 10 Feb 1931 p24

1181 Long Beach Sun 01 Feb 1931 p14

1182 Spokesman Review 01 Feb 1931 p15

357

1183 San Francisco Chronicle 10 Feb 1931 p24

1184 San Francisco Examiner 16 Jan 1931 p21

1185 Los Angeles Evening Express 31 Jan 1931 p17

1186 Oakland Tribune 01 Feb 1931 p25

1187 San Francisco Examiner 03 Feb 1931 p22

1188 Spokesman Review 02 Feb 1931 p10

1189 Los Angeles Evening Express 31 Jan 1931 p17

1190 Long Beach Sun 01 Feb 1931 p14

1191 Oakland Tribune 22 Mar 1931 p23

1192 Remembering Battling Nelson and his greatest fight, Pete Ehrmann,
Special to OnMilwaukee.com, Published Dec 08, 2017

1193 Dayton Daily News 18 Sep 1932 p33

1194 Dayton Daily News 25 Nov 1934 p35

1195 Oakland Tribune 22 Mar 1931 p23

1196 The Columbus Dispatch 01 Feb 1931 p27

1197 Trenton Times-Advertiser 01 Feb 1931 p25

1198 Oregon Sunday Journal 01 Feb 1931 p21

1199 Collyer's Eye 07 Feb 1931 p3

1200 Oakland Tribune 02 Feb 1931 p14

1201 Minneapolis Star Tribune 01 Mar 1931

1202 Coos Bay Oregon Times 08 Apr 1931 p2

1203 Morning Oregonian 06 Apr 1931 p15

1204 Sunday Oregonian 05 Apr 1931 p51

1205 The Sacramento Union 14 Mar 1931 p3

1206 Anaheim Bulletin 13 Mar 1931 p6

1207 Sacramento Union 15 Jan 1927 p2

1208 Marysville Appeal-Democrat 12 May 1931 p2

1209 Journals of the Legislature of the State of California. California State Assembly Committee Report on boxing 14 May 1931; p3820/3821

1210 San Francisco Examiner 26 Jul 1931 p32

1211 Oakland Tribune 26 Jul 1931 p23

1212 San Francisco Bulletin 28 Dec 1927 p15

1213 San Francisco Examiner 25 Feb 1933 p3

1214 Salt Lake Tribune 24 May 1931 p19

1215 Baby Face Nelson, "The Grand Haven Heist," 27 Dec 2023, Black Barrel Media, podcast, MP3 audio, 34:00, Black Barrel Media

1216 Salt Lake Tribune 24 May 1931 p19

1217 San Diego Union 08 Jul 1931 p13

1218 Las Vegas Evening Review-Journal 09 Jul 1931 p7

1219 Marysville Appeal-Democrat 08 Sep 1931 p8

1220 Oakland Tribune 19 Nov 1931 p30

1221 Oakland Tribune 25 Nov 1931 p13

1222 Oakland Tribune 24 Nov 1931 p24

1223 27 Jan 1932 Nevada State Journal p7

1224 Marysville Appeal-Democrat 24 Feb 1933 p1

1225 Cinderella Man, Jeremy Schaap, 2005 Houghlin-Miffin, Boston, MA, p141

1226 Edmonton Alberta Bulletin 02 Jun 1938 p12

1227 Boston Globe 27 May 1933 p7

1228 Los Angeles Times, 24 Dec 1996, Montalbano, William D., The Jews in Hitler's Military

1229 London Evening Standard 14 Jun 1935 p7

1230 San Francisco Examiner 18 Oct 1963 p58

1231 Sacramento Bee 10 Feb 1970 p24

1232 Marriage License No 15221, Douglas County, Nebraska

1233 Marriage License No 89, Laramie County, Territory of Wyoming

1234 Sacramento Union 01 Jul 1935 p8

1235 St. Louis Star and Times 05 Apr 1933 p20

1236 Washington Post 25 Jun 1993

1237 Lincoln Star 05 Apr 1933 p10

1238 Chicago Tribune 23 Jun 1934 p17

1239 The Boston Globe 09 Jun 1933 p22

1240 Oakland Tribune 15 Jan 1933 p1

1241 The Sacramento Bee 04 Apr 1933 p1

1242 Sacramento Bee 3 Jun 1933 p1

1243 Oakland Tribune 17 Nov 1930 p17

1244 Pomona Progress Bulletin 11 Aug 1933 p2

1245 Press Democrat 10 Nov 1933 p4

1246 Oakland Tribune 16 Nov 1933 p2

1247 Burbank Daily Evening Review 04 Jun 1932 p4

1248 Bob Shand, "Shand's Sport Sheet" Feb 1933 p3

1249 Miami Herald 14 May 1989 p684/1D

1250 Oakland Tribune 14 Jan 1933, Sat · Page 3

1251 San Francisco Examiner 23 Nov 1933 p3

1252 Los Angeles Daily News 28 Nov 1933 p3

1253 Supreme Court. State of New York, Appellate Division, First Dept, March 1934, p39-40

1254 New York Daily News 19 Sep 1935 p308

1255 Oakland Post Enquirer 09 Feb 1938 p1

1256 The Buffalo News 26 Jun 1934 p21

1257 Washington Times 11 Jan 1934 p24

1258 Los Angeles Examiner 24 Jun 1931 p21

1259 Cinderella Man, Jeremy Schaap, 2005 Houghlin-Miffin, Boston, MA, p154

1260 Buffalo Daily News 12 Jun 1934 p18

1261 Des Moines Register 16 Jun 1934 p9

1262 Pittsburgh Post-Gazette 23 Jun 1934 p15

1263 The Atlanta Constitution 15 Jun 1934 p20

1264 Minneapolis Star 15 Jun 1934 p21

1265 Scranton Times-Tribune 15 Jun 1934 p32

1266 Raleigh North Carolina News and Observer 17 Jun 1934 p17

1267 Los Angeles Times 17 Jun 1934 p59

1268 Liverpool Evening Express 23 May 1935 p7

1269 New York Daily News 16 Jun 1934 p32

1270 Chicago Tribune 23 Jun 1934 p15/17

1271 Philadelphia Inquirer 07 Jun 1934 p16

1272 San Francisco Chronicle 19 Aug 1934 p70

1273 San Francisco Chronicle 28 Aug 1934

1274 San Francisco Chronicle 2 Sep 1934 p70

1275 San Francisco Chronicle 09 Jan 1935 p21

1276 Oakland Tribune 03 Oct 1934 p20

1277 Oakland Tribune 18 Jul 1934 p9

1278 San Francisco Chronicle 02 Oct 1934 p20

1279 Oakland Tribune 03 Oct 1934 p20

1280 San Francisco Chronicle 10 Nov 1934 p13

1281 San Francisco Chronicle 15 Nov p20

1282 San Francisco Chronicle 20 Nov 1934

1283 San Francisco Chronicle 28 Nov 1934

1284 Kalamazoo Gazette 25 Nov 1934 p13

1285 San Francisco Chronicle 12 Dec 1934 p17

1286 Oakland Post Enquirer 03 Nov 1934 p5

1287 San Francisco Chronicle 05 Jan 1935 p17

1288 San Francisco Chronicle 25 Jan 1935 p19

1289 San Francisco Chronicle 26 Jan 1935 p11

1290 San Francisco Chronicle 06 Feb 1935

1291 Petaluma Argus-Courier 08 Feb 1935 p4

1292 Fresno Bee 07 Feb 1935 p12

1293 Oakland Tribune 16 Feb 1935 p8

1294 San Francisco Examiner 17 Feb 1935 p30

1295 Oakland Tribune 16 Feb 1935 p8

1296 New York Daily News 24 Mar 1934

1297 Ogden Standard-Examiner 23 May 1935 p9

1298 New York Daily News 09 Jun 1935 p33

1299 New York Daily News 11 Jun 1935 p46/48

1300 Tampa Tribune 13 Jun 1935 p11

1301 Sacramento Bee 14 Jun 1935 p22

1302 San Jose News 26 Apr 1978 p75

1303 Hemingway, Ernest, "The Million-Dollar Fright," Esquire, Dec 1935 p190b

1304 Phone interview Tony Hood, 17 Oct 2023

1305 Johnson City Chronicle [Tennessee] 14 Jun 1935 p8

1306 Oroville Mercury Register 19 Jul 1935 p6

1307 Brooklyn Daily Eagle 14 Jun 1935 p24

1308 The Daily Messenger 07 May 1935 p4

1309 Los Angeles Evening Post-Record 03 Jun 1933 p8

1310 San Francisco Examiner 10 Jun 1935 p17

1311 Brookville [Pennsylvania] American 20 Jun 1935 p2

1312 The Spokesman-Review 24 Aug 1935 p12

1313 Los Angeles Times 24 Aug 1935 p7

1314 Brooklyn Daily Eagle 25 Sep 1935 p27

1315 The Missoulian 01 Sep 1935 p9

1316 Nevada Appeal 08 Feb 2006

1317 Sacramento Bee 25 Sep 1935 p16

1318 New York American 15 Sep 1935 p23

1319 Franklin News-Herald 30 Sep 30, 1935 p9

1320 The Charlotte News 27 Sep 1935 p19

1321 Omaha World-Herald 14 Oct 1936 p25

1322 Portland Press Herald 26 Sep 1935 p12

1323 Miami Herald 25 Sep 1935 p9

1324 Chambersburg PA Public Opinion 30 Sep 1935 p4

1325 Atlanta Journal Constitution 15 Aug 1948 p15, Austen Lake, "Doping to Win"

1326 extremeweatherwatch.com/cities/new-york/year-1935

1327 Pampa Texas Daily News 24 Sep 1935 p1

1328 Brooklyn Daily Eagle 25 Sep 1935 p22/27

1329 Escanaba Daily Press 26 Sep 1935 p2

1330 Brooklyn Times Union 21 Sep 1935 p11

1331 Hemingway, Ernest, "The Million-Dollar Fright," Esquire, Dec 1935 p35

1332 Harrisburg Evening News 23 Jun 1938 p18

1333 Cedar Rapids Gazette 16 Apr 1937 p13

1334 Petaluma Argus-Courier 25 Sep 1935 p4

1335 Foxworthy, Donald F., The Foxworthy-Fallon Saga p4, 1989

1336 Fort Collins Express Courier 26 Sep 1935 p12

1337 Los Angeles Evening Post-Record 11 Oct 1935 p17

1338 Nevada State Journal 24 Feb 1936 p6

1339 The Montreal Star 22 Oct 1936 p31

1340 The Toronto Star 20 Oct 1936 p10

1341 Lafayette Daily Advertiser 29 Apr 1937 p6

1342 New York Daily News 10 Feb 1937 p56

1343 Pasadena Post 17 Apr 1937 p9

1344 The Lincoln Star 02 Jun 1939 p11

1345 Wewoka Times-Democrat 10 Jul 1938 p4

1346 Ogden Standard-Examiner 24 May 1936 p12

1347 The Montana Standard 02 Apr 1939 p45

1348 Oakland Tribune 06 Apr 1941 p12

1349 Calgary Herald 04 Apr 1941 p6

1350 Des Moines Tribune 16 Nov 1949 p20

1351 Dayton Daily News 15 Jul 1951 p52

1352 New York Daily News 13 Dec 1959 p6

1353 Interview November 2022 Diane Camilli Abraham

1354 Van Nuys News 31 Jan 1949 p11

1355 Siskiyou Daily News 23 Nov 1959 p3

1356 Sacramento Union 11 Dec 1943 p5

1357 Red & Blue Student Body Newspaper 12 Jun 1947

1358 San Francisco Examiner 13 May 1948 p26

1359 Register of officers and cadets - United States Military Academy, 1951 p105.

1360 The Honolulu Advertiser 18 Jan 1952, p12

1361 San Francisco Chronicle 23 Apr 1935 p24

1362 Report of AF Aircraft Accident 11 July 1953

1363 Virginia McConnell article in Taps Jan/Feb 2005

1364 Report of AF Aircraft Accident 11 July 1953

1365 Virginia McConnell article in Taps Jan/Feb 2005

1366 Tucson Citizen 01 Jan 1952 p1

1367 Arizona Republic 1 Jan 1952 p2

1368 Arizona Republic 1 Jan 1952 p1

1369 Tucson Daily Citizen 2 Jan 1952 p1

1370 Virginia McConnell article in Taps Jan/Feb 2005

1371 aviationarchaeology.com/listPages/tour_us/asp/toursus21_c47.asp

1372 New York Times, Richard Goldstein 22 Oct 1997

1373 San Francisco Chronicle 06 July 1931 p23/H3

1374 Peninsula Times Tribune 07 Jan 1989 p42

1375 Phone interview August 2008 Joanne Camilli Griggs

1376 The Daily Olympian 27 Jul 1938 p6

1377 Longview Daily News 24 Oct 1957 p15

1378 Oakland Tribune 06 May 1942 p20

1379 Hometown San Francisco – xxx Framm

1380 Los Angeles Times 05 Dec 1941 p5

1381 Phone interview August 2008 Joanne Camilli Griggs

1382 Phone interview July 2023 Diane Camilli Abraham

1383 Oakland Tribune 27 Oct 1930 p17

www.ingramcontent.com/pod-product-compliance
Lightning Source LLC
Chambersburg PA
CBHW051607120626
46551CB00014B/1702